Dat

PROTOCOL ANALYSIS

⅃ㄥ Bradford Books

Edward C.T. Walker, Editor. Explorations in THE BIOLOGY OF LANGUAGE. 1979.

Daniel C. Dennett. BRAINSTORMS. 1979.

Charles E. Marks. COMMISSUROTOMY, CONSCIOUSNESS AND UNITY OF MIND. 1980.

John Haugeland, Editor. MIND DESIGN. 1981.

Fred I. Dretske. KNOWLEDGE AND THE FLOW OF INFORMATION. 1981.

Jerry A. Fodor. REPRESENTATIONS. 1981.

Ned Block, Editor. IMAGERY. 1981.

Roger N. Shepard and Lynn A. Cooper. MENTAL IMAGES AND THEIR TRANSFORMATIONS. 1982.

Hubert L. Dreyfus, Editor, in collaboration with Harrison Hull. HUSSERL, INTENTIONALITY AND COGNITIVE SCIENCE. 1982.

John Macnamara. NAMES FOR THINGS. 1982.

Natalie Abrams and Michael D. Buckner, Editors. MEDICAL ETHICS. 1982.

Morris Hale and G. N. Clements. PROBLEM BOOK IN PHONOLOGY. 1983.

Jerry A. Fodor. MODULARITY OF MIND. 1983.

George D. Romanos. QUINE AND ANALYTIC PHILOSOPHY. 1983.

Robert Cummins. THE NATURE OF PSYCHOLOGICAL EXPLANATION. 1983.

Irvin Rock. THE LOGIC OF PERCEPTION. 1983.

Stephen P. Stich. FOLK PSYCHOLOGY AND COGNITIVE SCIENCE. 1983.

Jon Barwise and John Perry. SITUATIONS AND ATTITUDES. 1983.

Izchak Miller. HUSSERL'S THEORY OF PERCEPTION. 1984.

Elliot Sober. CONCEPTUAL ISSUES IN EVOLUTIONARY BIOLOGY. 1984.

Paul M. Churchland. MATTER AND CONSCIOUSNESS. 1984.

Owen D. Flanagan. THE SCIENCE OF MIND. 1984.

Ruth Garrett Millikan. LANGUAGE, THOUGHT AND OTHER BIOLOGICAL CATEGORIES. 1984.

Norbert Hornstein. LOGIC AS GRAMMAR. 1984.

Myles Brand. INTENDING AND ACTING: A NATURALIZED ACTION THEORY. 1984.

K. Anders Ericsson and Herbert A. Simon. PROTOCOL ANALYSIS. 1984.

PROTOCOL ANALYSIS

Verbal Reports as Data

K. Anders Ericsson

and

Herbert A. Simon

The MIT Press
Cambridge, Massachusetts
London, England

Publisher's note: This format is intended to reduce the cost
of publishing certain work in book form and to shorten the gap between
editorial preparation and the final publication.
Detailed editing and composition have been avoided by
photographing the text of this book directly from the authors'
word-processor output.

This book was set in Times Roman with Scribe^{TM} on
the Xerox Dover Printer at Carnegie-Mellon University.

Printed and bound in the United States of America.

Library of Congress Cataloging in Publication Data

Ericsson, Anders K.
    Protocol analysis.

    "A Bradford book."
    Bibliography: p.
    Includes index.
    1. Verbal Behavior—Research. 2. Cognition—Research.
3. Behaviorism (Psychology)—Research. 4. Psychology,
Experimental. I. Simon, Herbert Alexander, 1916-
II. Title.
BF455.E68 1984   153   83-24918
ISBN 0-262-05029-3

To

INGRID and KARL-OLOV ERICSSON

and
to the memory of

EDNA and ARTHUR SIMON

who taught us not to be afraid
to voice our thoughts.

CONTENTS

FOREWORD

In 1980, the authors proposed in *The Psychological Review* a theory on verbal thinking-aloud protocols as data, and provided substantial empirical support for the theory. The response to this article was so lively, and the interest in protocols that it revealed so widespread that we decided to enlarge our inquiry into a book. The book would make the theory as explicit and rigorous as possible, would explore the empirical evidence more thoroughly than we could in a single journal article, and would discuss the techniques of protocol analysis. This is that book.

The ideas set forth in this book have taken form over many years, beginning with a brief meeting between the authors in the Spring of 1975. Many people have spent countless hours discussing these issues with us in these years, and we would like especially to acknowledge William Chase, Gunnar Goude, and Robert Neches. A number of colleagues and friends have been kind enough to read drafts of the book and offer their suggestions for improving it. Among them are Micki Chi, Donald Fiske, Goran Hagert, Barbara Hayes-Roth, Walter Kintsch, Allen Newell, Stellan Ohlsson, Gary Olson, Richard Nisbett, and Ed Smith. We wish to thank them warmly and at the same time absolve them from responsibility for infelicities of the product.

We are also grateful to Betty and Henry Stanton of Bradford Books, who have greatly facilitated the transformation of manuscript into a bound book, and who have been understanding when deadlines have not always been met. Finally, we owe special thanks to Therese Groden, who has assumed responsibility for producing camera-ready copy from the raw manuscript, and in the course of doing so, has found her way through the thickets of word-processing systems and printers at Carnegie-Mellon University.

Work on this book has been aided by grants from the National Institute of Mental Health and the Alfred P. Sloan Foundation.

K. Anders Ericsson
Herbert A. Simon
November 28, 1983

PROTOCOL ANALYSIS

1

INTRODUCTION AND SUMMARY

After a long period of time during which stimulus-response relations were at the focus of attention, research in psychology is now seeking to understand in detail the mechanisms and internal structure of cognitive processes that produce these relations. In the limiting case, we would like to have process models so explicit that they could actually produce the predicted behavior from the information in the stimulus.

This concern for the course of the cognitive processes has revived interest in finding ways to increase the temporal density of observations so as to reveal intermediate stages of the processes. Increasingly, investigators record the directions of the subject's gaze (eye movements), and the intermediate behaviors (movements or physical manipulations of stimulus material) that precede the solution or criterion performance. Since data on intermediate processing are costly to gather and analyze, it is important to consider carefully how such data can be interpreted validly, and what contribution they can make to our understanding of the phenomena under study.

One means frequently used to gain information about the course of the cognitive processes is to probe the subjects' internal states by verbal methods. These methods are the topic of this monograph.

USING VERBAL REPORTS: SOME ISSUES

There are several issues that we must deal with if we are to use subjects' reports as fundamental data in psychological experiments. First, we must respond to the strong doubts that have been expressed by many psychologists in the past about the suitability of subjects' verbalizations as scientific data. Second, we must consider the processing that must take place in order to transform subjects' behaviors (whether verbal or not) into data. Third, we must examine how the encoding of behavior into data can be made objective and univocal, so that the resulting data will be "hard" and not "soft." Fourth, we must be explicit about the theoretical presuppositions that are necessarily embedded in the encoding process. Finally, we must specify the processes that allow us to go backward from the data to the behavior and thence to inferences about the subjects' thought processes.

We offer a few comments on each of these five issues. They will reappear frequently as recurrent themes throughout the monograph.

Doubts About Verbal Data

Since the triumph of behaviorism over "introspectively" oriented competing viewpoints, verbal reports have been suspect as data. More precisely, behaviorism and allied schools of thought have been schizophrenic about the status of verbalizations as data. On the one hand, verbal responses (or key punches that are psychologically indistinguishable from verbal responses, except that they are made with the finger instead of the mouth) provide the basic data in standard experimental paradigms. In a concept attainment experiment, the subjects say (or signal) "yes" or "no" when a possible instance is presented to them. In a problem solving experiment, they report the answer when they find it. In a rote verbal learning experiment, they say "DAX" when the stimulus syllable "CEF" is presented. The actual performance measures commonly used—latencies and numbers of items correct— are derived from these responses, and the former depend for their validity on the veridicality of the latter.

On the other hand, modern psychology has been dubious about verbalizations produced by subjects along the route to their solutions or final responses. Even more dubious has been the status of responses to experimenter probes or retrospective answers to questions about prior behavior. All of these sorts of verbal behavior are frequently dismissed as variants of the discredited process of introspection (Nisbett & Wilson, 1977). Introspection, it has generally been argued, may be useful for the discovery of psychological processes; it is worthless for verification. As Lashley (1923, p. 352) said, in a vigorous and widely cited attack on the method, "introspection may make the preliminary survey, but it must be followed by the chain and transit of objective measurement."

Extracting Data from Behavior

The notion that verbal reports provide possibly interesting but only informal information, to be verified by other data, has affected the ways in which verbalizations are collected and analyzed. If the purpose of obtaining verbal reports is mainly to generate hypotheses and ideas, investigators need not concern themselves (and generally have not concerned themselves) with methodological questions about data collection. As a result, there is little published literature on such issues, the data-gathering and data-analysis methods actually used vary tremendously, and the details of these methods are reported sketchily in research publications that make use of such data.

If we are to make rapid and continuing progress in understanding human cognitive processes, this state of affairs is wholly unsatisfactory. In the first place, no clear guidelines are provided to distinguish illegitimate "introspection" from the many forms of verbal output that are routinely treated as data—as passing the chain and transit test (see the examples above). On what theoretical or practical grounds do we distinguish between the subject's "yes" or "no" in a concept attainment experiment and his assertion that the hypothesis he is entertaining is "small yellow circle"? In the second place, no distinctions are made among such diverse forms of verbalization as thinking-aloud (TA) protocols, retrospective responses to specific probes, and the classical introspective reports of trained observers. All are jointly and loosely condemned as "introspection."

Soft versus Hard Data

Some investigators call verbal reports and verbal descriptions "soft data" in contrast to simple behavioral measures like latency or correctness of response, which are referred to as "hard." What does this distinction mean? In science one would like to maintain as clear a separation as possible between data and theory. Data are supposed to derive directly from observation; theories are supposed to account for, explain, and predict these observation-based data. Data are "hard" when there is intersubjective agreement that they correspond to the facts of the observed behavior.

Even psychoanalytically or existentially oriented psychologists will accept response latencies as data—even though being possibly irrelevant data for explaining behavior. When, however, an analyst codes a five-second description of a dream as "oral fixation," many psychologists would argue that this encoding is not a datum but a subjective interpretation of the data (i.e., of the verbal description of the dream). Surely, theory-laden inferences were required to derive the encoding from the verbal protocol. Data are regarded as "soft" to the degree that they incorporate such inferences, especially when the theoretical premises and rules of inference are themselves not completely explicit and objective. The problem with "soft" data is that different interpreters making different inferences will not agree in their encodings, and each interpreter is likely, wittingly or not, to arrive at an interpretation that is favorable to his theoretical orientation.

The hard-soft distinction is orthogonal to the distinction between verbal and non-verbal. The same problems of inference can emerge in observers' attempts to understand non-verbal events (e.g., sequences of physical movements, pieces of music). Such events may require as much interpretation as is required to understand verbal sequences.

Technological advances have enhanced our ability to treat verbal protocols as hard data. Until tape recorders were generally available, it was common practice for experimenters to take selective notes of verbalizations, paraphrasing and omitting whatever was "unimportant." In analyzing such notes further, it was impossible to distinguish the inferences from the original verbalizations. Using encodings of verbal protocols as data has often been made even more difficult because the theories employed, explicitly or implicitly, in the encoding were formulated in very general terms. The search for general mechanisms also led to overall interpretations of entire protocols with little concern for encoding and explicating individual protocol statements.

More recent research based on explicit information processing models of the cognitive processes has caused thinking-aloud verbalizations to be viewed in a new light. It is now standard procedure to make careful verbatim transcripts of the recorded tapes, thus preserving the raw data in as "hard" a form as could be wished. At the same time, information processing models of the cognitive processes provide a basis for making the encoding process explicit and objective, so that the theoretical presuppositions entering into that process can be examined objectively.

Theoretical Presupposition in Encoding

Clyde Coombs, in his book *A Theory of Data*, shows that raw data go through a typical sequence of steps on the route from initial observation to the edited and encoded form in which they are used to test theories or make predictions. These steps, which are not neutral with respect to theory, can be seen in the processing of protocol data as they can with other kinds of data. At the first step, theory delimits a small portion of the universe of potentially observable behavior as being relevant. This judgment of relevance determines what behaviors should be recorded. At the next step, these behaviors are encoded in a manner that is again determined on theoretical grounds.

In the case of verbal behavior, the process begins with a tape-recording, containing essentially all the auditory events that occurred during the experimental session. In producing from the tape a written transcript, some selection is required. After the temporal information, repetitions, and stress have been used to segment and parse the verbal stream, most of this information is usually eliminated from the transcript, except as it is captured by punctuation. We will refer to this transcription step as *preprocessing*.

At the next step, the preprocessed segments are encoded into the terminology of the theoretical model. This is often achieved by first determining coding categories, a priori, and then having human judges make the coding assessments. If each of the segments is to be treated as an independent datum, then the encoding of that segment must be made on the basis of the information contained in it, independently of the surrounding segments. In Chapter 6 of this book, we will discuss at some length methods for carrying out this kind of local encoding, and the conditions that must be met to make it possible.

Verbal protocols have been analyzed in two rather different ways. One method claims *not* to require the analysis of meanings, while the other does require it. In the first kind of analysis, subject and experimenter have agreed, by prior instruction, upon specific signals, which may be speech signals or button presses, for their communication. These signals are mostly arbitrary— a subject could say "cef" instead of "yes"; communication is possible only because of the agreement established between subject and experimenter. To analyze the recorded verbalizations under these conditions, the experimenter has only to categorize each speech signal into one of the agreed-upon categories. In theory, if not in practice, a coder should not even need to know the subject's language—assuring that no meaningful analysis or inferencing is involved. A large number of paradigms in psychology use this kind of analysis. For example, studies using scales and multiple-choice alternatives can all be seen as instances of this method.

In the second kind of analysis, the observed verbalizations are analyzed in terms of their meanings. Even in this case, the theory guiding the analysis limits the encoding to selected aspects and features rather than the full meaning of the verbalization. For example, in a typical concept attainment task, each instance or stimulus can be represented as a unique combination of features. Each distinct concept can be represented by some particular configuration of features. Then encoding simply requires the mapping of the verbalizations onto these concepts and features—usually a rather unequivocal matter. Although the space of logically possible different concepts may be very large, it is severely limited compared with the variability of natural language. Thus a verbalization like "red circles are cef's" can normally be encoded as identical with "blood-colored round ones are cef's."

The context of a particular theory and experiment greatly constrains the range of possible interpretation and allows the meaningful analysis of verbalizations to be selective and incomplete. If a theory of concept attainment is limited to the language of hypotheses, many verbalizations will not be encoded at all— statements like, "I wonder what I should do. I'll just guess on this one." Many examples can be cited of this kind of meaningful analysis, where verbalizations are mapped onto a priori formal alternatives. The analysis of memory for meaningful text has been studied by Kintsch (1974) and many others. Newell and Simon (1972) analyzed tasks, identifying formally defined knowledge states in terms of which subjects' thinking-aloud protocols could be encoded.

Many analyses of verbalizations do *not* fit the above scheme, including most analyses that seek to arrive at an understanding of the verbalizations. In less formal kinds of analysis, the encoding scheme is not defined formally and a priori, but the search for interpretations proceeds in parallel with the search for an appropriate model or theory. We recognize clearly the need for and value of such interactive processes in the search for theories in new domains, but in our own account here we will be concerned primarily with situations where the theoretical terms are fixed before the actual encoding begins.

Inferring Thought Processes From Behavior

It is sometimes believed that using verbal data implies accepting the subjects' interpretation of them or of the events that are reported. This issue of trust has its origins in our everyday experience and use of language. In order to communicate effectively with other people, we accept their word for many facts. If someone says that he has bought a new car, we generally accept his statement as true instead of asking him to produce the sales contract or a receipt. In a similar vein we trust people—at least our friends—to answer questions correctly and to give us the best advice they can. However, if the issue is important to us or we suspect ulterior motives in the responses, we may demand more details and may review all the available evidence ourselves. The same thing holds in scientific research; few scientists will accept another scientist's claim of finding conclusive evidence for ESP without wanting an independent review of the evidence.

Subjects' reports of their own mental states and mental processes raise slightly different issues of trust. According to a naive theory of consciousness, subjects have the sole *direct* access to their own mental states and processes. The subjective feeling of one's ability to report one's own mental experiences veridically is strong. For a great many reasons, this confidence is not shared by experimental psychologists, who have shown that under numerous circumstances such self-reports are unreliable.

However, the issue of the reliability of self-reports can (and, we think, should) be avoided entirely. The report "X" need not be used to infer that X is true, but only that the subject was able to say "X"—(i.e., had the information that enabled him to say "X.") By following this path, we can even show that there is an inverse relation between how much subjects need to be trusted and how much information they verbalize. For the more information conveyed in their responses, the more difficult it becomes to construct a model that will produce precisely those responses adventitiously—hence the more confidence we can place in a model that does predict them.

Consider, for example, the following possible interchanges between experimenter and subject:

1. Do you know the name of the capital of Sweden? *Yes.*

2. Which of these three, Oslo, Stockholm, or Copenhagen, is the capital of Sweden? *Stockholm.*

3. Name the capital of Sweden. *Stockholm.*

4. (A retrospective report as to how the subject arrived at an answer to Question 1): *First I tried to picture where Sweden is located on a map of Europe, then Oslo came to mind, but I remembered that it is the capital of Norway. Then Stockholm popped up and I remembered that is where the Nobel prizes are awarded; then I felt sure I could answer "yes."*

In the first case we have to trust the subject if we want to infer that he actually knows the capital, whereas in the third case it is unlikely that he could generate the correct name unless it were accessible from memory. The primary difference between second and third cases is that, for the second, one could conceive of a number of processes other than memory retrieval (e.g., guessing) that would account for the response. The fourth response, the retrospective report, also verifies that the subject has the name in memory together with some redundant information about it that gives him confidence in his answer. Of course we do not have to believe that he has given a veridical report of the process whereby he generated the name, although there is nothing implausible about the sequence of associations he reports.

Consider next a more controversial example, which has played a role in the psychological literature on learning without awareness. After a learning experiment, the experimenter asks the subjects whether they were aware of any relation between the stimuli and responses, on the one hand, and the reward contingencies on the other. Yes/no responses to this question are informative only if we trust the subjects. If a subject, however, describes the stimulus-response contingency for reward, we can be reasonably certain that he had access to this information while he was learning. On the other hand, if a subject is unable to report anything about the contingency, we *cannot* conclude that he wasn't aware of it during the learning process—we have solid evidence neither for nor against awareness during the experiment. Later, we will discuss the problem of making inferences from reports of lack of information.

These examples illustrate that the information externalized in verbal responses often provides the experimenter with data that eliminate the need for trust in the subject. The examples also show that verbal reports may be generated in many ways. To understand the reports, we must understand the processes by which they were generated. In none of these respects do data from verbal reports differ from data based on other types of observations.

Some Basic Assumptions

We can now summarize the basic assumptions that set the stage for our further explorations. Most fundamentally, we see verbal behavior as one type of recordable behavior, which should be observed and analyzed like any other behavior. The cognitive processes that generate verbalizations are a subset of the cognitive processes that generate any kind of recordable response or behavior. Hence, we would look for the same kind of "mechanical" and complete process description of verbal behavior as of other kinds of behavior, and we would not accept magical or privileged processes as explanations for verbalizations.

Whether one can and should trust subjects' verbal reports is not a matter of faith but an empirical issue on a par with the issue of validating other types of behavior, like eye fixations or motor behavior. A single invalid verbal report should not force us to discard analysis of verbal reports generally. Indeed, this monograph will undertake to build a theory of verbalization, so that we can then specify when, where, and under what kinds of instructions informative verbal reports can be obtained from subjects.

Postulating that the cognitive processes underlying verbalization are a subset of all cognitive processes implies that verbalization must comply with the constraints that have been identified, experimentally, to govern all cognitive processes. These information processing constraints will provide powerful guidelines for our attempts to specify how observed verbalizations could have been generated. We wish to account for verbally reported information by proposing a processing model sufficiently powerful to regenerate that information.

Plan of Attack

Our first task is to describe a general theory of cognitive processes and structure, which, we argue, accounts for verbalizations and verbal reports. For reasons that have already been stated, the analysis must be carried out within a framework of theory. This framework must be sufficiently general to permit us to relate, within a unified perspective, all the kinds of data that are commonly used in psychological experiments.

Usually, in choosing between theories, we want to pick the strongest one—the one that will make the strongest predictions. In the present case, where the theory we choose will influence the way in which we encode and analyze our data, we want to pick the weakest and most "neutral" one that can do the job. The fewer controversial assumptions we incorporate in the theory, the less we will be involved in the circularity of using theory-laden data to test our theories. Nevertheless, there appears to be no way of processing data that does not incorporate *some* theoretical assumptions about the system and processes that generated the data. Our particular strategy will be to set forth the theory in its most general, hence least controversial, form first, then add more specific hypotheses where they are required.

After presenting the theory as an information processing model of cognitive processes, we will survey the literature on verbal reporting and derive from it a taxonomy of reporting procedures. We will follow this survey with an historical review of earlier approaches to verbal reports. We will then take up the major issues surrounding the use and validity of verbal reports, discussing the empirical studies within the framework of a more detailed information processing model.

THE PROCESSING MODEL

Our purpose in presenting a specific processing model is to aid us in interpreting verbal data obtained from subjects and the relation of their verbal to their other behavior. Since the data (including the verbal data) are gathered in order to test theories about the human information processing system, we are engaged in something of a bootstrap operation. We need a model in order to interpret data that are to be used, in turn, to test the model.   Under these circumstances, our data-interpretation model should be as simple as possible, and it must not incorporate components that are themselves bones of theoretical contention. The model should be robust (i.e., compatible with a wide range of alternative assumptions about human information processing).

The specifications we are about to present are simple and robust in this sense, and, indeed, summarize the core that is common to most current information processing theories of cognition. Of course they are not entirely neutral, for they would be hard to reconcile with an extreme form of behaviorism that denied the relevance of central processes to the explanation of behavior. But they are not specific to the view of any particular "sect" within the general information-processing tradition. (For fuller discussion of the model, see Newell and Simon (1972, Chapter 14), and Simon (1979, Chapters 2, 3).

General Specification

The most general and weakest hypothesis we require is that human cognition is information processing: that a cognitive process can be seen as a sequence of internal states successively transformed by a series of information processes. An important, and more specific, assumption is that information is stored in several memories having different capacities and accessing characteristics: several sensory stores of very short duration, a short-term memory (STM) with limited capacity and/or intermediate duration, and a long-term memory (LTM) with very large capacity and relatively permanent storage, but with slow fixation and access times compared with the other memories.

Within the framework of this information processing model, it is assumed that information recently acquired (attended to or heeded)* by the central processor is kept in STM, and is directly accessible for further processing (e.g., for producing verbal reports), whereas information from LTM must first be retrieved (transfered to STM) before it can be reported.

This general picture is compatible with all sorts of specific hypotheses that have been put forth with respect to the details of the mechanisms. For example, some theorists propose that what we call "short-term memory" is not a separate, specialized store but simply a portion of LTM that is currently and temporarily activated (Anderson, 1976). Some theorists believe that information in STM extinguishes with passage of time, unless rehearsed; others that it is lost only when replaced. In general, these differences of detail do not affect the model at the level of specificity required for our purposes. The important hypothesis for us is that, due to the limited capacity of STM, only the most recently heeded information is accessible directly. However, a portion of the contents of STM are fixated in LTM before being lost from STM, and this portion can, at later points in time, sometimes be retrieved from LTM.

Our specification of the system is general, but it is not vague. Specific information processing models that incorporate these features have been constructed in the form of computer programs, and these have

---

*Because the phrase "attended to" is often stylistically awkward, we will sometimes use "heeded" instead. So we will say, more or less synonymously, that information was "attended to," was "heeded," or was "stored in STM."

been shown to produce a variety of behaviors previously observed in psychological laboratories. Verbal predictions of how such a system behaves can, thereby, be tested by using a computer program as a simulator. The principal model of this kind that guides our own thinking about these processes is the EPAM program, due to Feigenbaum (1963) and Simon, and discussed in some detail in Section 3 of Simon (1979).

We assume that any verbalization or verbal report of the cognitive processes would have to be based on a subset of the information held in STM and LTM. From this and the above hypotheses, the taxonomy of verbalization procedures shown in Table 1-1 follows in a straightforward fashion (Ericsson & Simon, 1980).

Table 1-1

A Classification of Different Types of Verbalization Procedures as a Function of Time of Verbalization (Rows) and the Mapping From Heeded to Verbalized Information (Columns)

| | | Relation between heeded and verbalized information | | | |
| | | | Intermediate processing | | |
Time of verbalization	Direct one to one	Many to one	Unclear	No relation
While information is attended	Talk aloud Think aloud			
While information is still in short-term memory	Concurrent probing	Intermediate inference and generative processes		
After the completion of the task-directed processes	Retrospective probing	Requests for general reports	Probing hypothetical states	Probing general states

The two dimensions of Table 1-1 represent two major distinctions. First, the time of verbalization is important in determining from what memory the information is likely to be drawn. Second, we make a distinction between procedures where the verbalization is a direct articulation or explication of the stored information, and procedures where the stored information is input to intermediate processes, like abstraction and inference, so that the verbalization is a product of this intermediate processing.

Detailed Specification

We now specify more fully the components of the information processing system that we have just sketched. The model draws upon a variety
of sources that are summarized in Newell and Simon (1972, Ch. 14) and
Simon (1979, Ch. 2.3). Few of the model's specifications are controversial. It makes no real difference, for example, whether we assume a
single homogeneous memory with different modes of activation (e.g.,
Anderson, 1976; Shiffrin & Schneider, 1977) or several discrete memory
stores (sensory stores, STM, and LTM). The important matters, which
can be described in either terms, relate to the amounts and kinds of
information that can be retained, and the conditions for accessing them
and reporting them verbally. We will use the conventional model of
multiple memories in our description.

Recognition. Information received from the sensory organs resides
for a short time in memories (iconic and echoic memories) associated
with the different senses. During this time, portions of the sensory information are directly *recognized* and encoded with the aid of information
already stored in LTM. Recognition associates the stimulus, or some
part of it, with existing patterns in LTM, and stores in STM "pointers" to
those familiar patterns. (The EPAM discrimination net is a model of this
recognition mechanism.) Intermediate stages of the direct recognition
process (the successive steps of discrimination), which may take only 10
to 100 msec, do not use STM to store their products.

Long-Term Memory. The LTM may be pictured as an enormous
collection of interrelated nodes. Nodes can be accessed either by recognition (through the discrimination net), as just explained, or by way of
links that associate these nodes to others that have already been accessed.
Information accessed in either way is then represented by pointers in
STM. Thus, information can be brought into STM from sensory stimuli
via the recognition process, or from LTM via the association process.
Association processes are much slower than direct recognition processes,
requiring at least several hundred msec for each associative step. Associative processes may use STM to store intermediate steps. So, for
example, in recalling a name that is not immediately accessible, a person
may use a sequence of cues to find an associative path, step by step, to
the sought-for name. Such processes may last tens of seconds, or even
minutes, and may leave numerous intermediate symbols in STM, where
they are temporarily available for verbal reports.

Short-term Memory. The central processor (CP), which controls and regulates the non-automatic cognitive processes, determines what small part of the information in sensory stimuli and LTM finds its way into STM. This is the information that is *heeded* or *attended to*. The amount of information that can reside in STM at one time is limited to a small number (four?) of familiar patterns (*chunks*). Each chunk is represented by one symbol or pointer to information in LTM (Simon 1979, Ch. 2.2). As new information is heeded, information previously stored in STM may be lost.

When a cognitive task (e.g., mental addition of a column of figures) is being carried out, the typical chunks in STM are pointers to the operands, operators, and outputs of the operations that are being performed. Thus, in adding 3 to 4, pointers corresponding to the symbols "3," "4," "PLUS," and "7" might at some time be present in STM. Since, in our culture, adding two digits involves a direct reference to LTM ("table lookup"), no further detail of the process would be heeded in STM or available for verbal reports. On the other hand, if the task were to multiply 17 by 45, STM might hold, at various points in the process "45," "17," "7," "TIMES," "3" (the carry in multiplying 45 by 7), "315" (the first intermediate product), "45," "1," "TIMES," "PLUS," "765."

We hold no brief for the details of the above description, which is intended merely as an example of the *kinds* of information we would expect to be heeded in STM, and to be available, potentially, for concurrent or retrospective reports. The specific details would depend on the particular strategies subjects used and the nature of the chunks they had stored in LTM (Simon, 1979, Ch. 2.4). STM would symbolize the process only down to some modest level of detail (corresponding to elementary processes of a second or two in duration), and we would not expect to find information there about simple, automated processes (e.g., the processes of retrieval from LTM or recognition processes), much less about neuronal events. Thus, the architecture of the control apparatus (CP) determines the fineness of grain of the representation of processes in STM.

Control of Attention. The flow of attention is diverted, from time to time, by interruptions through the higher control mechanism. Intermediate stages in these interruptions, not being symbolized in STM, are not reportable. Sudden movements in peripheral vision, loud noises, emotions operating through the reticular system are important causes of interruption and shift in attention (Simon, 1979, Ch. 1.3). While information heeded immediately before or after a shift in attention may sometimes allow subjects to give a relatively clear account of the interruption, we would expect such information to be less complete than reports of an orderly process that is induced by the successive content of STM itself (e.g., a thought sequence during which goals in STM are guiding the thought processes).

   Fixation. New information is retained in STM during the time the CP is attending to it. In order to create an LTM representation of new information that can later be recalled, associations must be built up by coding and imaging, as well as new tests and branches in the recognition network. These learning processes, including the storage of new information in LTM and the addition of new pathways in the discrimination net for accessing it, are modeled in some detail by EPAM (Simon, 1979, Section 3). Processing of the order of 8 to 10 seconds is required to assemble each new chunk from its familiar components in STM, and to store it in LTM as a new chunk (Simon, 1979, Chs. 2.2, 2.3).

   Automation. As particular processes become highly practiced, they become more and more fully automated. (Shiffrin & Schneider, 1977). Automation means that intermediate steps are carried out without being interpreted, and without their inputs and outputs using STM. The automation of performance is therefore quite analogous to executing a computer algorithm in compiled instead of interpretive mode. Automation (and compiling) have two important consequences. They greatly speed up the process (typically, by an order of magnitude) and they make the intermediate products unavailable to STM, hence unavailable also for verbal reports.

TYPES OF VERBALIZING PROCEDURES

The only feature common to the whole range of techniques used to obtain verbal data is that the subject responds orally to an instruction or probe. Because of the flexibility of language, there are virtually no limits to the probes we can insert and the questions we can ask subjects that will elicit some kind of verbal response.

   Within our theoretical framework, we can represent verbal reporting as bringing information into attention, then, when necessary, converting it into verbalizable code, and finally, vocalizing it. The crucial issue for verbal reporting procedures is what information is heeded. There have been studies showing that the response modality does not affect the frequency of different responses. Newhall and Roderick (1936) found no differences in frequencies between verbal reports, button presses with fingers, or pedal presses with the feet. This result indicates that the response is heeded symbolically, and then translated into the appropriate overt form. (See Chapter 5 for further discussion.)

Two forms of verbal reports can claim to being the closest reflection of the cognitive processes. Foremost are *concurrent verbal reports*—"talk aloud" and "think aloud" reports—where the cognitive processes, described as successive states of heeded information, are verbalized directly (see Figure 1-1).

We claim that cognitive processes are not modified by these verbal reports, and that task-directed cognitive processes determine what information is heeded and verbalized. We will evaluate this claim empirically in Chapter 2.

A second type of verbal report is the *retrospective report*. A durable (if partial) memory trace is laid down of the information heeded successively while completing a task. Just after the task is finished, this trace can be accessed from STM, at least in part, or retrieved from LTM and verbalized. Retrospective reports based on information in LTM will require an additional process of retrieval that will display some of the same kinds of error and incompleteness that are familiar from experimental research on memory. Both of these kinds of reports, we claim, are direct verbalizations of specific cognitive processes.

Recoding Before Verbalization

Various processes, and especially recoding processes, may intervene between the time information was heeded by the central processor (CP) and the time a verbalization is generated. When information is reproduced in the form in which it was heeded, we will speak of *direct* or *Level 1* verbalization. When one or more mediating processes occurs between attention to the information and its delivery, we will speak of *encoded* or *Level 2* or *Level 3* verbalization. A number of different kinds of intermediate processes between access and verbalization may modify the information. Among the important kinds are the following:

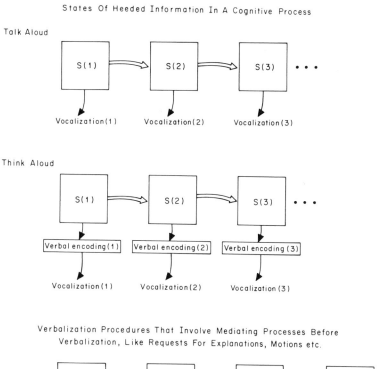

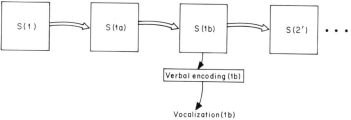

Figure 1-1

The Relation Between the Heeded States of a Cognitive Process and Verbal
Reports for Various Types of Verbal Report Procedures

1. Recoding into verbal code (Level 2 verbalization). When the internal representation in which the information is originally encoded is not a verbal code, it has to be translated into that form. Werner and Kaplan (1963) have shown that when subjects generate verbal descriptions of nonverbal stimuli for their own future use, the format is compact and incorporates many idiosyncratic referents. When verbalizations are generated to communicate information to another person, additional processing is required to find referents (Werner & Kaplan, 1963).

2. Intermediate scanning or filtering processes (Level 3 verbalization). When the task instructions ask for verbalization of only selected information, it is necessary to postulate additional processes that test if the heeded information is of the desired type. Such instructions are used, for example, in commentary driving experiments, in which the subjects are asked to report all perceived traffic hazards while they are driving a car (Soliday & Allen, 1972).

3. Intermediate inference or generative processes (Level 3 verbalization). The situation is even more complicated if the experimenter is interested in particular aspects of the situation that a subject would not ordinarily attend to. The issue of whether the instruction to verbalize calls for information not normally heeded by the subjects is central and directly related to the occurrence of intermediate inference and generative processes. Since we will return to this issue in more depth, only a brief summary will be given here of the types of information that are likely to require additional mediating processing for their generation.

In addition to verbalizing their ongoing thinking, subjects are sometimes asked for verbal descriptions of their motor activities, for example, what objects are moved where, or where they are looking. When this information is not heeded directly, as is often the case, the subject is required to observe his or her own internal processes or overt behavior to generate the information.

Experimenters are often interested in subjects' reasons for their overt behavior and consequently ask the subjects to verbalize their motives and reasons, which may not be available directly or even at all. In an excellent review of research on the effects of persuasive messages, Wright (1980) discusses a wide range of biases due to different verbal report procedures.

In sum, with Level 1 and Level 2 verbalization the sequence of heeded information remains intact and no additional information is heeded. On the other hand Level 3 verbalization requires attention to additional information and hence changes the sequence of heeded information.

Retrospective Reports

In the ideal case the retrospective report is given by the subject immediately after the task is completed while much information is still in STM and can be directly reported or used as retrieval cues. It is clear that some additional cognitive processing is required to ascertain that the particular memory structures of interest are heeded. Our model predicts that retrospective reports on the immediately preceding cognitive activity can be accessed and specified without the experimenter having to provide the subject with specific information about what to retrieve. In this particular case, the subject will still retain the necessary retrieval cues in STM when a general instruction is given "to report everything you can remember about your thoughts during the last problem." This form of retrospective verbal report should give us the closest approximation to the actual memory structures.

Even in this favorable case, some problems arise that are common to all kinds of verbal reports from LTM. First, the retrieval operation is fallible, in that other similar memory structures may be accessed instead of those created by the just-finished cognitive process. The probability of this occurring increases markedly if the subjects have just solved a series of similar problems. However, since most accessed memory structures contain redundant information beyond the cues used for retrieval, subjects may use this additional information to validate the retrieval as well as to increase their confidence in the veridicality of the retrieved information. In a subsequent section we will discuss this type of evaluation further and examine the relevant theoretical and empirical literature.

A second general problem when retrieving cognitive structures is to separate information that was heeded at the time of a specific episode from information acquired previously or subsequently that is associated with it (Mueller, 1911). For example, if a picture reminds one of an old friend, it may be tempting to use the stored information about that friend to *infer* what the person in the picture looked like. (In Chapter 3 we will discuss this issue in more detail.) It may be possible to eliminate this artifact by instructing subjects only to report details that they can remember heeding at the time of the original episode (Mueller, 1911). By imposing a requirement of determinable memory as a basis for reporting, we can avoid many subjects' tendency to fill in information that they can't remember but "must" have thought.

Inferential or Generative Processes

The most marked difference between concurrent and retrospective reporting is that retrospective reports refer to a cognitive process that is completed and cannot be altered and influenced. Hence, if subjects are requested to report information that was never heeded, they cannot possibly base their responses on direct memory. The subjects can answer that they don't know, but often they will infer and generate an answer on the basis of information provided in the question and other information accessible from LTM. Since retrieval from LTM may be an onerous task, even in situations where the information is potentially retrievable subjects may prefer to generate the information instead.

The most common probe that creates this problem is the why-question: for example, "Why did you do this?" or "Why did you prefer that product?" In an interesting discussion, Lazarsfeld (1935) points to many issues and problems in interpreting responses to why-questions, where subjects select one alternative out of several possibilities. Some of the alternatives may never have been heeded. If we wish to find out: "Why did you buy this book?" we may receive, out of the same concrete experience of the respondent, quite different answers, according to whether we stress "buy," "this," or "book." "If the respondent understood: 'Why did you BUY this book?' he might answer, 'Because the waiting list in the library was so long that I shouldn't have got it for two months.' If he understood: 'Why did you buy THIS book?' he might tell what interested him especially in the author. And if he understood: 'Why did you buy this BOOK?' he might report that he at first thought of buying a concert ticket with the money, but later realized that a book is a much more durable thing than a concert, and such reasoning caused him to spend his money upon the book" (Lazarsfeld, 1935, p. 29).

The example is instructive in showing that a person who did not actually buy the book, and hence had no specific memory of the associated cognitive processes, could give the same or similar answers as *plausible* reasons for someone else's buying a book. Hence, the answers can be generated (inferred) without access to a specific memory trace of the episode.

Directed or Specialized Probing

Verbal probes differ in the comprehensiveness of the topics to be reported and the generality or particularity of the events to be reported. Let us first consider topic specificity. In many studies, the investigator is interested only in particular aspects of subjects' behaviors. Then the verbal probe may be constructed to induce the subjects to generate information specifically relevant to the hypotheses under consideration. In order to help subjects retrieve the desired information from memory and to induce greater completeness of the verbal reports, the question or verbal probe often contains contextual information. To guard against subjectivity in analyzing verbal reports, the investigator often supplies subjects with a fixed set of alternative responses. In contrast, a general instruction to give verbal reports typically asks subjects to tell everything they can remember or are thinking of while performing the task.

In most cases, verbosity and absence of selectivity in subjects' reports is not an important problem. What the subject reports is likely to be less, rather than more, than we should like to hear. In no study known to us using general instructions has the investigator complained that subjects have reported too much information from actual memory.

One common difficulty in probing for specific information, especially when the subjects are offered a fixed set of alternative answers, is to know that the questions conform to the internal representations the subjects are employing in their thought. Probes for types of information that subjects don't have directly accessible, or probes that provide inadequate sets of alternatives may force subjects to intermediate and inferential processing, and hence produce verbal reports that are not closely related to the actual thought process. Moreover, when specific, fixed-alternative probes are used, there is no way to detect from subjects' responses that this has occurred.

Since providing contextual information and prompts to subjects may aid recall from LTM, in studies of LTM the use of prompts and context is frequent and relatively well-motivated. When subjects are asked to report on immediately preceding cognitive processes of relatively short duration, specific probes are more questionable and less useful. In a logical sense, the experimenter gets just as much information from the subject in the third as in the first two of the following three cases.

(1)   Directed probe 1
       Question: Did you use X as a subgoal?
       Answer: Yes.

(2)   Directed probe 2
       Question: Did you use any subgoals? If so, which?
       Answer: Yes, I used X.

(3)   Undirected probe
       Verbal report: ...I was first trying to get X and I...
       when I attained X...

The replies in all three cases provide evidence that the subject used X as a subgoal, yet the evidence is stronger in the third case than in the second, and in the second than in the first. The verbalization in the first case could easily be generated by processes independent of any memory for the actual thought processes. Comparing the second and third cases, the former communicates to subjects what information the experimenter expects them to report. It may encourage subjects to try to infer or guess what particular information the experimenter will accept, and to generate information accordingly.

In many cases, other criteria are available for estimating the validity of the reports. An analysis of the task (Newell & Simon, 1972) will often provide strong indications of the adequacy of verbalized information, especially in cases with many logical possibilities for response.

Finally, different kinds of probes may have different effects upon the behavior of subjects. Requesting a certain kind of information may suggest to subjects what aspects of the task are important. Subjects may also alter their normal ways of processing so as to be able to give the requested information to the experimenter on subsequent trials.

In studies that use retrospective verbalization, subjects are seldom asked what they can remember about specific instances of their cognitive processes. Rather, they are usually asked to retrospect about their thought processes in experiments with many trials or to answer general questions, and thus must try to synthesize all the available information after selective recall. In making judgments, subjects have access to an extremely large base of relevant knowledge. Tversky and Kahneman (1973) have demonstrated that subjects only retrieve a few events or pieces of knowledge and use this sample to infer frequencies and probabilities of events. Although the retrieved sample may often be representative and the inferred probability judgment fairly accurate, there are many factors influencing retrievability that do not reflect frequency. Hence, in many situations such cognitive processes will yield incorrect judgments about frequency. Even though all the specific information retrieved is accurate, the inferred probability may be seriously in error. Nisbett and Ross (1980) have given a recent comprehensive discussion of such biasing factors in human judgment.

Particular and General Reports

If the purpose of retrospective probing were to recover memory traces of subjects' processes, the appropriate instruction would be to ask them to recall their specific thought processes during particular trials of the experiment. For at least two different reasons, such a procedure is rarely used. First, after a series of trials, a subject's memory for individual cognitive processes will be poor and lacking in detail. Moreover, there is a tendency for recurrent cognitive processes gradually to become automatic, so that fewer or none of the intermediate states of the processes for the later trials of the experiment are accessible for recall.

Second, many experimenters, because they are interested in general characteristics of the thought processes and not in the episodic details of the individual trials, probe their subjects with questions of the type, "How did you do these tasks?" Such questions implicitly or explicitly request a general rather than specific interpretation of how the subjects were performing the tasks.

There are several different ways in which subjects might arrive at descriptions of their general procedures, as distinct from reports on specific behaviors during individual trials. One possibility is that subjects are aware of the general procedures, or "programs," they are using, use essentially the same programs on all trials, and can recall and report these directly without reference to the specific behavior they produced. Another possibility is that subjects remember some parts of their processes during particular trials, and generalize this information into a general procedure, which they then report. A different possibility is that subjects remember some specific tasks, regenerate—by redoing them—the processes used for these tasks, and use this information to infer the general procedures they may have used. Finally, subjects may draw upon various kinds of prior information, such as general knowledge on how one ought to do these tasks, to generate a verbal report describing a general procedure or strategy. In this case, the verbal reports may not bear any close relation to the actual cognitive processes (Nisbett & Wilson, 1977).

In areas of applied psychological research where verbal questioning has a long tradition, subjects are usually asked about specific events rather than for general information or conclusions. In the critical incident technique proposed by Flanagan (1954), the subjects were always asked to report their memory for specific events. For example:

... pilots returning from combat were asked "to think of some occasion during combat flying in which you personally experienced feelings of acute disorientation or strong vertigo." They were then asked to describe what they "saw, heard, or felt that brought on the experience." (Flanagan, 1954, p. 329)

Interpretive probing, unlike the critical incident technique, cannot be relied upon to produce data stemming directly from the subjects' actual sequences of thought processes. The probing procedures encourage or even require subjects to speculate and theorize about their processes, rather than leaving the theory-building part of the enterprise to the experimenter. There is no reason to suppose that the subjects themselves will or can be aware of the limitations of the data they are providing. Moreover, the variety of inference and memory processes that might be involved in producing the reports make them extremely difficult to interpret or to use as behavioral data.

TWO CHALLENGES TO VERBAL REPORTS

It will be useful, in order to get a perspective on the issues, to use the above analysis to examine two published papers that have sometimes been interpreted as providing strong evidence against trusting verbal reports as data from which cognitive processes can be inferred: the first, a paper reporting a study by Verplanck and Oskamp; the second, the review paper on retrospective verbal reports by Nisbett and Wilson. A discussion of these papers will show how the information processing model we have outlined can help us interpret the findings of experiments on verbalization.

Apparent Inadequacies of Concurrent Verbalization

In an often cited study (Verplanck, 1962), Verplanck and Oskamp claimed to have shown that verbalized rules are dissociated from the behavior they were supposed to control. By having subjects verbalize the rules they were following in sorting illustrated cards, the experimenters could reinforce either the verbal rule or the placement of cards (i.e., behavior). To make the contingencies less noticeable, the criterion trials were followed by additional trials with partial reinforcement. When correct placements were reinforced, the subjects were found to place

cards correctly in 71.8% of the trials; but they stated a correct or correlated rule in only 48.4% of the trials. When correct statement of the rule
was reinforced, the subjects stated a correct or correlated rule on 92.8% of
the trials, but placed the cards correctly on only 76.8% of the trials.

In a replication and analysis of this experiment, Dulany and
O'Connell (1963) were able to show that the above results could be attributed to two artifacts of the original experiment. First, in the case
where correct placement was reinforced, by making a correction for
guessing (the subjects had a 50-50 chance of placing the card in the
correct pile when they didn't know the rule), we can estimate that subjects *knew* the correct answer in 43.6% of the trials—a percentage very
close to the 48.4% in which they stated the correct rule.

Second, with respect to the reinforcement of rules, Dulany and
O'Connell found that the rules defined by Verplanck and Oskamp were
ambiguous for the card illustrations they employed. In fact, naive subjects who were told these rules explicitly misplaced the cards as frequently as did the subjects in the original experiment.

In a detailed analysis of the rules the subjects verbalized on each
trial, Dulany and O'Connell found that on all but 11 of 34,408 trials the
subjects put the card where they said they were going to. Hence, Dulany
and O'Connell impeached rather thoroughly the evidence put forth by
Verplanck and Oskamp for believing that the rules subjects verbalized
were inconsistent with their behaviors.

Numerous studies provide positive support for consistency between
verbalized rules, concepts, and hypotheses and immediately preceding
and succeeding behavior, before subjects receive feedback. When
Schwartz (1966) asked subjects their reasons for placing a card as they
did, the reasons given were consistent with the placements on all but 2 of
1,962 trials. Even more impressive, Frankel, Levine, and Karpf (1970)
obtained retrospective reports from subjects about the basis for their
responses to four earlier discrimination-learning problems with 30 non-
feedback trials each, and found that subjects could provide such reports
in more than 90% of the sequences of trials.

Apparent Inadequacies of Retrospective Reports

In a recent extensive review of studies permitting evaluation of retrospective verbal reports, Nisbett and Wilson (1977) have reported evidence
that appears at first sight to be very damaging to the utility of verbal

reports for inferring information processes. Since their paper has received widespread attention, it is important that we review their findings carefully. The authors summarize their main empirical findings thus (1977, p. 233):

> People often cannot report accurately on the effects of particular stimuli on higher order, inference-based responses. Indeed, sometimes they cannot report on the existence of critical stimuli, sometimes cannot report on the existence of their responses, and sometimes cannot even report that an inferential process of any kind has occurred.

First, we call attention to the frequent use, in their summary, of the qualifiers "often" and "sometimes." Nisbett and Wilson cite a large number of experiments that support their conclusions, but do not investigate in detail the *conditions* under which these conclusions do and do not hold. Moreover, they do not propose a definite model of the cognitive processes as a framework for interpreting the findings they survey. Their theoretical interpretations are entirely informal, resting heavily on an undefined distinction between introspective access to "content" and to "process," or, as they alternatively state it, (1977, p. 255), between access to "private facts" and to "mental processes." Their summary of the kinds of information to which subjects *do* have access is this (1977, p. 255):

> ... we do indeed have direct access to a great storehouse of private knowledge ... The individual knows a host of personal historical facts; he knows the focus of his attention at any given point of time; he knows what his current sensations are and has what almost all psychologists and philosophers would assert to be "knowledge" at least quantitatively superior to that of observers concerning his emotions, evaluations, and plans. Given that the individual does possess a great deal of accurate knowledge ... it becomes less surprising that people would persist in believing that they have, in addition, direct access to their own cognitive processes. The only mystery is why people are so poor at telling the difference between private facts that can be known with near certainty and mental processes to which there may be no access at all.

Nisbett and Wilson also observe that subjects "are often capable of describing intermediate results of a series of mental operations (1977, p. 255)" (i.e., that they hold in STM and can access the symbols that are inputs and outputs to such operations).

We may compare this list of "private facts" and intermediate results that, according to Nisbett and Wilson, *are* accessible to subjects with the kinds of information that our processing model would imply that subjects could report. The individual knows, they say, his focus of attention, his current sensations, his emotions, his evaluations, and his plans. He knows the intermediate results of his mental operations. But these are exactly the kinds of information that, according to our model, would be held in STM and be available for verbal reports.

Unfortunately, the studies reviewed by Nisbett and Wilson provide little data on what information is heeded during the thought processes, and what information is accessible from STM and LTM at the time of the verbal report. Nisbett and Wilson find that the subjects, when *asked questions about their cognitive processes*, frequently do not base their answers on memory for specific events at all, but "theorize" about their processes (1977, p. 233).

When reporting on the effects of stimuli, people may not interrogate a memory of the cognitive processes that operated on the stimuli; instead, they may base their reports on implicit, a priori theories about the causal connection between stimulus and response.

In reviewing the studies cited by Nisbett and Wilson, we can profitably raise the question of *why* and *when* subjects do not consult their memories of cognitive processes in answering questions about those processes. It is easy to draw the erroneous conclusion that this independence of verbal answers to questions about cognitive processes from the actual course and results of those processes implies a *general* lack of accessible memory for such processes, or even an unawareness of the information while the process was actually going on. But this sweeping conclusion appears not to be justified.

The accuracy of verbal reports depends on the procedures used to elicit them and the relation between the requested information and the actual sequence of heeded information. Invalid reports, like those discussed and obtained by Nisbett and Wilson, may be due to lack of access to thoughts (their claim), inadequate procedures for eliciting verbal reports, or requesting information that could not be provided even if thoughts were accessible. In a subsequent chapter (Chapter 3) we will describe in some detail what information will be heeded and hence reportable. Although some studies cited by Nisbett and Wilson did probe for such information, we will focus here on the deviations between the verbal report procedures used in many of the studies cited by Nisbett and Wilson and the procedures that, according to our model, would elicit valid retrospective reports of cognitive processes.

First, many of the verbal reports they discuss could be generated without accessing memory of the corresponding cognitive processes. In some of these studies, the questions presented to subjects contain considerable background information from which answers could be generated without consulting their memories. With questions like, "I noticed that you took more shock than average. Why do you suppose you did?" (Nisbett & Wilson, 1977, p. 237) It is not even clear to us, nor probably to the subjects, that memory for the cognitive process *should* be the information source for the answer. If subjects can generate their answers without consulting their memories (Nisbett and Wilson showed that control subjects could do exactly that), they might often prefer this method to retrieving information from memory.

Second, several aspects of the verbal report procedures reviewed by Nisbett and Wilson made the relevant thoughts less *accessible.* In most of the studies reviewed, the time lag between task and probe was sufficiently great to make it unlikely that the relevant information remained in STM. In Chapter 3 we will review the rather extensive literature from general experimental psychology showing that time and intervening thought activity between the cognitive process and its verbal report, as well as incentive to recall memories of the cognitive process, lead to dramatic declines in the accuracy of the verbally reported information. A recent chapter by Genest and Turk (1981) and a paper by Wright and Kriewall (1980) give references showing that such considerations of accessibility are powerful determiners of the accuracy of verbal reports for cognitive processes in tasks like those discussed by Nisbett and Wilson (1977).

A tendency to generate verbal reports without access to memories will be stronger, the less readily available the memory is. When the probe is not a good retrieval cue for the relevant aspects of the memory, the subject must attempt, through conscious processing, to recall sufficient information to give an appropriate answer. Since retrieval from LTM, even if possible, requires considerable time and effort, subjects, unless explicitly instructed to provide a relatively complete recall, may be disinclined to do so, especially if other ways of producing a response are open to them. A recent study by Wright and Rip (1980) provides strong evidence for an increase in accurate self-report when subjects were explicitly motivated to retrieve memory for thoughts in a judgment task.

Finally, in some studies reviewed by Nisbett and Wilson, subjects were asked to report information that cannot be given even with complete access to the thought processes (cf. why-questions regarding causes), and information that is far from a direct recall of memory of the cognitive processes. Our model predicts that information can be recovered by probes only if the same information would be accessed by undirected requests for concurrent or retrospective reports. For many of the studies in the Nisbett-Wilson review, our model would predict failure to obtain from the probes verbal information about particular instances of processes. For example, in between-subject designs, subjects obviously cannot answer from memory of their processes why they behaved differently from subjects in another experimental condition—the processes did not include such a comparison. Hence, this information can be derived, if at all, only by comparing the descriptions of the processes provided by different sets of subjects in the two conditions. In other studies the subjects were asked how they would have reacted if the experimental conditions had been different in a specified respect. Such probing for hypothetical states can never tap subjects' memories for their cognitive processes, since the information was never in memory. In still other studies, subjects were asked, explicitly or implicitly, to summarize or generalize the processes they used, rather than to report concretely the processes used on each trial.

Several articles have been published making similar criticisms of the Nisbett and Wilson (1977) paper, and raising other objections as well. Of particular interest are the papers discussing the problems with verbal reports in between-group designs. (Smith & Miller, 1978). Some recent studies have shown that in corresponding within-group studies, subjects are able to provide veridical verbal reports (White, 1980; Weitz & Wright, 1979; Wright & Rip, 1980).

In sum, we disagree with Nisbett and Wilson's interpretation that subjects simply were not aware of relevant information during the critical experiments. Instead, we claim that better methods for probing for that awareness (concurrent or immediate retrospective reports) would yield considerable insight into the cognitive processes occurring in *most* of the studies discussed by Nisbett and Wilson. On the other hand, we agree with Nisbett and Wilson's analysis of subject's reports in situations where the subjects do not have access to or for other reasons don't rely on memory for the cognitive processes in question. In such situations, Nisbett and Wilson propose that an experimental subject infers the causes of his own behavior by relying on common-sense theories and observable events—the same process that an observer would use to infer causes of behavior in an observed subject. By using experimental situations, where common-sense theory would lead to the incorrect assessment of causes, Nisbett and Wilson provide convincing evidence for their interpretation by showing that both experimental subjects and observers agree on the incorrect cause of the experimental subjects' behaviors. (For a nice presentation and extension of these arguments see Nisbett and Ross (1980).)

We think that Nisbett and Wilson's paper has been useful in forcing investigators like ourselves to think carefully about the relation of verbal reports to cognitive processes. Many verbal report procedures are justly faulted by their review. However, their results are consistent with our model of concurrent and immediate retrospective reports.

Concluding Remarks

Our examination of two of the most vigorous challenges to the usefulness of verbal reporting leaves intact our belief that such reports— especially concurrent reports, and retrospective reports *of specific cognitive processes*—provide powerful means for gaining information about such processes. The concurrent report reveals the sequence of information heeded by the subject without altering the cognitive process, while other kinds of verbal reports may change these processes. In retrospective reports of specific processes, subjects generally will actually retrieve the trace of the processes. In other forms of retrospective reporting, subjects, instead of recalling this information, may report information that they have inferred or otherwise generated. Hence, in the chapters that follow, we will pay particular attention to the two special forms of reporting—the one concurrent, the other retrospective—that are most likely to yield direct evidence of cognitive processes.

VERBAL REPORTS OF COGNITIVE STATES AND STRUCTURES

Although this book focuses upon cognitive processes, the model and concepts it employs can be extended to the non-cognitive aspects of verbal behaviors. There are several reasons for undertaking such an extension. It will permit us to identify common problems and issues in areas of psychology, like psychophysics, survey design, and measurement of personality traits, that traditionally have had little or no interaction with each other. In these areas, too, as in those we have been discussing, behaviorism has muted explicit examination of the status of verbal responses and reports.

First, we will propose a taxonomy of these other kinds of verbal reports, and will discuss briefly some examples of relevant research. Then we will consider two limited topics for more systematic discussion. The first of these is attitude assessment, the second is the historical development of verbal reporting, with particular emphasis on introspection. All of the verbal reports with which we will be concerned in this section are elicited by probes specifying what information is to be reported. Often, also, a set of alternatives is supplied from which the subject has to select a response.

Predictions from our model about the effects of verbal reporting on thought processes will depend on the circumstances under which the verbalizations are induced. We can classify verbalizations according to the memories that are tapped and according to the verbalization instructions the experimenter gives to the subjects. With respect to the memory source of the reported information, we can distinguish among (a) reports of stimuli that remain constant and available to the subject's senses while the report is being made, (b) reports of information retained in STM, and (c) reports of information from LTM. The next three subsections of this section will be devoted to the special problems that arise for each of these three kinds of reports.

Reporting of Sensory Stimuli

At any given moment, a large amount of external stimulation impinges on any human through the sensory receptors (visual, auditory, etc.), as well as from internal visceral sources. Normally this information is not heeded directly, but recognition processes access existing relevant LTM patterns, which provide higher-level descriptions and are in turn heeded. (In Chapter 3 we will discuss these recognition processes and their relation to attention in some detail.) In many circumstances attention can be directed toward the information in the sensory stores (cf. Kahneman, 1973). We can focus on marks on the page we are reading or listen for unusual faint sounds and so on. Many kinds of verbal reporting procedures rely directly on our ability to process sensory information selectively.

In most psychophysical studies, subjects are instructed as to the stimuli as well as the types of responses they will use. They are asked to rate how much pain the experience causes, how loud a certain stimulus is, how far away a certain stimulus is, and so on. This research has had a strong empirical emphasis and has been virtually unaffected by the drastic changes in theoretical views of mainstream experimental psychology. In our historical discussion, we will point to differences between the psychophysical methods and the analytic introspective methods, which also attempted to describe experiences in terms of the sensory units. Now we only want to sketch the relation of the psychophysical methods to our model of verbal reporting.

Since the primary goal of psychophysical research has been to describe the structural relation between physical stimulus and response, little attention has been paid to the mediating processes. However, selective attention is under attentional control and as reportable as is the final reponse. (The study cited earlier showing that subjects can substitute key pressing for verbal reports is a case in point.) The research methodology of psychophysics uses long sessions of trials to seek stable structural relations and highly automatized processes.

In a classic paper, Eriksen (1960) showed that the verbal report is the most sensitive index for basic perceptual processes, like discrimination. Hence, the results from psychophysical methods of report are quite consistent with our model of verbal reporting. We would, however, like to go a step further and argue that detailing the cognitive processes involved in generating psychophysical reports may prove quite useful. First, there is evidence that cognitive structures are involved even in simple judgments, like discrimination. A dramatic example is given by Binet (1969), who showed that the threshold for discriminating touch of two separate points of contact (compared to a single point of contact) could be reduced *10 times* by showing the subject the compass used. Second, different verbal instructions in judgments of size give different results (Carlson, 1977). Subjects give reliably different responses when asked to judge the objective size, the apparent size, and the size of the vertical projection of an object.

Converging support for the use of different cognitive processes in judgment of apparent and objective size was obtained by Epstein and Broota (1975), who found objective size judgments to be slower and a linear function of the distance to the stimulus object, whereas apparent size judgments were faster and unrelated to distance. Brunswik (1956) shows that instructing subjects to analyze the stimulus, as well as asking them to "be so certain that they could bet on the actual size," clearly influences the judgments. Finally, and probably most important, the observed improvement of psychophysical judgments with practice (see Gibson, 1969) appears to implicate cognitive mechanisms (see Chapter 3). Some recent results by Ericsson and Faivre (1982) show that performance in a perceptual learning experiment can be best described in terms of the acquisition of cognitive structures indentified from retrospective verbal reports.

A related class of learning situations involve control of body functions—like heart rate, audiomotor performance—through biofeedback. In a very interesting review, Roberts and Marlin (1979) discuss the fairly extensive research (with conflicting results) on how reported awareness mediates development of control of these body functions. They define *veridical content* as verbally reported information making reference to "activities or perceptual events that are correlated with target behavior and therefore with feedback presentation" (Roberts and Marlin, 1979, p. 81), and discuss circumstances favorable to the generation of such reports. They point to two main biasing sources. Instructions in these biofeedback tasks often explicitly tell subjects to avoid certain strategies, like regulation of breathing rate. Other instructions give subjects incorrect information (e.g., that rate of heart beats is unrelated to rate of breathing). It is clear that such instructions will bias the subject against reporting such information regardless of their thoughts. These studies indicate that subjects can report the strategies they use for achieving control of visceral functions.

In a subsequent study, Roberts, Marlin, Keleher, and Williams (1982) provide some supportive evidence for the claims of validity of verbal reports made by Roberts and Marlin (1979). In most other studies, subjects are informed what visceral function is to be controlled, but this information may induce inferential processing, and also eliminates the possibility of using statements on what function is involved to validate the verbalized thought. In two studies described by Roberts et al., (1982), subjects were not told which visceral functions were involved and were simply shown an indicator of the function to be controlled. Subjects gave written descriptions of how they achieved control immediately after training. All subjects developing control over the visceral function invariably showed evidence for accurate self-report regarding their processing, as assessed by blind judges of written descriptions.

Our framework for analyzing verbal reports also applies well to psychophysical experiments. Similar methodological and theoretical issues arise in the two domains, especially with regard to the instructions given subjects. Moreover, there is evidence of subjects' awareness of process even in the reports from these "simple" and "basic" psychophysical tasks.

Reports of Information in STM

Next we will review briefly some types of verbal reporting from STM that are closely related to those already discussed, but which have been used so frequently that they have emerged as separate procedures with separate literatures.

In *thought sampling*. an attempt is made to get data on subjects' thoughts while they are performing their daily activities. Subjects are given a portable tone generator, which generates tones at random times. When a tone sounds, the subjects are to stop their normal activity and write down their thoughts, and perhaps additional information.

Genest and Turk (1981) provide a nice review of the emerging research using this method. In most cases the method is non-directive, requesting a report of the heeded thought at the time the tone was heard. Yet, the report is retrospective and often a fair amount of time will intervene before the subject can make his written record. Kendall and Korgeski (1979) propose that subjects should be provided with portable tape recorders so reporting will be more immediate and less disruptive. Genest and Turk (1981) also discuss *event recording*, where subjects are asked to record all instances of a certain type of thought. It is not un-likely that such instructions will lead to conscious monitoring and in-crease the frequency of thoughts of the observed kind. Unlike thought sampling, event recording is mostly used with maladaptive thoughts, with the aim of identifying their content rather than measuring their fre-quency.

Another widely used technique is *thought listing*, where the subject is asked to write down all thoughts that occurred during an interval. This technique is in many cases indistinguishable from the retrospective reporting discussed earlier. It is different in emphasizing thoughts as distinguishable elements. Where thoughts are elicited through associa-tions to externally presented information, and are relatively disconnected from each other, one would expect reporting thoughts to be easy and unambiguous. Reports of the lists of thoughts from an interconnected thought activity like mental multiplication will undoubtedly be more difficult. In a nice review, Cacioppo and Petty (1981) note that most of the studies using thought listing have studied thoughts evoked by persuasive communication.

Reports of Information in LTM

Subjects are often asked to report information that has no relation to their immediately preceding thoughts. The general format is to ask the subject a question and often also to provide a set of alternative answers. According to our model, the subject needs to comprehend the question and retrieve relevant information from memory. Retrieval can in some cases proceed directly from comprehension of the question (i.e., "In what year were you born?"). More often the subject needs to generate retrieval cues to access relevant memory traces (i.e., "How many times have you been to a movie theater in the last two months?"). In Chapter 3 we will consider in more detail the process of retrieval of information and in Chapter 5 we discuss studies of the retrieval process using protocol analysis. Here we wish to show that simply by asking by what processes the subject can make his responses we can arrive at some useful conclusions about these matters.

Our model makes a major distinction between information directly stored in memory and information that is generated and produced. The first class comprises factual information and information about experiences and perceived events and behavior in past situations. The second class comprises information about reactions and behavior in hypothetical situations, including general and abstractly described situations.

Reports of Past Experience. When we ask somebody to report something they should know and the report is not accurate, we may be inclined to distrust the method of asking (i.e., the verbal report). Such evidence is, of course, particularly damaging if we lack methods to validate even occasionally the reported information. In surveys, subjects are often asked many different questions. One question that is fairly easy to validate is "How old are you?". Some studies have shown the reported information to be invalid in as many as 83% of cases (Parry & Crossley, 1950). At first glance, that may be rather surprising, as most people should know their age. Invalid reports might indicate premeditated lying, which of course is always a possibility. But asking for somebody's age is unfortunate, as age changes each year. If we rely on direct retrieval of our age, we may access information stored earlier which is no longer valid. Bjork (1978) has shown that a similar analysis can account for experiences of children appearing to grow very fast or parents aging very fast. When we see the child or the parent, we access an image of them, which was not the most recently seen image but one stored at an earlier time, hence the too big difference between perception and image. It is, of course, possible to derive one's age from one's birthdate, but the calculation requires mental effort, and can lead to errors and attempts to estimate the answer. This is especially true when the subject does not perceive the need to be completely accurate. Asking for somebody's birthdate would be much better as it remains fixed.

In other cases, the invalidity of reported information can be traced to issues of definition. In answering how many rooms they have in their house or apartment, subjects may differ in their ideas of what constitutes a room. Karlton and Schuman (1980) cite a study of the English census that showed that people were accurate in reporting the number of rooms according to their own definitions, but they simply did not use the census definition.

The problems in obtaining valid reports become more pronounced if the subject doesn't have the relevant information readily accessible in memory. When we ask subjects how often they have been to the doctor or the dentist, experienced various forms of crimes, or made airplane trips during some specified time interval, we would expect them to retrieve all these instances from memory, and attempt to verify that they occurred during the given time interval. However, if only the number of instances is to be reported, we have no way to monitor the subjects' retrieval activity and they may estimate rather than recall the instances.

When subjects are asked to recall instances, investigators have found the retrieved information to be valid. The common error appears to be inability to date instances and hence to determine whether they occurred within the given time interval. For highly salient and retrievable instances, this may lead to overreporting. By asking subjects to recall instances before as well as after the critical time period, such overreporting can be virtually eliminated.

A multitude of issues surround the use of fixed response alternatives to questions (see Schuman and Presser (1981) for an extensive review). In the ideal case, the subject retrieves his response and selects the appropriate response alternative. The results from studies using open-ended questions and fixed responses should then be very similar, but in many cases they are not. In an interesting analysis, Schuman and Presser (1981) showed that the main source of discrepancy was the unavailability of certain alternatives. By constructing the fixed alternatives from the open-ended responses in a preliminary study they showed that much closer correspondence could be obtained between the two types of responses in a subsequent study. In fact, providing the set of relevant alternatives may reduce retrieval failures and hence enhance the validity of responses. We will talk later about possible effects of bringing to mind certain kinds of information that the subject may not have thought of otherwise. It is interesting that in Schuman and Presser's (1981) study, subjects recalling the most preferred aspect of a job gave most responses with the same frequencies as when they selected the responses from alternatives.

The concern for achieving accurate recall of information is quite explicit in current survey research. Karlton and Schuman (1980) review three methods used by Cannell and his colleagues to achieve more accurate reporting. First, the subject should be given an explicit instruction to recall accurately. We know that people do better when they think carefully about each question, search their memory, and take their time in answering. People also do better if they give exact answers, and give as much information as they can. This includes important things as well as things which may seem small or unimportant (From Cannell et al., 1981, reviewed in Karlton and Schuman (1980, p. 16)). Second, the interviewer should give more sensitive feedback and, in particular, monitor the retrieval process. For example, when subjects gives quick responses, they should be encouraged to think and retrieve more. Last, the interviewer should try to get the subject to make an explicit agreement to respond accurately and completely.

Reports of Hypothetical and General Information. Verbal reports that do not specify a clear relation to retrievable experiences, events, or knowledge are of several kinds. We want to distinguish verbal reports on reactions or behavior in *hypothetical situations* from verbal reports on reactions or behavior towards persons, ideas, and experience *in general* without specification of more specific context or situation.

Occasionally, we find verbal reports about hypothetical situations used in experimental psychology. For example, in a study by Reed and Johnsen (1977), subjects were asked how they would solve a problem if it were presented to them again. Subjects in a study by Nisbett and Wilson (1977) were asked how they would react to a story if some passages had not been presented. However, the most frequent and important use has been opinion-polls, surveys and personality and attitude assessment. Personality and attitude assessment will be discussed later in a separate section.

We cannot offer a detailed model of the cognitive processes that generate a response to an attitude or opinion question. In fact, given our model, it is quite puzzling how somebody can access and integrate the multitude of relevant aspects and experiences at the time of the question. (The situation is, of course, quite different when the assessment has already been made prior to the question and can be directly accessed.) A possible view is that the question or statement serves as a retrieval cue to access a small subset of selected information, which is evaluated and used as a basis for responding. The consistency of accessed information and response to the same statement at different times will be determined by the organization of LTM—a point we will discuss in more detail in Chapter 3.

A review of the literature shows that such a simple association model has some support, especially for attitudes and opinions that are moderate and refer to non-central issues. Even when people are responding repeatedly to the same items within a relatively short time interval like a year, intercorrelations are relatively low (around 0.40) (Schuman & Presser, 1981). The principal exceptions are strong attitudes to central issues. The most likely locus of the variability between test occasions is in the information accessed.

More direct evidence for the selective cueing of information comes from the extensive body of research showing effects of wording questions in different ways. For example, subjects are much more willing "not to allow" public speeches against democracy than to "forbid" such speeches. Schuman and Presser (1981) shows similar effects for "not allowing" vs. "forbidding" other activities. Even in laboratory studies where subjects are exposed to the same events and information, the wording of the question (i.e., How long was the film? vs. How short was the film?), yields reliable differences, even when the same response alternatives were used. Although we lack evidence about what information was accessed, the direction of the influence is consistent with the hypothesis of selective access of information.

In a situation where subjects' attitudes and opinions are measured, the retrieved information will not simply reflect the current question, for information retrieved on preceding questions will be more accessible and more likely to be retrieved if similar cues are reinstated. The procedure used to study the influence of answering preceding questions is to manipulate the order of presentation of questions and compare the responses to the same question in the different orders. Although most questions or items do not show such order effects, or at least sufficiently large effects to be statistically reliable, there are several examples where the effects are quite large. Schuman and Presser (1981) discussed two items where the interpretation of the effect appears quite straightforward.

Communist reporter item:
   Do you think the United States should let Communist newspaper reporters from other countries come in here and send back to their papers the news as they see it?

American reporter item:
   Do you think a Communist country like Russia should let American newspaper reporters come in and send back to America the news as they see it?
   see it?

The effect of interest is that subjects are more likely to be favorable to letting foreign reporters operate in the USA if they have previously answered the item regarding letting American reporters operate in Communist countries (see Schuman and Presser (1981) for a comprehensive review of similar effects). Interesting effects of previous questions are also shown in a recent study by Bishop, Oldendick, and Tuchfarber (1982). They were able to show that subjects' assessed general interest in politics and the coming election was markedly influenced by preceding questions on facts regarding the election, like names of candidates for President, and voting records of their representatives in Congress.

In two experiments Bishop et al. (1982) showed separately that easy preceding questions (tapping information most people know) led to higher assessed interest levels, and hard preceding questions led to a decrease in assessed interest levels. The effects interacted with the knowledge people had about politics and the election. Highly knowledgeable subjects were unaffected by preceding easy questions, whereas subjects with less information were affected. Hard questions had a rather uniform effect of reducing subjects' assessed interest in the election and politics.

Admittedly, our discussion of cognitive processes in these unstructured verbal report situations is rather speculative. As far as we know, almost no attempts have been made to determine with the aid of verbal reports what information is accessed in such situations and by what processes. However, there is evidence suggesting that this would be feasible. First, open-ended questions where subjects are asked to name aspects and issues have been quite successful. Second, Schuman (1966) showed that asking subjects to elaborate their closed-choice selections for randomly selected items (random probe technique) was useful in evaluating understanding of the item when it was translated and used in a different culture. Finally, some of the tasks used by Karl Buhler (1908a,b) are rather similar to deciding one's opinion on a statement. He found subjects able to provide informative sequences of thoughts about their opinions. A more complete empirical analysis of the thought processes should yield interesting implications for improvement and redesign of the methods used to assess attitudes, opinions and other general constructs. Below we will consider in more detail psychological research concerned with assessing attitudes and its relation to verbal reporting.

VERBAL REPORTS IN ASSESSMENT STUDIES

In discussing various forms of verbal reporting that claim to elicit currently heeded information or cognitive structures that remain in memory, we have indicated how several different kinds of cognitive processes might generate the reported information. One of our major assertions is that verbal reports can be, and should be, understood in exactly the same way as we understand other kinds of responses.

As a concrete application of our approach to a major area of psychological research, let us see what a first-pass analysis of verbal reports in questionnaire-answering might yield. In particular, let us look at the assessment research aimed at measuring and describing individual differences, especially differences in cognitive structure. This research has adopted many of the ideas advocated by Watson. The approach has been to search for aspects of behavior that remain invariant over some class of situations, yet discriminate one individual from another. Collecting observations and discovering behavioral regularities (especially with the help of correlational techniques) have been emphasized over theoretical analysis. Much of the research has been directed towards useful "real-world" applications: selecting people for education, jobs, and various forms of clinical treatment.

It has been customary to interpret invariant aspects of behavior that are found by assessment in terms of postulated internal states or traits. General abilities, like numerical skill, are associated with traits as are many stable aspects of personality, like aggressiveness. In the approach described above, which we will term indirect assessment, the invariant structures are induced from many specific observations.

Within the same framework, attempts have been made to gain information about these general invariant structures more directly. Instead of time-consuming observation of subjects' behaviors in concrete situations (e.g., while selecting food dishes), one could ask for their reactions to a verbal description of a general class of situations (e.g., "Do you like to eat fish?") and thus seek to access general preferences directly.

Alternatively, one can ask subjects after they have exhibited some behavior why they did it, hoping to receive a report of a general motive that could explain or predict their behavior over a wide range of situations. This research has taken a basically empirical approach to finding behavioral regularities, and it has not attempted to specify the cognitive mechanisms that both generate behavior and are accessible for verbal questioning. Implicit reference is made to the common-sense notion that people are aware and rational and therefore able to answer questions about the cognitive structures responsible for their overt behavior.

Data

In consistency with the behaviorist viewpoint, the research on direct and indirect assessment has not collected observations and data about the processes that generate the target behavior. Concurrent verbalizations, retrospective reports, and latencies have been collected and analyzed only very sparingly.

Indirect assessment methods have been used primarily and most successfully to assess cognitive abilities. In ability tests a sample of representative tasks for the ability in question is generated, and the subjects' responses are evaluated for correctness. A given subject's ability is then assessed in terms of his or her pattern of success on the items. The cognitive structures are inferred only indirectly.

To create representative situations that will elicit behavior reflecting hypothesized traits—like preference, aggressiveness, and other personality-based characteristics—is much harder. Some research has employed observers to record subjects' behaviors in natural environments or in semi-controlled group interactions. However, most of the research has employed more direct assessment procedures. We have distinguished four methods that produce different kinds of data for assessing traits. Some of these distinctions have been proposed by Olson (1976).

1. In the first type of assessment procedure, observers who study the subjects' behavior in one or several types of situations afterwards make direct estimates of the "levels" of certain traits for the subjects. These ratings by the observers constitute the data.

2. In the second type of procedure, the subjects' memories are probed for their previous behavior or covert reactions in particular classes of situations. The subjects are generally asked to respond with one alternative from a predetermined set, which asks about the frequency (e.g., "never," "occasionally," "often," etc.) of the behavior.

3. A third type of procedure obtains subjects' reactions to verbal stimuli or their predicted actions in general situations verbally described. We give an example of a stimulus and an excerpt from an instruction given to subjects (taken from Mischel, 1968, pp. 61-62):

> I enjoy social gatherings just to be with people. (Item from California Psychological Inventory.)

> Your first impression is generally the best so work quickly and don't be concerned about duplications, contradictions or being exact. (From instructions to the Leary Interpersonal Check List.)

The data in this case are the categories (e.g., "very much," "not at all," etc.) that the subject selects, and the responses are not conceptualized as introspective reports about the associated traits.

4. In the fourth type of procedure, subjects are asked for explanations of, or motives for, their observed behavior. When the subjects are asked *how* they were thinking throughout the experiment or *why* they exhibited particular behavior, the experimenter seeks to learn directly from them the underlying cognitive structure that produced the overt behavior.

Effectiveness of Assessment

Indirect assessment of cognitive abilities has been found to be very successful in predicting behavioral differences in real-world situations. This stands in rather stark contrast with the controversies surrounding assessment (direct or indirect) of personality traits and direct assessment of cognitive structures in general. Correlations between different methods and tests for assessing the same personality traits are often unsatisfac-torily low (e.g., Campbell & Fiske, 1959). Reported reasons for behavior are unrelated to experimentally induced variations in behavior (e.g., Nisbett & Wilson, 1977). Reported attitudes do not correspond to actual behavior (e.g., Calder & Ross, 1973; Schuman & Johnson, 1976; Wicker, 1969).

In trying to explain the relative success of indirect assessment of cognitive abilities as compared with other types of indirect assessment, we consider the differences in the cognitive processes involved and the cognitive structures accessed.   Unfortunately, there has been little research directed toward uncovering processes, most analyses having been made on data representing the final result of the processes. Lacking extensive data on the relevant processes, we will proceed by making assumptions derived from other areas of cognition where more such data have been gathered. First, we will note some general differences between the kinds of cognitive processes evoked by ability tests and the kinds evoked by personality tests and direct assessments. Then, we will turn to a discussion based on a more detailed explication of the cognitive processes underlying probes to assess cognitive structures directly.

Processes Evoked by Assessment

There are at least three marked differences between the cognitive processes evoked by items in an ability test and those evoked by items in a test to assess traits by self-reports. The first difference concerns the likelihood that the relevant cognitive processes and structures are actually evoked or accessed. The "first impression" requested by the instruction, quoted above, for self-reports and the emphasis that responses are neither right nor wrong, stand in stark contrast to the instructions for ability tests, where responses are considered carefully before being produced and are either correct or incorrect. In order to generate the correct answer or response in an ability test, the information has to be processed carefully by the relevant sequence of operations. The probability that a subject can generate the answer by guessing or some short-circuiting procedure like first impression, is small. There is, thus, much more experimental control for ability items than for self-report items over the cognitive processes and structures that are activated to generate a response.

For self-report items, uninteresting response processes (like always agreeing with the statement or simply selecting the socially desirable alternative) often appear to account for a sizeable fraction of the variance. However, by careful selection of questionnaire items, more recent studies have reduced the extent to which subjects can rely on such criteria as social desirability in choosing their answers.

The second difference between ability tests and others derives from the relation between the test item and the "real" situation in which the actual non-test behavior occurs. Many symbolic tasks occurring in the "real" situations, like arithmetic, are rather accurately represented by a test item. By contrast, verbal description of a social interactive situation is usually a rather poor representation of the situation, which fails to communicate many essential aspects that would influence the actual non-test behavior. We will return to this issue later.

Memories versus Inferences

The frequent low correlations between different assessment tests of the same trait provide grounds for scepticism about verbal reports.

Inaccuracy has been attributed mainly to a variety of distorting motivational forces, including deliberate faking, lack of insight, and unconscious defensive reactions, all of which presumably produce inaccurate self-descriptions (Mischel, 1968, p. 69).

However, Mischel (1968) points to research supporting other possibilites, which are consistent with the notion that subjects are able to describe and predict specific behavior with minimal interpretation of its meaning. The self-reports described so far require the subjects' global interpretations of their own general behavior patterns, rather than descriptions of specific behavior. Likewise, the attributes assessed by observers are mostly high-level traits that require considerable inference. Correlations could be low between different assessments because they elicited different inferences rather than because of conflict of evidence at the level of description of specific behavior. In support of this view, Mischel (1968) cites research showing that inter-coder reliabilities increase rapidly as the necessity for complex inference decreases. For further discussion of the special problems of assessments by observers see Fiske (1978) and Mischel (1968).

Remembered versus Anticipated Behaviors. In a more detailed analysis of the cognitive processes occuring in assessment procedures, we need to distinguish probing subjects' memories for past processes and occurrences of acts and reactions, on the one hand, from probing for subjects' anticipated responses in verbally described situations or to described classes of objects or people.

First we will address probing for subjects' memories. We will assume that information about specific past behavior and covert reactions is generally stored in episodic form in LTM. This implies that a statement about occurrences of a certain kind will require access to the memory of all relevant specific occurrences of that kind. For simplicity, we will not discuss the exceptions, where subjects have been asked similar questions before, or have, by their own reflective activity, already generated the corresponding general information, which then can be accessed directly.

From general research on recall, we know that ability to recall specific events—especially with detailed information—deteriorates rapidly with time (see Cannell & Kahneman, 1968). Recall depends very much on the availability of retrieval cues. Since general verbal descriptions of classes of events most often will be insufficient as cues for retrieving specific events, subjects will have to supply additional information to generate more specific cues, like the relevant time period and specific situations in which the activity might have occurred. If the experimenter specifies the relevant time period and particular type of events to be recalled, recall increases considerably (e.g., Biderman, 1967). This type of recall is very time consuming and can hardly take place in the time allotted for filling out a questionnaire, unless the relevant episodes were few and easily retrieved because of recency.

If the subjects were able and motivated to retrieve all relevant episodes, they would face the problem of converting the information into fixed alternatives, like "often," "frequently," etc. Mischel (1968) cites a study by Simpson, that demonstrated that a wide range of percentages were associated with such words, when presented out of context. For example, one fourth of Simpson's subjects associated "frequently" with events occurring over 80% of the time, whereas another fourth associated it with events occurring less than 40% of the time. The processing activity that would be needed for accurate responses to questions about past overt and covert behavior—given the limits of recallability—appears to be incompatible with the relatively fast responses requested.

Causes of Behavior. Let us now turn to the questioning of subjects about the reasons or causes of their behavior. In terms of our model, legitimate probes for reasons and motives for observed behavior in a given process are just one kind of cue for retrieving information selectively from the memory trace of that process. From studies of current verbalization of heeded information, we know that subjects often generate goals in solving problems, hypotheses in concept-formation experiments, and evaluations in decision making. It should be possible to elicit these by probes of *why* a specific overt behavior occurred.

One should not assume that the subjects can assess directly that specific responses were "caused" indirectly by more general goals or hypotheses. Cognitive processes often involve attention to specific information, which is *not* a specification of heeded general structures like goals. Information is heeded in other cases as a result of direct recognition processes without any intermediate states entering consciousness. In these cases the subject cannot answer a *why* question by direct retrieval from memory.

Much of the research cited by Nisbett and Wilson (1977) and reviewed above concerns experiments where the subjects have been questioned about a long series of experimental trials. When subjects are asked about their average behavior or motives, they obviously cannot answer the questions by retrieving a single motive or episodic memory. The behavior on different trials may correspond to very different cognitive processes, and it may in any event be difficult to retrieve them all from memory. Therefore, it is reasonable to assume that the subject either infers general motives or processes from retrieved selected episodic memories, or tries to rationalize his behavior using other sources of information than the memory of the processes.

Smith and Miller (1978) noted that in many of the experiments cited by Nisbett and Wilson the subjects were asked why their behavior in one condition of the experiment differed from other subjects' behavior in other conditions of the experiment. In such a situation, it is not clear to subjects that their memory is relevant for answering the question, as shown by the following initial step of a typical dialogue:

> Question: I notice that you took more shock than average. Why do you suppose you did?
> Typical answer: Gee, I don't really know . . . Well, I used to build radios and stuff when I was 13 or 14, and maybe I got used to electric shock. (Nisbett & Wilson, 1977, p. 237)

The subject appears to understand the assertion to mean that he took more shock than other subjects in the *same* condition, and he therefore probed his memory for explanations that would be independent of the situation, and hence of his processing activity. If the subject, to give a valid report, has to rely on his memory for his earlier processing, it would be necessary for him to have experienced *both* experimental conditions to explain any differences in behavior between them. Inferring what one would do in a new situation should not be confounded with reporting actual memory of completed processes.

Predictive Responses. In the case of asking subjects for their reactions to classes of persons or objects or their expectations of their behavior in verbally described situations, we have little data on what cognitive processes and structures are evoked. It is most plausible to assume that the subject forms some kind of representation or "image" of what is verbally described, and uses this to determine his hypothetical reaction or behavior. LaPiere (1934) questioned the extent to which subjects in many situations are able to represent internally the crucial aspects of the verbally described situations. Any such failure will make their conceived behavior different from actual nontest behavior.

> Thus from a hundred or a thousand reponses to the question "Would you get up to give an Armenian woman your seat in a street car?" the investigator derives the "attitude" of non-Armenian males towards Armenian females. Now the question may be constructed with elaborate skill and hidden with consumate cunning in a maze of supplementary or even irrelevant questions yet all that has been obtained is a symbolic response to a symbolic situation. The words "Armenian woman" do not constitute an Armenian woman of flesh and blood, who might be tall or squat, fat or thin, old or young, well or poorly dressed—who might, in fact, be a goddess or just another old and dirty hag. And the questionnaire response, whether it be "yes" or "no," is but a verbal reaction and this does not involve rising from the seat or stolidly avoiding the hurt eyes of the hypothetical woman and the derogatory stares of other street-car occupants. (LaPiere, 1934, p. 230)

In his classic study, LaPiere (1934) studied attitudes and behavior towards Orientals. Six months after a large number of hotels and restaurants had been visited by an Oriental couple, the same places were sent a questionnaire with the question, "Will you accept members of the Chinese race as guests in your establishment?" The overwhelming majority of the places visited answered "no," with a smaller number saying "under some circumstances." Similar disassociation of verbal responses to symbolic situations from real behavior has been found by, for example, Kutner, Wilkins, and Yarrow (1952).

In information processing terms, LaPiere's hypothesis is that, in the cases where the generated internal representaton contains all relevant aspects appropriately portrayed as in the "real" situation, the behavior and verbally reported behavior will be consistent. When the "real" situation is more or less symbolic, as in the case of voting, accurate predictions can usually be made for actual behavior on an aggregate level from verbal reactions to questions (see Schuman & Johnson, 1976). Similarly, Katona (1975, 1979) has found that sampled subjects' reports of their expectations of future prices, future income, and so on, give valid information for predicting changes in purchasing behavior for the general population to which they belong. Ajzen and Fishbein (1977) show in a recent review that when the attitude measurement situation corresponds closely to the situation in which the behavior to be predicted occurs, high agreement between attitudes and behavior is found. Fazio and Zanna (1978) have found that extended direct experience with specific entities leads to better defined attitudes (and stable internal representations evoked by the questionnaire items), which can better predict subsequent behavior. When the information in focus of attention is taken into account, attitudes appear to be consistent with each other and with behavior (Taylor & Fiske, 1978).

This brief overview of controversies about direct assessment by verbal probing and questioning shows clearly that a detailed model of cognitive processes and cognitive structures is needed for making decisions on when and how to use this type of assessment procedure.

We know of only two studies that collected concurrent reports (Schneider-Duker & Schneider, 1977) or retrospective reports (Kuncel, 1973) for thinking during responses to personality tests. Although the results from these studies are promising, much more must be done to understand how personality tests should be constructed to measure cognitive structures.

HISTORY OF VERBAL REPORTS AND INTROSPECTION

A good test of the adequacy and usefulness of our analysis of cognitive processes involved in verbal reporting is to see whether such an analysis can shed light on why some forms of verbal report, like introspection, were problematic, while other forms of verbal report, like psychophysics judgments, gave uniform and accepted results. This discussion of the early forms of verbalization will show that many of the difficulties arose from the requirements imposed on subjects in generating the reports.

Early speculations about the human mind and human subjective experiences were closely related to religious and philosophical questions about the nature of man. The human mind was generally viewed as beyond understanding in scientific terms. However, individual philosophers did attempt to inquire about the mechanisms responsible for acquiring new knowledge and the correspondence between the external world and subjective experience.

The basic source of information for these inquiries was observation by philosophers of their own cognitive processes—that is, introspection. The analyses were directed towards very general issues and questions about the mechanisms and structure of human mind, and were primarily speculative, with little concern for establishing empirical support for the proposed ideas. Speculations and self-observations were inextricably mixed, for they were all the products of the same individual. Although many of the proposals for mechanisms became influential in subsequent theorizing, this type of inquiry gradually became suspect as not conforming to scientific method.

One could observe a similar pattern of speculation for extending our knowledge about the physical environment before a distinctive scientific approach emerged to the analysis of physical phenomena. The scientific approach distinguishes between facts and theories, regarding as facts only "indisputable" observations. Methods of controlled observation and experimental manipulation are essential components of the scientific method. It was several centuries after the emergence of the natural sciences before scientific methods began to be applied to the study of mind and human behavior.

Considerable effort has been devoted in psychology, as in other sciences, to specifying what constitutes "indisputable evidence." Since all observations are made by humans, it was important to secure general agreement on what kinds of observations reflect the external world rather than idiosyncrasies of the individual observer. Complex assessments were questioned or discarded as empirical evidence, for they were judged to embody inferences and knowledge not shared by all observers. Complex assessments were also thought to be sensitive to the expectations and subjective biases of observers. By contrast, simple perceptual judgments based on sensory qualities, like colors, were found to be invariant over different observers and, in principle, independent of such biasing factors as differences in knowledge and earlier experience.

Introspection

In the early years of psychology, the direct observation of mind in operation was taken as the primary method for obtaining information about the mind and its contents. William James used introspection (broadly construed) naturally and unself-consciously as a major tool of investigation.

> *Introspective Observation is what we have to rely on first and foremost and always.* The word introspection need hardly be defined—it means, of course, the looking into our own minds and reporting what we there discover. (James, 1890, p. 185)

Another pioneer, Binet, went so far as to make the definition of psychology contingent in terms of the introspective method.

> Introspection is the basis of psychology; it characterizes psychology in so precise a way that every study which is made by introspection deserves to be called psychological, while every study which is made by another method belongs to some other science. (In Titchener, 1912b, p. 429)

At the turn of the century there was a consensus about the value of naive introspection.

> We need not hesitate to admit, on the other hand, that a roughly phenomenological account, a description of consciousness, as it shows itself to common sense, may be useful or even necessary as a starting-point of a truly psychological description. (Titchener, 1912c, p. 490)

However, as we shall see, naive introspection was soon deemed to be as unscientific as casual observation of natural events would be for the natural sciences. In order to provide facts about the mind, more rigorous and systematic methods of introspection were required.

Structuralism. The main aim of Titchener's research was to gather facts about consciousness (the content of mind), and in the process to uncover its structure. The facts consisted of subjects' direct descriptions of consciousness, whereas inferences and generalizations based on conscious experiences were not accepted.

> But the data of introspection are never themselves explanatory; they tell us nothing of mental causation, or of physiological dependence, or of genetic derivation. The ideal introspective report is an accurate description, made in the

interest of psychology, of some conscious process. Causation, dependence, development are then matters of inference. (Titchener, 1912c, p. 486)

Titchener proposed to separate theory from facts by letting the subjects only describe their experienced conscious content, leaving the inferential process to the experimenter.

To the question of how the contents of consciousness should be reported, Titchener proposed a description in terms of the sensory components of thought. There appear to be at least two partly different reasons for this choice. The first is theory-based and should be seen as a hypothesis. Titchener, like Wundt, held the hypothesis that all mental states and experiences could be described in terms of their sensory and imaginal components. Wundt's thesis was that human experience of external stimulation has two phases. First, the invariant sensory attributes of the stimulation are immediately experienced. Then, mediating processes occur, relating the sensory stimulation to existing general knowledge and prior experiences. According to Wundt, it is the result of the second phase that constitutes the cognitive phenomena we call consciousness.

Wundt assumed that we are born with the sensory components of the first stage already fixed, and that they remain unchanged throughout life. Changes in the way we experience the same sensory stimulation are due to changes in the associations evoked by the stimulation (i.e., are the result of the second stage). Assuming that all knowledge is ultimately derived from experience (the assumption of Locke's empiricism), and that all experience corresponds to a conglomerate of sensations, it follows that the structure of mind and consciousness, including thought, could be described in terms of sensory components. In the search for intersubjective invariants and general psychological laws, it was therefore natural to concentrate on the structure of the immediate sensations.

The second reason for Titchener's choice of a vocabulary of consciousness is basically methodological, and derives from the difficulty of transmitting the conscious experience without contaminating it through words with imprecise meanings.

I quote an illustration from Titchener; a half-trained student reports in an experiment a feeling of "perplexity." Now perplexity is clearly a complex experience. A group of processes is present, some of which we can experience in other contexts, disjoined from each other. True, I have a fair idea of what he has experienced. But only a *fair* idea. The description should be so full and complete that one can imaginatively or sympathetically reconstruct the experience. (English, 1921, p. 406)

Titchener's proposal was that consciousness should be described in terms of its elementary components.

By the "description" of an object we mean an account so full and so definite that one to whom the object itself is unfamiliar can nevertheless, given skill and materials, reconstruct it from the verbal formula. Every discriminable part or feature of the object is unambiguously named; there is a one-to-one correlation of symbols and the empirical items symbolised; and the logical order of the specifications is the order of easiest reconstruction. This, then, is what we mean by "description" in psychology. (Titchener, 1912a, p. 165)

This procedure is analogous to transmitting a picture as a pattern of dots—as on a TV screen—where no biasing semantic descriptors are required. The analogy may be considered a fair approximation to Titchener's idea, for he says "the record must be photographically accurate" (Titchener, 1909). This view harmonizes well with the conservative criteria for simple perceptual observations used in the natural sciences, and with the notion that introspection is analogous to inspection in physics, but with consciousness as its target of observation.

In their efforts to find the elementary units of thinking, the structuralists searched not only for the elements of thought-content, but also for the elementary processes involved in thinking. Relatively early, Wundt started to pursue research along the lines of Donders, who is seen as the pioneer in the analysis of cognitive processes by means of observed latencies. Donders' central idea was that more complex processes could be viewed as compounded additively from simple reactions and the other cognitive processes. Three different tasks were proposed by Donders to estimate the durations of the most basic cognitive processes (i.e., stimulus discrimination and response selection). The simplest is *simple reaction time*, where the subject responds with a given single response, like a button-press, as soon as a stimulus is presented (*a-reaction*). In the *c-reaction* the subject responds only to a certain type of stimulus with a given single response. The c-reaction was assumed to differ from the a-reaction by requiring an initial discrimination of the stimulus. For the *b-reaction* the subject responds for each stimulus with a different response, and thus is required not only to discriminate but also to select the correct response. Wundt extended this method by proposing an additional reaction that we will discuss in the next section.

Data. Titchener relied primarily on introspective reports given after the completion of the processes, but the latencies of the cognitive processes were also used in his analyses. The introspective reports requested by Titchener were very different from the phenomenal accounts provided by naive introspection. Subjects required extensive practice to break away from their habits of giving phenomenal accounts. They had an initial tendency to commit the "stimulus error," which was to report information reflecting previous experience and knowledge from the second stage (for example, to report "seeing a book"), instead of reporting the sensory and imaginal components of the thought or presented stimulation. The extent of training required is indicated by Boring (1953), who mentions that Wundt required his subjects to have 10,000 supervised practice trials before they could participate in any real experiments.

In the Structuralist view, the contents of the self-observations or introspections are considered to be facts or data. From an information processing point of view, on the other hand, the fact or datum is that a subject *said or reported "X"*. In the former interpretation we are obliged to trust that the subject is honest and capable and that the words and the sentences are understood in the same way by the subject and the experimenter. In the latter interpretation, it is sufficient to reproduce or account for the report or aspects of it. Taking it literally as an observation is just one of many alternative interpretations.

Another crucial aspect of classical introspection is that in the direct description of the sensory components it wasn't obvious what were to be taken as the elementary units of sensation. Much introspective research activity was devoted, therefore, to determining the characteristics of these units. In this kind of analysis the observers made decisions about which of several proposals for sensory units correctly reported direct judgments and evaluations of hypotheses. This kind of introspective analysis is very different from the direct description advocated by Titchener, and was also particularly plagued by extensive disagreements between different laboratories.

Latencies of cognitive processes were considered interesting as a separate source of data on the structure of thought processes. Donders' proposal, discussed earlier, for three types of reactions was extended by Wundt. He suggested that the c-reaction, where the subject gave a fixed response to only a certain type of stimulus, involved not only a discrimination but also a choice of whether to respond or not. As a consequence of this criticism, Wundt proposed the *d-reaction*, in which the subjects respond as soon as they have made a cognitive discrimination of the stimulus. As the subjects didn't have to make a choice to respond or not (they always responded, as discrimination of a stimulus invariably occurs) this d-reaction would be a pure measure of the time taken to discriminate or to cognize the stimulus.

Issues and Discussion.   Titchener's type of introspection was severely criticized on at least two major counts. The Wuerzburgers and the Gestalt psychologists claimed that many aspects of consciousness could not be reduced to sensory and imaginal components, and that, consequently, the method of analytic introspection was inadequate and should be replaced with phenomenal reports. In addition, the researchers at Wuerzburg collected phenomenal evidence rejecting the assumptions underlying the subtraction method for measuring the duration of cognitive processes.

The behaviorists with Watson reacted against the direct observation of consciousness, and claimed that only observable behavior could be used as facts or data. Watson pointed out the lack of reproducibility of analytic introspections from different laboratories (i.e., disagreements on issues like "existence of imageless thought," "whether the primary colors are three or four" and "which are the fundamental attributes of visual sensation"). At the same time he acknowledged the reliable and robust results obtained by introspection in psychophysics. These two lines of critique suggested other methods of study, which we will consider later. First, we will discuss why the difficulties with analytic introspection of thought did not prevent reliable results from being obtained in psychophysical studies. Then we will review briefly the unsuccessful attempts of the structuralists to measure the speed and duration of the basic cognitive processes.

Analytic Introspections.   We wish now to describe and reinterpret in information processing terms the cognitive processes involved in making analytic introspections and observations of the sensory and imaginal components of thought. Unfortunately, there is very little explicit discussion of these processes by the introspectionists themselves, and our explication will therefore be partly inferred. The first phase hypothesized by the structuralists, involving the sensory attributes, appears to be very similar to the processes atttributed to the sensory stores in the human information processing model. Classical introspection was aimed at describing the contents of these sensory stores at discrete time intervals, like photographic snapshots (to be interpreted generally to include non-visual sensations and imagery).

Observation, as we have said above, implies two things: attention to the phenomena, and record of the phenomena. The attention must be held at the highest possible degree of concentration; the record must be photographically accurate. (Titchener, 1909, p. 24)

From the point of view of attention this means that the subject, if he can, must redirect attention intentionally from the spontaneously emerging thought content of STM to a single sensory store in order to register rapidly the active sensory components. Let us assume for the moment that this is possible. Each recognized pattern in STM would correspond to a very large number of independent sensory components, which would all have to be retained in STM or stored in LTM until they could be reported. However, storage of information in LTM with usable retrieval cues requires considerable time—estimated at 8 seconds for each chunk (Simon, 1979)—which would basically exclude the possibility of storage in LTM in this case.

Span of attention was known by contemporary research to be limited to a small number of elements (see Woodworth, 1938). It was possible to retain much more information if familiar patterns or organizations were recognized, yet encoding in such patterns would violate the notion of a description directly in terms of sensory and imaginal components. This raises the question of how all these sensory components could be registered and then stored awaiting their reporting, as reporting is known to take considerable time.

Strange to say, a ten-second period of thinking sometimes required as many minutes to recount and make clear to E. (Woodworth, 1938, p. 783)

Evaluating the completeness, objectivity, and veridicality of the "psychological description" of thought contents raises serious methodological problems, since the experimenter lacks external control of, and independent access to, the thought content described. One answer to the problem of the brief availability of thought content is tachistoscopic presentation of visual stimuli. By providing experimental control over the stimuli, this technique allows assessment of the veridicality and accuracy of the "psychological descriptions." In a noted study in 1904, Kuelpe (Chapman, 1932) found that with tachistoscopic presentations of colored letters, an instruction to report certain aspects first (e.g., the colors of the letters) caused a serious decrement in the subsequent reportability of other aspects of the stimulus (e.g., the positions of the letters).

Kuelpe's study doesn't discriminate between incomplete encoding of the stimuli and decay of memory for the information that wasn't reported immediately. In a later study Chapman (1932) demonstrated that informing the subjects about the aspect to be reported prior to the tachistoscopic presentation yielded more accurate reports than informing the subjects immediately after the stimulus was presented. Still more recently, Sperling (1960) measured the duration of these initial "iconic" recordings of sensory stimuli, and demonstrated that though they endured only a fraction of a second, their content exceeded the capacity of STM. (The units of reporting in Sperling's studies were not elementary sensory components, but letters or digits.)

Clearly, then, reportability depends on what information is heeded, and hence upon the task (Aufgabe). Not only is the capacity for retaining information limited, but ability to report it can be affected by an initial bias to search for particular information. Introspective reports are subject to several sorts of selective bias including the theoretically based training of observers, the uncontrolled use of questions (Humphrey, 1951), and the fact that subjects (often faculty and graduate students) are often not naive to the hypotheses addressed in these studies (Comstock, 1921). Taking these possible biases into account, it becomes difficult to accept the reports as scientifically valid evidence. In fact, it was proposed in the case of imageless thought that the observers simply overlooked the actual images and kinesthetic sensations,

> ...so quick is the process of thought and so completely is the attention of the subject likely to be concentrated on meaning. We have a parallel case in the neglect of after-images and double images ... in everyday experience when other things are in the focus of attention. (Comstock, 1921, p. 211)

Psychophysical Judgments. In contrast with the dubiousness of the method of analytic introspection, high reliability is usually imputed to the results obtained from introspective analysis of psychophysical relations. Yet the standard data in psychophysics are introspections. The explanation for the difference is simple; the experimental situation for making psychophysical judgments of sensory stimuli is very different from the one described above. The observer is instructed in advance when to attend and what to attend to; the stimulus is simple and presented over an extended interval of time. Moreover, the judgments, generally being comparative, are reports of highly encoded stimuli that say nothing about the raw sensory components. Essentially, no additional memory is required for the observation before it can be reported. On the basis of these differences, it is not difficult to accept psychophysical introspections as reliable, but to reject analytic introspections.

Latencies. The Structuralists' research on latencies was criticized on basically the same grounds as was analytic introspection. Some initial research with Wundt's d-reaction, where the subjects responded as soon as they had discriminated the stimulus, gave very reliable estimates for the times taken to cognize stimuli. Then a series of studies (see Woodworth, 1938) showed the d-reaction to take as much time as the simple reaction. Berger (Woodworth, 1938) explained these results by pointing out that the response in the d-reaction is independent of the discrimination, in that the subject *always* responds, as in simple reactions. Hence, there is no objective criterion to assure that the subject waits until the stimulus is discriminated before responding. In fact, unless the subject is to make his motor response contingent on the result of the discrimination, there seems to be no way to ensure that the motor response is not initiated earlier and in parallel with the perceptual processes. Again it appears that subjects were asked to do an impossible task.

Analyses of latencies were discarded on more general grounds when evidence was found against Donders' crucial assumption that the stages of discrimination and response selection in the b- and c-reaction were simply inserted additively in the a-reaction. Ach and Watt from the Wuerzburg laboratory found from retrospective reports that the processes of preparing for these several reactions were very different in terms of what was attended to prior to the presentation of the stimuli (Woodworth, 1938). These different types of reactions should thus be seen as wholly distinct procedures, and the differences in duration among them could not be used as estimates of the durations of unique component cognitive processes.

Watson's Attack on Introspection

Just at a time when the classical introspectionists were becoming increasingly self-conscious about methodological issues (Titchener, 1912a, 1912b, 1913), Watson (1913), in the influential paper "Psychology as the Behaviorist Views it," launched a total attack on the study of consciousness. He criticized the introspective method and its results, and argued that psychology, as a natural science, could do without introspective data and mental constructs.

It is important to note that Watson's (1913) critique is not directed against all uses of verbal reports as data, but specifically against the analytic methods and results of the classical introspectionists. When he points to the lack of reproducibility of analytic introspections from different laboratories, he refers to the issue of "imageless thought," "whether the primary colors are three or four" and "which the fundamental attributes of visual sensations are." Watson is even more disturbed that laboratories try to discredit opposing evidence by attributing it to lack of training of the observers in the competing laboratories.

Although Watson did not mention Comstock's (1921) objection that the observers were not, in general, naive to the hypotheses under study, he did stress the additional problem of communicating meaning. How can we be sure that the introspecting observer uses language in the same way as the interpreting experimenter? Especially when an observer is learning new distinctions of consciousness without any feedback or objective control, there is a problem of ensuring common reference between observer and experimenter. Watson (1920) argues, with evidence, that the introspective verbal report is untrustworthy for scientific purposes.

> After having made as searching analysis as we like upon several players' playing of golf, what will be left out of the individuals' own accounts? Again suppose we take down their overt responses to any questions we may ask and incorporate them into our record. They are of relatively little value. No one since objective studies upon golf have been made trusts the verbal report of a golf player. He will tell you that he never takes his eyes off the ball when making a stroke. The camera shows that he is a prevaricator. (Watson, 1920, pp. 100-101)

It should be noted that the kind of questioning illustrated by this example does not refer to the subject's memory of a specific instance, but to how he thinks he performs activities in general when he is asked about them. Watson made a clear distinction between analytic classical introspection, verbal questioning of a subject, and thinking aloud. His views on the veridicality of the latter kind of verbal report were quite different from his views on the first two. In fact, of course, his view was that thinking consisted primarily of subvocal speech (Watson, 1924), and to give evidence on this point, Watson (1920) demonstrated that thinking can be made overt.

The present writer has often felt that a good deal more can be learned about the psychology of thinking by making subjects think aloud about definite problems, than by trusting to the unscientific method of introspection. (Watson, 1920, p. 91)

After presenting the first documented analysis of thinking-aloud activity, Watson (1920) summarizes his arguments for the opinion just quoted —that the overt verbalizations in TA correspond to the normally covert thought activity—by making reference to observations from numerous individuals thinking aloud while working problems. Watson was quite clear about distinctions among modes of verbalization that have since become muddled. These distinctions were also quite apparent to the Gestalt successors of classical introspectionism. In their phenomenological observations, naive subjects were used, and the subjects were allowed to give their own spontaneous descriptions in their own language.

The behaviorists' suspicion of verbal reports was reinforced by their emphasis upon overt performance rather than mediating processes. Even if introspective information was not necessarily incorrect and uninformative, it was unnecessary and could be replaced by appropriate behavioral measures (Watson, 1913). With this point of view, questions of the adequacy and validity of verbal reports, and of methods for obtaining them, were simply irrelevant. It is not surprising, therefore, that this methodology was not studied extensively.

Later Views

When Woodworth (1938), twenty years later, discussed verbal reports, he emphasized the distinction between describing thoughts and expressing them. In response to Titchener's notion of excluding meaning from reports, he presented a case for a more direct and natural reference to complete thoughts (Woodworth, 1938, p. 785):

Even though reference to the object is a very incomplete description of a particular instant of experience, a series of such statements does describe the *general course* of a thinking process—just as naming the towns through which you have driven maps the route you have taken. If O reports "I thought of A, and B, of C, noticed that I was drifting away from the problem and went back to A," he gives a picture of the course of his thinking (Selz, 1913).

And as a more concrete illustration of the type of verbal report he had in mind, he gave (Woodworth, 1938, p. 786) the following example from Binet (1903, p. 14):

I thought of the pump in the garden which someone was operating and said to myself that it must be the cook, then I heard a rooster crow and thought of this rooster.

I asked myself whether Polly would be willing to lend me her bike so that Marge could take mine to ride with us to Fontainebleau.

Note that this immediate retrospective report of thoughts has many of the same attributes as the phenomenological description that followed classical introspection—where untrained and naive subjects verbalize their immediate impressions. This view of immediate retrospective reports as something quite distinct from classical introspective analysis seemed, through the subsequent years, to have faded away, so that verbal reports came to be viewed, without distinction or discrimination, as something inadmissible.

In the relatively small number of studies since the advent of behaviorism that sytematically collected verbal reports, the following criticisms were either raised or investigated empirically: (a) Verbal reports are incomplete, and important behavioral and performance changes are not reflected in them (Greenspoon, 1955; Rees and Israel, 1935); (b) The instruction to give verbal reports and/or their production changes the cognitive processes under study (Phelan, 1965); (c) The verbal reports are inconsistent with other observable aspects of behavior (Verplanck, 1962); (d) The verbal reports are unreliable and idiosyncratic, and they do not carry any information that is generalizable or that can further our understanding of performance (Nisbett & Wilson, 1977). We have already seen that many of these criticisms are either unsupported or overgeneralized.

Thinking aloud has many features in common with the phenomenological observation that succeeded classical introspection. Instead of the analytic steps and the self-observation of introspection these new methods sought for a *direct expression* of the thoughts.

While the introspecter makes himself as thinking the object of his attention, the subject who is thinking aloud remains immediately directed to the problem, so to speak allowing his activity to become verbal. When someone, while thinking, says to himself, "One ought to see if this isn't—," or, "It would be nice if one could show that—," one would hardly call this introspection. (Duncker, 1945)

By having the subjects verbalize their thoughts at the time they emerged, the difficulties and sources of error associated with keeping thoughts in memory or retrieving them from memory could be eliminated (Claparède, 1934). With a TA instruction, naive and inexperienced subjects could be used, since the subjects were asked simply to express their thoughts, a skill which, it was thought, should be part of every subject's normal repertoire.

Several investigators (Bulbrook, 1932; Claparède, 1934; Duncker, 1926; Smoke, 1932; Watson, 1920) started more or less independently to ask subjects to "think aloud" or "talk aloud." This method did not produce a real breakthrough until the verbalized information could be given explicit meaning in terms of a formal model of the thought processes that could be simulated on a computer (Newell, Shaw, & Simon, 1958).

These newer methods of inducing subjects to give verbal reports have also been criticized frequently. One of the main criticisms is that giving verbalizations concurrently with the cognitive processes, or even knowing that one is to give retrospective reports after the experiment, changes the performance and hence the cognitive processes studied. This criticism will be referred to as the *effect-of-verbalization* argument. A second criticism, called the *incompleteness* argument, is that the subject may fail to verbalize a considerable part of the information that passes through his STM, or that he uses in the task he is performing. In this case, the TA protocol will fail to track the actual path of the activity, as revealed by other observations or inferred from theory. This criticism applies also to the cases, primarily in retrospective verbalization, where subjects, for lack of knowledge or memory of the activity, refrain from giving a full verbal report. A third criticism, which we will call the *epiphenomenality* or *irrelevance* argument, is that the verbalizations may report an activity that occurs in parallel with, but independent of, the actual thought process, hence provides no reliable information about the latter. Putting all these criticisms together, they amount to the accusation that the TA procedure changes subjects' thought processes, gives only an incomplete report of them, and mainly reports information that is independent of, hence irrelevant to, the actual mechanisms of thinking.

SUMMARY AND PROSPECT

In this introductory chapter, we have set forth the hypothesis that verbal behavior is to be accounted for in the same way as any other behavior, that is, by developing and testing an information-processing model of how information is accessed and verbalized in response to stimuli. We have surveyed a wide range of different verbal reporting tasks to show how they can be accommodated within this framework, and to show how we can use our model to resolve some of the controversies that have arisen about the interpretation of verbally reported information.

In the remainder of the book, we will focus largely upon a few kinds of verbal reports, particularly thinking-aloud protocols and immediate retrospective reports, that reflect the cognitive processes in the most direct way. We will survey, as comprehensively as we can, the literature on such reports in order to show how they can be used as valid data about cognitive processes and structures. In principle, our analysis is not limited to reports of these particular kinds, but it will also serve as a foundation for the understanding of other reporting tasks and procedures.

We will exclude studies of very unconstrained tasks (fantasizing, imaging, free association) and most clinical studies. We do not consider ourselves sufficiently familiar with clinical theory to interpet it using information processing terms. Furthermore, two recent books have done a good job of discussing this literature (Kendall & Hollon, 1981; Merluzzi, Glass & Genest, 1981). We have not made any other conscious exceptions or exclusions, and have tried hard to capture all the relevant literature within the bounds of our enterprise.

The next chapter will discuss the effects of verbalization upon task performance, and will show that instructions to think aloud do not alter the sequence of cognitive processes significantly. Chapter 3, which discusses the incompleteness of verbal reports, will show that verbal concurrent and retrospective reports provide a nearly complete record of the sequence of information that is heeded during task performance. Chapter 4, which discusses the issues of epiphenomenality and idiosyncracy of verbal reports, will demonstrate that verbally reported information is as regular and valid as other types of data. Chapter 5 presents a detailed model of verbalization processes under think-aloud and talk-aloud instructions. Chapter 6 uses the theoretical model of verbalization to examine and evaluate coding schemes and procedures, and to describe methods of analysis that are reliable and valid. Chapter 7, the final chapter, provides a number of detailed examples of various ways in which protocol analysis can be carried out within our information-processing framework.

2

EFFECTS OF VERBALIZATION

We must now consider verbalization in the context of our general model of memory. Information may reach, and be stored in, memory in a variety of encodings—visual, auditory, tactile. In first approximation, at least, the aural (afferent) encoding and the articulatory (efferent) encoding of oral language can both be represented as strings of phonemes. Without trying to decide whether the encodings are identical or simply nearly isomorphic, let us designate both as the *oral* encoding. Now our fundamental assumption is that, when the CP attends to or activates a structure in memory that is orally encoded, then this structure can at the same time be vocalized overtly without making additional demands on processing time or capacity. At any time when the contents of STM are words (i.e., are orally encoded), we can speak those words without interference from or with the ongoing processes. This is, of course, an empirical assumption, which we will need to test against experimental data.

VERBALIZATION AND THINKING

In a variety of situations, adults have been observed to speak aloud spontaneously without intent to communicate. An interesting example of this is given by Sperling (1967), who found that his subjects vocalized during presentation of visual (verbal) stimuli and during a waiting period until delayed recall, especially in the presence of external noise. He proposed that in response to the visual presentation a corresponding articulatory code was activated and executed, leaving an *internal* auditory trace which was stored in the normal auditory sensory store. When noise was present, the articulation was made overt, thus entering the auditory sensory store by the *external* route as well.

In the noise condition of a similar study by Hintzman (1965), the subjects did not report awareness of their overt verbalizations, suggesting that little or no additional processing was required for them, and possibly that the suppression of vocalization is monitored by feedback. Spontaneous vocalization or noticeable silent articulation have been observed in studies of rather different cognitive activities, for example, in routine work under exposure to noise (Morgan, 1916), in reading difficult passages, especially in foreign languages (Gibson & Levin, 1975), and in memorizing (Bartlett, 1932). Even when the verbalization is not audible or the articulation directly observable, there is evidence for oral encoding of the stored information. Confusion errors in immediate recall of visually presented verbal stimuli are similar to those obtained from auditory presentation of the same stimuli, which suggests that they are stored in a similar (i.e. oral) code (Conrad, 1967; Estes, 1973; Hintzman, 1965).

Although spontaneous vocalization provides evidence for a close relation between internal activation of orally coded information and the corresponding vocalization, we are skeptical of Watson's proposition (Watson, 1920), that thought is internalized speech. It is more likely that internal activation may occur without peripheral activation—which would mean that the overtly verbalized information is a subset of the internally activated oral information. In the discussion of central versus peripheral thought, evidence from a number of studies makes the notion of a peripheral locus highly implausible. Thorson (1925) found no structural relation between tongue movements during vocalization of a word and tongue movements observed in subjects instructed to think about the same word. However, Max (1934) attributed Thorson's results to lack of sensitivity and resolution of his recording techniques.

More modern techniques for recording EMG activity of the speech-producing organs show a pattern of results consistent with measurements of covert speech processes (McGuigan, 1970; Sokolov, 1972). By feeding EMG activity back, Hardyck and Petrinovich (1970) showed that subjects could learn to read without EMG activity in the speech organs, at least with simpler texts. (With more difficult texts, comprehension was poorer with suppression of EMG.) Cole and Young (1975) found with a similar training procedure that subjects can learn to suppress EMG activity during a memory task without change in the processes involved.

According to the hypothesis of a peripheral locus for thought, it should be possible to eliminate task-relevant thought by occupying the

vocal system with reciting irrelevant phonemic patterns, like "la-la-la ..."
or "hiya-hiya ..." Indeed, in an early review Pintner (1913) noted in many
studies a marked decrement in performance caused by such concurrent
verbalization. However, Pintner (1913) showed in his own experiments
that, with practice, subjects could learn to count (i.e., recite 14, 15, 16, 17,
14, ...) while reading a passage without a decrement in recall for the
content of the passage. However, more recent work by Levy (1975, 1977)
clearly shows that concurrent counting markedly affects memory for the
text read, even after extensive practice. In these studies the subjects were
not only asked to recite digits (in this case 1 through 10), but to do it as
fast as they possibly could.

In our view, this does not demonstrate the peripherality of thought.
The processes required for the recitation occupy not only the vocal system but also the central system for activating oral information, and the
time to activate internal information can plausibly be assumed to equal
the time for overt production. The demonstration (Smith, Brown,
Toman, & Goodman, 1947) that curare, which inhibits all skeletal
muscles (including those in the vocal system), has no effect on higher-
level thought processes is further evidence against peripheral activation.

We will now examine our model more closely in terms of (1), the
peripheral activity of the vocal systems and the receiving sensory systems
and (2) the internal activation of orally coded information.

Interference From Auditory Stimulation

First, since our model assumes that the activated oral code resides in a
portion of the auditory memory system, we would expect, at least under
some conditions, interference from simultaneous auditory stimulation
while retrieving such information during rehearsal. Poulton (1977) suggested that effects of noise on performance in many studies may be due
to a masking of inner speech. The observations presented earlier, that
many subjects tend to vocalize noticably in noise to improve the signal-
to-noise ratio, support Poulton's hypothesis. In tasks involving only
maintenance of items in STM, some studies have found no effects of
white noise (Hintzman, 1965; Murray, 1965). Poulton showed that such
results are consistent with intensified rehearsal as a response to noise, and
noted that in a study by Hamilton, Hockey and Rejman (1977) the noise
condition was advantageous only for the most recently presented digits
and disadvantageous for earlier presented digits.

Colle and Welsh (1976) proposed that white noise doesn't have an effect because it is not phonemically encoded, and demonstrated that short-term recall was impaired by having subjects listen to phonemically encodable noise (i.e., irrelevant German). From studies of selective attention to different speakers (e.g., the cocktail-party phenomenon), we know that a listener can separate speakers on the basis of location and pitch. Introspective reports of subjects in a study by Weber and Bach (1969) suggest that the internal rehearsal is perceived to be of high pitch and to be located in the "middle of the head." Colle and Welsh propose that discrimination for location and pitch could explain the differences in interference obtained by Crowder (1973) between consonants and vowels. Furthermore, these cues may be used by subjects to differentiate covert and overt rehearsal, when they are not masked by external noise.

Irrelevant Covert and Overt Articulations

The second empirically testable implication of our information processing model has to do with interference between the covert and overt articulations. If there is a unitary mechanism for activating orally coded information, it should be possible to occupy this mechanism with accessory tasks. A wide range of different tasks requiring irrelevant concurrent verbalization have been used to study the effects on task-directed processes.

As a complete review of all these studies is impossible here, we will simply make three points. First, most studies are not very explicit as to what type of information processing would actually be required to generate the prescribed concurrent verbalizations, and what role the internal activation of oral information has. In some cases (e.g., Estes, 1973) the information to be verbalized concurrently is presented visually, and thus requires both attention and recoding in order to activate the oral code. When, as is usually the case, the information to be verbalized is available in LTM, it becomes important whether the information forms a single chunk, or is part of a familiar list (e.g., the alphabet or the natural numbers), or a list of so many items that it constitutes several chunks requiring successive retrieval. The observed decrease with practice in interference from concurrent verbalizing might result from the sequence to be verbalized having been chunked. The rate of verbalization is also a crucial variable. Maximum interference would be expected when the rate of overt verbalization parallels the rate of internal activation. Another important condition is a requirement to verbalize items at a regular pace, which would eliminate the possibility of internal activation of larger speech units and most likely require additional processing.

Second, some important processes involving internal activation of oral codes are reduced or totally inhibited by certain concurrent verbalization tasks. Levy (1975) showed that rapid concurrent recital of numbers decreased recoding of visually presented verbal information. Her data showed clear differences in memory for text between groups of concurrently verbalizing subjects given auditory and visual presentations, respectively. Recoding of visually presented digits into oral code was eliminated when subjects pronounced visually displayed numbers (Estes, 1973) and when they recited nonsense words (Levy, 1971). Rehearsal of orally coded information disappeared (Baddeley, Thomson, & Buchanan, 1975) when subjects concurrently counted from 1 to 8 at a regular rate of three digits per second.

Third, overt verbalization of non-oral information is impeded by tasks requiring extensive rehearsal of orally coded information. In a series of experiments Brooks (1968) demonstrated that when subjects had to make word category judgments (e.g., "noun" or "article") for each word in a sentence, they took longer to make verbal responses (i.e. "yes" or "no") than to point to visually available response words. The fact that the subjects had to maintain the surface form of the relatively long (ten-word) sentences in memory was crucial, for the effects disappeared when the sentences remained visually available during the ouput of the word category decisions. The verbal labels associated with the word category judgments had to use the same limited-capacity STM system as the rehearsal of the words of the sentence and the information for keeping track of the next word to be categorized.

Time Requirements for Vocalization

A third implication of our model is that, in activating the oral code, articulation and vocalization follow without requiring additional time. If the code is oral, there is thus not any difference in time taken for overt and silent rehearsal or activation. There are some suggestions (Gibson & Levin, 1975) that, due to the redundancy of language and verbal structures, inner speech may not require complete articulation. In most available relevant studies, complete internal activation in the silent case is assured by using non-redundant oral code or by instructing the subject.

In a frequently cited study, Landauer (1962) found that implicit recitation speed for well-learned lists like the alphabet, the sequence of natural numbers, and the pledge of allegiance was no different from overt recitation speed, especially after practice in overt verbalizing. Weber and Bach (1969) found no difference in speed between recitation of the alphabet silently and aloud, and their study showed no practice effects over a sequence of ten trials. Chase (1977) found that overt rehearsal of letter combinations was about 15 percent slower than covert rehearsal, requiring an additional 30 msec per letter, but suggested that further practice might eliminate that difference. In a study of metered memory search, Weber and Blagowsky (1970) found that instructing one group of subjects to verbalize the intermediate steps (i.e., the list items between the stimulus item and the response) produced no differences in performance and latencies, as compared with silent control subjects and subjects instructed to say the steps silently to themselves.

EXPERIMENTAL STUDIES OF VERBALIZING WITHOUT RECODING

The model we have described implies that verbalization will not interfere with ongoing processes if the information stored in STM is encoded orally, so that an articulatory code can readily be activated. The implications of the model can be tested in a wide variety of situations where the subject is explicitly called upon to verbalize.

We will begin by examining studies where the tasks are fairly simple in structure and where evidence is available to suggest strongly a spontaneous oral encoding of the information. Such evidence includes data on confusion errors in retention and indications of spontaneous verbalization, as well as information about how the task was originally learned. For example, in the early learning of many skills—like reading and arithmetic—performance of the task is accompanied by overt verbalization. After a discussion of these studies, we will turn to thinking-aloud studies of more complex tasks, where we have less knowledge about how the task information in STM is encoded.

Simple Tasks With Oral Codes

In the tasks considered in this section, the subject is instructed to retain information presented to him. Since the information is presented by the experimenter, we know that it can be heeded, and we can make reasonable assumptions as to how it is encoded internally. Typically, the subject is presented with letters, digits, or words, which we have assumed will be held in STM in an oral encoding. Under these conditions, verbalization should be effortless, and should not interfere with task performance. However, in most studies, the instruction is *not* just to verbalize the stimulus information, but to produce specified verbalizations based on it (e.g., to read the stimuli aloud one by one, to rehearse the stimuli aloud when they are presented, etc.) As any change in the sequence and frequency with which information is heeded by the subject will change the cognitive process, we must scrutinize the verbalization instructions as to their effects on attention.

The requested verbalizations may be *selective* and result in selective attention to the stimulus displays, especially when there are multiple stimuli. Instructions to verbalize sometimes specify the *units* of information to be verbalized, thus biasing attention towards those units. For example, subjects instructed to verbalize individual digits in a stimulus sequence may pay less attention to patterns of digits than uninstructed subjects. Instructions sometimes prescribe a short *time interval* for producing the verbalization, which may not correspond to the time during which this information would otherwise be heeded. The instructions sometimes prescribe the *pace* of verbalization, and thereby influence the duration of attention to each piece of information; this, in turn, may affect processes associated with fixating information in LTM. Furthermore, an instruction to keep a fast pace may bias the subject to retrieve information from STM as opposed to LTM because of the differential retrieval times for the two stores.

In the following studies, unless the contrary is explicitly mentioned, the inter-stimulus intervals are identical between the verbalizing and the silent group. This means that the time available for subjects in the two groups is identical, so that performance can be compared directly in terms of amount of information retained, and so forth.

Vocalization at Presentation

In the present section, we study memory-span tasks where stimuli are presented rapidly and recalled almost immediately. There is strong evidence that, in response to a visual presentation of a verbal stimulus, an oral encoding is normally activated (e.g., Conrad, 1967; Estes, 1973; Hintzman, 1965) and thus could be vocalized.

When subjects vocalize visual stimuli, immediate recall for the last-presented items is improved over the silent condition (Conrad & Hull, 1968; Crowder, 1970; Murray, 1965; Routh, 1970). The same effect is found if the experimenter, instead of the subject, verbalizes the stimulus, as well as under the condition of auditory presentation (Crowder, 1970; Penney, 1975). Since visual stimuli are, by the assumptions of our model, also orally encoded, this "modality effect" suggests that it is not the encoding of the stimulus, but hearing and storing an articulation of it, that enhances recall of the recent items. This interpretation is supported by studies by Murray (1965) and Tell (1971), which show that the magnitude of the effect depends on the degree of articulation (e.g., whispering versus pronunciation aloud). Murray did not find any difference between silent articulation (i.e., mouthing) and the non-articulating control group. Furthermore, Levy (1971) showed that mouthing did not produce as large an effect as auditory presentation. Thus, the effect of vocalizing visual stimuli appears to be due primarily to the auditory feedback from vocalizing. Let us now look at this effect in more detail.

The effect on immediate recall of vocalizing with visual presentation is largest with fast presentation rates (Murray, 1965) and decreases when there is irrelevant interpolated verbal activity (Crowder, 1970; Tell, 1971). For normal presentation rates and vocalization of each stimulus, the effect is limited to the last couple of stimulus items (Conrad & Hull, 1968; Crowder, 1970). A somewhat longer effective range has been observed for recognition tasks (McNabb & Massaro in Massaro, 1975). A more complete discussion of the range and character of the modality effect is presented in Penney (1975).

Vocalizing stimuli at presentation can have at least two other effects. First, sometimes vocalizing produces *worse* performance than silence. When the visual stimuli are not presented individually, but simultaneously in groups, subjects in the silent condition perform better (Penney, 1975; Slak, 1969). In these experiments, the vocalizing subjects are instructed to pronounce the stimuli one by one (i.e., digit by digit), while the silent subjects can group the stimuli for their covert rehearsal.

Thus the instruction forces the verbalizing subjects to use an inferior coding format.

Second, some studies show a decrement in performance when subjects are instructed to vocalize auditory stimuli (Mackworth, 1964), and in particular, a decrement in retention of early items (Crowder, 1970; Ellis, 1969). In the case where the stimuli are presented orally, immediately reactivating the just-presented item to generate the required vocalization does not seem efficient, and probably occurs at the expense of other processing, like rehearsal of earlier items.

Verbalizing Rehearsal Processes

We turn now to experiments where the subject is instructed to rehearse aloud information held in memory. Such rehearsal may take place under two quite different circumstances: when the information rehearsed is being held in STM, and when the information is rehearsed as an aid to fixating it in LTM. The effects of these two kinds of rehearsal upon task performance may not be at all the same. We must also consider the possibility that the subject may change his strategy to take advantage of the improvement in short-term retention produced by vocalization, and may by that change affect his performance of the task. This is especially likely to happen when the instructions emphasize the requirement of vocalization rather than retention of the stimulus material.

In confronting our model with studies of the effects of verbalization, then, we must take careful account of the verbalization instructions given to the subject. Three dimensions of variation in the instructions may be noted:

(1) In some studies the subject is asked to rehearse or pronounce words at a *specified pace*, while in other studies, he is instructed simply to vocalize covert rehearsal (i.e., "to say out loud any word on the list he was thinking about while he was thinking about it") (Geiselman & Bellezza, 1977).

(2) In several studies the subject is constrained to rehearse *only* the items presented, or some subset of them. A more subtle and common restriction is to constrain the subject to verbalize *individual stimulus items*, instead of recoding them as higher-level chunks. Although in a few studies subjects were explicitly told that there were no restrictions on their encodings of list items (Brodie, 1975; Brodie & Murdock, 1977), recoding would still imply a discrepancy between the verbalized information and the internal encoding.

(3) Last, but not least important, subjects are generally required to rehearse or verbalize *frequently* (Horton, 1976), or instructed to fill the presentation interval with their rehearsals (Einstein, Pellegrino, Mondani, & Battig, 1974; Kellas, McCauley & McFarland, 1975; Rundus, 1971; Rundus & Atkinson, 1970). Even without such instructions, the observed rate of rehearsal is rather high, around 1 rehearsed item per second (Brodie & Murdock, 1977; Geiselman & Bellezza, 1977). Since retrieval from long-term memory is known to take considerable time—of the order of seconds (Simon, 1974) —one might anticipate that a requirement of frequent rehearsing would bias the subject toward retrieving items from STM. We might also anticipate a bias toward maintaining information in STM, which is achievable by rehearsing items serially. This would likely improve performance on short lists, but degrade performance on longer lists.

Analyzing the results of Brodie and Murdock (1977), Kintsch and Polson (1979) noticed that subjects selected items for continued rehearsal inefficiently and rehearsed some items much longer than would be necessary for the memory performance. It would be informative if studies recording rehearsals would analyze the temporal structure and selection of items, but such information is seldom reported. Other indices of the rehearsal process, like eye fixations, have been found to vary with instructions for overt rehearsal (Geiselman & Bellezza, 1977).

It has been suggested that, under additional instructions regulating their verbalizations, subjects will rehearse list items serially more often than will control subjects (Kellas et al., 1975). In support of this hypothesis, Kellas et al. found that differences in study time between verbalizing subjects and controls decreased substantially when recall conditions were changed from free to serial recall. They also found that, in free recall, verbalizing subjects followed the serial order of the stimuli more closely than controls did. Murray (1967) found that differences in performance were much smaller with forced serial recall than with semi-free recall. Geiselman and Bellezza (1977), using simultaneously presented items, found their verbalizing subjects were better than controls at recalling the two leftmost items, a result which they interpreted as evidence for more serial processing among the former. In an interesting developmental study, Kellas et al. (1975) found no difference between verbalizing and control subjects for students below the 7th grade. They interpreted this finding as marking the age at which children first acquire the more sophisticated encoding strategies, which would give an advantage to the control subjects.

The hypothesis, that the verbalizing subjects with a bias toward serial rehearsal would have an advantage in recall of short lists and a disadvantage in recall of longer lists, gets some support from the fact that Geiselman and Bellezza (1977) found superior recall with verbalization for a list of 8 simultaneously presented items; Horton (1976) and Roenker (1974) found no difference in immediate recall for lists of 12 and 15 items; while Fischler, Rundus & Atkinson (1970) and Einstein et al. (1974) found a significant decrement with verbalization in recall of lists of 20 and 24 items. It should be noted that in Roenker's study the words were presented auditorily, which might reduce the difference in processing between vocalization and control conditions; in all the other studies, the words were presented visually.

There is some evidence that how much information will be stored in LTM, and how much will be retained in STM, depends on the modality (visual or auditory) in which the stimuli are presented (Penney, 1975).

Geiselman and Bellezza (1977) found that when subjects were informed that they would be asked to remember the stimulus items for delayed recall, their rates of verbalizing dropped by 30 percent. This suggests that an intention to fixate information in LTM leads to slower rehearsal, and furthermore, that regulating the rate of verbalizing and rehearsing by instruction may produce significant processing differences.

In a study comparing covert and overt rehearsal (Brelsford & Atkinson, 1968), recall of paired associates was investigated with a continuous presentation technique. Verbalizing subjects showed a clear advantage over controls for lags between presentation and recall of paired-associate items up to five or six items, that is, about up to the span of STM. This result is consistent with a strategy, among the verbalizers, of maintaining information primarily in STM to allow easier updating.

There are several experiments where the instruction to verbalize was used to control rather than simply monitor rehearsal processes. In a study on incidental learning, Mechanic (1964) showed that instructions to repeat the pronunciation of the stimuli aloud increased retention. Even more interesting, he showed that, using the same pronouncing procedure, instructions to memorize the words did not improve retention. However, subjects not required to use the pronunciation procedure retained the material better with an instruction to memorize than without it.

In several studies (Einstein et al., 1974; Fischler et al., 1970; Glanzer & Meinzer, 1967), where subjects were instructed to vocalize frequently or to rehearse the just-presented item, their recall was always much poorer than that of controls. In two of these studies, the more intriguing comparison can be made between overt rehearsal of any item and restricted overt rehearsal. In Fischler et al., the overall performance is about the same in both conditions. In Einstein et al., using a somewhat longer list, the recall is somewhat better under conditions of restricted verbalization.

These results would again be expected because of the difference between processing that is directed toward fixating information in LTM and processing that maintains information in STM. Under the restricted rehearsal condition, we would expect subjects to encode in LTM the item being rehearsed repeatedly, while with unrestricted rehearsal, they would tend to maintain the items in STM. Such a difference in strategy would produce the observed relative advantage of the LTM encoding strategy with longer lists of items.

Verbalizing With Multiple Stimulus Displays

Not all the studies discussed below use verbalizations directly to monitor the cognitive activity. But since they specify rather clearly the verbalizations required of the subject, they will serve to illustrate some of the effects of such procedures. With one exception (Geiselman & Bellezza, 1977), the studies discussed earlier have presented one stimulus at a time, so that problems of competition of attention among different stimuli can be disregarded. The most direct example of multiple stimuli is discrimination learning with two stimuli.

In a study on discrimination learning with words, Wilder (1971) found that requiring subjects to utter the correct choice aloud led to faster learning of the list of discriminations. From our earlier discussion it would be reasonable to assume that hearing one's own voice and elicited associations may be a useful memory cue for recognizing the correct response on subsequent trials. This was possible with a relatively small number of responses per list (16) and a relatively short interval between recurring discrimination items, for the presentation of the list took about a minute. Ghatala, Levin and Subkoviak (1975) showed that the same increase in performance as found for subjects verbalizing the correct items could be obtained by instructing subjects to use imagery.

A similar study was conducted by Carmean and Weir (1967) with visually presented drawings as stimuli. An instruction to describe or

name the visually portrayed object should require a verbally coded name
to be generated for the object. One might argue that stimuli like those
used in this experiment automatically elicit a verbally coded name, but
this cannot be taken for granted in the general case. In this study subjects
were instructed to vocalize the name of the visual stimulus according to
five different instructions. The degree of correlation (either positive or
negative) between the correct response and the overtly named stimulus,
which was regulated by the different instructions, was strongly related to
the speed of learning in the discrimination task. In the immediate recall,
a clear relation was found between the stimuli verbalized and stimuli
recalled, and an overall better recall was found for the verbalizing conditions as compared to the control condition. These general results have
been replicated by Weir and Helgoe (1968).

The relation between verbalizing names of visually displayed objects and long term retention (one week) was investigated in a now classic
study by Kurtz and Hovland (1953). The subjects were presented with a
four-by-four matrix of objects, which were selected so that subjects could
label them without ambiguity. In the control condition the experimenter
would point to one of the objects and ask the subject to make a circle
around that object on a photo of the stimulus. When the experimenter
pointed to an object in the experimental condition, the subjects were to
find the name of the object in a four-by-four matrix of names arranged
exactly like the matrix of objects, encircle the word and pronounce it
overtly. When the subjects were, a week later, given a recognition test or
a written test of recall, the experimental group showed superior retention
on both tests.

In evaluating the effective element in the above procedure, a study
by Rosenbaum (1962) is helpful. It differed from the others mainly in
that the control group encircled words in the matrix and thus behaved
just as the experimental group did, apart from the pronounciation of the
word. Rosenbaum found subjects pronouncing the word to have superior retention on tests of recognition and recall, and furthermore, silent
subjects exposed to somebody else's pronounciation to show a similar
increase in retention. Even though it can be argued that the structural
isomorphism of objects and words could have made it possible to do the
task without cognizing the word, the primary cause of these changes in
retention is not likely to be the elicitation of a verbal internal code,
especially not with carefully selected objects. From these results, we
infer that the causal agent in these studies is *not* the production or
generation of the overt verbalization but rather the internal processes
elicited in response to the instructions to verbalize.

Verbalizing Associated With Mental Arithmetic

In mental addition and multiplication, the subjects are presented either visually or orally with numbers and the mathematical operators and must generate the answer without recourse to external memory. There is convincing evidence from the way these skills are learned that the internal code of the numbers, operations and internally generated products is either used or readily elicited. Our model predicts that it should be possible for the subjects to verbalize the heeded information, especially as all new mental content is generated sequentially. The available studies on the effects of the instruction to verbalize are sparse and will be dealt with individually.

A study on mental arithmetic by Wegner (Merz, 1969) investigated the existence and possible nature of the effect of verbalizing. To separate the effects due to producing the vocalization from the effects due to hearing it, the subjects wore ear phones with a noise level that prevented them from hearing their own voices. In one of the verbalization groups their amplified voices were superimposed on the noise, in the other they were not, thus eliminating the feedback of the voice. It was found to be more difficult to instruct the subjects in the non-feedback condition to refrain from verbalizing, which suggests that verbalizing is a normal behavior in such a noisy environment (Hintzman, 1965). Feedback of the voice was found to be the crucial factor, as there was no improvement without it.

In the arithmetic task, three digits, which were available to the subject only one at time on a kind of memory drum, had to be subtracted from or added to each other. Temporary storage of the intermediate results appeared to be the major difficulty, with feedback of the voice proving to be exceptionally helpful in at least two respects. First, the subjects without feedback and the control subjects went back more often to look at the digits presented earlier in the triple, which took additional time and led to completion of fewer problems. Second, the subjects without feedback obtained more incorrect subtotals than the subjects with feedback. In accord with the results presented earlier, hearing the overt verbalization seemed to be the important factor in improving short-term retention and performance.

Fryer (1941) was primarily interested in the role of articulation in automatic mental work. In a number of experiments with a test involving writing down totals of very simple additions (the sums never exceeded nine), he found that instructing the subjects to refrain from articulation impeded performance markedly. Retrospectively, subjects judged it to be almost impossible to avoid articulation. Instructing subjects to vocalize the answers before writing them down, or to whisper them silently led to a consistent and reliable decrement in speed of performance. However, since the average decrement was no more than about one percent, Fryer suggests that it may be attributed to the extra monitoring required to assure the articulation for each answer.

In a study of mental multiplication, Dansereau and Gregg (1966) asked a subject to verbalize each step during the solution process. Whenever the subject remained silent too long, the experimenter would urge him to talk. On a wide range of problems varying in difficulty, no reliable differences in speed of performance were found between a silent control condition and the verbalizing condition. In spite of this finding, the subjects judged introspectively that verbalizing slowed down the process but facilitated the necessary fixation and storage of intermediate results in memory.

In a subsequent study, Dansereau (1969) reports that, with increased practice, two of his better subjects gave overt verbalizations only of intermediate results and the initial problem, and they reported introspectively that complete verbalization interfered with retrieving information. Dansereau suggests that these subjects used overt verbalization as a retrieval cue for accessing important information. To what extent the subjects felt that verbalizing slowed them down is not reported, nor is a comparison provided with performance under a silent control condition.

Some Conclusions

In nearly all the studies reviewed in this section, performance time was the same in verbalization and control conditions, both when trials were paced by the experimenter and when the subject determined the pace. Our model, agreeing with these findings, predicts that overt verbalization under thinking-aloud instructions will not affect the speed of performance unless the verbalizations have to be queued. With a few possible exceptions, the empirical studies do not provide any evidence that queuing occurs.

We have identified few studies where subjects are simply instructed to verbalize the heeded information; in most studies, specific requirements are imposed on them with respect to the timing, frequency, and content of their verbalizations. There is evidence that when subjects try to comply with such requirements, the normal course of their internal processes is altered (e.g., rote serial rehearsal may increase and attention may be shifted).

Apart from the effects of imposing specific requirements for verbalization, hearing overt verbalizations generally facilitates memory retrieval and storage. The first component of this effect is most likely the greater durability of the accoustical sensory store, which only spans a couple of seconds and is furthermore subject to masking by subsequent verbalizations. The second, longer-term, component is a facilitation in retrieval, due to the specific cues supplied accoustically by the overt verbalization. The strength of the second effect would depend on how selective the overt verbalizations were with respect to the retrieval task. Increases in the verbalization of material other than that which was to be remembered should decrease this effect.

THINKING-ALOUD PROCESSES

In the previous section we reviewed experiments in which the subject was instructed to verbalize or rehearse the actual stimuli. Only in the arithmetic tasks was the subject required to verbalize thoughts that he himself generated in the course of performing a task. We turn now to our main concern, thinking-aloud (TA) instructions, where the subject is specifically ask to vocalize those self-generated symbols while he performs his task. Again, we will be seeking evidence on the extent to which the TA activity affects the performance of the main task.

Thinking-aloud activity is not entirely alien to everyday life, and almost all subjects have probably had some experience of it before they come to the laboratory. Students at school occasionally have to explain their solutions of problems aloud to their fellow students in order to show how the solutions were generated. In other situations, people explain or describe their solution attempts to others, so that the listener can tell them where their thinking is in error. Even more frequently, people just communicate their thinking to others. In many cases, at least, such verbalization requires considerable intermediate processing prior to articulation, and is distinctly different from the verbalization of ongoing cognitive processes. In order to characterize the differences, we will describe three different levels at which a subject can verbalize his thought processes and their content.

Levels of Verbalization

1. A first level of verbalization is simply the vocalization of covert articulatory or oral encodings, as required in the tasks we have presented in the previous sections. At this level, there are no intermediate processes, and the subject needs expend no special effort to communicate his thoughts. A distinction must still be made, however, between cases where the subject is directing his communications to himself, and those where he wishes to communicate with other people. The self-directed verbalizations have been found to be more idiomatic and to use more idiosyncratic referents than communications directed to others (Werner & Kaplan, 1963). In which category a particular example of verbalization falls may depend on the subject's interpretation of the instructions, as well as upon their actual content.

2. A second level of verbalization involves description, or rather explication of the thought content. We assign to this level verbalizations that do not bring new information into the focus of the subject's attention, but only explicate or label information that is held in a compressed internal format or in an encoding that is not isomorphic with language (e.g., information about odors). We will have to add to our model the requisite recoding processes. We will refer to verbalization requiring such recoding as Level 2 verbalization.

Since explication or recoding requires processing time for the subject but does not replace other processing involved in the task performance, a subject who is verbalizing at this second level can be expected to take more time for the task than one who is not verbalizing. However, we would hypothesize that such recoding does not change the structure of the process for performing the main task.

3. A third level of verbalization requires the subject to explain his thought processes or thoughts. An explanation of thoughts, ideas, or hypotheses or their motives is not simply a recoding of information already present in STM, but requires linking this information to earlier thoughts and information attended to previously. Level 2 verbalization does not encompass such additional interpretative processes.

If, in the normal course of task performance, a subject pays attention to the relational or generating processes that are bringing new information into his STM (and insofar as he *can* pay attention to them), the verbalization would fall within the compass of Level 2 verbalization. But if the subject does not attend to these processes, then he will have to make intermediate inferences, which may or may not represent correctly his actual motives or the actual causes linking his thoughts. Moreover, an instruction requiring a subject to explain his thoughts may direct his attention to his procedures, thus changing the structure of the thought process.

Alternative Thinking-Aloud Instructions

The subject's TA protocol and (specifically whether it will correspond mainly to Levels 1, 2, or 3) may well be influenced by the exact wording of the TA instructions. We will begin by examining the instructions given by the two psychologists, Duncker and Claparède, who are usually credited with introducing the method of thinking aloud. In describing their instructions, we will distinguish a *main* part from some *complementary* parts.

The main part of the instruction to think aloud is usually very short, making reference to a procedure that is presumed to be already familiar to the subjects.

> "*Try to think aloud.* I guess you often do so when you
> are alone and working on a problem." (Duncker, 1926; italics
> in original)

> "Think, reason in a loud voice, tell me everything that
> passes through your head during your work searching for the
> solution to the problem." (Claparède, 1934.)

Thus the subjects are asked just to vocalize their thoughts, which are apparently presumed to have the form of inner speech. If the presumption is correct, it is not surprising that such short instructions could elicit the desired behavior. Verbalizing, under this assumption, would be quite simple (Level 1), because of the oral code and sequential structure of the internal speech.

In Claperède's instructions, however, the subject is asked to verbalize "everything that passes through [his] head," whether encoded orally or not. In order to comply with such an instruction, the subject would in many cases have to label and encode the content of STM, thus requiring the kinds of recoding processes that are postulated in Level 2 verbalization.

TA instructions frequently contain other information or requirements, which we have already refered to as "complementary." One complementary instruction that is often included is a request for *completeness.* Here are two examples:

"The chief thing is to talk aloud constantly from the minute I present the picture, for I want to get everything you happen to think of, no matter how irrelevant it may seem." (Patrick, 1935)

"I am not primarily interested in your final solution, still less in your reaction time, but in your thinking behavior, in all your attempts, in whatever comes to your mind, no matter whether it is a good or a less good idea or a question. *Be bold!* I do not count your wrong attempts, therefore speak them all out." (Duncker, 1926; italics in original)

There appear to be at least two ways in which this instruction could be implemented by a verbalization procedure: (a) A superordinate monitoring process could be incorporated in the procedure to guarantee that every item would be verbalized; (b) In quite an opposite direction, the effect of the instruction could be to eliminate any censorship process intervening between awareness of STM contents and their vocalization. Some TA instructions imply the presence of, and require the elimination of, such censorship:

"Don't plan what to say or speak after the thought, but rather let your thoughts speak, as though you were really thinking out loud." (Silveira, 1972)

Another kind of complementary instruction is a request for *explanation.* In order to get as full an understanding as possible of the subjects' processes, they are asked to explain their thinking:

"In order to follow your thoughts we ask you to think aloud, explaining each step as thoroughly as you can." (Smith, 1971)

As follows from our earlier discussion, inducing the subject to explain his solution very likely changes the structure of his thought processes. In a school situation with mathematics tasks, where the students were accustomed to explaining their solutions aloud, Krutetskii (1976) took special pains to warn his subjects against confusing the instruction to think aloud with that of explaining the solution:

"Do not try to explain anything to anyone else. Pretend there is no one here but yourself. Do not tell about the solution but solve it." (Krutetskii, 1976)

Relatively frequently, complementary instructions are included to influence the *content* of the verbalizations.   Investigators are sometimes specifically interested in certain types of mental content or mental processes, and ask their subjects to take special care to report instances of such content or processes (Johnson, 1964; Scheerer & Huling, 1960; Webb, 1975). Other investigators have asked subjects to verbalize what they are doing physically as well as what they are thinking (Hafner, 1957; Mayzner, Tresselt, & Helbock, 1964). Still other investigators have asked subjects to verbalize what they are perceiving visually (Farley, 1974; Huesmann & Cheng, 1973). In many of these studies, the exact wording of the instructions is not reported, which makes it difficult to discuss what verbalization procedures are necessary to comply with them. In most cases, however, it would be necessary to scan for specific content and to encode it for vocalization when found. Such monitoring would be, in fact, self-observation at the third level we described earlier.

One can only conjecture to what extent subjects pay attention to, understand, and comply with TA instructions, especially their complementary portions, and especially when the instructions are only presented at the beginning of sessions that may be an hour or more in length. There are many other conditions in a TA experiment that may affect the verbalization procedures of subjects as much as or more than instructions do. We turn next to these additional factors.

Effects of Training and Reminders

In many TA experiments, the subject is given initial warm-up problems to acquaint him with the experimental situation and accustom him to the microphones and tape recorders. In some studies, more extensive warm-up procedures are used explicitly to *train* the subjects to conform to the TA instructions.

During warmup, the experimenter feels free to interfere with and disrupt the subject, while during the experiment, he is very concerned not to interfere. An essential merit of TA as compared with introspection, however, is that the former is a normal mode of processing that does not call for the extensive training needed for the latter. Hence, the training in TA paradigms is negligible compared with that employed in classical introspection experiments.

The experimenter is generally, though not always, present during TA experiments. In the earlier studies, the experimenter had to be present, since there was no other means for recording the subject's verbalizations. Although tape recorders are now used almost universally, the experimenter is still usually present, primarily to monitor the verbalizations by reminding the subject to speak when he lapses into silence.

These reminders, given after 15 sec to 1 min pauses (the interval being different in different studies), are generally standardized, taking the form of "keep talking" or "what are you thinking about?"

In some studies the experimenter also monitors the content of the verbalizations, and when necessary, asks the subject to explain what he means by something, and/or asks him to explain his solution processes. One may conjecture that the mere presence of the experimenter may induce some subjects to provide descriptions or explanations that they would omit in a non-social situation.

Reminders to verbalize of the "keep talking" variety should have a very small, if any, effect on the subject's processing. However, a reminder of the type, "what are you thinking about?" is more likely to elicit a self-observation process or produce an other-oriented description as a response. In cases where it is desired that the subject produce specific kinds of verbalizations (see the previous section), the experimenter's prompts may elicit the desired behavior, while the subject may be less likely to comply if only initial instructions are given.

Some investigations use TA procedures where the experimenter is not present (Klinger, 1974). It is technically feasable by automatic means to detect pauses that exceed a given length, and to remind the subject by means of an (auditory) signal to resume verbalizing.

REVIEW OF EMPIRICAL STUDIES

In this review of empirical studies that employ TA procedures, we will be concerned primarily with studies that meet the criteria of Level 2 verbalization, for most of the experiments in the literature de-emphasize speed and instruct the subject to "take your time and concern yourself with performance." This does not mean that verbalizing cannot remain at Level 1, even for complex tasks, but in most cases the additional information obtainable when recoding is permitted is judged to be more important than strict invariance of performance.

Studies of Level 2 Verbalization

The criteria for Level 2 verbalization are that only the information attended to (i.e., held in STM) should be verbalized, and that the recoding of this information for purposes of vocalization should not otherwise alter the processing involved in the task performance. It is often difficult to evaluate whether the criteria of Level 2 are satisfied in a given experiment, but in some cases the trace of the solution for a control condition of "silent" subjects provides sufficient information to permit a comparison of the structure and course of their solution process with that of vocalizing subjects.

In only a few experiments explicitly designed to study the effects of verbalizing, have experimental and control groups been exposed to identical conditions. After describing these studies we will go on to others, where experimental and control conditions, while not identical, are closely similar.

Roth (1965) investigated the effects of TA instructions upon performance in a series of problems. In order to test some hypotheses about how much verbalization would be elicited under different conditions, he varied factorially: (1) warm-up or pretraining for verbalizing, and (2) the extent to which subjects were allowed to manipulate objects while generating the solution. Here we will concern ourselves only with performance on the problem. Roth found no difference in time to solution that could be attributed to verbalizing. Since he did find significant differences due to problems, and to an interaction between problems and allowing manipulation of objects, his experimental measurements were not insensitive to manipulations of conditions.

In a study of discrimination learning, Karpf (1972) compared 40 subjects who were instructed to think aloud with 20 control subjects. The subjects were divided into two matched groups on the basis of ten preliminary problems, and were then given 15 experimental problems where the experimental group was asked to think aloud. Finally, five problems were given, where *all* subjects were instructed to be silent, to detect after-effects of thinking aloud. No reliable differences in number of correctly solved problems were found between the TA group and the control group, for either the experimental problem or the final problems. However, the TA group took about 50 percent more time than the control. Karpf gave some evidence suggesting that the effect of verbalization may have differentially affected the subjects (i.e., helping some and impeding others). This kind of effect will be discussed later.

Walker (1982) instructed subjects, under TA and standard recall conditions, to recall members of familiar categories (e.g., automobiles, soups, detergents). There were large differences among categories in the numbers of members recalled, but no differences between the TA and silent conditions. As would be expected from our theoretical analysis, the verbalizations of TA subjects consisted of retrieval cues and previously recalled names.

When Carroll and Payne (1977) compared TA with control subjects in a study of parole decision-making, no reliable differences were found for speed of decision, type of decision, or information requested while making the decision. In another study, Smead, Wilcox, and Wilkes (1981) had subjects choose between brands of coffee-makers, while confronted either with the products or with verbal descriptions of their attributes. Eye fixations were recorded, and subjects were asked afterwards to rate the realism and difficulty of the judgments and their certainty in their final choices, and also to state what attributes were most important in their choices. No differences between TA and control subjects even approached significance, though several differences were found between subjects shown actual products or verbal descriptions, respectively.

In another experiment (Johnson & Russo, 1978) the subjects were making choices among consumer items, some of the subjects with an additional instruction to think aloud. In a subsequent test for memory of the stimulus information, no differences attributable to thinking aloud could be found either in accuracy or latencies. Feldman (1959) studied a single subject's predictions in a binary choice situation with a TA instruction. Two large control groups of subjects were run in the same condition without instruction to think aloud. No differences in types of choices and number of correct predictions were observed. In a study on the effects of covert modeling of assertive behavior, Kazdin (1976) included a comparison between a silent condition and a condition where subjects narrated aloud their ongoing imagery during the correct modelling. Due to insufficient specification of the instruction to verbalize, we are not certain that it should be seen as a pure TA instruction. Still, it is informative that no differences due to the instruction to verbalize were found in an extensive analysis of the effects of the covert modeling.

Several studies allow comparisons between a silent and a vocalizing group, for identical or similar tasks, and with only slightly different experimental conditions for the two conditions. In some instances, these studies measured success or speed in solving problems, in others, they also reported data on the solutions paths that were discovered.

In several studies, evidence can be found that verbalizing had no effect on the basic performance measures or the gross structure of the thought process. The proportion of subjects solving Duncker's candle problem did not differ between a TA condition and a silent conditon in a study by Weisberg and Suls (1973). In a study of intransitive preferences, Montgomery (1977) replicated a study by Tversky (1969), but with the addition of a thinking-aloud instruction, and found approximately the same choice distributions. Studying anagrams at different levels of difficulty, Sargent (1940) was able to show, by correlational techniques, that difficulty level produced changes in the types of processes used in *both* silent and TA subjects. No more detailed comparisons were made.

More detailed comparisons of the structures of the thought processes were made by Newell and Simon (1972) on problems in propositional logic, by Bulbrook (1932) on insight problems, by Ericsson (1975b) on a block puzzle, and by Flaherty (1974) on algebra word problems. For subjects discovering proofs in propositional logic, Newell and Simon compared the number of solutions and the detailed solution paths of their seven TA subjects with the solutions (collected by different investigators at Yale) to the same two problems by 64 subjects under silent conditions. With so few subjects in the TA condition, it could not be expected that differences could be found between the two conditions in gross measures of performance, nor were they. More significant is the fact that when the detailed structures of the solutions (i.e., the specific proof steps) were examined and compared between the two groups, no differences were found. Both groups explored essentially the same parts of the problem space with about the same relative frequencies.

For a large number of different insight problems, Bulbrook (1932) found close agreement between the solution patterns reflected in subjects' TA protocols, and answers by a large group of silent subjects to a retrospective questionnaire.

In Ericsson's (1975b) study on problem solving with the Eight Puzzle, two separate experiments were conducted for the two conditions, but the same sequence of puzzles was presented to the subjects in both conditions. In one experiment, the subjects were instructed to think aloud and had to tell the experimenter what tiles to move; in the other experiment, the subjects, sitting alone, pressed keys on a teletype to make the computer change the puzzle configuration. Differences in the structures of the solutions could be investigated through analysis of the sequences of moves, which were recorded in both conditions (Ericsson, 1975a, 1975b). No differences were found in the subjects' attainments of objectively defined subgoals and subrelations of the goal, nor in the structure of the search trees. However, the mean number of moves was significantly larger for the verbalizing subjects for the first couple of problems. Ericsson (1975b) attributed this difference to a change in the effort that subjects devoted to mental planning, induced, in turn, by differences in the design of the two experimental conditions. In the study with the TA instruction, the subjects had to tell the experimenter what moves he should make for them, while in the "silent" study, the subjects were alone and inputted their moves on a teletype. This difference alone is enough to explain the observed difference between the numbers of moves in the two conditions.

Flaherty (1974) studied the effects of practice and verbalizing in a factorial design with algebra word problems. Flaherty used an extensive coding schema of 17 variables to describe the TA solutions; ten of these variables could also be assessed from the written solutions of the silent subjects. Analysis of variance showed no effects on problem solving performance of either practice or verbalizing. The verbalizing subjects did not even take a longer time to solve the problems. T-tests for the ten coded variables showed only one significant difference between verbalizing and silent subjects: the verbalizing subjects made more computational errors. Since, unfortunately, the silent subjects solved their problems in groups and their written solutions constituted the data, while the TA subjects were tested individually by the experimenter and their written solution as well as the verbal protocol made up the data, it is difficult to know whether the observed difference in number of mistakes is due to verbalizing or to the other differences in experimental conditions or the data available for analysis.

In several studies using verbalization, models have been constructed on the basis of the verbal data, and used to predict the subjects' behavior in subsequent silent situations. In a study on consumer choice, Bettman (1970) showed that his formalized decision-net models of two consumers, based on TA protocols obtained on earlier shopping trips with these subjects, could predict 85% to 90% of the products selected by the subjects. Clarkson (1962) studied and modeled a trust officer's selection of portfolios of securities on the basis of several TA protocols. When, a year later, the trust officer selected four different portfolios, the model predicted (without interaction with the subject) the companies whose shares he would buy with 80% to 85% accuracy. These results suggest that the information provided by the TA protocols for the model building does accurately reflect the normal course of the thought processes.

Finally, we describe a couple of miscellaneous results that have implications for our problem. In a study by Marks (1951) where all subjects were thinking aloud, performance was significantly affected by asking subjects, "What are the elements of the problem?" This result suggests that thinking aloud does not by itself enforce an analytical approach, as has sometimes been alleged.

Subjects have occasionally been asked to judge the effects of their verbalizing. No interference was reported by subjects who were making decisions (Svenson, 1974). The experimental setup, including the TA requirements, was judged representative by most artists and non-artists engaged in writing poems (Patrick, 1935) and drawing pictures (Patrick, 1937). Some of Dominowski's (1974) subjects reported that verbalizing led them to more careful information processing.   However, Dominowski's experiment may not have met the criteria of Level 2 verbalization, for he instructed his subjects to describe the stimuli and to give reasons for their classification responses, even though guesses and other informal explorations were explicitly said to be acceptable.

Differential Effects of Thinking Aloud

Several investigators (Claparède, 1934; deGroot, 1965) have observed marked differences in the spontaneity and richness of TA protocols and suggested that these may be related to the ease and skill with which subjects transform non-orally coded information to external speech. Johnson (1964) noted individual differences in the pattern of verbalizing, some subjects giving fluent verbalizations and some adopting a "think-then-summarize" procedure. Some subjects may transform automatically, whereas others may require a conscious effort for this transformation and verbal production. These differences may be due to the compatibility of codes, some subjects using visual images while others are more verbal. Although there are no studies of individual differences across tasks requiring different codes, some support for the transformation hypothesis can be found in an observation by Klinger (1971) that only highly verbal females could give good verbalizations in a reverie condition, which is known to employ mostly visual images.

An instruction to verbalize and think aloud could help some and impede others. We know of only two studies that have found reliable differential effects on subjects. Flaherty (1973, 1974) separated subjects who were sensitive to the fact that some problems were physically impossible from subjects who were not sensitive (the latter presumably relying mainly on verbal cues for generating the solution). She found a reliable difference in performance between these two groups of subjects only in the think-aloud condition. She suggested that subjects who were verbally oriented problem solvers would be impeded by having to perform a second verbal task (i.e., thinking aloud). However, a reanalysis of Flaherty's (1973) data shows no reliable difference (p > .15 two-tailed t-test) between verbally oriented problem solvers in the TA and the control conditions, which would be the proper test for her hypothesis.

In the study by Karpf (1972) discussed earlier, the subjects were asked after the experiment whether thinking aloud helped, had no effect, or interfered. He found reliable differences between the "no effect" group and the "interference" group for the experimental problems requiring them to think aloud, but also for the final problems when *no* subject verbalized. One may have considerable doubt whether the subjects could assess that their worse performance was due to verbalizing, especially since their performance did not improve during the final "silent" trials.

Unless the experimenter, by constant probing, tries to eliminate the differences in completeness of verbalizing between subjects, thus possibly changing their cognitive processes, there appears to be little reason to anticipate differential effects of verbalizing. All the studies reviewed above support the conclusion that the observable structure of cognitive processes is not affected significantly by the instruction to think aloud when the experimental conditions are consistent with the criteria for Level 1 or 2 verbalizations. These findings suggest that the internal structure of the thought processes also is not changed as a result of the additional verbalizing activity. The few differences that were encountered in the published reports were not of major importance, and where differences appeared, they were very likely attributable to differences in the experimental conditions. In evaluating our conclusion, it is important to know that we have included all comparisons in studies complying with the conditions of Level 1 and 2 verbalization that we have discovered in the literature.

Studies Not Conforming With Level 2 Conditions

In the review of studies meeting the criteria of Level 2 verbalizing, we found no evidence of changes in the course or structure of the cognitive processes induced by verbalizing. We would not expect this result to hold in studies where the subject is asked to verbalize information that would not be heeded in the normal course of processing, or that would not normally be encoded in an oral code.

This distinction bears on the completeness of verbalizations. Our model assumes that *only information in focal attention* can be verbalized. In most theories of the structure of the human information processing system a distinction is made between fast, automatic processes that are not necessarily conscious (and which are often thought to proceed in parallel) and the slow serial processes that are executed under cognitive control—a distinction, that is, between pre-attentive and focally attended processes (Neisser, 1967), perceptual and cognitive processes (Simon, 1975), and automatic and cognitively controlled processes (Shiffrin & Schneider, 1977). In our discussion, we will adopt this distinction. We will also assume that with increase in experience with a task, the same process may move from cognitively controlled to automatic status, so that what is available for verbalization to the novice may be unavailable to the expert.

Several types of processes generally occur automatically, in this sense, and rapidly (in a matter of tens or hundreds of milliseconds): perceptual-encoding processes (recognition), memory retrieval processes, and motor processes. There are many instances during thinking-aloud studies where a subject acquires hypotheses "instantaneously" and directly, without evidence of prior related or intermediate stages; for instance, interpretations of complex pictures (Claparède, 1934), and "insights" in geometry problems (Henry, 1934). Retrospective reports of sudden acquisition of hypotheses are common in experimental settings (Woodworth, 1938) and in more informal demonstrations (Miller, 1962).

We have observed that there is no fixed and stable boundary between automatic and focally attended processes. With extensive practice, cognitive processes will develop into fixed automatic processes; and there is suggestive evidence that practice leads to a successive fading from consciousness of information about the process. There is such evidence, for example, in retrospective reports after each trial in experiments by Ach and Watt (Woodworth, 1938).

The fact that processes can continue to occur after retrospective reports about them have disappeared is urged by Leeper (1951) as a principal argument against the validity of verbal reports as data about processes. Even without retrospective reports, the Shiffrin and Schneider (1977) study makes it abundantly clear that an automatic process is very different from its cognitively controlled antecedent in terms of modifiability, speed, and so on. The automatic processes can be seen as units or chunks, and Schneider and Shiffrin suggest that the growth of skill can be viewed as the development of successively higher-level codes and organizations of lower-level processes. Hence, we should expect the verbalizations of highly skilled individuals to be less complete than those of less skilled ones.

If information is available (the process not automated) but not held in an oral code, then verbalization will require recoding (Level 2), and this recoding will have to *share focal attention* with other task-directed processes. We hypothesize that, in the case of such competition, the task-oriented processes will have priority over the recoding and verbalization processes. There is supporting evidence for this hypothesis in three different types of situations:

1. Subjects tend to stop verbalizing in conditions where they are giving indications of being under a high cognitive load. Such indications may take the form of reorganizations of the problem representation or strategy (Durkin, 1937), or direct expressions of feeling difficulty (Johnson, 1964).

2. When subjects attend to information that leads to direct recognition of appropriate actions, this information tends not to be verbalized (Duncker, 1945). In Maier's research on the pendulum problem (1931), subjects were retrospectively questioned on solving a problem just after being given a hint. Subjects who described the solution as emerging in a single step did not report any memory of the hint; while subjects who mentioned several steps in the solution all reported the hint that had been administered. With the available data it is not possible to determine whether all were aware of the hint *at the time it was given.*

3. In situations where the subject is judged not to have any competing task-directed processes, verbalization tends to be relatively complete. Ericsson (1975b) calculated how regularly an observable feature of the process (e.g., reversal of a pair of moves) was associated with a specific kind of verbalization, and found a very high correlation (e.g., on each occurrence of a reversal, the subject verbalized a negative evaluation of the original moves).

There are broad areas of cognitive behavior, however, where investigators consistently experience difficulties in obtaining rich verbalizations from subjects. We will focus on two of the most important kinds of processes where verbalization is poor: perceptual-motor processes, and visual encoding processes. These will be taken up in the next two sections. A small number of miscellaneous studies relating to other processes will be discussed in a third section.

Verbalization of Perceptual-Motor Processes

The problems of verbalizing perceptual-motor processes are most clearly visible in problem situations where the problem is represented physically (e.g., the disks and pegs of the Tower of Hanoi puzzle), and performance involves manipulation of this physical representation.

Thomas (1974) found that TA protocols from a variant of the Missionaries and Cannibals puzzle provided insufficient information on the course of the solution to specify a definite model of the process. Other studies with different kinds of puzzles (Ruger, 1910) and instructions to think aloud (Durkin, 1937) have shown that subjects have difficulties in expressing their thoughts verbally in these situations, and are biased towards direct manipulation of objects. Manipulation appears to lack a mediating symbolic representation that can readily be encoded into the verbal code. In the study by Durkin, many subjects expressed the feeling that thinking and manipulation were distinctly different, alternative, activities, even when both were directed to the solution of the problem.

From a study by Klinger (1974) using pure TA instructions, it appears that the amount of verbalization that occurs is not significantly less in these kinds of tasks than in others, but that there is a significant difference in the verbalized mental content. In manipulative tasks there is a relatively high frequency of higher-level evaluations of unverbalized solution attempts (e.g., "Yep," "Damnit," etc.), and of verbalizations denoting attention to control processes (e.g., "Let's see," "Where was I?"). When engaged in perceptual-motor manipulation, the subject does not appear to be aware of, and does not verbalize, the lower-level content or structure of his thought processes.

In order to increase verbalization of content, some experimenters using the TA method have changed the task by constraining the manipulations partially (Durkin, 1937) or wholly (Benjafield, 1971), thereby forcing the subjects to form an internal representation of the content that can be verbally encoded. When this is done, more of the content of the thought processes is, in fact, verbalized.

From a behavioral point of view, constraining manipulation significantly changes the task, for the overt moves have now become covert and are no longer amenable to direct observation. The subjectively perceived polarity between thinking and manipulation, mentioned above, may very well correspond to this difference between covert and overt trials. Duncan (1963) showed that giving subjects an explicit instruction to *think* resulted in significantly fewer overt trials in a switch-setting task, but an actual increase in solution time. Hence, the covert processing, in the condition that induced more planning before manipulation, took longer than the corresponding overt trials. A similar tradeoff was noted by Shipstone (1960) in a concept-learning task, with an instruction to "slow down and use logical procedures." In a switch-setting task, Ray (1957) found that an instruction that required the subject to tell the experimenter what he was going to do before he started to manipulate the switches significantly decreased the number of overt trials to solution. Ray does not report the corresponding solution times.

Most of these results could be explained by the hypothesis that, in response to the instruction to "think" or verbalize, the subject did not change the structure of his processing, but simply substituted overt trials (the measured index of performance) for non-observable covert trials. However, it is reasonable to assume that the internal representation generated for the covert processing improves memory and the organization of the processing.

Our theoretical model predicts that an instruction to verbalize motives or reasons for one's thinking will likely change the course of processing. In general, when the thinking-aloud instructions do not re quire such verbalizations, the protocols do not contain them. We now review three studies where subjects were specifically instructed to report motives or reasons for their actions.

The study by Gagné and Smith (1962) with the Tower of Hanoi problem was aimed at investigating the effects of different verbalization instructions upon performance during some training tasks (two-disk to five-disk problems), and upon transfer to a similar but more complex task (six-disk problem). One of the two factorially combined manipulations during the training tasks required the subjects to state verbally a reason for each move. This requirement greatly improved performance on the transfer task, both as to number of moves required and time taken to find a solution. As a second manipulation, the subjects in one pair of conditions were also instructed to search for a general principle behind the different versions of the problem. This instruction did not affect performance on the transfer task.

In the training tasks, the verbalization group produced more efficient solutions (solutions having fewer moves), indicating that the instruction to verbalize the reasons induced more deliberate planning, in addition to its effect on transfer. Although no formal record was kept of the time taken for each move, the experimenters judged this to be longer for the overt verbalization group, but they reported that this extra time was "filled with the articulation of the reasons for the moves." They suggested that the instruction to verbalize the reasons for the moves affected performance by "forcing the subjects to think."

In a follow-up study with the same basic design, Wilder and Harvey (1971) investigated whether the overt verbalization was crucial, or if equivalent results could be obtained with a firm instruction to state the reasons covertly; in addition they checked the time taken to achieve solutions during the training tasks. The results showed no difference between the two verbalizing conditions, but a clear reduction in the number of moves in both those conditions as compared with a control condition. The time to solution did not differ among the three conditions, during either the training tasks or the final task. This finding eliminates the hypothesis that the advantage in transfer shown for the verbalization condition in this experiment was attributable to extra learning time during the training sessions.

In another follow-up of Gagné and Smith, Davis et al. (1968) included the presence of the experimenter as an additional dimension in a factorial design. In this study the subjects were instructed to verbalize their reasons at the beginning of the experiment, but the instruction was not repeated; in the earlier experiments, the subjects were closely monitored during the entire session to make sure they followed the instructions. In the Davis study, verbalization had no effect on the training task (5-disk problem), but significantly reduced the number of moves required to solve the test problem (6-disk problem). The experimenter's presence increased verbalization on the training problem, but not on the test problem. There was no interaction between amount of verbalization and presence or absence of the experimenter. Unfortunately, no information is given about the solution times.

These three studies show that a requirement to verbalize reasons and motives has substantial effects on both immediate performance and learning, and thus indicates that generating verbalized reasons brings about changes, at least in manipulative tasks, in the normal course of the processes. Here, as in the studies discussed earlier, we do not know to what extent forcing subjects to give reasons for their actions simply causes them to substitute overt trials for non-observable covert trials and planning. The negative result of the Davis et al. experiment is most readily interpreted as showing that, in a problem-solving situation with a heavy cognitive load, initial instructions may be disregarded by subjects unless they are monitored by the experimenter. An analysis of the content of the verbalizations, not provided by the authors, would be required to test the plausibility of this explanation. Finally, we may conjecture that the presence of alternative solutions to the Tower of Hanoi problem probably increases, in comparison with other tasks, the sensitivity of thought processes to instructions to verbalize reasons.

Verbalization of Visual Encodings

There is compelling evidence to support the distinction between a visual representation or code and an oral or symbolic representation or code when subjects are presented with drawings or pictures. An instruction to describe a visual scene verbally should require an oral encoding of the picture, which will imply extensive processing.

The task of viewing a novel visual scene has been studied to detect effects of imposing an additional verbalizing task, in this case to describe the scene verbally. A study by Freund (Loftus & Bell, 1975) showed that subsequent recognition of scenes was much improved by the verbalizing requirement as opposed to viewing without it. On the other hand, when an unrelated verbal task, like counting backwards by threes, is imposed, the subsequent recognition of scenes deteriorates as compared with normal viewing, but not to a chance level (Loftus, 1972; studies of Freund and Szewczuk described in Loftus & Bell, 1975).

Loftus and Bell (1975) have studied the process of recognizing pictures viewed with the instruction to remember them for subsequent recognition. At the time of judging whether or not a picture had been presented before, the subjects were asked if their judgment rested on a specific detail or on general familiarity with the picture. Performance was very much better when a detail could be named than when the subject simply cited general familiarity. From recordings of eye movements during the initial presentation of the pictures in an earlier study, Loftus (1972) found that the detail verbalized during the recognition trials was the detail that had received most fixations at the initial presentation. Loftus and Bell propose that all these results can be explained by the notion of two different codes. The nonverbal encoding is direct and independent of the verbalization instructions. The extent to which an oral encoding is also generated is influenced by the instruction to give a verbal description.

Evidence supporting the distinctness of the two codes comes from an investigation by Schuck and Leahy (1966) on fragmenting visual images. They found that subjects reporting the disappearances verbally tended to report omissions of meaningful complete segments, while control subjects who traced the disappearances on an outline of the image did so to a lesser degree. However, subjects in the two conditions were not treated identically. The verbalizing subjects gave reports continuously, while the others were given time to trace images when they appeared. Schuck (1973, 1977) carried out some subsequent experiments that equated the two conditions more carefully, and then found no statistically reliable differences between the two groups of subjects. It would appear that when sufficient time is allowed them, and the degree of detail that is wanted is specified, the verbal descriptions that subjects give of fragmented images are basically veridical. This is especially interesting since the task obviously calls for recoding of the perceived stimulus.

Studies on concept formation using the Vigotsky test (Hanfmann, 1941; Hanfmann & Kasanin, 1937) have identified interindividual differences in strategies which have a bearing on the effects of instructions to describe stimuli verbally. The test employs a number of blocks varying in color, shape, and size. Each block has one of four names written on its reverse side, and the subject is to find the characteristic that serves as basis for the naming. Subjects classified as "conceptual" did not inspect the blocks visually very much, but spent most of their time in thinking, using a symbolic representation of the blocks in terms of their attributes. In this group, for example, the hypothesis that color might be one of the relevant characteristics is checked by counting the colors rather than moving the blocks. This group showed a strong preference for shape as the relevant attribute, and were disappointed with the solution, which was based on color.

The subjects classified as "perceptual" constantly manipulated the blocks, and appeared to get their ideas for organizing the blocks from looking at them. Typically, they first made groupings by manipulating the blocks, and then discovered or formulated a general principle. Retrospective reports from these subjects on how they found the solution were particularly scanty, and they often had no more to say than that it seemed natural to group the blocks as they had. These subjects seemed to favor color and size as the relevant characteristics, and were fully satisfied with the solution based on these characteristics. Consistently with this preference, the perceptual subjects were significantly better at the task than the conceptual subjects.

A reasonable hypothesis about the effect of requiring subjects to verbalize explanations in such a task would be that subjects with a preference for perceptual processing would alter their processing strategy, and hence their performance. In a study by Brunk et al. (1958), subjects were given an initial test of the Vigotsky type, and then a second, similar test. In one condition on the second test, each subject was "requested to tell why he placed each block where he did." In a control condition, no such explanation was requested. The correlation of subject scores between initial and second test was significantly lower under the instruction to explain than under the control condition, as the hypothesis would predict.

Using several highly perceptual tasks, like the Rorschach, the stencil test and a block test, Goldner (1957) was able to identify in data from TA protocols consistent individual differences along the perceptual-cognitive dimension (in his terminology, between processing wholes and parts of the stimulus information). For the stencil test, Hafner (1957) found (though the differences only approached significance) that instructing subjects to verbalize what "they were thinking and doing" improved their test performances, but also required more time. His instruction to verbalize is poorly documented, but the theoretical context of his study suggests that there were important differences from the assumptions of Level 2 verbalization. Hafner's results seem to reveal the same effect as Brunk et al.'s (1958) study.

In a series of studies reported in Merz (1969), the effect of verbalization on performance in intelligence tests was investigated. In a study by Kesting using the Figure Reasoning test, the 13- to 17- year-old subjects who always had to say aloud how the figures were alike or different were significantly better than the subjects who were asked to say the same thing to themselves silently; but they were also significantly slower. In this study, there were also two other conditions with additional verbal interference tasks; one group of subjects had to say "eins, eins ..." rhythmically, while another group had to sing "la, la ..." while solving the test items. These conditions have the same performance (in terms of number of correct solutions and time required) as the silent verbalizing condition; which suggests that the same processes, mainly nonverbal in character, were used in all three conditions.

This oral-encoding interpretation is supported by Waszak (reported in Merz, 1969), who showed that hearing one's own voice in a heavy noise condition does not eliminate the improvement associated with verbalizing. The crucial mechanism underlying these results appears to be that the instruction to explain answers increases the tendency to encode figures and their differences verbally. This interpretation is also supported by the observation of Merz that it is difficult to induce subjects to verbalize in this kind of perceptual task.

To test the hypothesis that the instruction to verbalize made the subjects assume a more analytic problem-solving style, Hofgren (Merz, 1969) compared performance on a parallel form of the Figure Reasoning test between a group that had previously verbalized on an initial form and a control group that had not. The verbalizing group performed significantly less well when not required to verbalize, but still somewhat better than the control group, whose performance hardly differed between the two occasions. Merz suggests that the loss of performance by the "verbalizers" on the second occasion was due to transfer of thought content, as the verbalizing subjects solved more test items on the first occasion, rather than to transfer of a more analytic style of thought. Supporting evidence is given in a study by Waschke (Merz, 1969): the verbalizing and control groups performed equally on the first occasion, when simple items were used; and the performance of both groups was the same on the second occasion, with respect to time and number of items correct. These investigations indicate that the instruction to verbalize forces subjects to encode the figures orally, and that this, in turn, induces verbal symbolic processing that is especially well adapted to discovery of the prescribed solutions in the Figure Reasoning test.

In the above studies, performance was averaged over subjects and different tasks. We now consider evidence of differences between individuals, and of differential effects, on performance with tasks of varying difficulty. Merz (1969) reports a smaller study showing that with simple test items, verbalization did not help the subject and amounted more or less to a retrospective description of the solution "seen" immediately. The verbalized description was only helpful with more difficult items that required some search for the right solution.

Inner speech, measured by electrical activity in the speech apparatus with Raven's Progressive Matrices items and without verbalization shows a similar pattern, in that inner speech activity increased with difficulty of the items (Sokolov, 1972). Analyzing the protocols from verbal reconstructions of the problem-solving process, Sokolov showed that the simple items were solved in a predominately visual way, while with the more difficult problems, verbal designations of some features of the figures were used to aid solution. In outlining a scheme for the interplay of visual and verbal processes in solving such problems, Sokolov points to the influence of verbalization in attending to features that would have gone unnoticed in the purely visual analysis. In this interpretation, the directed verbalization provides the subject with additional noticed features, which in turn facilitate performance.

There is little evidence as to whether directed verbalizing has a general or a differential effect on subjects. A general effect is suggested by the fact that the variance of the increased performance with verbalizing is equal to or less than the variance of performance under control conditions in the studies of Kesting and Waszak and Hofgren (Merz, 1969). The investigation by Sokolov indicates differences between subjects, leading Sokolov to propose a differential reliance on verbal and visual processing; but this result is not incompatible with the idea that there may also be general effects upon all subjects.

In this context we also want to discuss the well-known effect of providing verbal labels to visual stimuli, which was originally demonstrated by Carmichael, Hogan, and Walters (1932). We will rely heavily on the relevant parts of Riley's (1962) excellent discussion of memory for form. Carmichael et al. showed clearly that naming one of two possible labels for an ambiguous stimulus before its presentation led subjects to draw the pictures more like the label in a subsequent memory test. A series of studies have shown that this effect is not a purely perceptual one, at least when the presentation time is sufficiently long for complete perception (Bruner, Busiek, & Minturn (1952) found effects for presentations shorter than a tenth of second). Hanawalt and Demarest (1939) showed that verbal labels presented at recall gave similar effects when the pictures had been unlabeled at presentation. Prentice (1954) showed that presenting verbal labels with the pictures produced no bias in perception.

Additional insight into the effects of labels is provided by a study by Herman, Lawless, and Marshall (1957), who included a control group that was simply shown the pictures. (The original study by Carmichael et al. had a very small control group.) Herman et al. (1957) found that the subjects in the control group showed as much tendency as the others to distortions of memory. However, in the control group the memories were distorted equally in the directions of the two labels, while in the experimental groups, they were distorted mainly toward the label that was presented. Yet even in the experimental groups a few subjects deviated toward the verbal label that was *not* presented. Hanawalt and Demarest (1939) found that subjects who were not given a verbal label at presention reported meaningful associations to the pictures, and a substantial number of these associations were similar or even identical to the labels used originally by Carmichael et al. Herman et al. (1957) confirmed this by asking a new group of 29 subjects to give free associations to the pictures. On the average, 63 % of the associations were identical to or very similar to the ones used by Carmichael et al. Furthermore, Herman et al. (1957) showed that the effects of the labels could be markedly reduced if subjects were told in advance that they would be asked to draw the pictures later. In sum, the original effect observed by Carmicheal et al. appears to be caused by inducing subjects to use certain associations at the expense of others. Hence, it is entirely possible, even likely, that subjects could easily perform this memory task with TA or retrospective report instructions without changes in performance.

Other Verbalization Studies

None of the studies that remain to be discussed employ highly manipulative tasks or pictorial stimuli. In a study on clinical judgment (Baranowski, 1975), the subjects, who were psychologists, made two successive series of judgments. On the first occasion, all subjects performed the task under identical conditions. On the second occasion, the subjects were divided into: (a) a group working under the same instructions as on the first occasion, and (b) a group instructed to verbalize and monitored by the 'experimenter who asked the subjects questions whenever "a particular profile could use more explanation" (1975, p. 21). There was no difference between control and verbalizing conditions (measured by variance accounted for by linear and non-linear models). However, the cross-validated linear models over the two occasions accounted for significantly less variance for the verbalizing group than for the control, suggesting that the instruction to verbalize changed the utilization or subjective weights of the cue-variables.

   In a related study, Fidler (1979) had subjects choose for admission to graduate study between two students described in terms of several attributes. Subjects gave both concurrent and retrospective reports. (Unfortunately, the concurrent reporting instruction asked subjects to provide certain specific information, like the reasons for judgments, how they evaluated information, and so on.) Retrospective reports were elicited by asking subjects how they had reached their decisions. Fidler compared the performance under different reporting instructions (including no verbal report at all). No reliable differences in choice were observed, nor were subjects more consistent in making choices on repeated trials with verbal report instructions than without such instructions. When regressions were estimated to determine each subject's decision model for verbal-report trials and no-report trials, respectively, no reliable differences were found for 10 of the 13 subjects. The reliable differences in the rules for the three remaining subjects could be traced to stable changes in their decision rules that occurred in the transition between blocks of report and no-report trials. Whether these changes in decision rules were induced by the reporting instructions or other factors is not certain. Fidler proposes that it may be due to the inexperience of the subjects. Since they were not experts at the judgment task, they were aware of their decision rules, hence could report them. The consistency between reported reasons and decision rules, on the one hand, and actual choices (even on no-report trials) lends further support to that interpretation.

In a concept-learning study by Bower and King (1967), one group of the subjects was required to verbalize their hypotheses before classifying the stimuli, while a control group was not. In preparation for the experiment, the subjects described the stimuli, in order to ensure that subject and experimenter agreed in their descriptions. Under these circumstances, we would expect that no further oral encoding need occur in the verbalizing condition. The number of irrelevant dimensions of the stimuli was varied, although the instructions indicated which two features were relevant to the solution in each case. The requirement to verbalize hypotheses improved performance significantly (i.e., number of responses to criterion), but only for the first problem. Bower and King found that variation in the number of irrelevant features or dimensions was only effective on this initial problem, suggesting that the verbalizing of hypotheses helped the subjects initially to ignore the irrelevant attributes. It should be noted that no training trials were used in this study. Karpf and Levine (1971) found no effect on performance in a discrimination learning experiment from asking subjects to repeat their hypotheses verbally before each trial.

In a cue-probability learning task, Brehmer (1974) required one group of subjects to describe the rule underlying their predictions just after each prediction was made, but before feedback was received. The subjects' descriptions should be so explicit that another subject could understand and use it; if they did not meet this standard, the experimenter prompted for more information. Explanations like "I guessed," or "I remembered from the previous trial," were accepted as verbal descriptions. An analysis of variance showed no significant effect or interactions associated with verbalization. In a subsequent study (Brehmer, Kuylenstierna & Liljegren, 1975) the subjects wrote down their current hypotheses in a booklet at the beginning of the test blocks, without any significant effect on performance.

According to our model, requiring verbal explanations of behavior should not alter the normal processes unless the information required for the verbalizations would not otherwise be generated. Unfortunately, there is little evidence for the tasks used in the above studies about the content of undirected verbalizations. In the cue-probability experiment of Brehmer (1974) with very simple stimuli (a straight line varying in length), the number required for explaining the rule was most likely consciously generated even in the silent condition. That the effects of verbalization were limited to the first trial in the Bower and King (1967) experiment could be attributed to the fact that verbalizing helped the subjects ignore irrelevant features. Alternatively, one might speculate that verbalizing may have speeded up the generation of an internal representation, thus making the subject more independent of his direct perceptions. In the study of Baranowski (1975), unlike the other studies, the subjects were highly skilled. In our model, verbal explanation of automated activities would be cumbersome and change the course of the processing from a largely perceptual (recognition) to a more cognitive one. In support of this hypothesis, the time taken by the clinical psychologists to perform the task with verbalization was two or three times the time taken in the silent condition.

Effects from Retrospective Verbalization

We turn now to some experiments that are often cited to show that verbalizing information (even retrospectively) may change and deform it, and hence affect subsequent task behavior. Hendrix (1947) showed that an instruction to describe a concept or principle verbally after learning reduced ability to use the concept in a transfer situation. The results were substantiated in subsequent work by Schwartz (1966) and by Phelan (1965). Careful analysis shows that these studies do not address the question of verbalization, as such, but rather verbalization of explicit and logical concepts. There are two issues. The first is that if the subjects do not normally organize what they learn in these experiments in verbalizable concepts and general principles, then verbalization forces them to generate such concepts and principles from whatever information is currently available to them. The reformulation may not at all reflect the way in which the learning was actually encoded. For example, Phelan found that the verbal descriptions of certain pictorial stimuli tended to contain discriminative features different from those that defined the concept the

subjects had learned. In Chapter 3 we return to the issue of what information should be reportable in such cases.

The second issue relates to the detail and explicitness called for by
the instruction to verbalize. Sowder (1974), examining the effects of
various sorts of verbalizations of learned generalizations, found no differences as compared with a control condition. He also cited two studies
that found no effects of producing written descriptions of learned
generalizations. Sowder proposed that the important differences between his study and Hendrix's was that Hendrix (1947) specified
precisely the content of her subjects' verbalization (quantifiers, domain,
and so on), while he did not.

Rommetveit (1960, 1965) and Rommetveit and Kvale (1965a,
1965b) studied concept formation in a situation where 12- and 13-year-
old subjects played on a wheel of fortune, different pictures being displayed when subjects were to win or lose, respectively. They found that
instructing the subjects that they were subsequently to describe differences between the "win" and "lose" figures, as opposed to just playing
on the wheel, influenced retrospective descriptions of the two figures.
Other procedural variations—like demonstrating before the experiment
how the figures differed (Rommetveit, 1965)— tended to eliminate a
(correct) tendency toward associating roundness with good figures. In
these studies, therefore, the effective variable is not verbalization per se,
but directing the cognitive processes by instructions. Without such direction, verbalization appears to have no effect on the cognitive processes.

The fact that encoding and reporting verbally takes time creates a
procedural difference, which is important in some studies, between the
reporting and control conditions. Time is known to be an important
variable in LTM phenomena. Boersma, Conklin, and Carlson (1966)
allowed their subjects in the verbal report condition an additional minute
to specify their encodings of each stimulus. Retention scores were superior for the verbal report condition, but the experimental design con-
founds the effect of the additional time with effects of generating a written description of the stimulus.

In sum, the empirical data from the modest number of systematic
studies of the effects of verbalizing (e.g., Brehmer, 1974; Brehmer,
Kuylenstierna & Liljegren, 1974, 1975; Karpf & Levine, 1971; Wilson &
Spellacy, 1972) support consistently our assertion that producing verbal
reports of information directly available in propositional form does not
change the course and structure of the cognitive processes. However,
instructions that require the subjects to perform additional cognitive

processes to generate or access the information to be reported may affect
these processes.

New Research on Effects of Verbalization

The renewed interest in psychology in using verbal reports as data has
generated new research activity aimed at casting further light on the
effects of verbalization upon cognitive processes. This new work seeks to
go beyond proving the presence or absence of effects of verbalization,
and to measure the extent and nature of these effects under different
experimental conditions. We will conclude our discussion by a summary
of three important recent studies of this kind.

In a dissertation, Karat (1983) analyzed the verbalizations of subjects solving the Tower of Hanoi with TA instructions. He found that
subjects verbalized plans and goals before making some, but by no
means all, of their moves. If subjects were required to give reasons for
each move, as in the original study by Gagné and Smith (1962), they
would have to generate these reasons through additional cognitive
processing. Since Karat found no effects due to TA, the effects found by
Gagné and Smith can very likely be attributed to their more specific and
demanding verbalization instructions.

The most ambitious attempt to explore and document effects of
instructions to verbalize is an unpublished study by Russo, Johnson, and
Stephens (in preparation). In their study, 24 subjects performed 55 trials
of 4 different tasks with 5 different instructions. The five instructions
included a control condition, concurrent verbalization, retrospective
reports with the problem still in view, retrospective reports without any
stimulus information, and retrospective reports cued by the eye-
movements recorded during the immediately preceding solution. In the
following, we will only discuss the data for the control condition, and for
concurrent and retrospective reports without stimulus information. The
four tasks were: selection between gambles, items from Raven's progressive matrices, mental addition of three 3-digit numbers, and anagrams.
For each task 55 items were selected to yield an average percent correct
of 75%. The eye movements of subjects were recorded on every trial.

In this thorough study, the only reliable over-all effect of verbalization was that solutions took longer with concurrent verbalizing than in
the silent condition. Although the average solution times with verbalization were longer for all four tasks, a post-hoc analysis showed that the

differences were statistically significant only for gambles and anagrams, and the differences were also small relative to the variability of the solution times. For gambles, the solutions with TA took 7.5 seconds longer than the average of solutions (44.6 seconds) under the silent condition, an increase of about 17 per cent.

The analysis of accuracy of solution showed that with concurrent verbalization subjects performed the gambles task a little better than silent subjects (p < .01), while in the addition task concurrent verbalizers performed slightly more poorly than silent subjects (p = .06). Hence concurrent verbalizing leads subjects to take longer and perform better on the gambles task, and to take longer but perform more poorly on the additions task.

To help us pinpoint the sources of differences, E. S. Johnson (personal communication) reports results from a preliminary analysis of the data. "We did not find any differences between conditions for the first ten practice trials, but control subjects subsequently increased their accuracy in the addition task more rapidly than subjects giving verbal reports. Both concurrent and retrospective subjects improved over trials in their selection of gambles, while control subjects gradually speeded up but maintained constant accuracy levels."

While awaiting the complete analysis of the protocols, eye-movement sequences, and errors, we can only speculate about the reasons for the differences in final performance. A comparison of the verbalizations during practice trials and test trials should reveal the changes in processing that took place in the gambling task. It is noteworthy that retrospectively reporting subjects, who did not have to think aloud, improved in performance in that task just as concurrently reporting subjects did. The difference for mental additions is especially surprising in view of the fact that earlier studies showed no effects of verbalizing in mental multiplication. From a preliminary analysis of numbers of protocol statements (Russo et al., in preparation) it appears possible that concurrent subjects failed to speed up because they continued to verbalize simple operations that could be elicited by recognition. This "superfluous" verbalization could slow down performance and interfere with recall of intermediate steps. Verbal reporting might not alter initial performance, but might slow down changes toward automaticity during continuing practice.

In sum, Russo et al. (in preparation) found reliable effects of concurrent verbalization for gambles and additions, but the differences reported are small in relation to other variability in the performances.

Since the effect was virtually the same for the concurrent and retrospective verbalization conditions, and since there was no effect of verbalization in the early trials, we are rather uncertain as to the real causes for the differences that were observed.

A recent dissertation by Gerhard Deffner (1983) provides additional extensive information about the effects of concurrent verbalization. Using anagrams, a geometric puzzle, and the N-term series problem (see Ohlsson (1980) for a description), and varying task difficulty and amount of perceptually available information, he found that thinking aloud increased solution times, but did not affect average numbers of solutions, and did not interact with the other experimental variables. Deffner's analysis of his subjects' strategies, and rate and content of their verbalizations will be discussed elsewhere in this monograph.

SUMMARY

The picture that emerges from our review of empirical studies of verbalization is quite clear and consistent. We have seen that the effects, or absence of effects, of verbalization depend upon characteristics of the tasks and of the verbalization instructions in ways that can be predicted from our model of the processing system.

When the instructional procedures conformed to our notion of Level 1 or Level 2 verbalization, the studies gave no evidence that verbalization changes the course or structure of the thought processes. A small number of minor differences between verbalizing and silent subjects can most plausibly be attributed to procedural differences between the experiments conducted with the two groups.

Studies that deviated in task, instructions, or experimental procedure, from the criteria of Level 2 verbalization were mainly experiments on perceptual-motor tasks and tasks requiring visual encoding processes, and experiments where specific verbal content was asked for by the instructions. Evidence was presented, for these kinds of experiments, that the information requested by the experimenter was not normally available to the subject in an oral encoding, and hence that producing the verbalization required intermediate processing that changed the course and structure of the thought process.

From our review of the evidence, we conclude that the processes subjects use to verbalize while thinking are neither illusory nor elusive, but can be understood and modeled. The processes associated with verbalization should be treated as an integral part of any model of the cognitive processes for a given task whenever the articulation takes the form of direct verbalization (i.e., vocalization of heeded information). The model should also include the processes for storing information in LTM, to account for the phenomena of retrospective verbalization at the end of experimental trials. The gross model we have proposed is focused on the verbalization of ongoing cognitive processes, but the postulated close link between information attended to and information stored should make it a relatively straightforward matter to model retrospective verbalization.

Finally, in the review of studies comparing different instructions to verbalize, we found substantial evidence that differences in performance were induced by telling the subject *how* to verbalize. In order to verbalize the information called for by the instructions, instead of the information he would normally have attended to, he had to change his thought processes.

3

COMPLETENESS OF REPORTS

An important problem arises in using verbal reports as data: the processes underlying behavior may be unconscious and thus not accessible for verbal reporting, or at least may be reportable only very incompletely. Closely related to the problem of incompleteness is the possibility that verbalizations, when present, may not be closely related to underlying thought processes—may not be veridical reports of those processes or may be epiphenomenal. In the course of the chapter, we will consider these issues of veridicality and epiphenomenality also, but our central concern will be with the completeness of reports.

We begin by viewing the issues in historical perspective. Then, we extend the model of the human information processing system proposed in previous chapters to encompass the processes associated with verbalization. Finally, we take up the evidence on completeness of reports under four different headings:

1. Ability of subjects to report their own cognitive states;
2. Reports of recognition processes;
3. Retrospective reports of previous cognitive processes;
4. Insight.

THREE VIEWPOINTS

The completeness, veridicality, and epiphenomenality of verbal reports can be viewed from quite different perspectives. On the one hand, behaviorism is generally skeptical about the accessibility of internal states. On the other hand, a perspective that postulates that all human thinking is rational and logical finds it hard to account for verbalizations that appear not to have these qualities, and to account, also, for sudden leaps of "intuition."   We need to consider each of these perspectives in turn, and to relate them to our own information processing perspective.

The Behaviorist View

The strongest behaviorist objection to treating verbal protocols as veridical is the *epiphenomenality* claim— the claim that the processes involved in generating a verbal report are totally independent of the process that generates the task behavior of the subject. A slightly weaker form of the objection is the argument that *certain types* of cognitive processes are not conscious, hence that these processes and their contents cannot be reported. In his famous *Psychological Review* article, Watson (1913) opposed extensive theorizing about cognitive structures and processes. The only acceptable facts and data were behavior and recordable events that could be observed by an independent observer, as opposed to introspection. Emphasis was placed on collecting and analyzing such facts, and theorizing was treated as a subordinate activity.

> [Behaviorism] may never make a pretense of being a *system.* Indeed systems in every scientific field are out of date. We collect our facts from observation. Now and then we select a group of facts and draw certain general conclusions about them.   In a few years as new experimental data are gathered by better methods, even these tentative general conclusions have to be qualified. (Watson, 1930, p. 18)

Of particular interest is Watson's view of cognition. He opposed the structuralists' attempts to study cognitions directly and questioned the need for postulating cognitive structures and mechanisms beyond describing them in terms of stimulus-response connections.   Watson wanted very strongly to eliminate the magic surrounding unobservable cognitive structures by showing that they could be understood in terms of observable events or at least potentially observable events. As his account represents an extreme, yet important, viewpoint, we will describe it briefly without critical comments.

Watson proposed that memory can be accounted for adequately by established S-R bonds, which could have been observed at the time of their acquisition. He explicitly refutes the need for "memory" as a construct.

> The behaviorist never uses the term "memory."   He believes that it has no place in an objective psychology. (Watson, 1925, p. 177)

By "memory," then, we mean nothing except that fact
that when we meet a stimulus again after an absence, we do
the old habitual thing (say the old words and show the old
visceral-emotional behavior) that we learned to do when we
were in the presence of that stimulus in the first place.
(Watson, 1925, p. 190)

Watson proposed that thinking can be seen as sequences of S-R
connections that are primarily verbal. These covert verbal responses can
be observed either by asking the subject to think aloud, or by sensitive
registration of the muscular activity of the larynx and the speech organs.

The behaviorist advances the view that *what the
psychologists have hitherto called thought is in short nothing
but talking to ourselves.* (Watson, 1925, p. 191)

Watson views verbalization as behavior, rather than as expression
or description of a corresponding cognitive structure. In support of his
argument, he notes that the verbalizations associated with many activities, like playing golf, are totally detached from actual
behavior—hence, it is possible to talk about golf-playing, and even to
describe verbally how one should do it, without being able to play.
Verbal reports on behavior can therefore be generated without any relation to the actual behavior.

The behaviorist assumes that different types of behavior are
generated separately, rather than being different expressions of common
cognitive structures and processes. It was even proposed that verbal
reports could be conditioned independently of behavior (Verplanck,
1962). A study by Hull (1920) is often cited as showing that a subject's
ability to describe a concept is not related to his ability to behave according to the concept.

Since behaviorism had no model of the structure of the cognitive
system, it made no attempt to specify the locus and characteristics of
awareness. Research, exemplified by a frequently cited study by
Greenspoon (1955), has claimed to show that changes in behavior and
learning can occur without awareness as assessed by verbal reports.
Other research has suggested that changes in attitudes may be unconscious, hence, unreportable. Subjects, when asked after an experiment
how they did the task, sometimes give reports that are inconsistent with
their recorded behavior. All of these results were used by behaviorists in
support of their position that awareness is incomplete and
epiphenomenal. They will be discussed at length in the section of this
chapter on learning without awareness.

Rationalism

The rationalist position, almost at the opposite pole from behaviorism, seeks to describe human thinking in terms of formal models from logic. Poincaré's (Ghiselin, 1952) discussion of mathematical creation is, for several reasons, a good example of the rationalistic point of view. First, Poincaré is a proponent of the necessity for assuming unconscious processes during creative thinking. Second, he is very explicit in urging a rationalist explanation for thinking.

A first fact should surprise us, or rather would surprise us if we were not so used to it. How does it happen there are people who do not understand mathematics? If mathematics invokes only the rules of logic, such as are accepted by all normal minds; if its evidence is based on principles common to all men, and that none could deny without being mad, how does it come about that so many persons are here refractory? (Ghiselin, 1952, pp. 22-23)

In order to explain how people sometimes make logical mistakes, Poincaré evokes the fallability of memory. He argues that errors do *not* occur in making inferences from premises but result from forgetting the earlier premises on which the later inferences rely, or remembering them only inexactly. Thus, we may have forgotten a step in a proof or may recall inaccurately an item in the multiplication table.

Poincaré attributes the superior mathematical skill of mathematicians to their better memory for mathematical entities, making it easier for them to follow and generate mathematical proofs. He points to the existence of a higher-level representation as crucial for memory.

A mathematical demonstration is not a simple juxtaposition of syllogisms, it is syllogisms *placed in a certain order,* and the order in which these elements are placed is much more important than the elements themselves. (Poincaré, 1952, p. 24)

He clearly makes the point that "better memory" and higher-level representation are intimately related to each specifically developed skill—in this case in mathematics—and do not imply better memory in general for other kinds of material.

With his explanations of individual differences in terms of representation or memory, Poincaré (Ghiselin, 1952) can retain his view that logical inference and rational conscious search for alternatives is the main vehicle for human problem solving. In accounting for discoveries of mathematical relations, however, he finds such reasoned activity insufficient, and suggests that we must assume unconscious processes. We will return later to a fuller discussion of his empirical findings and his theories of unconscious processes.

More recently Polanyi (1969) has argued that logical inference and explicit knowledge do not span all types of knowledge available to people. Polanyi points to perception and recognition of objects as the primary examples of tacit knowledge (i.e., knowledge that is not explicitly specified or specifiable). Polanyi argues, primarily on the basis of psychological evidence, that recognition is not an explicit reportable operation because subjects are, in general, unable (1) to report what particular information they relied on to make the recognition, and (2) to state what the necessary perceptual attributes are for identifying instances of that category.

> We certainly recognize a human face at first sight and can say only from a subsequent analysis, and then rather inadequately, by what particulars we recognized it. (Polanyi, 1969, p. 169)

> The meaning of a disease is doubly unspecifiable. (1) We cannot identify, let alone describe, a great number of the particulars which we are in fact noticing when we diagnose a case of the disease. (2) Though we can identify a case of the disease by its typical appearance, we cannot describe it adequately, ... (Polanyi, 1969, p. 132)

While the evidence Polanyi adduces would create difficulty for a theory that assumes all thought processes to be applications of the rules of logic, it is not in any way incompatible with the model of thinking we are proposing here. We have assumed that LTM is indexed by a net of tests that can be applied to stimuli in order to discriminate among and recognize them. Nothing in this assumption implies that the person making a recognition has conscious access to these tests, or can state what they are—and, indeed, the empirical evidence shows pretty clearly that there is no such access.

As to the ability or inability of a person to describe an object or person he has just recognized, our model is silent. Such a description can be generated if (1) the descriptive characteristics have been noticed consciously at some time in the past and have been stored in LTM, and (2) these characteristics have been indexed so that access can be gained to them at the time the description is called for. A failure in ability to describe a recognizable stimulus can result from failure to attend to its characteristics (even when learning to recognize it), and it can also result from an inability to retrieve these characteristics on request.

Moreover, the characteristics that a person uses to recognize a stimulus may or may not bear a close relation to the characteristics he has stored in memory and can retrieve if asked to provide a description. Anyone who has studied the taxonomy of some phylum or order of plants or animals knows that his mode of recognizing particular species on sight bears little relation to the characteristics of those species as recorded in formal taxonomic keys. In fact, the characteristics given in the keys often cannot be observed without the use of the microscope and scalpel, hence cannot possibly provide the basis for direct recognition.

The unconscious processes postulated by Poincaré and the tacit knowledge hypothesized by Polanyi both have genuine support in empirical evidence, but this evidence can, as we have now seen, be interpreted in a way that is not inimical to the information processing hypothesis. It does imply that verbal reports, however complete they may be in other respects, will not cover the microstructure of recognition processes. They will not enable a subject to report how a recognition he has just achieved was accomplished.

On the other hand, there does not seem to be any basis for Poincaré's expectation that the conscious and reportable component of the thought processes should bear any close resemblance to the laws of deductive thought laid down in formal logic. The laws of logic state conditions that a piece of deductive reasoning must meet in order to be valid. It says nothing about the processes used to discover or arrive at the valid conclusion.

Discovering a logically valid conclusion, as distinct from *testing its validity*, once discovered, is an inductive and not a deductive process. It may be achieved by recognition, in which case the details of the recognition process will not generally be reportable. Or it may be achieved by heuristic, selective search; in which case intermediate stages of the search process will usually be stored temporarily in STM, and hence will be accessible for verbal reports.

The Information Processing View

What can we say about the completeness of verbal reports from the viewpoint of the information processing model we have adopted in this volume? In this model, we emphasize the difference between the limited capacity of STM (the limits of attention) and the vast, essentially un-limited, storage capacity of LTM. Information held in STM will be available directly to the subject, while information in LTM will not be unless it is accessed and brought into attention. The three to five unre-lated information structures that can be held simultaneously in STM are best thought of as labels or pointers to nodes in LTM, where the actual information is stored. Hence, bringing such a pointer into STM is equiv-alent to activating, in other models of memory, the corresponding node or nodes in LTM.

Accessing Information in LTM. Just as information stored in an encyclopedia can be found readily only if appropriate entries are con-sulted in the index, so information can be accessed from LTM only if an appropriate accessing symbol is held in attention. Stating the conditions under which relevant information can be retrieved from LTM requires specifying the class of relevant information (index entries) that will en-able the system to identify this information and discriminate it from the rest.

For people who have expertise in a particular domain of knowledge, access to relevant information appears to be almost instan-taneous. Acquiring expertise involves developing a very systematic way of indexing information, at the time of storage, by attending to ap-propriate, usually multiple, indexing characteristics. When some knowledge is required to solve a problem or answer a question, the avail-able indexing terms will determine the desired information, so that it can be accessed directly or its absence identified.

Access can be either direct or indirect (that is, by association). If asked to report the third word of the national anthem, most persons would access "national anthem" directly, but would have to count down the first verse, associatively, until the third word was encountered. Un-less exactly the right stimulus (i.e., index entry) is provided, retrieval from LTM may require some problem solving to find an access path, and very often a stimulus may not define univocally what memory contents are wanted. Reports from LTM cannot, therefore, be "complete" in the sense of guaranteeing that all relevant items have been retrieved. Only that can be retrieved which can be accessed through cues held in atten-tion.

Storing and Indexing in LTM. It is even more obvious that infor-mation can be retrieved from LTM only if has been stored there previously, and retained. The hypothesis about storage (fixation) that seems to us most defensible in the light of the empirical evidence is that if and only if information is heeded in STM for a sufficient interval of time will it be stored (and indexed) in LTM. Attention (in a sufficient amount) provides the necessary and sufficient condition for learning. This hypothesis implies that learning does not occur without awareness, and that the information available in LTM is a subset of the information that, at some earlier time or times, was held in STM.

The general hypothesis that attention leads to fixation does not indicate how the stored information will be indexed, and what stimuli will be effective in eliciting it. Woodworth (1915) carried out a number of verbal learning experiments to determine the conditions under which one item, attended to in temporal juxtaposition to another, would be likely to serve as an effective stimulus for evoking the other.

Things become associated only when they are contiguous in experience. But is it a sufficient condition? There is little in the experimental work on memory to indicate that it is sufficient, and much to indicate that it is not usually depended on to accomplish results. The things to be connected must be together, in order to arouse the reaction connecting them; but unless they arouse some such reaction, they do not become connected, except it be very weakly. (Woodworth, 1915)

In a well-known experiment, Woodworth read subjects a list of forty words with the instruction to learn them in pairs so that they could respond with the second member of a pair when the first member was provided as stimulus. They were then tested on their ability to respond with the *first* item of a pair when the second item of the *previous* pair was provided as stimulus. They succeeded in only 7% of the trials.

Thorndike (1932) subsequently replicated Woodworth's results and demonstrated their generality. In one experiment, two groups of 100 and 140 subjects were read ten sentences in the same order 10 times with instructions to "listen to what I read with moderate attention, as you would listen to a lecture" (Thorndike, 1932, p. 66). Afterwards, subjects were given one or more words from a sentence and asked what word followed. Subjects in the two groups were 73% and 81% accurate, respectively, in reporting the word that followed a sentence's subject; but being probed for the first word in a sentence by being given the last word of the previous sentence, they were correct in only 2.3% and 2.8% of the cases, respectively, a level attributable to guessing.

In another experiment, Thorndike (1932) read pairs of words and numbers to subjects. He designed a list of 1,304 pairs so that certain word-number sequences like "beaver-86 charade-17" were presented 24 times each. Subjects asked to give the numbers following words could respond correctly in 38% of the cases, but asked to give the words following numbers, were correct in only .5%, a result no better than guessing.

Recognition Processes. The process we know as "recognition" is simply the special case of retrieval from LTM where the stimulus is some set of characteristics of the object retrieved. When something is retrieved by recognition, there is also retrieved, of course, all sorts of other information associated in LTM with the item retrieved. What is not retrieved, however, are the internal steps of the recognition process itself—hence, our inability to say *how* we recognized something.

In our model we assume that new memory structures are generated by bringing together the contents of focal attention with information accessed from LTM. As a result, a new structure is formed, and when this structure is accessed, it will provide a memory of the corresponding thought episode.

Since retrieval requires those cues to be present that were indexed to the LTM content at the time of learning, recall is most likely to be successful if the cuing stimulus is encoded in the same way at recall as it was at the original presentation. This leads to the interesting prediction, in paired associate learning, that the subject must recognize having seen the stimulus item in order to exceed chance in his recall of the response member of the pair. This prediction was confirmed by Bernbach (1967) and Martin (1967), using visual and oral stimuli, respectively.

That the encodings of the stimulus must be essentially the same at presentation and test for correct recognition was nicely demonstrated by Rubin (see Woodworth, 1938). He showed reversible figures to his subjects: either half could be seen as figure or as ground.

Depending on whether the black or the white field is seen as figure, the stimulus will be encoded and perceived in two different ways. Subjects were instructed to treat one color as figure, the other as ground. When they were subsequently presented with old and new stimuli for recognition judgments, with instructions to view either the same, or the other, color as figure, their performance depended on whether or not the color treated as figure was the same or had been reversed. In the former condition, 49% of the figures were recognized; in the latter condition, only 9%—almost the same as the percentage (6%) of false recognitions of new figures not presented previously.

Tulving and his colleagues (cf. Tulving & Thompson, 1973) have presented considerable evidence to show that, for successful recognition and recall of paired associates, stimuli must be encoded in the same way at time of test as at time of original presentation. Bower and Winzenz (1969) demonstrated that digit sequences were only recognized as previously seen if the digits were grouped in the same subsequences at both presentations. The extensive body of research showing the close relation between the perceptual and conceptual encoding of the stimuli and subsequent recall is very nicely described in Bower and Hilgard (1981, Chapter 10).

Some of the strongest evidence for the direct relation between heeded information and memory comes from the extensive research on memory that is incidental to performing certain tasks. Because excellent reviews of this literature already exist (Saltz, 1971; Smirnov, 1973), we will only summarize the main findings. The information committed to memory corresponds closely to the aspects of the stimuli that must be heeded in order to perform the task (Smirnov, 1973). Incidental memory from some tasks is so good that explicit instructions to commit the information to memory do not improve performance on subsequent memory tasks. All of the above studies test only memory for physically present stimulus information; later, we will discuss memory for thoughts.

Thus, there is a wide spectrum of possibilities between the extreme SR view, which assumes that unique cues are linked to unique responses, and the extreme rationalist position, which assumes that all information is semantically integrated, and all possible inferences are drawn (and stored) when new information is encountered. The information processing view, which we have just sketched, takes an intermediate position, making specific predictions about the conditions under which information will be stored and the conditions under which it will be available for recall.

Extensions of the IP Model

The information processing model describes the cognitive processes as producing a sequence of states, each marked by a small collection of information in attention and STM. For the moment, we will disregard information from the external environment that is available in sensory stores, and simply consider the successive states of heeded information in STM.

Formally, we can represent the time course of information in STM as a sequence, each element of which is the *output* of the process that operated on its predecessor and the *input* to the process that will produce its successor. We deliberately omit further description of the process that creates these input-output relations because, from the viewpoint of attention and consciousness, this process is opaque and its intermediate states are not reportable.

Cognitive tasks vary dramatically in well-definedness and specificity, as do the relations between inputs and their outputs. If the task is to find the sum of 2 and 3, the subject will usually access and retrieve the correct answer, 5. In this case, the output is determined, at least semantically, by the input and process. However, if a subject is asked to name a word starting with "A," the input is insufficient to determine what word will be selected. Subjects report that a word simply "occurs." (Most college students retrieve the same word, "apple.") The retrieved word is determined by the structure and organization of LTM. The same opaque retrieval process makes it impossible for subjects to report veridically why they responded "red" when asked to name a color—although they are quite willing to speculate about the reasons.

Our hypothesis is that the subject is only aware of input and output of such processes, and has no further direct information about the process itself. He does not know which elements in the stimulus, which cues, were functionally important for access to the response information. This doesn't mean, of course, that subjects have no cognitive control over the responses they generate. They can evaluate and process in other ways the information they access before responding with it. A subject, for example, may retrieve several words starting with "A," then retrieve additional information in order to make a selection among them. Subjects may also retrieve and apply additional constraints to the response before it is verbalized (e.g., "word should be unusual," "part of book title"). In such circumstances, subjects can report additional information (the additional information they have retrieved and stored temporarily in STM) beyond the stimulus and response.

There is considerable evidence that subjects can and do conform to task instructions (the *Aufgabe*) in responding. If asked for a beverage they will respond with the name of a beverage. Hence information in attention and STM imposes constraints on accessed information and cognitive structures, even though it does not always determine uniquely which specific structure will be accessed. The general and basic point is that subjects *cannot* gain access to information in LTM without bringing that information into STM, hence into attention.

The model we are proposing has strong implications for recognition and learning which we wish to examine in some detail. In the next section, we will examine experiments on recognition processes. Then we will review evidence that suggests strongly that only information in attention is committed to memory, and evidence on the effect of automation of responses through practice upon reportability.

RECOGNITION PROCESSES

By recognition processes we mean the processes or mechanisms by which sensory information is encoded and familiar patterns and structures are identified. The Structuralists assumed that complex patterns were recognized by identifying their elements, and thus assumed that elements were identified prior to recognition of the pattern. The Gestalt psychologists argued that the complex patterns were recognized prior to identification of their parts. We agree with the Gestalt position to this extent: that in many situations, a complex pattern is accessed without prior conscious awareness of its parts. Whatever use is made of features in the recognition process itself, these features need not be accessible to awareness.

Generally, we recognize familiar faces, words, and objects directly, that is, without storing in STM the features extracted from the stimuli and used for discrimination. There is evidence, also, for direct recognition of more complex patterns and relations, especially when the presentation is visual. Claparède (1934) found that his thinking-aloud subjects did not report intermediate stages when generating interpretations and hypotheses for complex visual stimuli. Similar findings are reported for subjects noticing relations in geometry problems (Henry, 1934).

In recall and retrieval of familiar information, unless it requires problem solving with the aid of successive associations, processes leave only the final product as trace in STM. The phenomenon is so familiar that it appears not to have been tested by experiment. There was ample evidence, however, from introspective reports directed at the issue of the existence of imageless thought for Woodworth (1938, p. 787) to reach the conclusion that "what is imageless is not thought as much as recall."

Evidence for One-Stage Recognition

We have argued that recognition is a one-stage process, whose intermediate products are not available in STM for verbal reports. Let us look at the evidence for this position, which is in direct opposition to that held earlier by the Structuralists. We will show, first, that in the recognition of complex patterns, lower-level components cannot generally be recognized prior to recognition of the larger pattern, and, second, that relatively fragmentary perceptual information often suffices for recognition of a whole complex pattern.

With respect to the first point, Johnson (1975) has shown that subjects cannot recognize a single letter faster than the complete word containing that letter. There is even more extensive evidence for the second point. Elements of a pattern sometimes do not even need to be *presented*, much less heeded, for successful recognition of the pattern. Warren (1970) presented subjects with a recorded sentence, replacing one or more phonemes with pure tones. Subjects almost never noticed the substitution. Warren and Warren (1970) showed that subjects could hear the correct word in a sentence even when context had to be used to disambiguate the stimulus. For example, the stimulus "eel" was recognized, appropriately, as "wheel," "peel," or "heel," depending on context. Similar results have been obtained by Cole (1973). See also, Best, Morrongiello, and Robson (1981).

Strong evidence for the opacity of recognition comes from some research inspired by Kulpe, who was intrigued by trained introspective observers' occasional confusions of imagined with perceived images. In these cases the subjects were unaware of the inputs that caused them to retrieve familiar structures. Replicating an original study by Perky (1910), Segal (1971) showed that subjects instructed to form images of familiar objects in front of a white screen were influenced in their imagery when, without their knowledge, images were projected on the screen. For example, if subjects were asked to imagine a coke glass, they were more likely to describe a glass with "Coca-Cola" written on it when such a glass was dimly projected on the screen than when it was not.

In another study, (Segal, 1968), two incomplete red squares were projected dimly while subjects were forming an image of either a plant or a violin. When questioned afterwards, only one of 33 subjects reported noting any projected images; twenty of 32 subjects (about one standard deviation above chance) answered correctly whether the image was projected while they were imaging the violin or while they were imaging the plant. Subjects making correct judgments would report the following kinds of grounds for their decisions:

Before the image of the plant that I reported, I imagined a pot of geraniums—I think that was projected.

or

The image I had of a plant was funny, so I think that was projected. (Segal, 1968, p. 394)

Subjects thought that the projected images were images of plants and violins, and were confused when given a verbal description of the actual images which were neither plant-like nor violin-like. Hence their responses provide no real evidence for awareness of the projected images.

In a followup study by Segal and Fusella (Segal, 1971), 64 subjects generated three different images; an image was projected during one of these mental imaging tasks. Subjects were able to guess the period when the image was projected only at about chance level. When half of the subjects were shown a picture of the projected image, their ability to infer when it was projected was almost doubled. When the other subjects were given a verbal description of the projected image, "a triangular-shaped design of 3 green bars," their ability to infer the period of presentation was reduced to less than half. The authors argue that the perceptual similarity between projected image and remembered displayed image allowed subjects to make more accurate judgments. It should be pointed out that the projected images are easily detected when subjects are given only a discrimination task, and not a separate imaging task (Segal, 1968). Thus, although the projected image is visible, it is not separately perceived during the image-generating task.

In an early study, Pillsbury (1897) investigated the ability of trained subjects (among them Titchener!) to recognize misprints in briefly presented words. Subjects were better able to detect omission of letters than blurring or substitution of letters—operations more likely to preserve the shape of the presented word. Of course people frequently find typos and recognize the intended word from partial and misleading information. Perhaps more interesting, Pillsbury's subjects reported seeing letters that were not presented. For example, a subject shown "disal," responded "deal," and reported, "There may be something between "e" and "a," but I am not sure" (Pillsbury, 1897, p. 377).

Pillsbury also attempted to facilitate recognition of the intended word by giving a synonym before presenting the stimulus. In this condition, the number of mispellings correctly identified decreased by ten to twenty per cent. Subjects occasionally saw the spoken synonym, or part of it, rather than the word presented. When "dwelling" was spoken and "aesidance" displayed, a subject read "dwelling" and claimed to have seen the letters "... welling." Sometimes the words that subjects saw reflected quite different meanings from those intended. When "pane" was spoken and "winxow" presented, one subject responded "ache," and claimed to have seen "aiche."

Pillsbury also found evidence that parts of recently presented words occasionally intruded and were "seen." Much of Pillsbury's research has been supported and extended with more modern experimental techniques, but without the use of verbal reports to capture the heeded information (cf. Morton, 1964; Neisser, 1967).

In an interesting study, Ellis, Shepard, and Davies (1979) showed that subjects were able to recognize famous peoples' faces from partial information, either of features or of contour. We can extend this analysis to reading as well. For simple text, comprehension may be almost immediate, without intermediate steps in awareness. If texts are vague or ambigious, they may provide cues for triggering personal experiences, a mechanism that can account for the "predictive" ability of horoscopes (cf. Snyder & Larson, 1972; Ulrich, Stachnik & Stainton, 1963).

In sum, there is strong evidence that the recognition process is opaque, so that subjects cannot report what cues allowed them to retrieve information from LTM or what part of the recognized structure was actually contained in the stimulus. Of course, subsequent to recognition, the recognized structure can be matched against information available to the senses. It is only under special circumstances (especially, the requirement of rapid response after brief presentation of the stimulus) that the report of the recognized structure does not reflect the presented information veridically.

"Spontaneous" Recall

According to our model, retrieval of information from LTM is a direct function of the information heeded—the information accessed in LTM will be associated with some subset of the heeded information. We showed earlier that the goals and task information that are heeded can effectively prevent irrelevant information from being accessed without conscious intermediate states or intent ("incidental" or "spontaneous" recall). Hilgard (1948) describes empirical demonstrations of "spontaneous recall" by Kohler and von Restorff (1935) and Bartel (1937). Kohler and von Restorff let subjects solve an arithmetic problem, then showed them a shortcut for certain multiplication problems: $(a-b)(a+b)=a^2 - b^2$. Half of the subjects were given a series of other arithmetic problems, while the other half were given match-stick problems and then both were given a new arithmetic problem, where the short-cut method could be used. Seventy-two percent of the subjects in the match-stick group spontaneously applied the short-cut method, while only 26% of the others did so, indicating that in the absence of interference from intervening material "spontaneous" recall of the short-cut occurred.

Kohler and von Restorff give the following protocol excerpts (translated from page 78) for spontaneous recall of the short-cut.

Here you can do this again – $(a+b)(a-b)$. Right? But I am still not sure of that.

Perhaps I could come up with your method by myself.
(Kohler & von Restorff, p. 78)

The subjects who failed to use the special method all recalled it when they were specifically probed for it afterwards. The information was in memory and was sometimes (not always) used without conscious intent—that is, by *recognition* of its relevance to the new task. Kohler and von Restorff (1935) and Bartel (1937) demonstrated the same phenomena in experiments using a mechanical construction set.

Experts in their domain of expertise display spontaneous and immediate recall of similar and relevant information (Chase and Ericsson, 1982). In contrast, novices have difficulty in retrieving, or even knowing that they know, relevant information (Bloom & Brooder, 1954; Allwood & Montgomery, 1981, 1982). Hence, access to relevant information depends on the adequacy of the encoding. A rich "indexing" of information may eliminate the necessity for a consciously driven search for adequate retrieval cues.

Recognition and Inference

From recognition of faces, it appears that people rely on only a subset of cues to recognize acquaintances. They make many errors of recognition, and can often recognize individuals with beards shaved off or hair style changed (sometimes without noticing the change). We can therefore conclude that people, through recognition, gain access to an LTM structure that contains more information than was used in accessing it from the stimulus. With brief presentations of stimuli, where there is no time for attending to the stimulus after recognition, subjects obtain essentially no information about what features actually evoked the recognition.

Hess (1975) showed a group of twenty men two photographs of an attractive young woman. The only difference between the two pictures was that one had been retouched to make the woman's pupils larger than in the other. The men responded (as measured by the sizes of their own pupils) twice as favorably to the picture with the larger pupils as to the other. When questioned afterwards, no subjects reported noticing the sizes of the pupils. Some reported that one photograph was "more feminine" or "prettier" or "softer" than the other. The study demonstrates that one can be influenced by stimulus features without being able to detect which ones are responsible for the effect.

In naturalistic situations (especially outside the laboratory), people can make many ecologically valid inferences about the stimuli they encounter. If they see a house, they can infer validly that it has a door, even if they don't notice the door. Subjects may generate invalid reports about stimuli by reporting these inferred features, which may or may not have actually been noticed. In normal perception there is no clear boundary between explicit observation and inference from the observation. When a subject reports seeing a stage magician make an object disappear, this is clearly an inference rather than a direct observation. Laboratory studies make clear the role played by this interaction between observation and inference in the recognition process.

Bruner and Postman (1949) showed subjects normal and altered playing cards for short durations in a tachistoscope. Subjects reported seeing (i.e., recognizing) normal playing cards even when the cards had been altered so that suits and colors were mismatched. Subjects, on observing a red four of Spades, reported seeing either the four of Hearts or a black four of Spades. Whether suit or color determined their choice appeared to be idiosyncratic for each individual.

In another study, Postman, Bruner, and Walk (1951) showed subjects strings of letters, where some strings contained a single reversed letter. The reversed letters were correctly identified or recognized with shorter latencies than were required to recognize that the letters were reversed.

Assessment of Recognition Processes

Our postulate about recognition processes allows us to argue against reportable intermediate states for such processes. However, to avoid circularity, we need to be able to assess independently when recognition processes occur.

The sorts of independent evidence for recognition discussed in the previous section almost all related to open-ended tasks, or tasks where the time constraints were too severe to allow sequences of successive states to be heeded. In most cognitive tasks studied in the laboratory, there is a unique response that is "correct." In such cases, sufficient information must be extracted from the stimulus to generate the correct response reliably. Hence, at some prior time, learning with feedback must have occurred; the cognitive structure that is accessed by recognition must exist already in LTM. These two criteria give us some rather powerful means to discriminate recognition processes from the conscious processes for which verbal reports of intermediate states would be available.

In order to sharpen our characterization of recognition processes, we turn now to a discussion of the automatization of cognitive processes, and the emergence of recognition processes.

Automation of Responses

Although we hypothesize that attention is necessary for learning or changing cognitive structures, it is no longer necessary when the same cognitive process has been executed many times. Only a few studies have attempted to capture changes in reported information as a function of degree of expertise and experience with a given type of process.

There appears to be a close (negative) relation between degree of practice and awareness of intermediate stages of a process. The early work of Ach and others suggested that the conscious content disappeared with extended practice and growing automaticity of the processes. More recently, Dean and Martin (1966) found that overlearning in paired-associate learning leads to a decrease in the number of reported mediating associations. The work of Schneider and Shiffrin (Schneider & Shiffrin, 1977; Shiffrin & Schneider, 1977) suggests that there are clear differences between automatic and controlled processing, in terms of speed and of accessibility for modification and learning. From all this evidence, it seems necessary to postulate, as we have, that many highly overlearned processes operate automatically without leaving any more trace than their final result in STM.[*]

We may distinguish between automatic processes that subjects already possessed prior to an experiment, as part of their cognitive skills, and processes whose intermediate stages became more automatic, and hence less reportable, during the course of the experiment. In the case of the latter, reports from the automated processes at the end of the experiment will omit information about intermediate states of which the subjects were aware at the beginning of the experiment. We will later provide some concrete examples of this phenomenon.

Recognition automates cognitive processes for a specific task. Since this task is represented cognitively, the subject can change it at any time. If he does, recognition will no longer determine the responses. It might be thought that if a response were strongly established, it would resist the owner's attempts to define the task. Ach (research reviewed by Ryan, 1970) thought he had demonstrated precisely this—the response to a stimulus could be explained as the outcome of a competition between previous rooting of the response and its appropriateness to the current task. But more recent research appears to show that he was mistaken. Lewin (reviewed by Ryan (1970)) demonstrated that as many as 300 repetitions of the initial associations did not cause false responses to later, different, tasks, nor lengthen the reaction times. Ach's early results probably resulted from subjects' confusions or misconceptions of what tasks they had actually been asked to perform.

Rather similar evidence has been obtained from experimental analysis of the Stroop effect. In the Stroop Test, subjects are instructed to name the color of the ink used to print words that spell the names of other colors. It appears (Glaser & Dolt, 1977) that in spite of the instruction to name the color of the ink, the response corresponding to the printed word first comes to the subject spontaneously, and has to be rejected actively. However, if the printed words are semantically

---

[*] This effect of automation may be explained thus: Before overlearning has occurred, processes have to be interpreted, with substantial feedback from intermediate stages in STM. Overlearning amounts to compiling these processes, so that fewer tests are performed when they are being executed, hence less information is stored at intermediate stages in STM. Experience with compiling in computer languages shows that automation typically speeds up a process by an order of magnitude, at the expense of making it less flexible, and its intermediate stages less available for report.

unrelated to color words the effects are small or non-existent (Klein, 1964; Keele, 1973).

Let us focus more directly on the development of recognition-like processes in a given task as a function of amount of practice. The initial instructions to the subjects communicate only roughly what the task is. Beginning with the first trials, the subjects will notice or actively seek regularities and constraints in the particular examples presented by the experimenter. When subjects discover redundancy in the information presented (syntactic constructions are constant, the responses stand in some rule-bound relation to information presented [Einstellung], or responses share a common characteristic that is not made explicit [set]), they can use these regularities to improve the efficiency (and the stereotypy) of their response processes.

Quinton and Fellows (1975) studied the emergence of changes in subjects' cognitive processes with practice in solving three-term series problems (e.g., "Ben is taller than George; Dave is shorter than George; Who is tallest?"). They observed that most of their subjects gradually shifted to a perceptual strategy that depended on recognizing problem types. Associated with the change in strategy, they observed a dramatic reduction in solution time.

Wood and Shotter (1973) asked subjects to respond with the appropriate kinship term to questions like, "What relationship to a man is his father's sister's daughter?" They found that, with practice, subjects tended to go from meaning to formal properties. The kinship terms were reported as organized in a spatial image. As one subject described it (Wood and Shotter, p. 509), "I was imagining in levels . . . I go up for father, across for sister . . . I go up and down and across in levels. After a while, up-across-down *means* cousin."

In an interesting study, Wood, Shotter, and Godden (1974) showed that with more practice, subjects became less able to answer unexpected questions about the information presented. After presentation of a number of five-term series problems, subjects were asked unexpectedly about the order of two items, which was different from the order in the original problem. When this unexpected question was asked after the first problem, 55% of the subjects gave a correct answer, but after the 21st problem, only 10%. A control group was presented with twenty problems, but asked to arrange the terms in alphabetical order before they received their first five-term series problem and their unexpected question. In this case they answered the unexpected question correctly in 70% of the cases. These studies show evidence of a movement, with practice, from complete awareness of problem-solving steps toward more efficient solution by recognition.

Luchins' (1940) classical experiments showed that subjects, given a series of problems with the same rule for solution, solved test problems by a "blind" application of that rule, even when a much simpler solution was possible. Evidence indicates that the effect is not the result of inadvertent mechanization, but results from subjects' deliberate choices of strategy. A number of experiments have reduced the Einstellung effect by marking the test problems as separate problems rather than a continuation of the sequence of problems presented before (Jensen, 1960). Moreover, a single extinction trial (a problem solvable with a different rule) is sufficient to eliminate the effect. Luchins and Luchins (1959) supported this interpretation in an extensive review of Einstellung:

> What seemed to be important was not the recency of the E method, or that the test tasks immediately followed the E tasks, but the subject's attitude: that is, whether or not he viewed the tasks as belonging together, as members of a homogeneous series. (Luchins & Luchins, 1959, p. 333)

There is evidence for Einstellung effects in the performance of experts, in whose responses recognition processes should be prominent. When asked to "give the mathematical expression for all numbers that, when divided by seven, yield a remainder of 89," mathematically trained subjects were more likely than novices to notice the semantic contradiction in the question and produce the syntactically correct formula (Krutetskii, 1976). Wertheimer (1945) found that mathematically trained subjects tended to use the complex general solution of a problem requiring them to calculate the area of an altar window, while novices selected a simple and "insightful" solution.

The reason experts rarely do worse than novices, we conjecture, is that their recognition processes are carefully "debugged" during their extensive learning experiences. Moreover, the expert can always fall back on a systematic and conscious search for a solution, which should always give him an advantage over the novice.

Perceptual-Motor Processes

Research on perceptual-motor processes also demonstrates that in these we normally have access only to certain higher-level intermediate results.

In a recent paper, Broadbent (1977) presents empirical evidence for a hierarchical organization of such processes. Most studies of perceptual-motor processes using thinking-aloud protocols and other verbal reports have examined problem solving with puzzles. As we reported in Chapter 2, in tasks allowing physical manipulation, Klinger (1974) found frequent higher-level verbal evaluations of unverbalized solution attempts (e.g., "Yep," "Dammit," etc.), and verbalizations of attention-control processes (e.g., "Let's see," "Where was I?" etc.). When engaged in perceptual-motor manipulation, subjects did not verbalize, and appeared not to be aware of, the lower-level content or structure of their throught processes. Ruger (1910) found that subjects could often solve one of his mechanical puzzles several times, yet provide only a limited high-level account of the intermediate steps leading to the solution. It has been suggested that physical manipulation is different from thinking in not employing any internal (i.e., STM) representation (Durkin, 1937).

INFORMATION ABOUT COGNITIVE STATES

In this section we will examine the assertion that STM contains all the information that is available for report. We will first discuss subjects' reports of being close to remembering something (tip-of-the-tongue), and their subjective feeling that they could recognize information they cannot recall (feeling-of-knowing). We will ask whether such reportable states, having testable behavioral consequences, can be represented in terms of structures in STM and how these structures can be used to help extract the information presumably present but currently inaccessible in LTM. Then we will ask how subjects can be confident about the adequacy and correctness of information they have recalled. A strict interpretation of our model argues that the subject only knows what cues and task information he heeded just prior to heeding the retrieved structure.

Tip-of-the-Tongue

James (1890) is generally credited with first describing the tip-of-the-tongue phenomenon. Early research relied primarily on analyzing situations in which such phenomena occurred spontaneously. Woodworth (1938) found that in such situations, the subjects almost invariably had additional information about the items they sought, beyond the mere "feeling" that it was in LTM. This additional information (e.g., knowledge of some syllables, number of syllables, initial letter) could usually be verified as valid partial information about the word being sought.

A more systematic and controlled study by Brown and McNeil (1966) showed that subjects expressing a "tip-of-the-tongue" feeling, but unable to recall a word, were able to report some of the letters in the word, the number of syllables, and the location of the primary stress, with much better than chance probability.

Yarmey (1973) studied the tip-of-the-tongue experience in naming famous people presented in pictures. When he asked his subjects to supply information in any one of several categories, they tended to mention first the place where they had seen a picture of the person, then when they had last seen one. Attempts to recall initial letters and numbers of syllables of names had no clear order preference. The amounts of such information retrieved were substantial, regardless of whether the subject succeeded in recalling the name, or even recognized it when the experimenter presented it.

Koriat and Lieblich (1979) demonstrated that subjects had better-than-chance records in guessing the letters and number of syllables even of words they didn't know. Apparently these subjects used information about the attributes that would be typical for such words. Hence, memory for specific items and events can be confounded by inference from more general memory.

In a couple of studies Hart (1965, 1967) studied the validity of subjects' feelings of being able to recognize an item they couldn't recall. The questions he put to his subjects involved general knowledge like, "Which planet in our solar system is the largest?" Hart found that subjects were able to predict reliably whether they would subsequently recognize the unrecallable answers. They were also able to predict, although with lower accuracy, their ability to recognize learned paired associates.

Blake (1973), using brief presentations of trigrams followed by an 18-second distractor task, found that feeling-of-knowing judgments were markedly related to number of letters recalled correctly. The judgments were also related to ability to recognize the correct answers, even after differences in recall were held constant. These results were confirmed in a second experiment that eliminated the effect of the number of letters recalled initially. The result implies that the encoding of the trigrams was not entirely in terms of the component letters.

Wellman (1977), using a paradigm similar to Hart's, with pictures to be named, asked his subjects (kindergarten, 1st grade, and 3rd grade students) (1) to make judgments of "feeling-of-knowing," (2) to tell what they knew about the thing pictured, and (3) to report if they had seen the pictured items. Judgments that they had seen an object proved to be better predictors of subsequent recognition than "feeling-of-knowing" judgments. The verbal comments showed a clear relation between amount of knowledge about the object, on the one hand, and a feeling of knowing and successful recognition, on the other.

All of the above experiments provide evidence that the ability to make accurate judgments about one's memory or feelings is associated with the availability of related knowledge that can be accessed prior to those judgments.

Retrieval Without Direct Recognition

The research on both tip-of-the-tongue and feeling-of-knowing show that LTM is highly organized. Subjects often know how stored information is encoded and generate the appropriate retrieval cues to access it. Similarly, subjects often know when they don't have information in memory, because they find that the information is not available where it should be stored. For example, one can know that one doesn't know the phone number of the White House. If it were present, it would surely be associated to the stimulus, "White House phone number," hence would be recalled.

The appropriate storage of relevant information with reasonable cues is not mysterious within our proposed model, which views LTM as a richly indexed and cross-indexed data base. When a subject is presented with new information, he will access (by recognition) the relevant LTM structures and store some subset of the heeded information. At the same time, new recognition access routes to the information will be created (new "index entries"). This continuing processing and storage of heeded information will allow direct access by recognition to many important pieces of information.

Machotka (1964) argues that our ability to judge and evaluate objects and people rapidly must be attributed to unconscious processing. We would argue, on the contrary, that relevant information can be accessed directly because it was heeded on a previous occasion and stored with appropriate access paths. When the new stimulus is presented, these paths can be used without the requirement of an unconscious review of previous experiences.

Subjects often have to retrieve information that cannot be accessed directly—that has not been indexed. Everyone has stored a vast number of personal experiences, thought episodes, and pieces of detailed information that can only be recalled via an active search for retrieval cues and an active evaluation of the retrieved LTM structures. Only in this way can people recall how often they have gone to the movies in the past year, or have been swimming, or the names of all the different cars or detergents that they know. (See Chapter 5 for a discussion of these recall processes and associated verbal reports.)

When subjects are questioned about information stored in LTM, their responses depend not only upon the presence or absence of that information, but also on whether the cues that are present are adequate for its retrieval. Inability to retrieve a memory structure is not equivalent to its absence from memory. One of the most reliable effects in the literature on human memory is the difference between the number of stimulus items that a subject can *recall* and the number of items that he can *recognize* as having been presented. Recognition that something has been seen before is the most sensitive test that an information structure is in LTM.

The cues provided for memory retrieval may be consistent or inconsistent with the way in which the stored information is indexed. When appropriate cues are available, immediate recognition is triggered. In other cases, some of the information in the cueing stimulus may enable a successful heuristic search to be made for the information, while the remaining information is used to check proposed answers for adequacy. For example, if asked to supply an 8-letter English word whose 6th letter is *e*, a subject might narrow the search by seeking word endings of the form *e—*, finding *ent*, and then seeking words ending in *ent*. Having found one (e.g., "dissident"), it is tested for length and rejected. Another (e.g., "accident") is accepted. The entire memory retrieval can thus be seen as an initial retrieval specification, use of some part of this specification to access a memory structure, and verification that the memory structure is consistent with the entire specification (Norman & Bobrow, 1979).

What is heeded and thus reportable in memory retrieval without direct recognition? The retrieval cues have to be heeded and kept in STM. What are reportable in recognition, according to our model, are only the input (the cueing stimulus) and the output (the accessed LTM structure). If the answer is not immediately recognized, the cueing stimulus may be augmented by heuristic search and other problem-solving efforts, and the intermediate products of these efforts can also be reported. Which retrieval cues were effective in accessing the LTM structure can only be reported in retrospect by recall of these intermediate products or by inference from the nature of the information recovered.

Within this framework we are able to capture rather nicely the inability of subjects to give informative reports for some of their cognitive processes. In recognition, the subjects simply do not have any information in STM to report. When pressed for a "reason" for their responses, they have no recourse but to rationalize (i.e., to infer after the fact what the effective cues must have been). When retrieval involves intermediate search steps, however, subjects can report various items that were held temporarily in STM as the "reasons" for their responses.

Turning to the positive side, what can subjects report about their retrieval processes and their memory structures? First, they can assess, with some reliability, which of the items of information they recall is accurate, and also their correctness in making recognition judgments. Moreover, subjects have some ability to predict whether they possess certain information in LTM even in situations where they are unable to recall that information.

Judgments of Confidence

Subjects can evaluate their confidence in the correctness of information recalled if they can retrieve additional information that is redundant with it, hence permits it to be checked for veridicality. A subject who has the response "Monrovia" simply indexed to the stimulus "Capital of Liberia" may be unable to assess the accuracy of his response. If Monrovia, however, evokes "Monroe was President of the United States when Liberia was founded," this provides a reason for confidence in the answer. Thus, without any direct evidence from the *process* of retrieval, confidence can be judged. Speed of retrieval might also be a partial basis for judgments of confidence, so that even the (rapid) immediate recognition may be judged correct with high confidence. In a recent paper Koriat, Lichtenstein, and Fischhoff (1980) discuss the relevant research showing that people can successfully assess the correctness of their memories with a few exceptions. However, they are overconfident in the correctness of their answers caused by overemphasizing evidence justifying the selected alternative and disregarding evidence contradicting it. Hence, confidence judgments can be improved by asking subjects to list reasons, contradictions, then choices. Judging confidence involves accessing and reviewing relevant knowledge, and bias in confidence judgments is due to biased retrieval of such knowledge.

In laboratory research, ratings of confidence in recall and recognition have frequently been shown to be predictive of correctness (e.g., Wearing, 1971). In research on eye-witness testimony, however, the relation between confidence and accuracy is *not* uniformly positive (Deffenbacher, 1980). However, in a thorough review, Deffenbacher shows that in studies with high recognition accuracy, indicative of substantial memory, a strong relation is found between accuracy and rated confidence. It is only in studies with lower (yet reliable) recognition accuracy that there is no relation between accuracy and rated confidence.

Apparently the circumstances that yield high accuracy also provide subjects with information on which to base their ratings. Some studies have sought to discover what that information is.

Loftus and Bell (1975) have studied the process of recognizing pictures that were viewed with the instruction to remember them for subsequent recognition. At the time of judging whether or not a picture had been presented before, the subjects were asked if their judgments rested on a specific detail or on general familiarity with the picture. Performance was very much better when a detail could be named than when the subjects simply cited general familiarity. From eye-movement records during initial presentation of the pictures in an earlier study, Loftus (1972) found that the detail verbalized during the recognition trials was the detail that had received most fixations at the initial presentation.

How can we account for the numerous demonstrations that subjects' responses to memory probes (especially leading questions and providing response alternatives) can be altered by the experimenter (Loftus, 1975, 1979)? These demonstrations of experimenter influence uniformly pertain to situations where the accuracy of recognition is low. In such situations, the actual evidence available in memory is compatible with a number of alternative responses, so that the one selected may depend on the experimenter's probe (compare Kubovy & Psotka, 1976; Kubovy, 1977). We are not aware of any such demonstration for information that subjects have memorized so thoroughly that they can assess confidence reliably. These results are highly consistent with our model.

WHAT *IS* REPORTED?

We have now reviewed the evidence for an information-processing model of cognitive processes that characterizes the information that is in attention and STM at any point in time. We have shown that such a model is consistent with, and indeed supported by, a wide range of empirical evidence about recognition processes. In fact, we have been unable to identify any directly conflicting evidence. However, in the pages that follow, we will discuss a number of studies that have argued against various assumptions of our model by claiming incompleteness and nonveridicality of verbally reported information. We will see whether these arguments invalidate the picture we have drawn thus far.

Our model proposes that verbal reports are based on information currently held in STM, or information retrievable from LTM that was at some previous time held in STM. In order to avoid circularity, we must be able to state, from independent sources of evidence, what kind of information is heeded, and hence passes through STM.

Although it may be very hard, in general, to know what information is in a subject's STM at a particular time, the assumptions of the information processing model do allow fairly strong predictions to be made. First, the model claims that subjects' memories of earlier thoughts and information are a subset of the information to which they attended. No new memory structures can be stored in LTM or subsequently retrieved unless they were heeded when presented. The information that will be heeded, for example, in generating a mathematical proof or solving a mathematical problem will be different if the subject already has memory access to similar proofs or to relevant special methods or theorems than if he doesn't. With a knowledge of prior theorems, the subject may short-cut many steps in the proof.

The existence of enormous individual differences in the knowledge held in memory means that predictions of verbalizations must be contingent on the retrievable information of each subject. In many experimental studies of thinking, investigators have tried to avoid this difficulty by using "naive" subjects—that is, subjects who did not have any prior experience with the problem domain. Gestalt psychologists were alluding, in part, to the difference between naive and experienced subjects in their distinction between productive and reproductive thinking.

In cases where we can rule out reproductive, or recognition-based cognitive processes, we can make strong predictions that any information that is recalled must have been heeded in the experimental situation.

Perhaps the best example of a situation where we can make this prediction is learning under experimental control, where a subject changes his behavior into behavior determined by the experimenter. Under our hypothesis, such learning can always be traced by concurrent reports of heeded information. We begin our review of evidence bearing on this prediction with studies using different kinds of verbal reports in learning experiments. We will then review all studies of which we are aware that contain apparently damaging evidence against our model.

LEARNING WITHOUT AWARENESS

The mechanisms and processes that emerged from the associationist and behaviorist analyses of learning were so simple that it must have been very tempting to propose that these processes were unconscious and inaccessible for verbal reports. Some influential theorists, like Thorndike (1932, 1933), argued that an association could be strengthened without the subject knowing what it was, hence that the subject should not be able to report it. In an experiment by Thorndike and Rock (1934), evidence was found that appeared to support such a view. By way of introduction to our topic, we will describe that study and some follow-up studies that refute the argument. Thorndike and Rock had subjects generate words as fast as possible in response to stimulus words. Subjects were told "wrong" if the response word was meaningfully related to the stimulus word (synonym, opposite, etc.). They were told "right" if the response formed a sequential connection with the stimulus (e.g., yours → truly, up → stairs, etc.). For ambiguous or unclassifiable responses, the subjects received no feedback at all. The subjects showed gradual and variable learning, which to the experimenters implied lack of insight. Insight, they argued, should lead to abrupt, single-trial improvement in responses.

The last assertion is not correct, as shown by a follow-up study by Irwin, Kaufmann, Prior, and Weaver (1934). Subjects after *explicit* instruction as to what words constituted correct responses, did not learn faster than subjects not receiving any instruction. In further experimentation, Postman and Jarrett (1952) found that both informed and uninformed subjects showed gradual learning. The informed subjects learned more rapidly than the uninformed. A detailed analysis of the behavior of uninformed subjects provided a wholly parsimonious explanation of this difference. Sometime during the experiment, the large majority of the uninformed subjects were able to verbalize the correct principle. Subjects unable to verbalize the principle showed *no* improvement. Dramatic improvement was observed on and after the trial on which the principle was first verbalized. However, a much smaller, yet statistically reliable, improvement was found for trials preceding the first verbalization of the correct principle. Postman and Jarrett argue that this improvement could be due to learning without awareness, or to partially correct verbalized principles. An alternative hypothesis that would account for the results observed is that subjects who incidentally made a couple of correct responses were more likely to access or induce the principle. This study illustrated, incidentally, the potency of concurrent verbal reports.

Concurrent Verbal Reports of Learning

In Chapter 1, we reviewed the study in which Verplanck and Oskamp claimed to have shown that verbalized rules are dissociated from the behavior they were supposed to control. When correct behavior was reinforced, they made 71.8% correct responses, but only stated the correct rule for the behavior in 48.4% of the trials. When correct statement of the rule was reinforced, they stated the rule correctly on 92.8% of the trials, but took the correct action in only 76.8%.

Dulany and O'Connell (1963) showed these results derived from two artifacts. First, the data analysis did not correct for guessing; making this correction reduces the percentage of correct responses in the first case to 43.6%, close to the percentage of correct rule statements. Second, they showed that Verplanck and Oskamp's rules were sometimes ambiguous. Taking account of the ambiguity, in all but 11 of 34,408 trials the subjects did exactly what they said (in the rule statement) they were going to. Hence, the experiments provide no evidence whatsoever that the rules verbalized were inconsistent with the behaviors.

Numerous studies document the support for consistency between verbalized rules, concepts and hypotheses and immediately preceding and succeeding behavior, before subjects receive feedback. In Schwartz (1966), where subjects were asked their reasons for placing a card as they did, reasons consistent with placements were given on all but 2 of 1,962 trials. Even more impressive, Frankel, Levine, and Karpf (1970) obtained retrospective reports from subjects on the basis of their responses to four earlier discrimination-learning problems with 30 non-feedback trials each, and found that subjects could provide such reports in more than 90% of the sequences of trials.

In an attempt to differentiate between an incremental S-R theory of concept attainment and a cognitive theory, Prentice (1949) had subjects think aloud during concept attainment. In an experimental group the correct response was reversed after 20 trials. Prentice predicted (cognitive or one-trial learning theory) that if no mention of the relevant hypothesis was made by the subject prior to the reversal there would be no difference between groups in learning times. When all subjects mentioning the relation in their protocols were deleted from the analysis, the difference between groups was about 20 trials as compared to a cognitive theory's prediction of no difference and an S-R theory's prediction of 40.** Prentice thus infers that there are nonconscious processes operating.

A critical reading of Prentice shows that the difference between the groups is barely significant. To infer, therefore, that the difference is 20 trials is clearly unwarranted. The concept-learning situation in Prentice's study involves only 8 different stimuli, each capable of taking on 2 different values—16 instances in all. Prentice reports that most subjects usually considered explicit hypotheses, and the solution emerged while they were summarizing the results of the last three or four trials. That attention to stimulus attributes is a primary component in learning is shown by the fact that experimental subjects attending to the right relation before reversal required about 15 trials *less* than average to learn after reversal.

In all other studies coming to our attention where it is claimed that the learning process is unconscious, hence not reportable, the verbal reports were not given concurrently with the responses. In interpreting these studies, we must therefore make further assumptions about memory in order to relate the verbal reports with the criterial behavior. In particular, it is risky to assume that awareness during a learning experiment can be determined by questioning after the experiment is over.

** The prediction from S-R theory was based on the assumption that a concept learned during the first 20 trials would take another 20 trials to undo, thus amounting to 40 trials difference. An S-R theory with one-trial learning would predict no difference.

Assessing Awareness from Post-Experimental Questioning

We consider next the situation where a subject is probed for information that is not then available in STM. Then the information must be retrieved from LTM. Memory retrieval is fallable, sometimes causing access to other related, but inappropriate, information. Further, what information can be recalled depends on what cues and probes are provided. Hence the completeness of the information retrieved will vary with the probing procedures.

The controversy over whether learning can and does occur without awareness, as evidenced by retrospective verbal reports from subjects, has recently been reviewed by Brewer (1974). Drawing on his work, we will seek to interpret the differences, primarily methodological, that distinguish studies finding learning without awareness from studies not finding such learning. One type of study has been criticized repeatedly for poor documentation of probing procedures and brief post-experimental interviews, which are sometimes not given after the learning trials but after an additional series of extinction trials (Spielberger, 1962). This design does not eliminate the possibility that subjects retain in STM the information about the reinforcement contingency until it is lost during overlearning or extinction trials. To ensure a relatively complete verbal report, the probing should occur just after the last learning trials, preferably before the subject is told that the experiment is over. Many of the studies of this first type seem little concerned with these considerations. Furthermore, the verbal probes used have been global questions, like "What did you think the experiment was about?" (Brewer, 1974) In our framework, such probes will not elicit retrospective memory of the subject's own cognitive processes so much as encourage him to generate hypotheses about the experiment, which may or may not be related to those processes.

A second type of study, which has responded to the above criticisms by probing subjects just after the last learning bloc of trials and explicitly asking them for their memories of their cognitive processes during the preceding trials, has generally been unable to find evidence for learning without reported awareness of the reinforcement contingency. The studies of this type have been criticized, in turn, for asking leading questions. We have already discussed this issue in the section on effects of probing. The need for specific probes is not well documented, but a general motivation for it is given in Dulany (1962). Another important consideration is that the subjects often report contingencies that, while not identical with the one the experimenter reinforces, are correlated with it (Dulany, 1962). Here failure to report the experimenter's version of the contingency may simply mean this is not the version the subject is using, and may not at all imply incompleteness in the report of the contents of STM.

In a third type of study, subjects are asked to verbalize during conditioning experiments according to a technique suggested by DeNike (1964), in which the subject writes down "any thoughts that come to you that have any relation to the experiment" (p. 523). Using this procedure, DeNike was able to extend the claim of consistency between written thoughts and behavior, finding that subjects' behaviors changed on the trial in which they wrote down their first correct hypothesis about the reinforcement.

Also using DeNike's technique, Kennedy (1970, 1971) found that the behaviors changed *before* subjects wrote down that they were confident of their hypotheses or their verbal hypotheses were confirmed. Brewer (1974) points out that Kennedy's finding, that behavioral changes were associated with trying out or modifying verbal hypotheses, does not challenge, but supports the validity of the verbalized information.

Comparing different probing techniques with each other indicates that the written thoughts elicited with DeNike's technique are incomplete as compared with information obtained with Dulany's postexperimental questionnaire (Sallows, Dawes, & Lichtenstein, 1971). There is also some evidence that the incompleteness may be caused by the requirement of written responses. Silveira (1972) found a marked difference in number and character of responses elicited during a creativity test between written and oral response conditons. Writing the responses or ideas, as contrasted with giving them aloud, led to evaluation and censorship.

It has been assumed implicitly that the contents of STM after the last learning bloc are representative of the contents during the preceding trials. This is a reasonable assumption for concept learning, and for experiments with deterministic reinforcement schedules, where there is no inducement for the subject to reject a correct hypothesis. Several studies have shown that subjects are unlikely to change hypotheses in response to positive feedback (Heidbreder, 1924; Karpf & Levine, 1971). However, since subjects are highly likely to change hypotheses in response to negative feedback, the assumption of stable hypotheses is less tenable for probabilistically determined feedback conditions.

In a recent study by Williams (1977), all subjects who learned were assessed (by a procedure of the Spielberger type (1962)) to have been aware of the reinforcement. However, in a second experiment with probabilistic relations, Williams found evidence of learning without awareness (assessed by the same procedure). During the experiment, subjects were explicitly (and falsely) told that "All the sentences I said 'correct' to met the same necessary requirements" (Williams, 1977, p. 93). These instructions would encourage subjects to abandon correct and correlated hypotheses when negative feedback was encountered. A study by O'Connell (1965) shows clearly that if the subjects verbalize their hypotheses on each trial, the verbalized reports account for their behavior even in a non-deterministic environment with partial reinforcement.

There is a related issue of awareness of mediating associations. A series of studies (Bugelski & Scharlock, 1952; Horton & Kjeldergaard, 1961; Russel & Storms, 1955) have found that paired-associate learning can be facilitated by prior exposure of the subjects to the proper mediating associations. Subjects who first learned lists of paired associates of types A-B and B-C learned lists of type A-C faster than control groups. In all these studies informal post-experimental questioning gave no evidence that the subjects were aware of using any mediating B-list items. "None of the Ss was able to report any correct appreciation of the nature of the experiment and most assuredly did not verbalize a pattern of A-B, B-C, A-C in learning the third list (Bugelski & Scharlock)." This was interpreted as evidence for unconscious mediation in learning.

However, the above studies can be criticized on the same grounds as the studies purporting to demonstrate concept learning without awareness; and typically we find different results in more recent studies that probe for retrospective information in a more controlled and ambitious manner. In a study by Dean and Martin (1966), the subjects, after reaching criterion for the third list, read each stimulus of this list and were then asked to tell the experimenter exactly what came to their minds when they saw the syllable on the screen. The subjects were then shown the entire list of paired associates and asked how the list was learned. Dean and Martin found that a majority of the subjects reported using at least one mediating term from the previously learned facilitating lists. An analysis of learning rates for each of the reported mediation types (other than A-B-C mediation) showed clearly that the effective difference among groups was attributable to the occurrence or non-occurrence of A-B-C mediation. When Dean and Martin had one experimental group overlearn the paired-associate list for ten extra trials, they found a significantly lower occurrence of reported mediation, thus suggesting that direct and automatic processing had developed as a result of additional practice.

In a study following a procedure similar to that used in Horton and Kjeldergaard (1961), Horton (1964) used a direct question: "Did you notice any relationship between the pairs you just completed and the ones you learned earlier in the experiment?" Horton assessed three levels of awareness, where the highest level required naming the actual mediating items. With a variety of experimental manipulations, he found a consistent relation between mediation (facilitative effect of previously learned PA lists), and assessed awareness. There are many differences between the studies reporting awareness of mediating items and those that report no awareness. Horton suggested that the difference between his study and Horton and Kjeldergaard stemmed from the factors in the experimental situation stimulating awareness. The two groups of studies also differ in the strictness of the learning criterion, which might have affected the retrievability of the mediating links. However, the most obvious difference, in our view, lies in the probing procedure.

Sorting Without Awareness of Concept

In concept learning, it has been observed that subjects can select appropriate instances in test trials without being able to state the concepts they are using (Heidbreder, 1934, 1936; Phelan, 1965; Smoke, 1932). Although these studies have been cited in support of the notion that the verbalized information is incomplete, a more reasonable interpretation is that the subjects cannot formulate the concept as it is defined by the experimenter, although they can differentiate instances from non-instances by recognition. Correct selection of instances could be mediated by processes like memorizing exemplars or a set of correlated discrimination features without using a rule expressed in terms of common features. A concept-formation task can employ a large number of different strategies. If the number of different stimuli is fairly small (20 or less) subjects might even memorize them or use a mixture of memory for exemplars and rule learning. If a subject were actively employing a hypothesis, we would expect him to be able to report it. If he were relying on memory for exemplars, we would not expect him to be able to report them, for they would not all reside simultaneously in STM.

Under these circumstances, the concept attainment task is a recognition task, and we know that recognition does not imply ability to recall.

There is evidence that subjects sometimes perform concept-attainment or rule formation tasks by relying on similarity between the stimulus instance and evoked exemplars in memory (cf. Brooks). None of these processes for concept attainment can be ruled out a priori, and in fact, verbal reports during performance might be the most useful data for discriminating among them.

When Smoke (1932) asked subjects to identify the concept used by the experimenter from verbal descriptions, he found in four experiments that 20-25% of the verbal descriptions of the successful subjects were defective, and "usually too inclusive" (p. 20). This study, and other related ones, do not address the incompleteness problem as we would state it: Is the verbal report a complete and sufficient description of *the information the subject actually has and uses?* In Smoke's study the subjects who were classified as unable to verbalize the concept could "almost invariably" (p. 20) draw two instances of the concept from memory correctly; but this does not imply that they had a complete and correct (though unverbalizable) criterion for making the selections.

The question of completeness has been put to a more direct test in an interesting study by Wilson (1973, 1975). Here, the subjects wrote down their rules for positive instances at each trial, and were then asked to sort a test series of instances. Wilson then assessed the information transmitted in these verbal descriptions by having the same subjects a week later make re-sorts from the descriptions. In addition, naive subjects who did not participate in the learning experiment were asked to sort the test series on the basis of the individual descriptions provided by the original subjects. The results showed that the sorts made by subjects after a week's delay agreed less closely with their original sorts during the concept learning experiment than they did with the sorts made by the naive subjects. This is evidence that the subjects had more information at the time of the original experiment than they gave in their verbal reports. However, the correspondence between all the sorts was high, especially considering that the verbal rule was not always applicable to all instances in the test series.

In a second experiment, Wilson (1974, 1975) found that the degree of incompleteness of descriptions varied with the stage of concept learning at which the verbalization of the rule was obtained. For rules verbalized either at the very beginning of the experiment or at criterion, almost complete agreement was obtained between sorts; but more discrepancies were found for rules verbalized at intermediate stages of acquisition. Wilson attributed these results to subjects' difficulties in verbalizing the complex hypotheses they entertained during intermediate learning stages, and this interpretation was further supported by the greater length of the verbal descriptions for these stages.

One alternative explanation, suggested previously, would be that the instructions used by Wilson ("to verbalize a rule"—the average number of words per rule was about 8) were inadequate to tap the subjects' total information about positive instances. Another possible interpretation is that instances in the test series may have served as cues for retrieval and recognition of previously presented items that were not available to the subjects when they generated the verbal report. Some supporting evidence is given by a study on discrimination learning by Frankel, Levine and Karpf (1970), where the subjects could give a retrospective description of "on what basis they had responded" (p. 346) that described more than 90% of their responses.

Lack of Access to Relevant Knowledge

In the preceding section we showed that subjects may perform correctly on a concept-attainment task, yet use the process of recognizing exemplars without generating the abstract concept. This is an example of a more general principle: subjects do not, in many or most situations (and even if they are able to access all the relevant information), integrate all the information and abstract the higher-level relations the experimenter has built into the stimuli.

Several studies have shown that subjects sometimes can report very different amounts of knowledge relevant to the task, without corresponding differences in performance (Broadbent, 1977; Hull, 1920). Other studies show that subjects can report accurate knowledge at the time of probing, yet while executing a cognitive process that should access that knowledge, they report *not* heeding this information or report accessing some inconsistent information instead (Allwood & Montgomery, 1981, 1982).

These findings are inconsistent with our model only under a couple of (dubious) assumptions. Specifically, one must assume that exactly the same information is retrieved and heeded in the probing situation as when performing the task. In everyday experience, one often does not recall information that, if recalled, would be relevant (e.g., while

shopping, or in conversation with others). Only for highly skilled per-
formers can we be reasonably certain that relevant knowledge will always
be retrieved when required. A second assumption is that the knowledge
deemed relevant by the experimenter can be and is used by the subject to
complete the task. Broadbent (1977) mentions an extreme case:
Newton's Third Law of Motion is logically relevant to riding a bike, yet it
is unlikely that anyone would use it to learn how to ride. In the following
discussion we will be concerned primarily with showing that in the
studies discussed earlier these assumptions are not satisfied, and hence
that the findings are consistent with our model. A more refined model,
of course, would predict the deficiencies in recall as a function of task
conditions and subjects' skill levels.

One line of research demonstrated that subjects may differ considerably in what relevant information they report, yet not differ discern-
ably in performance. In his classical study, Hull (1920) presented
Chinese characters that had one of several simpler signs (radicals) embedded in them. In one experiment, Hull investigated whether learning
was facilitated by presenting the radicals in association with their correct
responses, thus eliminating the process of abstracting these from the
compound characters. At the end of the learning trials there was no
reliable difference in correct assignment of concepts between the condition in which the radical was presented and the control condition.
However, when half the subjects were asked to draw a picture of crucial
features corresponding to the concept names, the concepts presented
with the radicals were described twice as well as the others, as assessed by
independent judges. Hull concluded:

> The power to define is thus in some cases at least a very
> inadequate index of the functional value of a concept (Hull,
> 1920, p. 84).

This study is frequently cited, we think incorrectly, as evidence that
the observable behavior is not generated by accessible cognitive structures. We will argue that in this experiment the information that allowed
subjects to draw a picture of the crucial features of the concepts was only
partially accessed, if at all, in actually generating the concept-naming
behavior. Only 7% to 14% of the variability of the subjects' performance
in Hull's data can be accounted for by the difference in their ability to
define the concept (this quantity is not statistically significant). It is
abundantly clear that the knowledge from the presentation of radicals
was insufficient for learning the complex concepts. Identifying the embedded radicals was not an obvious matter. Hull (1920) showed that

marking the radical in red in the character led to considerable improvement in performance.

Broadbent and his collaborators (Broadbent, 1977) have shown that subjects learn to control computer simulations of traffic and of an economic system without generating any verbalizable knowledge about the interrelationships of the independent variables.   In one task (Broadbent, 1977), subjects were given control over the transport in a city by allowing them to alter the time interval between buses and to set parking fees for cars.   A simple computer model of this traffic system (unknown to the subjects) determined from the two parameters the average number of people on the buses and the number of empty parking spaces.   The subjects were asked to achieve some specified level of usage of buses and parking spaces by changing the variables under their control.   Before and after their control experience, subjects were asked about simple relations (e.g., "Will a rise in parking fee increase or decrease number of empty parking spaces?"), and cross-relations (e.g., "What effect will a rise in parking fees have on the load on the buses?").

With experience of the complete system, subjects improved in their ability to answer questions about simple relations, but ability to answer questions about cross-relations decreased with experience.   No relation was found between subjects' ability to control the system and their ability to answer questions.   The lack of such a relation may be due, at least in part, to the high level of accuracy of the subjects' questionnaire responses (half of the subjects answered all of the questionnaire questions correctly at the end of the experiment).   Although we do not have concurrent reports on the subjects' cognitive processes during the task, it is clear that they did not find the correct combination of parameters by mental planning, for they would have needed to try out, on average, six combinations of parameters before the correct one was found.   It is likely that the subjects relied directly on the effects of the last parameter change in selecting new parameter values, and hence explicit memory for the cross-talk relations may not have been necessary for their solution generated through successive approximation.

In both Hull's and Broadbent's studies, there is no inconsistency with our model, in that there is no evidence that the unreported knowledge was crucial for the cognitive processes involved in the respective tasks, hence no reason for generating it or storing it in LTM.

The unreliability of retrieval of relevant knowledge is nicely demonstrated by people's ability to detect their own errors. Allwood and Montgomery (1981, 1982) have studied subjects detecting errors in their solutions to problems in statistics. They found that subjects were able to find errors spontaneously without a directed effort to verify their solutions (Allwood, 1982). More errors could be detected if the experimenter focused the subjects' attention to some problem-solving steps. The principal factor in retrieving the correct knowledge was a broader and more intensive retrieval effort than occurs during normal problem solving. It is important to note that these subjects were not very skilled in statistics, and did not have their knowledge of statistics well integrated.

Being able to access knowledge in some form is not equivalent to being able to apply that knowledge correctly. This is particularly true for knowledge that is presented to the subject and acquired "passively." When the subject can generate the knowledge himself, the generation process assures that the knowledge is integrated with other knowledge. In instruction in motor skills, it is particularly obvious that being told, for example, how to hit a tennis ball is not sufficient for the hitting. Subjects may even disregard the verbal instruction and attempt to discover a way to achieve a realization of the procedure by themselves. At the same time, they may be able to retrieve the original verbal instruction.

Even for cognitive skills, like mathematics, subjects are often as effective in learning without instruction (i.e., by discovering the procedure) as in learning from explicit verbal instruction to use a specified procedure (cf. Kersh & Wittrock, 1962). A similar result was obtained by Duncker (1945) in his analysis of subjects solving the problem: Why are all six-place numbers of the form 276 276, 591 591, 112 112 divisible by 13? Most of the hints given to subjects were ineffective, although they clearly specify the general form of the solution (e.g., "If a common divisor of numbers is divisible by 13, they are all divisible by 13."). Duncker's account of the successful and unsuccessful hints was that subjects were unable to break up the pattern abc abc and realize that it is mathematically equivalent to $1001 * abc$.

Hayes-Roth, Klahr, and Mostow (1981) give a detailed analysis showing how advice given to a person playing a card game like Hearts requires a remarkable elaboration and inferential activity using relevant knowledge about the task before it can help the player guide his actions.

RETROSPECTIVE REPORTS OF EARLIER COGNITIVE PROCESSES

In this section we will elaborate on the model described earlier for retrospective reporting, and introduce more processes, mainly inferential, that subjects rely on to generate information about earlier cognitive processes and previously heeded information. First, we will review briefly our model of retrospective reporting and show that memory for the just preceding cognitive process appears to be markedly better than for earlier processes. Then we will turn to a discussion of the most frequent kind of retrospective questioning: questioning after the completion of an experiment session with many trials. Finally, we will discuss some other processes that can be used to make reliable predictions about earlier cognitive processes without retrieving episodic memory for those processes.

Model of Retrospective Reporting

Our general model assumes that the cognitive processes leave in LTM a subset of the originally heeded information in the form of a retrievable trace of connected episodic memory. Retrospective reporting involves retrieval of these episodic memories and verbalization of their content.

If the subjects are asked to report retrospectively on their last previous cognitive process, it appears that considerable episodic memory can be retrieved from information and cues in STM. Further, because of the redundancy of recent episodic memories, incorrect information about them is not likely to be produced. Mueller (1911) pointed out, however, that subjects sometimes confuse other retrievable information with information actually heeded during the processes being recalled. For example, a subject might report an unheeded feature of a (heeded) object (recalled from previous experience with the object).

Reports of General Cognitive Processes During Experiments

Requesting recall of general processes appears to be the most common procedure for collecting retrospective reports, and appears also to be the major source of evidence cited by people who doubt the usefulness of verbal reports as scientific evidence. In this type of reporting situation, the subject is asked after the experiment to tell the experimenter, for example, "How did you do these problems?" or "Can you tell me what you were thinking about during the experiment?" The rationale for asking such general questions is that any investigator would like to have their answers—namely, a compact veridical description of the subjects' cognitive processes while performing the task.

Our model predicts that such questions can be answered by direct retrieval of the information only if the subject has, during his performance of the task, already generated this kind of general description of his own cognitive processes. There is no reason to suppose that subjects generally do generate such information. To summarize veridically their cognitive processes, subjects would have to retrieve the entire episodic trace of their processing to provide an appropriate data base. Let us consider some of the difficulties with an "ideal" reporting model of this kind.

Finkenbinder (1914) let subjects solve a series of over 30 problems, obtaining introspective reports during and after the solution. The subjects were later asked to recall the problems and their solutions, and the information recalled was compared with the earlier reports. Finkenbinder did not quantify the results, but reports that while subjects, especially when given cues, did recall a good deal of information, they hardly ever recalled correctly short-cuts or erroneous solution attempts.

In a couple of studies by Smirnov (1973) subjects were unexpectedly asked to give retrospective reports of what they remembered experiencing and thinking during different episodes, for example, as they went from their house to the office. The question was put unexpectedly one or two hours after the subject reached the office. Below is a transcript of the first part of a typical report:

First of all I remember the moment I left the subway. What precisely? I thought that I must quickly take up the necessary position to get out of the subway and walk fast, since I was late. I remember I was in the last car. Therefore, I could not get out quickly and had to go into the crowd. Previously the people leaving the car took up the whole width of the platform. Now, in order to secure a passage for those entering the cars, officials are stationed who turn the public from the edge of the platform. It caught my eye that at each post stood a man for this purpose; otherwise the public would walk at the edge of the platform. (There follows a description of several men standing at the pillars, not letting the passengers to the edge of the platform.) I think I did not look at the clock. The road further is a blank. I remember nothing about it. There is only a hazy recollection from previous trips. I walked to the gates of the university without noticing anything. Don't remember what I thought of. When I entered the gate I noticed someone was hurrying. Who precisely, a man or a woman, I don't remember. More I don't remember ... Now about the first half of the way. I do not remember leaving the house.

Summarizing the reports of all subjects, Smirnov (1973) notes that virtually all the recalled information referred to experiences related to *walking* to the office. However, subjects were subjectively certain that they must have thought about other things, yet only thought related to walking to the office could be retrieved. Such a selective retrieval can be easily understood from the assumption that subjects could only access retrieval cues related to the walking and the physical environment traversed. Within this framework, we can also account for highway hypnosis (Natsoulas, 1970) where people suddenly realize that they remember nothing of the last twenty or thirty miles of the highway driven. If we assume that subjects are primarily thinking or fantasizing using internal cues during this time, and are able to perform the driving task nearly automatically, no memory trace of the environment would be expected. In such cases, subjects even lose the retrieval cues to what they were thinking about, thus leaving a total blank.

It is fallacious to assume complete retrievability of episodic information. All available data on subjects' memory for previously presented information and their cognitive processes in experiments with long series of similar trials shows subjects' memory to be poor. If it were not so, verbal learning experiments would take only a single trial.

Experiments using distinct types of stimulus material for different trials appear to yield much better recall (Frankel, Levine & Karpf, 1970; Burack, 1950), a result easily explainable in terms of distinctiveness of retrieval cues. If subjects used exactly the same processes on all trials, the failure to recall some of them would not be fatal, but we know that subjects frequently change their strategies in the course of an experiment, and may also solve different problems with different methods. A further complication is that subjects rely more and more on recognition to solve problems as an experiment proceeds, hence may find it harder and harder to recall their most recent cognitive processes.

How does the subject go from the retrieved episodic segments to generalizations about his processes? Inferences will generally be required, hence the veridicality of reports produced in this way has little relevance for the veridicality of reports of directly heeded information. Subjects may commit other types of errors. They may combine episodic memories from several different processes into a single structure. They may also make guesses as to the likely processes when they cannot remember them (cf. Mueller, 1911).

Several situations are documented where subjects do not recall all relevant information but short-circuit the retrieval. When subjects report on the frequency or representativeness of a solution procedure, they may very well rely on inferential or heuristic rules. Tversky and Kahneman (1973) have shown in several experiments that frequency judgments are closely related to ability to recall. In one experiment subjects were presented with a list of names of well-known people of both sexes. When the persons of one sex were more famous than those of the other, subjects overestimated the proportion of that sex in the list. Subjects also tend to judge consonants, like r and k as being more frequent in first than in third position, because words are easier to recall when their initial letters are given. Yet, in fact, consonants like r and k are more frequent in third position. On much the same grounds, subjects may infer that the particular solution procedures they recall are representative of all such procedures.

In a review article, Smedslund (1969) claims that verbal reports did not provide useful information on rapid mental processes in an arithmetic task he had studied (Smedslund, 1968). He described two reports that could be proven inconsistent—one with the subject's performance and speed in solving the test items, the other with the types of items actually given. In the original paper, however, Smedslund does not mention inaccuracy in the verbal reports, and actually quotes those reports to support some of his general results. In Smedslund's study the conditions for verbal reporting were far from optimal, for the subjects were asked after a relatively large number of trials to tell how they did the tasks. Even under these unpromising circumstances, the verbalized information, with a few exceptions, seemed to satisfy the author as basically consistent with his observations of subjects' performance.

In a study on the implicit learning of grammar, Reber and Lewis (1977) explicitly claimed inadequacy of retrospective reports:

> These reports were replete with statements that con-
> formed with neither the rules of the grammar nor the
> subjects' own behavior. (Reber & Lewis, 1977, p. 353)

First, a brief description of their experiment. On the first day, subjects were asked to memorize 15 patterns of symbols, like VSSXXVV. The subjects were then told that these patterns were generated according to rules and asked to construct new patterns from scrambled symbols conforming to these rules. On this anagram-like task the subjects were given no feedback.

For three more days, the subjects were first shown the 15 exemplars and then asked to do the anagram-like task. After completing this task on the fourth day, the subjects were shown a set of patterns and asked to decide whether they conformed to the rules that generated the 15 sample patterns. During this test, subjects were asked to verbalize reasons for each judgment as it was made. Finally, after the test the subjects were asked to write and describe in as much detail as possible what they knew about the rules and to describe special strategies they used in the experiment.

Thus, two types of verbal reports were collected in this study, neither of which corresponds closely with our notion of retrospective reports. It is interesting that Reber and Lewis almost exclusively criticize the general reports collected after the experiment rather than the verbalized reasons given after each judgment. Let us first discuss their evidence against the post-session rule descriptions, which is given in the form of a detailed analysis of an "average" subject.

The subject's performance in the anagram-like task improved steadily from day to day, providing clear evidence that his cognitive processes changed and that he did not apply the same rules at all times. Reber and Lewis compared reported regularities with the properties of proposed solutions to the anagram task, with the notion that prominent features recalled should also show up as parts of the anagram solutions. Although they found that features that were reported also appeared reliably as parts of anagram solutions, as expected, they also found that some admissible combinations were not generated. But in analysing the data, the experimenters pooled all anagram tasks from day 1 to day 4. Hence, we would expect regularities discovered late in the experiment to have a low frequency of occurrence in the anagrams; this would constitute no evidence of epiphenomenality. One reported pattern involved a combination of symbols that could not occur in the anagram tasks (although it occurred in one of the 15 learning examples). Given the large number of sequences exposed in the course of the experiment, and the consequent possibilities for errors of recall, the subject's reports appear to exhibit a rather high level of validity. Further, in 69% of the cases where a subject rejected a pattern correctly and verbalized a reason for the rejection, this reason was "correct" in terms of the experimenter's grammar. There is no evidence that in the remaining 31% of the cases the reasons given were inconsistent with the *subjects'* rules.

Apparent inconsistency of responses may simply be due to the fact that on successive occasions of retrieval, slightly different cues and context lead to different responses. Reber and Allen (1978) give the following example from a protocol:

> An M-sandwich [the subject's term for an item beginning and ending with M]. I know the last time I saw that I said no to it. But this looks right. Perhaps you can have an M-sandwich. I'll take it this time. (Reber & Allen, 1978)

Without additional evidence, there is no reason to suppose that the subject is not reporting the actual information ("This looks right") that leads him to his response. (Reber & Allen, 1978)

Reber and Allen (1978) point rather clearly to problems of retrieval as the source of inconsistency and "incorrectness" of verbalized reasons. They note that most of the "incorrect" rules concerned features that a pattern cannot have. These rules were often discovered spontaneously, as shown by the following protocol segment:

> RM? I don't remember seeing RM before. Perhaps that's not right. No, you can't have an RM (Reber & Allen, 1978, p. 215)

Most recently Dulany, Carlson, and Dewey (1983) replicated the learning study of Reber and Allen (1978). Along with their judgments of grammaticality, the subjects were instructed to underline the part of the letter string that made it well-formed or cross out the part that made it ungrammatical. Dulany et al. found that the rules as (imperfectly) understood by subjects accounted for the individual subjects' performances completely. Hence, imperfect rules or patterns that the subject has learned account for his responses.

Other Processes Without Awareness

In this section we will show that all instances that have been cited of lack of awareness with or without contradictory inferential reports can be traced to recognition processes. We will discuss first some studies involving stimuli that readily elicit responses. Then, in the next section, we will turn to the rather extensive literature on insight in problem solving and thinking. We will argue that insight involves direct access to pre-existing cognitive structures in LTM. Finally, we will discuss subjects' uses of inferential strategies to extract information about previous experience as a substitute for episodic memory of cognitive processes.

In situations where subjects' spontaneously generated behavior is studied, we cannot rule out recognition processes based on S-R links that have been established previously. If we knew the subject's entire prior history, we should, in principle, be able to identify the association that is later retrieved. Let us discuss a study by Rommetveit and Kvale (1965b) already considered in Chapter 2.

Patterns were displayed to signal to subjects playing a wheel of fortune whether they would win or not. When the experimenters asked a boy to describe the differences between positive and negative patterns, he said he did not know, although he had been able to anticipate the rewards correctly on previous trials. When pressed by the experimenter, he finally attempted a verbal description and gave one that was inconsistent with the actual signals. In this and many other similar accounts, it seems appropriate to attribute the error to absence of the information from memory rather than to inconsistency between memory contents and verbal reports of them. When information is not in memory, it cannot be reported verbally.

However, it still remains to show that recognition processes are sufficient to account for the performance. First, observe that subjects needed only to make a binary prediction, "win" or "lose," so that any accessed information implying likelihood of winning would suffice. In fact, subjects achieved their better-than-chance predictions by selecting figures characterized by roundness as "winners" (Rommetveit, 1965). But subjects might already have in LTM an association between "roundness" and "goodness."

Moreover, experimental variations, like telling the subjects that they will have to describe the figures afterwards and showing the subjects initially how the figures differed, may very well have changed their perceptions of the figures, and hence changed the cues that otherwise led to recognition of some figures as 'good'. Such an explanation is consistent with our earlier characterization of recognition processes.

We can use the same type of explanation for the finding by Rees and Israel (1935) that subjects, solving a series of 15 anagrams having identical structure, would select, for items with multiple solutions, the solution fitting the common structure, without reporting awareness of that structure. The anagrams all used the simple permutation, 54123.

Six out of ten subjects did not report awareness of the permutation common to all the solutions, suggesting that they did not have this information at the time they made their report. How can we explain how the four of these six subjects who made no errors selected the same permutation in 15 consecutive trials without retaining knowledge of the structure in STM?

We would attribute the result to the special properties of the permutation, 54123, used in this experiment. Subjects did not have to learn this particular pattern, but could decipher the anagram by using their normal visual scanning strategies, long since learned and automated: fixate at the left or near the middle of the stimulus, and scan from left to right. This strategy would reveal the anagram after only a couple of trials—probably in less than a second.

If this explanation is correct, then if more complex permutations were used, subjects would be aware of the structures of the solutions. This is exactly what Rees and Israel found in their study.

Kaplan and Schoenfeld (1966) recorded subjects' eye movements while they solved relatively simple permutation anagrams. The letters in the anagram were spaced so that the subject was able to fixate only a single letter at a time. From the eye fixations they were able to determine when subjects anticipated a certain permutation. They found perfect agreement between anticipation and reported awareness of the permutation structure: two subjects both displayed anticipation and reported noticing the structure, whereas one did neither.

In various problem-solving tasks, ample evidence has been recorded for pre-established scan or motor behavior. For example, Lindley (1897) studied subjects tracing a figure without repeating any line or starting over. Subjects tended to start in the left-hand corner of the figure, which made a solution impossible. It took subjects considerable time to become aware of the difficulty and change their behavior—a consequence of their established habits of writing and reading.

We propose a rather similar account for a series of experiments by Wason and Evans (1975) that they take as evidence for an unconscious response generation process coupled with a separate process for giving justification or reasons for their responses. It is entirely possible for subjects, especially if forcefully prompted, to generate reasons for responses evoked by recognition. Even when the response process generates intermediate reportable states, subjects may provide reasons that are more acceptable socially than those actually responsible for generating the response. However, in experiments where the subjects' responses cannot be accounted for in terms of immediate recognition, we feel obliged to scrutinize the evidence that suggests a dissociation between heeded information and reported reasons.

The principal task environment in which experimental psychologists have proposed a dissociation between generating responses and giving reasons for them is logical reasoning, in particular, in tasks testing the understanding of the implication relation (Evans & Wason, 1976; Wason & Evans, 1975). In these experiments, all subjects with formal training in logic are screened out. Subjects are told that the problem has to do with four cards, each card having a letter on one side and a number on the other. The subjects are then given the following rule: "If there is a D on one side, then there is a 3 on the other side." They are then shown one side of each of four cards, showing a D, B, 3, and 7, respectively. They are then told, "I want you to list for me those cards, and only those cards, that you must see in order to find out whether the rule is true or false." In general, subjects want to see the cards with D and 3, while the "correct" cards are those showing D and 7.

In the model proposed by Johnson-Laird and Wason (1970), it was proposed that subjects could be divided according to degrees of insight. Subjects without insight would select the cards showing symbols mentioned in the rule. With partial insight, subjects would also select instances where the card could falsify the rule. With full insight, subjects would rule out the card (the one showing 3) that was irrelevant to falsifying the rule. Goodwin and Wason (1972) found support for this model by analyzing subjects' verbalized reasons for selecting cards. Requiring subjects to give written reasons had only a small effect toward inducing correct solutions. In fact, some subjects even changed from more nearly correct solutions to less correct solutions. This was interpreted by Goodwin and Wason as evidence that the subjects' understanding fluctuated.

Wason and Evans (1975), studying subjects' responses to different rules (e.g., "If P, then not Q"), found that most subjects chose to look at cards with symbols named in the rule regardless of the form of the rule. They advanced the hypothesis that the choice is based on a simple matching process identifying the names of the symbols in the rule and another process of rationalization to provide the justifications. Evans and Wason sought to test this two-stage hypothesis by telling subjects (correctly or falsely) which cards should be chosen, and asking them to give reasons for the choices. Subjects were most confident in their reasons when the cards selected by the experimenter were those that they themselves would have chosen, except that they were about equally willing and able to generate reasons with confidence that the 3 should be chosen as that it should not be. Subjects giving a reason for not selecting the 3 cited irrelevance. Subjects forced to give reasons for selecting it gave as the reason a possibility for falsification.

This result has been claimed by Evans (1975) to show that verbal reports do not reflect cognitive processes. We interpret it differently. Subjects presented with the original choice task usually fail, as we have seen, to carry out a thorough enough analysis to arrive at the correct answer. On the other hand, when presented with an answer they believe to be correct, they carry out additional analysis to discover *why* it is correct, and from that analysis, they are able to provide a justification for the answer. It is presenting an "answer" to the subject that changes the cognitive processes. Evans (1982) has recently presented his own interpretation of these experiments which is consistent with ours. Both he and we interpret the original decision process as a recognition process, so that subjects cannot report the intermediate steps—their "reasons."

A study by Brunswik and Herma (1951) appears to be a cornerstone in Brunswik's (1956) argument for lack of awareness in learning of probabilistic relations between cues and outcomes. In order to understand fully the results of this study, we have to discuss how information about previous stimulus events may influence subsequent perceptions. Brunswik and Herma presented their subjects with weights of two different colors, one to be held in each hand. For some pairs of weights, the subjects were asked "which of the two objects appeared heavier at the first moment of lifting??" (Brunswik & Herma, 1951, p. 284) Immediate impressions were to be expressed as a snap judgment. The subjects were allowed to judge the weights as equal, yet discouraged from doing so. Each subject always held weights of a given color in the same hand, although the color varied among subjects. In one experiment, the weights of one color were heavier most (80%) of the time. Interspersed were trials where the weights were equal. During these test trials subjects tended to judge weights in the hand that normally received the lighter weights as heavier. Brunswik and Herma attributed these systematic responses to learning of a cue-response relation.

After the completion of the 72 test and learning trials, subjects were asked, "In your opinion, which objects were on the average heavier, the green or the red?" (Brunswik & Herma, 1951, p. 288), and also a similar question regarding the weights in the right and left hands. (Remember that color and position were perfectly correlated.) Most of the subjects (about 75%) answered *both* questions incorrectly, but, of course, thereby reported correctly for the relation in the test trials. (Subjects did not have to make a judgment for the trials where the weights were objectively different.)

Brunswik and Herma (1951) note that "some" subjects explicitly asked if the question referred only to test trials, or to all trials, and were told the latter. As no separate analysis was made of these subjects, we simply don't know whether most subjects misinterpreted the question or in fact did not remember the relative weights in the trials without a test. Moreover, there is no evidence from the study's data that the subjects learned *anything*, if by learning we mean a stable change in behavior.

Uznadze (1966) shows that contrast effects of stimuli, like those exhibited in the Brunswik-Herma experiment, can be obtained for a variety of stimuli—pressure, loudness of auditory stimuli, illumination, and weight. Theories explaining these phenomena have been proposed, most notably Helson's (1964) adaptation-level theory. These theories can account for the subjects' behavior in terms of short-term shifts in the perceptual and sensory systems, without learning. In particular, it can account for their demonstration of "reversal learning" (Brunswik & Herma, 1951). In this experiment, the authors showed that after providing lighter weights to one hand (and eliciting the judgment of "heavier" when equal weights were provided on test trials), the judgments could be reversed by giving heavier weights to that hand.

An adaptation-level theory can also account for the "one-trial learning" effects that puzzled Gibson (1969) in her discussion of this study. After a single presentation of unequal weights, subjects show a 90% tendency to give a biased judgment on the subsequent test trial of equal weights. Lacking evidence against the adaptation-level theory, we argue that it provides a more parsimonious explanation of the behavior than does cue-response learning. In Gibson's review of studies on learning stimulus-response relations in probabilistic environments, she finds very strong support, except for Brunswik and Herma's study, for the necessity of awareness in order for learning to occur.

INSIGHT AND ACCESS TO SOLUTION IDEAS

Apart from cases where the subjects rely on automatic processes, there are other forms of incompleteness in reports where information that was once in focal attention (in STM) is not verbalized. Information in STM is easily obliterated. In a few seconds, the contents of STM can be destroyed or made inaccessible by requiring subjects to perform certain types of tasks—for example, repeatedly subtracting 7 from a given number (Brown-Peterson paradigm). With any shift in the locus of attention, of which this paradigm provides an example, the previous contents of STM become unavailable. If an intermediate result in a sequence of processes causes a direct execution of other processes that make full demands on STM, the intermediate result may reside for only a brief moment in STM, and may be lost before being reported. Under thinking-aloud conditions, it has been observed (Duncker, 1945) that information leading to the direct recognition of the appropriate action often tends not to be verbalized. Similar observations have been made (de Groot, 1965) about the reports of chess grandmasters considering possible moves in chess positions.

A frequently cited study by Maier (1931) on subjects' retrospective reports about a hint given during solution of the Pendulum Problem gives some evidence for the same phenomenon. Subjects who described the solution as emerging in a single step did not report any memory of the hint. A result of Maier's study that is less often mentioned was that *all* subjects who mentioned more than one step in the solution of the problem reported that the hint had been administered.

The two related mechanisms mentioned thus far—the absence of intermediate stages of acts of recognition from STM, and failure to report transient contents of STM—are fully adequate to account for the phenomena of sudden "insight" that are the subject of so many anecdotes in the literature of creativity (Nisbett & Wilson, 1977, pp. 240-241). The studies cited in support of sudden insight are based on retrospective accounts of "real" creative acts, often reported many years after the event. Fortunately, a number of studies have addressed this topic in a more controlled experimental environment. Durkin (1937) sought to create favorable circumstances for "insight" with subjects thinking aloud while solving block puzzles. While subjects occasionally reported insights, the background steps leading to the emergence of the insightful ideas could always be determined from the concurrent thinking-aloud protocols. Of this kind of insight, Durkin (1937, p. 81) says:

> When it occurs, it comes with an onrush that makes it seem very sudden —an "out of the blue" experience. But it can always be found to have developed gradually. The suddenness must be regarded as due to the concealment of the background. It does not bring in a new *kind* of process. (Durkin, 1937, p. 81)

For geometry proofs (Henry, 1934), and for a variety of "insight" problems (Bulbrook, 1932), the thinking-aloud protocols showed that the progress to solution was either gradual or was determined by trial and error. In neither case was it necessary to postulate additional kinds of processes.

Insight or illumination of a creative idea was by many early investigators described as the result of a period of unconscious work, or *incubation*, following on preliminary work in becoming familiar with the problem (*preparation*). During this period of alleged incubation, these accounts go, the scientist or inventor has laid the problem aside in favor of other activities. However, it has been suggested (Woodworth, 1938) that during the period of incubation, the scientist will occasionally lapse into thinking about the problem, even while working on a different task. Woodworth (1938) cites a study by Platt and Baker that suggests that subjects are not aware of the durations of these unplanned episodes of concentrated thought on the problem. Clearly, such unanticipated thought processes, if they occur, will be very difficult to retrieve in retrospect. Generally such episodes are terminated, often abruptly, by external demands—as, for example, in a driving situation. It is also possible, as has been suggested by Simon (1966) that no new ideas are generated during incubation, but instead, Einstellung effects that keep attention directed toward unproductive lines of search are dissipated by forgetting during this period.

There is considerable evidence, though most of it is anecdotal, that many "creative" ideas are, in fact, reproductions of ideas from memory derived from the ideas of other people. Machotka (1964) mentions an art student who "generated" a poster design that she later recognized as having previously seen in the window of a store. According to Lowes' (1927) analysis of Samuel Coleridge's phrases and imagery, it can be seen that many of them came from reading, without Coleridge being aware of the sources of most of them. If other people's ideas can be mistaken for novel creative ones, so can ideas that actually were generated by the subject himself at some earlier time.

From research on daydreaming (Singer, 1975) and undirected thought (Klinger, 1971), there are suggestions that such thought episodes are difficult to recall fully unless the retrospective reports are obtained shortly thereafter, or unless the subjects label or rehearse the thought content for subsequent recall. Studies using concurrent verbalization (Bertini, Lewis, & Witkin, 1964; Kazdin, 1976; Klinger, 1971) provide detailed and informative accounts of undirected thought processes. In sum, thinking that is not closely related to the external environment can sometimes be retrieved with situational clues, but seldom otherwise, except when it is verbalized concurrently with the thought process.

Insight as Recognition

Let us now review the evidence we have surveyed as to whether recognition processes, as we defined them earlier, are sufficient to account for the phenomena reported above. The most important hypothesis in our model is that recognition processes simply access an existing structure in LTM, without modifying, altering, or generating old or new cognitive structures. In Maier's (1931) problem-solving experiment, there is no disagreement that subjects had the pendulum solution available in LTM. The evidence in Durkin's (1937) study is even clearer. An experimental group of subjects first solved several small block puzzles with different configurations, while a control group did not. The large block puzzle now given to all subjects could be broken up into subproblems, which corresponded to the smaller puzzles given earlier to the experimental group. Thus, only subjects in the experimental group had in LTM accessible cognitive structures corresponding to the subproblems; and predictably, only these subjects had insight experiences, with solution ideas corresponding closely to the earlier generated solution to the subproblems.

In many complex tasks it is, therefore, likely that a subject will generate information that cannot all be held in STM, but is accessible from LTM. In some tasks, such partial results will be useful and recognized, in other tasks, they may be of limited use and hard to retrieve—because of similarity confusions or other reasons. Durkin (1937) suggests that sudden insight occurs precisely in those tasks where the relevant information is too extensive to be all retained in STM. Sudden reorganization, which resembles closely the usual descriptions of insight, can, when the problem situation is beyond the subject's "apprehension span," be found to be related to previous responses (p. 84).

Is it necessary to postulate unconscious processes to explain the sudden emergence of problem solutions? There are at least two phenomena that must be accounted for. First, the subject, in solution by "insight," does not perceive his success as being a result of conscious cognitive processes. Second, subjects feel confidence that the suddenly appearing thought is the solution. Thus it might be claimed that both the solution finding processes and the testing processes were unconscious.

The source cited most widely in support of the importance of unconscious processes is Poincaré (Ghiselin, 1952). A critical reading of Poincaré does not provide any evidence for unconscious processing, nor for the belief that Poincaré himself favored such an interpretation.

Poincaré, discussing mathematical creation from the viewpoint of a completely "logical" mind, makes some observations, strikingly similar to those currently emphasized by information processing psychology, about the limitations of humans. He points to the limits of short-term memory as an explanation of occasional errors in generating proofs, and observes that the primary component of mathematical skill is a finer representation of mathematical knowledge that yields better effective memory, yet is restricted entirely to the mathematical domain. Mathematical creation, according to Poincaré, is "making new combinations with mathematical entities already known." He concludes that a mechanical combination of all possible alternatives is practically impossible, because of the large number of alternatives and he asserts that mathematicians only consider combinations that have a potential for yielding interesting results:

> Never in the field of his consciousness do combinations appear that are not really useful, except some that he rejects but which have to some extent the characteristics of useful combinations. (Poincaré, 1952, p. 25)

Consistent with both of these observations is the view that the objects of mathematical thought are abstract entities and patterns rather than detailed realizations of strings of symbols and the like.

Poincaré (1952) describes some circumstances in which he had sudden insights into mathematical relations. We note with interest that in the cases he cites, the insight involves seeing a correspondence between his current problem and some other developed domain of mathematics that was stored in, and accessible from, his LTM. In these retrospective reports (recorded long after the original experience), he has, of course, no memory of his thoughts just prior to his insights—the ideas emerging in response to heeding the suddenly emerged solution may well lead to loss of accessibility of such prior heeded content. He only mentions his memory of the general social situation in which the sudden insight occurred. He makes the important observation that:

> These sudden inspirations ... never happen except after some days of voluntary effort which has appeared absolutely fruitless and where nothing good seems to have come, where the way taken seems totally astray. (Poincaré, 1952, p. 27)

Further, the subjective feeling of certainty of the correctness of the solution is occasionally mistaken:

> We almost always notice that this false idea, had it been true, would have gratified our natural feeling for mathematical elegance. (Poincaré, 1952, p. 29)

Although Poincaré considers the possibility that unconscious processing continues after the conscious work and delivers the resulting solution, he rejects this proposal as unreasonable. He points out that in no case do the "unconscious processes make any calculations." In his experience they simply point out the similarity of two existing structures in LTM.

In his final proposal, Poincaré (1952) suggests that during the active conscious processing that preceded insight the inventor activates and generates a lot of mathematical structures "from which we might reasonably expect the desired solution" (p. 30). This model of the process is quite consonant with our model of problem solution by recognition. Poincaré's explanation requires no more unconscious processing than the unconscious steps in the recognition process that we have discussed before.

Regeneration—Hypotheses

We will argue that for the most part our behavior is mediated by cognitive processes that generate actively the responses that are sought. This is true even when the same task is presented repeatedly. In many cases where the same behavior is required again and again, the conscious level of control is changed to a monitoring role, and the corresponding memory trace may become weak or disappear. In the common case where one is wondering, for example, whether one turned off the stove or locked the door to one's house, unless some explicit attempt was made to memorize this event or some deviation occurred from the normal course of events, one is generally unable to retrieve any episodic memory even a few seconds later. Most people have returned to the door to check whether it was locked, and found it to be so, which shows that the process was actually executed.

Even in situations with rather full retrospective reports, subjects often have difficulty in retrieving the corresponding episodic memory. However, this doesn't imply that they cannot give valid reports on "what they must have done." When repeating the same task, like multiplying two 2-digit numbers in one's head, a subject is highly likely to encounter the same information each time. We might call memory of this information "regeneration memory" to distinguish it from memory of the individual episodes. Regeneration memory, of course, is simply contained in LTM, and does not constitute a separate specialized memory. For the most part, regeneration memory provides a good source for determining how we did behave when the behavior concerns responses to invariant knowledge structures or stable aspects of the environment. The answers that subjects give to questions like, "Name the current President of the United States," or "Give a word starting with 'A'," can be retrieved from regeneration memory as well. Regeneration memory would provide invalid reports if the identity of the President had meanwhile been changed, or if some other word starting with "A" had occurred immediately before.

The possibility that subjects may be relying on regeneration memory rather than episodic memory should be ascertainable through retrospective reports. We believe that subjects are able to discriminate between the two types of memory. However, there also are paradigms that will differentiate the two. It is possible to present the subject with incomplete information so as to eliminate reprocessing, yet to present sufficient information to serve as a retrieval cue for episodic memory. For example, regeneration memory would not provide an answer to: "I asked you for the name of a certain kind of famous person. What kind of person was I asking for?" or "I asked you for a word starting with a letter. Which letter was it?" Although we do not find in the literature experiments that support directly the idea of regeneration memory, we would like to discuss some results that provide indirect evidence for such a mechanism.

The first result is that subjects "unconsciously" change their attitudes as a result of being asked to argue for an opposing view. The change is unconscious in the sense that subjects don't report being aware of changing their attitudes and perceive themselves as having had the same attitudes even before the experimentally induced argument (Bem & McConnell, 1970). The experimental results can be understood if we assume that generating an attitude judgment involves retrieving relevant facts from LTM, yet does not leave a retrievable episodic memory trace. After arguing against their original views, subjects in making the postexperimental attitude judgments may retrieve some of the newer facts, and thus be biased in the direction they had argued. If we now assume that the subjects don't have any episodic memory of their previous judgment or judgment process, they may explicitly regenerate the process, or possibly realize that it would be the same as their current attitude. (The correlation between recall and current attitude is very high: .96 to .98.)

Control subjects without any experimental manipulation behave as if they make two attempts to generate attitudes—one for the recall and one for the current attitude. We can also account for the finding that the subjects who remembered the instruction to give evidence against their prior attitude showed less attitude change. (The number of subjects forgetting this component of the instructions was remarkably high.) Remembering the restriction might reflect memory of difficulty in suppressing counter-arguments that were accessed at the time for making the attitude judgment.

In an interesting series of studies, Fischhoff (1975,1977) has demonstrated that being informed about the answer to a question or the outcome of a situation changes subjects' perceptions of how well they knew the answer (knew-it-all-along effect), or how likely they judged the outcome of the situation to be (hindsight). Fischhoff (1977) had little or no success in getting subjects to disregard the information and eliminate the bias, by different kinds of instructions. The information presented appeared to integrate irrevocably with prior information (Fischhoff, 1977). We think that these results should be interpreted in terms of reprocessing. Subjects do not have accessible episodic memory of their cognitive processes for a judgment—the judgment is generated anew each time. This is consistent with the finding that when information relevant to the judgment is changed, so is the judgment process and its outcome, without any reportable change in the process.

This reprocessing view can also account for Fischhoff's observation (1977) that subjects can "remember" or regenerate many of their original judgments an hour later, when they are *not* given additional information. The subjects were instructed to remember their original responses, but we don't know if the subjects would have been equally accurate if they were simply asked to answer the question again (i.e., asked explicitly to reprocess the answer).

A similar analysis can account for the surprising observation that training and treatment will not change self-report measures taken prior and subsequent to treatment, even when objective changes are demonstrated (Howard, 1980). Howard (Howard, 1980; Howard, Ralph, Gulanick, Maxwell, Nance, & Gerber, 1979) suggests that information used to generate the ratings changes along with the training and treatment. Hence, the posttraining ratings will not employ the same scale as the pretraining ratings (response-shift bias).

Item 13: In a heated discussion I generally become so
absorbed in what I am going to say that I forget to listen to
what others are saying.

Subject at Pretest: "I listen to what other people say when I'm
talking to them. I'd say—2 (I disagree on the whole)."

Subject at Posttest: "All these group exercises made me realized that I don't listen to people. I should have put +3 (I
agree very much) the first time I filled this out. But the group
really opened my eyes and helped me to try to be more of an
active listener and so while I still sometimes forget to listen to
people, overall I'm not doing nearly so badly now. I'll put
−1 (I disagree a little)." (Howard et al., 1979, pp. 3-4)

In order to ascertain that pretraining and posttraining ratings are
judged on the same scale, subjects are asked to make both judgments
after the training or treatment. Using retrospective pretest and posttest
comparison, Howard (Howard, 1980; Howard & Dailey, 1979; Howard
et al., 1979) finds reliable differences attributable to the training and
treatment. The primary difference between the changes due to training
and the previous two changes is that subjects will heed and hence have
explicit memory for acquired and changed memory structures, which
allows them to assess the change attributed to training and treatment.

CONCLUSION

In this chapter, we have marshalled the evidence for a simple hypothesis
that is at the core of our model of human information processing: the
information that is heeded during performance of a task, is the information that is reportable; and the information that is reported is information that is heeded.

We have examined all of the studies of which we are aware that
have been cited as challenging this hypothesis, and have found that they
do not, in fact, refute it. We have also examined a great many studies on
recall, not designed with this hypothesis in mind, and have found that
they, too, are compatible with it. We conclude that the hypothesis
provides a substantially correct basis for understanding and interpreting
verbal reports.

One kind of information that subjects clearly *cannot* report, because it is not available in STM, are the cues that allow them to recognize

stimuli.   The *result* of the process of recognition (i.e., the thing recognized) is heeded and can be reported, but not the intermediate steps in the recognition *process*. Inability to report recognition cues must not be confused with failure to report contents of STM.

Many of the other claimed gaps in verbal reports are attributable to memory failures or confusions, especially when subjects are asked to make general retrospective reports, rather than to report specific recent episodic memories. Likewise, when subjects fail to recover from LTM information that has been requested of them, they may reason about the situation and report the results of their inferences instead of memories.

With this basic hypothesis in hand, we are now in a position to discuss the kinds of inferences that experimenters are justified in making from verbal protocols taken concurrently with performance of a task. This will be the topic of the next chapter.

4

INFERENCES FROM VERBAL DATA

In this chapter we will consider how verbal data can help us understand the structure of cognitive processes and observed performance. Data do not speak for themselves, especially in a system containing a memory that prevents observations from ever being exactly replicated. They must always be encoded and interpreted in the framework of a theoretical structure. We shall be much concerned with the objectivity and validity of the encoding process.

REQUIREMENTS FOR USING VERBAL DATA

In Chapters 2 and 3 we have dealt with two basic objections that have been raised against using verbal reports as data: first, that the reporting process might alter task performance; second, that reports may yield a very incomplete record of the cognitive processes. Our techniques for using verbal reports must be fashioned to meet these objections, and at least three others as well.

1. One argument is that verbal reports are *epiphenomenal*—that is, are generated independently of the cognitive processes that produce non-verbal behavior and performance. In Chapter 3 we showed that, indeed, some kinds of verbal reports are generated in complete independence of the accompanying cognitive processes. Here we are concerned only with concurrent and retrospective reports for which our model explicitly predicts a direct correspondence between cognitive processes and verbalization. When such a correspondence exists, and epiphenomenality can therefore be refuted, we will refer to the verbalizations as being *pertinent* to the cognitive processes.

2. A more moderate objection is that verbal reports are *idiosyncratic*, reflecting the unique experiences of individual subjects and hence not usable for general theory development. For example, different subjects often employ different strategies, a fact that makes it difficult to frame simple general laws. Under these circumstances it seems implausible that pooling data across subjects should reveal general patterns. Of course the difficulty here does not lie in verbal reports, but in the existence of individual differences. Using other methods that conceal these differences does not solve the problem.

3. The third argument, primarily methodological, is that *encoding* of verbal protocols cannot be made objective and sound. Coding categories are derived from theories, hence infect the encoded data with theoretical presuppositions. We will treat this objection more fully in Chapter 6.

Encoding and analyzing empirical data—whether verbal reports or other kinds of data—always takes place in some kind of theoretical context. In coding and generalizing we cannot ever achieve complete independence from theory. We can, however, employ theoretical assumptions that are as weak and uncontroversial as possible, although there is a trade-off between the weakness of our assumptions and the strength of the inferences we can draw from the data, stronger assumptions allowing stronger inferences. We will start our analysis here with weak and relatively uncontroversial assumptions, addressing the issue of epiphenomenality versus pertinence of verbal reports. Then we will introduce further assumptions in order to address the issues of reliability and generalizability of verbal report data.

When data can be shown to be pertinent to ongoing cognitive processes, they can then be used as evidence for the course and nature of these processes. Hence, our inquiry here into the pertinence of verbal data will also include a consideration of the kinds of inferences about process that can be drawn from these data.

The epiphenomenality argument is that verbal reports are generated by a different process from the one that generates the target behavior (e.g., the problem solution in a problem solving task). To understand how a subject solves a problem or generates an answer, we need to propose at least one processing model that is capable of generating the answer or solution. We need also to account for verbalizations and verbalized information by proposing processes and processing models that can generate, and in a sense verbalize, the same information. If we can show that the information processes that are needed to reproduce the verbalized information are also required and/or sufficient to generate the answer or solution, the argument for epiphenomenality is essentially refuted. Whenever verbalizations correspond to plausible intermediate states in a processing model for the problem solving activity, we can plausibly infer that this information is actually used in generating the problem solution. If a processor capable of solving the problems would *have* to generate the intermediate steps verbalized in the observed verbal reports, then it would not be parsimonious to postulate two independent processes, one to produce the reports, the other to produce the problem solution.

Since we can seldom demonstrate that a particular processing path is unique, we will usually have to be satisfied with weaker criteria for assessing whether the verbalizations are pertinent to the solution process. We will consider three such criteria, which may be regarded as necessary conditions to be satisfied by verbal data if they are to be used to infer underlying cognitive processes.

Relevance Criterion. The verbalizations should be relevant to the given task.

If all the observed verbalizations were irrelevant to the task, we could not claim pertinence of the verbalizations. It is not necessary to make commitments to specific models for cognitive processes to judge whether the verbalized information is relevant or not. For many kinds of tasks, an a priori task analysis will reveal what sorts of information are relevant to task performance (Newell & Simon, 1972). Relatively unconstrained cognitive activities, like free association or day-dreaming, cannot be subjected to this kind of analysis, but should meet another criterion.

Consistency Criterion. The verbalizations, to be pertinent, should be logically consistent with the verbalizations that just precede them.

If the items in a sequence of verbalizations were not related to each other or consistent, then independent and possibly random processes would suffice for generating them. This would argue strongly against the verbalizations' corresponding to goal-directed and cumulative processes with potential for generating answers and solutions. Conversely, conformity to the consistency criterion implies a higher-level control and organization of the processes underlying the verbalizations. Again, judging consistency does not require a specific processing model.

For both task-directed and undirected cognitive processes, we can postulate a third criterion.

Memory Criterion. A subset of the information heeded during task performance will be remembered.

When subjects are thinking aloud or giving retrospective reports, much of the information that comes to conscious attention will be remembered and available for subsequent retrieval. We can identify verbalization of the same information at two different parts of a protocol without a specific model of cognitive processes generating or accessing this information.

If the verbalizations meet these criteria, they could only be produced by a processing mechanism similar to the one performing the task, hence it would not be parsimonious to assume epiphenomenality. The strong form of the epiphenomenality argument would amount to the implausible claim that a subject could solve a problem (e.g., a logic problem) as well while thinking aloud about a different problem (e.g., mental multiplication) as while thinking aloud on the logic problem.

Let us now turn to a review of how various kinds of verbal protocols can be checked for conformity to these criteria, and how process models can be inferred from them.

Verbal protocols are usually first segmented into individual statements (assertions, propositions). This simple encoding is seldom difficult or problematic. Four tests of its validity can be applied at once. First, if a verbalization describes a situation that the subject can perceive directly, its correspondence with the stimulus can be checked. Second, its relevance to the task and to plausible steps toward a solution (as determined by task analysis) can be assessed. Third, its consistency with just previously verbalized information presumed to be in STM can be checked. Finally, whenever there is reason to believe that verbalized information will be committed to memory, its presence in memory can be tested by subsequent demands for recall or recognition.

In what follows we will distinguish three kinds of verbalized information: information available perceptually to the subject, information retrieved from memory, and all other information. These categories will be associated with different procedures for evaluating the pertinence of the information, and also different processes to account for its regeneration. We will first discuss verbalization of perceptually available information.

Perceptually Available Information

Since information available to the subject's perceptions is also available to the experimenter, the correspondence of reports with stimuli can usually be established easily. Two cases may be distinguished. In situations where subjects have access to the information externally (e.g., printed instructions, problem text), it can be verbalized by reading without more than transitory internal representation. Where subjects must verbalize pictorial information presented in non-verbal form, or where they paraphrase the information presented, more complex processes are involved. In either case, we can infer from the verbalization that the perceived information was heeded.

Independently of verbalizations, we can assess what information is heeded by recording eye fixations. In a dissertation, Winikoff (1967) related thinking-aloud verbalizations and eye movements for subjects solving problems in cryptarithmetic, chess, and letter series completion. He constructed and tested two sets of predictions of the subjects' eye movements. His "naive" predictions assumed that the subject would fixate on everything designated or referred to in the verbal protocol. His theory-driven predictions were derived from a Problem Behavior Graph of the entire protocol, where certain operations recorded in the graph were predicted to cause fixation on the information required for input to these operators.

Using several different procedures to map the eye movements on to simultaneous protocol segments, and using an adaptation of signal-detection theory as a statistical model, Winikoff (1967) showed that the predicted and observed fixations agreed at levels much higher than chance. (All differences were significant beyond the .01 level.) These results show that the eye movements correspond to the verbalizations, and also to the processes inferred from the information processing description of the problem solving.

In his study of anagram-like tasks and puzzles, Deffner (1983) recorded both TA protocols and eye fixations. (For more details see Chapter 2.) From the protocols all verbalizations describing or making reference to parts of the displayed information were encoded with respect to when the verbalization was made and which part was referenced. Similarly, the eye fixations were encoded with respect to what information was fixated and when the fixations were made. Based on the results from earlier research on the temporal relation between information fixated visually and its verbalization (i.e., the eye-voice spans) Deffner (1983) found that over 90% of verbalized references to a displayed piece of information could be linked to a fixation of that piece. This finding provides mutually validating evidence for TA and eye fixations.

There is some other converging evidence on the relation between eye fixations and heeded information, both in cases of concurrent and of retrospective verbalization. For subjects memorizing a list of items presented visually, Geiselman and Bellezza (1977) found a marked correlation between the number of times items were rehearsed aloud and the number of times they were fixated visually. In an immediate recall condition, the correlation was .74, and in a delayed recall condition it was .53. In a study on decision making, Russo and Rosen (1975) asked subjects to give a verbal retrospective report on their decision processes, and at the same time prompted them with a display of their eye-movements during the process. In 94% of the cases where the eyes fixated alternately on the two decision alternatives, subjects reported they were making comparisons.

Information Generated and Retrieved

To avoid strong theoretical commitments in our interpretations, we prefer to apply simple tests in judging the pertinence of verbal reports—tests like the relevance of information reported to the problem posed, consistency among various pieces of information reported, and consistency between the information and the task.

Only rarely have investigators analyzing verbal protocols actively considered the possibility that the verbalizations might be epiphenomenal or made explicit analyses of relevance and consistency. Most of the (indirect) evidence we have found on these matters requires reinterpretation and occasionally recalculation of the published data. The kinds of analyses we have in mind involve placing side by side the task information that is presented and the raw verbalizations. Below, we take as examples all the studies we have found for three kinds of tasks.

Tasks vary greatly in the extent to which the solution is implicit in the task information, on the one hand, or calls on extensive information stored in LTM, on the other. An example of a task that requires the evocation of the relevant structures in LTM is anagram problem solving. In this task, some letters are presented, together with the information that, by rearrangement, they can be made to form an English word. In solving anagrams, subjects rely on their knowledge of the frequent letter combinations in English and about possible patterns of vowels and consonants.

A very different task is concept attainment. The exemplars and non-exemplars presented to subjects consitute substantially all the information that is relevant—except in cases where the subjects are informed as to what kinds of rules to consider.

An intermediate class of tasks are mathematical problems, like algebra word problems, or physics problems. In these problems, a considerable amount of information is presented, but subjects need to evoke a lot of additional knowledge in order to solve them. We will start our discussion with this latter category of problems.

Mathematical Problem Solving. Explicit instruction in subjects like mathematics and physics biases subjects toward certain solution structures. Often, relatively little information need be retrieved from LTM, and it is reasonable to assume that subjects can generate the information in a few different ways. When paper and pencil are used, it is fairly easy to trace the successive input-output relations that lead to the solution. These written records are generally both relevant and consistent, especially when they lead to the correct answer. A thinking aloud protocol taken while a subject is generating a solution is different in many respects from the final written solution. Subjects are often explicitly cautioned not to explain what they are doing (as they are sometimes asked to do for written solutions) but simply to verbalize their thoughts. As a result, logically distinct steps are sometimes aggregated, in the verbal protocol, into single psychological steps (Krutetskii, 1976) and a single solution process often corresponds to a succession of gradually improving solution attempts (Montgomery & Allwood, 1978).

Several investigators have analyzed the information that is logically required to solve specific problems. This approach is probably best exemplified by Sokolov (1972) and Krutetskii (1976). Sokolov analyzed each problem into a logical and valid sequence of judgments and operations leading to the solution. The verbalizations corresponding to these steps were identified in the protocols, as well as errors and breaks in the sequence of inferences. In the sample of protocols that Sokolov reported, the verbal information can be mapped fairly easily onto the logically derived states, thus supporting a hypothesis of relevance and consistency.

Krutetskii (1976, pp. 271-275) performed a similar analysis, based on his best subject's detailed accounts of the steps that were logically necessary for solving the problem. Protocols from other subjects were then successfully mapped onto these steps (only the results of the analysis and not the protocols were published), except that able subjects took several steps at a time and poor subjects took additional unnecessary and sometimes incorrect intermediate steps.

Newell and Simon (1972) produced detailed analyses of three tasks —logic problems, cryptarithmetic problems, and chess—and analyzed numerous protocols against the background of these task analyses, demonstrating both relevance and consistency of the protocols.

In a series of studies of physics problem-solving (Larkin, McDermott, Simon & Simon, 1978) a complete enumeration of relevant physical principles was made for task domains, like kinematics and simple dynamics. The protocols of both expert and novice problem-solvers in physics could be described as sequences of applications of these principles. The expert subjects applied the principles in tightly organized and predictable sequences. Even novice subjects' verbalizations could in most cases be described as moving toward solutions by means-ends analysis. Hence, the protocols were both relevant and consistant.

The Semi-Automated Protocol Analysis (SAPA) system of Bhaskar and Simon (1977) can be conceptualized as an analysis of the information required for all tasks in a subdomain of thermodynamics. The core of SAPA is a formalized sequence of operations and judgments that, given the correct information input, yield a complete formal description and solution of the problem presented to it. The fact that SAPA can predict successfully and accept the verbalizations that appear in a protocol is clear evidence of the relevance and consistency of that information.

Let us turn now to studies analyzing larger numbers of protocols. Kennedy, Eliot, and Krulee (1970) had 28 high school students think aloud while solving six algebra problems. For each problem, they identified a sequence of content-defined steps like, "write or state that mixture is 20% anti-freeze now," "compute amount of water at end." The protocols were then coded as sequences of these steps. Nearly all subjects verbalized steps involving restructuring of the information presented and recognizing relations between problem elements. Subjects at higher ability levels showed greater ability to generate logical and physical inferences from the problem statements.

Most of the large-scale analyses of protocols (Flaherty, 1973, 1974; Kantowski, 1974; Kilpatrick, 1968; Webb, 1975) have aimed at identifying general processes rather than encoding heeded information, but they do provide some indirect evidence on pertinence. For example, Kilpatrick (1968) encoded solution attempts in three categories: inference from conditions, setting up equations, and trial and error. He also recorded the results of these attempts and identified errors, including structural errors like retrieval and generation of inconsistent information. Flaherty (1973, 1974), Webb (1975), and Kantowski (1974) extended Kilpatrick's encoding scheme to other problem domains and older subjects. Kilpatrick, Flaherty, and Webb showed that assessments like those described above can be made with high inter-judge reliability. Flaherty and Webb report low frequencies of structural errors, suggesting that verbalizations were consistent. Kilpatrick reports a somewhat higher frequency of structural errors, perhaps because his subjects were less skilled and younger. Flaherty and Kilpatrick report very strong correlations between the score on solutions and the frequency of structural errors, while Webb found a weaker relation of the same kind.

Montgomery and Allwood (1978) showed that subjects' knowledge of definitions required for a task, assessed independently, could predict erroneous solutions. Even in the absence of such differences in knowledge, they found that verbalization of incorrect definitions was associated with incorrect solutions.

In their study of algebra word problems, Paige and Simon (1966) found that verbalizations may be consistent with information in the problem statement, or consistent with prior knowledge, but pertinent in either case. Most subjects verbalized equations that were consistent with the information presented in the problem. However, for one type of situation (physically impossible problems) some subjects systematically reformulated the equation for the problems so that a physically possible solution was created. Evidence for the two types of consistency was obtained from the protocols of subjects who noticed and verbalized the inconsistency and the physical impossibility of the solution.

Retrieval from LTM: Anagrams. Retrieving information from LTM is a component of practically all cognitive processes. In anagram tasks, memory retrieval of the desired word is central, hence these tasks are especially well suited for discussing the general issues involved in LTM retrieval.

In recognizing familiar objects we employ fast processes that generally do not provide reportable intermediate states (see Chapter 3). Recognition is usually highly reliable (i.e., reproducible by repetition of the same stimulus) and the information presented generally determines what will be recognized. Patterns in LTM can often be evoked by very incomplete information. Subjects have no difficulty in responding to a request like, "Name one kind of mammal," with an answer like, "Dogs." Similarly, subjects can rapidly generate "apple" in response to a request like, "Give me a word starting with the letter A." Much research, especially around and just after the turn of the century, searched for inter-subject regularity in these associations and relative frequencies of response. Extensive attempts to identify intermediate internal states through introspection have been largely fruitless. In recognition tasks, the stimulus information will often be insufficient to determine uniquely what LTM structure is evoked. In a subsequent part of this chapter we will return to this discrepancy between input and output in our discussion of claims for unconscious processing.

We can discuss anagrams in the context of these considerations. In order to evoke the desired word it is not generally necessary to generate the complete sequence of letters or phonemes; a subset is often sufficient. In our analysis of verbal protocols for anagram tasks, we will distinguish between verbalization of cues and verbalization of word hypotheses.

Sargent (1940) collected ·anagram-solving protocols with the specific aim of showing how interindividual differences in the solution process could account for the low correlations between ability for solving anagrams at different levels of difficulty. Sargent did not define precisely his assessment criteria nor estimate inter-coder consistency. However, from the published sample of protocols and assessments, these decisions appear relatively straightforward. Sargent judged, for each word hypothesis that subjects generated, whether it was sensitive to the information presented (the stimulus letters). As an example, Sargent judged "slacker" and "climate" as being insensitive to the anagram "SCLIAO." Slow solvers generated "farfetched" associations in only about 20% of the problems, and fast solvers in only about 5%. Sargent reports that fast solvers generated about six hypotheses per minute while slow subjects generated about three.

Mayzner, Tresselt, and Helbock (1964) found from protocols that the word hypotheses their subjects produced were a rather constrained set of all possible letter combinations. In fact, the mean frequency of letter combinations (e.g., digrams) in the word hypotheses was highly correlated with the digram frequency in English, for all serial positions of word hypotheses and for words as well as non-words. These two studies show clearly that the verbalized word hypotheses respond both to the stimulus information and to well-known characteristics of the pattern sought (e.g., its being an English word).

We turn now to analyzing how the cues derived from the stimulus letters lead to evoking the right word. To evaluate the sufficiency of cues, Sargent (1940) identified all the cases where the subject generated and verbalized "good" cues. (Sargent does not provide an explicit definition for "good cues.") The cues might be part of a word hypothesis (e.g.,

SCLIAO → so-call) or a substring of letters (e.g., SCLIAO → SOC). In only about 20% of the cases where fast subjects verbalized "good" cues, they did not then evoke the solution word; for slow subjects, the corresponding number is about 30%.

Sargent, using both thinking-aloud protocols and retrospective reports, distinguished solutions with immediate reorganization, where the solution appeared rapidly within the first couple of seconds and without any prior consideration of letter combinations, from solutions with sudden reorganizations, where the solutions appeared suddenly after some mediating consideration of letter combinations and more than ten seconds after the presentation of the anagram. For each type of solution Sargent (1940) recorded if the subjects reported a cue emerging prior to the solution word. Immediate reorganizations were associated with verbalized cues in around 80% of the cases for the fast subjects and in about 60% for the slow subjects. Cues were reported for sudden reorganizations in about 95% of the cases for fast subjects and in around 85% for the slow. In sum, Sargent (1940) presents overwhelming evidence for the importance of useful cues in accessing solutions for anagrams, and for the pertinence of the verbalizations of these cues.

Concept Attainment. The majority of studies collecting thinking-aloud protocols during concept-attainment experiments have been interested primarily in building complete models that can regenerate the subjects' performance (Laughery & Gregg, 1962; Huesmann & Cheng, 1973; Johnson, 1964; Newsted, 1971). In these analyses of protocols, no clear line is drawn between theoretical assumptions and verbalized information. We will direct our own discussion to ways of evaluating relevance and consistency without making controversial theoretical assumptions about the protocol data. Moreover, the only components of the protocols we will consider are verbalized hypotheses that subjects propose about the concept they are seeking.

The question of consistency involves three kinds of relations. First, there are relations between the exemplars presented as stimuli and the hypotheses generated by subjects. The evidence actually presented to the subject contains much less information than is logically required to determine the correct hypothesis. The process of forming a hypothesis draws on information beyond the immediate stimulus. Second, there are the relations between hypotheses held by subjects and their predictions of whether a new instance is or is not an exemplar of the concept. These straightforward relations do not require further discussion. Third, there are the feedback relations from the predictions made on given trials to the decisions to retain hypotheses or generate new ones. (It is usually assumed, on logical grounds, that subjects will retain their hypotheses if they are confirmed, and reject them if they are not.)

Few concept attainment experiments have used standard think-aloud instructions, Karpf (1973) being the principal exception. Other studies, however, have required subjects to state their rules or justifications for their decisions. No differences have been found between studies that employed such probes and those that did not (Brehmer, 1974; Karpf & Levine, 1971). Variations in instructions ("guess" versus "state") do not affect performance, but do affect what information is verbalized (Wilson, 1974). These results are exactly what we would expect if the information verbalized in response to the probe was already available in STM.

Let us turn now to the relation between the verbalized hypotheses and the previously presented instances. Cahill and Hovland (1960) and Bourne, Goldstein, and Link (1964) have shown that the rules subjects announce are consistent with the most recent, still visible, item presented to them, but that the probability of inconsistency with previous items increases with the lag. These inconsistencies between hypotheses and previously presented stimuli can be greatly reduced or even eliminated by leaving the items in view. Coltheart (1971) has shown that subjects have little memory, as measured by recognition and recall, for the items presented, but excellent memory for the hypotheses they have generated. This finding can account for their generation of hypotheses inconsistent with earlier stimuli. Incomplete memory for earlier stimuli and hypotheses can also account for the increased probability of inconsistency with longer presentation lag.

The relation between verbalized hypotheses and subjects' predictions for specific instances has been given considerable experimental attention because of its importance for claims of the pertinence of verbalizations. We have already alluded to some of these experiments in discussing learning without awareness in Chapter 3. Karpf (1973) found that, when single hypotheses were encoded from the thinking aloud protocols, the subsequent choices were consistent with the hypothesis in 99% of the trials. When subjects were probed for their hypotheses on each trial, Karpf and Levine (1971) also found that the predictions were consistent with the verbalized hypotheses in 99% of the cases. Schwartz (1966) found that in only 2 out of 1,962 trials did the subjects not place cards according to their verbalized hypotheses.

Frankel, Levine, and Karpf (1970) asked subjects about their hypotheses during four problems, each involving 30 non-feedback trials. Independently, the hypotheses were inferred from their choices on the trials. In 77 of the 79 cases where a hypothesis was consistent with all the choices, it was identical with the hypothesis reported by the subject, and only in one case was there a difference. In the remaining cases, where no single hypothesis was consistent with all 30 responses, the subjects reported in 97% of the cases a simple hypothesis that was consistent except for one or a few errors. In some of these cases subjects even reported making errors in applying their hypothesis.

Coltheart (1971) found that of 114 hypotheses recalled by subjects only 15 did not correspond to hypotheses inferred from sequences of non-feedback trials. Of these 15, 11 could be accounted for by inadvertent errors in applying hypotheses, thus suggesting correct recall in 96% of the cases. In cue-probability learning, rules verbalized by subjects correspond well with the rules determined from regression analysis of subjects' responses (Brehmer, 1974; Brehmer, Kylenstierna, & Liljegren, 1974, 1975). The correspondence was even better when their rules were predicted by an observer from a graph of their choices.

In the experiments we have been describing, no new information about the correct hypothesis is conveyed to the subject by the mere presentation of an instance to be predicted. However, in the early experiments on concept attainment (e.g., Heidbreder, 1924), where subjects were not informed in advance about the population of stimuli, a new instance could display new features and make earlier hypotheses inappropriate. Moreover, although subjects rarely change their hypotheses after a correct choice, it is not necessarily illogical for them to do so, since more than one hypothesis may be consistent with preceding exemplars.

Keeping these points in mind, we now review evidence for subjects' retaining hypotheses on trials in which they receive positive feedback, and changing hypotheses when they receive disconfirming feedback. Disconfirming feedback appears to lead consistently to change in hypothesis. From his think-aloud protocols, Karpf (1973) found that subjects changed their hypotheses with negative feedback in 97% of the cases. Using probes, Karpf and Levine (1971) found changes in 98% of the cases. Schwartz (1966) found changes in all but 2 of over 1,900 cases. From retrospective reports, Heidbreder (1924) found that the current hypothesis was rejected in 89% of the cases of negative feedback. A further analysis of the deviant cases showed that, in about one fourth the subjects felt that their prediction was incorrectly generated from their hypothesis, and in half of the cases, the subjects felt unable to generate a better hypothesis, although they knew their current one was incorrect.

As would be expected, subjects' behavior is less consistent in the case of confirming feedback. Karpf (1973) found from his think-aloud protocols that the subjects retained their hypotheses in 97% of the cases where feedback was positive. Karpf and Levine (1971) found no change in 94% of the cases. Without feedback, Frankel, Levine, and Karpf (1970) found that subjects retained their hypotheses in more than 90% of the cases. In all these studies, the subjects were instructed to use simple disjunctive hypotheses and knew about the relevant attributes.

On the other hand, Schwartz (1966) found that hypotheses were retained only in 50% to 85% of the cases with positive feedback. Likewise, Heidbreder (1924) found that hypotheses were retained only 62% of the time. But Heidbreder's subjects were not informed prior to the experiment about the relevant stimulus features, while Schwartz asked his subjects to guess the rule, even when they felt uncertain. Wilson (1974), comparing subjects' responses when asked to "guess" or to "state," respectively, what the concept was, found that "guesses" were more complex and less closely related to the information presented than "statements." This suggests that an instruction to guess might influence subjects to go beyond the information about which they were confident, and thus increase the frequency with which they would change their hypotheses. From her retrospective reports, Heidbreder (1924) inferred the reason for changing hypotheses after confirming feedback. In more than one third of the cases, the subjects faced stimuli with new attributes, different from those on which their earlier hypotheses were based. The subjects reported that new and earlier heeded hypotheses occurred to them in about half the cases. Some changes corresponded to generalizations and simplifications of the current hypothesis.

All of the studies we have just reviewed contain strong evidence that verbalizations of hypotheses in concept attainment experiments are consistent with the subjects' responses to instances, and hence that these verbalizations are pertinent to the ongoing problem-solving processes.

MEMORY AS EVIDENCE FOR HEEDING

We discussed earlier the assertion that instructions to heed information will lead to retrievable memory for a subset of that information. Here we will reverse the argument and claim that if information is recalled from memory then it must have been heeded. This implies that a model accounting for retrospective reports must also account for the original storage and the recall of the information in the reports. Information retrievable from LTM when requested by instruction should also be available to the subject when found useful in other situations. In these cases it seems unlikely that the stored information would be epiphenomenal in relation to the processes going on when it was stored.

Alternative Models and Processes

Unlike memory for externally presented information, demonstration of memory for thoughts is far from trivial. Ability to regenerate, on separate occasions, the intermediate sums in a mental multiplication, given memory for the numbers to be multiplied, is not evidence for memory of those sums—they might be recalculated on each occasion. However, if the sums could be recalled without memory for the numbers to be multiplied, memory for the sums would be demonstrated.

Tasks, like memorizing for subsequent recall or generating free associations, impose hardly any constraints. Hence, we are unable to place any a priori delimitations on the relevance of thoughts. If a subject reports that in memorizing the paired-associate COW-BALL he was thinking of a cow kicking a ball, there is no direct way to validate that he actually had such thoughts. Our model, however, predicts that the mnemonic, as heeded information, will often be stored along with the stimulus words in LTM, and should usually be retrievable and reportable when the response word is accessed.

Most studies of mnemonic encodings have relied on retrospective reports. With such data, it is hard to refute the hypothesis that the mnemonic was actually generated at the time of the later recall. If we could show that the *same* mnemonmic that was used at presentation was retrieved at the time of recall, we could rule out that possibility. Let us review the experimental evidence on this point.

Montague, Adams, and Kiess (1966) gave their subjects 15 or 30 seconds to write down mnemonic codings for items in a series of 96 CVC pairs. If the subjects did not record a mnemonic encoding, the corresponding item was classifed as learned by rote. A day later, the subjects were asked to recall the response CVC and the mnemonic coding they had generated. When the same mnemonic was recalled as had been recorded originally, the CVCs were recalled correctly in 72% of the cases, but in only 2% when a different mnemonic was recalled. The latter score was slightly worse than the score for items learned by rote (i.e., without a mnemonic encoding recorded). Similarly, Boersma, Conklin, and Carlson (1966) found remarkable agreement among successive reports of mnemonic encodings—93% agreement after a 20-minute delay, and 83% after seven days.

This evidence does not guarantee that the mnemonic encoding, at the time of recall, is not generated from the CVC response, rather than being recalled from LTM. However, if the mnemonic is reported in cases where the correct CVC response is not produced, this indirect process is ruled out. Montague et al. (1966) found that for paired associates with reported menmonic encodings, the subjects recalled the encodings in 26% of the cases, while the response CVCs were only recalled in 20% of the cases. Hence, in one-fourth of the cases the mnemonic encoding was recalled correctly without access to the correct response word. A similar result was obtained by Kiess (Montague, 1972) for a brief interval between presentation and recall. He found that probability of recall of the mnemonic encodings was 97%, and in the remaining 3% of the cases, recall of the response words was no better than chance.

INFERENCES FROM VERBAL REPORTS

High-level encoding of verbal information, particularly encoding that abstracts from the substantive content of the protocols, can only be carried out if we make certain basic assumptions about human information processing. The fundamental assumption is that any cognitive process can be described in terms of the sequence of information processes that are attended to during its course. Information is brought into STM in a strictly sequential manner by information processes driven by information in STM and externally presented information.

A second assumption is that attending to information takes time. Where just previously heeded information is prerequisite for accessing or generating the currently heeded information, we assume that the time interval between these two acts of attention corresponds to the time taken by the corresponding information process. It follows that, if A and AB are two sequences of heeded information, with AB including A, the latency in reporting AB will be longer than the latency in reporting A alone.

The third assumption is that the number of symbols that can be heeded and held in STM simultaneously is severely limited, and independent of the particular content and type of information. The amount of information that subjects can hold in STM will therefore be a direct function of how much information they can encode in single symbol (*chunk*). This assumption allows us to abstract from the verbalized information the maximum number of different patterns or chunks into which it is encoded.

In the following sections we show how, on the basis of these assumptions, inferences about LTM can be drawn from verbal reports. First, we will consider inferences about LTM structures, including images, then predictions of episodic memory, and finally, predictions of latencies.

Identification of LTM Structures

We discuss first some experimental evidence on the structure of LTM chunks that does not rely directly on verbal reports to demonstrate the limited capacity of STM. These experiments involve situations where the nature of the chunks, or familiar units, available to subjects can be estimated a priori. For example, "apple" and all other familiar words are single chunks; so is a familiar saying like, "A bird in the hand is worth two in the bush."

In his classic paper, "The Magical Number Seven Plus or Minus Two," Miller (1956) showed that STM capacity was to be measured in terms of numbers of such familiar units, or chunks. By practicing recoding triplets of 0's and 1's into octal numbers, his subject increased his memory span 40 binary numbers while the number of recoded octal numbers remained virtually constant, but that the chunks in LTM denoted by these symbols may be almost arbitrarily large. The experiment suggests that the maximal number of symbols in STM, whether coded in binary or octal form, remains constant. Simon (1974) explored this hypothesis further. Relying on a single subject, he showed that the memory span for words was essentially independent of the numbers of letters and syllables, and the memory for familiar phrases like, "Four score and seven years ago," was nearly as great as for single words or unrelated letters.

Ericsson, Chase, and Faloon (1980) found that digits in a memory span task were grouped in the same way in retrospective reports as when the groupings were assessed by a coder listening to intonational patterns and pauses occurring during the recall of the digits.

In a review of the literature on exceptional memory and large memory spans for digits, Chase and Ericsson (1981) examined all cases where subjects had given retrospective reports from their thoughts during the digit-span task. All subjects with exceptional digit spans reported grouping the presented digits in groups of 3 to 5 digits. These groups were, in turn, related to multi-digit patterns already present in LTM. These data showed that even these exceptional people could not hold more than three to four chunks, familiar LTM structures, in STM simultaneously. In a series of experiments, Chase and Ericsson (1981) tested the validity of a single subject's reports of forming groups of digits and mnemonic associations to digit groups. The verbal reports in all of these studies give rich evidence of how information is chunked and otherwise structured in LTM.

Glanzer and Clark (1963a,1963b) presented visual symbols to subjects (strings of 0's and 1's) and asked them to describe the strings. They found the mean number of words generated for a given stimulus to be highly reliable over different groups of subjects. This does not imply that the subjects coded the strings verbally, but simply that simpler patterns were consistently describable in fewer words.

Using complex patterns of black and white objects (Glanzer & Clark, 1963a), binary numbers (Glanzer & Clark, 1963b), and conventional line drawings (Glanzer & Clark, 1964), Glanzer and Clark found subjects' ability to reproduce the stimuli after brief exposure to be strongly correlated (negatively) with the mean number of words used by a different group of subjects to describe these stimuli. Glanzer and Clark (1964) extended their results also to more complex schematic drawings.

Earlier, Fehrer (1935) had obtained a measure of the difficulty of reproducing a number of different figures after a brief exposure. For a subset of these figures, Glanzer and Clark (1964) had subjects write complete descriptions, whose sufficiency was tested by having the subjects reproduce the drawings from a selection of their descriptions. The mean number of words in these descriptions was highly correlated ($r = .8$) with Fehrer's assessed difficulty in reproducing the same figures. Glanzer and Clark also had subjects rate the anticipated difficulty of reproducing the figures, finding these ratings to be slightly less highly correlated with the actual difficulty of reproduction than was the length of the descriptions. In all of these studies of stimulus complexity, subjects' verbalizations are predictive of other measures of complexity of the information stored in LTM.

A long series of studies has explored the relation between reported imagery types and performance on maze learning tasks. In one series of studies (Cox, 1928; Husband, 1928, 1931; Perrin, 1914; Scott, 1930; Warden, 1924), retrospective reports indicated that different subjects relied on different types of information, the differences perhaps being related, it has been suggested, to types of imagery. Several of these investigators have been able to relate the assessed imagery type (verbal vs. motor vs. visual) to large differences in errors to solution. Warden, for example, suggests that a verbal code is associated with explicit counting (e.g., encoding a maze as "one right, two left, three right"), while spatial representation is associated with trial and error solution.

In early assessments of imagery type, subjects were often probed for the modality of their cognitive activity, rather than its content (Fernald, 1912; Davies, 1932). Correlations were found between imagery type and the relative difficulty of mazes of different structure (Warden, 1924). Additional support was obtained for the verbal-spatial distinction when subjects sketched their solutions on paper. However, there is more direct evidence that differences in imagery types may not correspond to differences in the strategies employed. Subjects tend to convert to verbal coding as a result of practice (Husband, 1928; Scott, 1930), and imagery types are strongly correlated with general intelligence (Warden, 1924; Scott, 1930).

Even with these qualifications, subjects were able to provide considerable information, correlated with performance, about the methods they had used. Warden (1924) distinguished three methods from subjects reports: verbal (encoding the direction and order of turns as verbal symbols), visual (imaging the maze), and motor (relying on kinesthetic "feel" for direction). According to Warden's analysis, subjects mainly use the first two methods. Subjects relying on visual images almost invariably reported using one of the other two methods as well. The performance differences between subjects reporting using the different methods were striking. Subjects using the motor method were *all* worse than *all* of the subjects using the verbal method. On the average, the motor subjects required four times as many trials to learn the maze to criterion as did the verbal subjects.

Warden (1924) showed that the reported methods accounted for many other interesting differences between the two groups of subjects. For example, when subjects were asked to reproduce the maze on paper, over 75% of the motor subjects reproduced the maze without any angular turns (see Figure 4-1, Exhibit B), while the remaining motor subjects depicted only a small number of turns. All of the verbal subjects reproduced the maze with angular turns (Figure 4-1, Exhibit A), and about 80% of them protrayed most of the turns in the actual maze. Performance of the visual subjects was intermediate between the other two. Another observation was that the motor subjects had much more difficulty in learning *where* to change direction in the maze. At the point of change, motor subjects made many more errors than verbal subjects, whereas other kinds of errors were made with about the same frequency. Visual subjects were again intermediate.

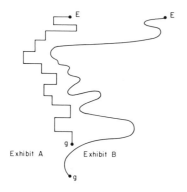

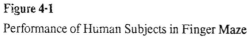

Figure 4-1
Performance of Human Subjects in Finger Maze

From a careful analysis of the verbal reports we are thus able to understand the performance differences, originally attributed to inherent "imagery types" of subjects, in terms of the LTM encodings and representations they used.

LTM Traces as a Function of STM Patterns

If episodic memory in LTM is a subset of information that was attended to, then we should be able to predict the structure of the memory trace in LTM whenever we can identify the patterns heeded in STM. In this subsection we will discuss some attempts at predictions of retrievability on the basis of assessed *structural* properties of the LTM trace. Note that these predictions involve abstraction from the specifics of the information.

We return to the topic of mnemonic encodings in learning non-sense syllables. The following analysis rests on the assumption that at the time of recall, the mnemonic asociation is retrieved first and the required response is retrieved from it. From this assumption it follows that the more closely related the stimulus and the mnemonic coding, the easier the retrieval process and the more accurate the recall.

We can use the results of early studies as evidence against the epiphenomenality of verbally reported natural language mediators (NLM)—mnemonic codes using linguistic patterns and units. If we can show that the retrieved NLM is a familiar chunk in LTM (a single word or word combination) and overlaps with the letters or phonemes of stimulus and response, then a claim of epiphenomenality is highly implausible.

Mattock (Underwood & Schultz, 1960) found that 86% of the reported NLMs could be seen as generated in a single step from the stimulus. Bugelski (1962) found that over 70% of the NLMs in his experiment were encoded as single words or meaningful word combinations (e.g., "jacket" for GAC-QET, or "says man" for CEZ-MON).

Schaub and Lindley (1964) compared the associations given to high- and low-meaningful trigrams. For the former, subjects in over 90% of the cases generated a single word, usually employing the trigram letters in corresponding locations (e.g., "honey" for HON). For the low-meaningful trigrams, the subjects generated a single word in less than half the cases (45.5%). Further, these latter associations rarely used letters corresponding to those in the trigrams.

In a short-term memory experiment with consonant trigrams, Groninger (1966) found that success in recall was very different for trigrams with high and low association values. He also found that very different NLMs were reported for the two types of trigrams. The NLMs for trigrams with high association values were primarily single words; trigrams with low association values were generally treated as acronyms. In cases where no NLM was reported, there was essentially no difference in recall between trigrams of high and low association value; while for trigrams with reported NLMs there was a clear difference.

At least two major attempts have been made to analyze the structure of more complex NLMs. In a study by Martin, Boersma, and Cox (1965), seven different association strategies could be assessed reliably from subjects' retrospective reports on how they formed the associations of each pair. The strategies were ordered by complexity from no associations and simple rehearsal to embedding elements of the stimulus in syntactical structures and sentences. This ordering by complexity was monotonically related to the probability of correct recall. In a study by Montague and Wearing (1967), a (negative) relation between complexity of strategies and number of errors in recall was also found. The failure of Boersma et al. (1966) to replicate the relations found in Martin et al. (1965) was attributed by the former authors to the use of a different type of stimulus and procedure. Hence, we need to analyze the nature of the relation between the complexity of the encodings and the recall accuracy in more detail to be able to reconcile these findings.

We believe that the complexity variable studied by Martin and his colleagues can be understood in terms of the relations among NLM and stimulus and response words. More overlap between stimulus and NLM and between NLM and response·would facilitate recall, and the opportunities for overlap grow with the complexity of the NLM. Montague (1972) interprets the results in a similar way.

Probably the most ambitious and formal effort to relate reported NLMs with stimuli is that of Prytulak (1971). He defined a set of transformations that would regenerate the stimulus word from the NLM, and that would show how the NLM could be accessed from the whole or part of the CVC (e.g., from "wonder" we get "wond" by deletion of suffix, and then "WOD" by deletion of consonant). Using his formal system of transformations, Prytulak assessed how many transformations were required to regenerate each CVC from the NLM reported by a subject. He found a strong correlation between the number of assessed operations and failure to recall.

In sum, we can differentiate two notions of complexity. A mnemonic encoding is "subjectively" complex if it corresponds to several pre-existing patterns (chunks) in LTM to be merged into a new memory trace. Probability of recalling the complete mnemonic encoding and then the response will be a function of the number of components (i.e., complexity of the mnemonic encoding). Notice that a subject may be able to access a single pre-existing pattern in LTM that will be formally as complex as one generated by merging many components in LTM. On the other hand, "objective" complexity of the encoding or the amount of information embodied in the mnemonic encoding will facilitate recall and/or reconstruction of the response in so far as the associational relation or overlap is strong.

Predictions of Latencies

Information processes operate on the information in one state to generate or access information from LTM, which is used, in turn, to generate the succeeding state. For many tasks, a combination of task analysis and analysis of data permits the sequence of cognitive processes executed in the task to be specified. Such a model can predict the sequence that will be followed for all tasks within a given class. For different classes of tasks, the model will predict different sequences of processes. If we know the processing sequence, hence the successive contents of STM, we should be able to predict what information subjects can report, either concurrently or retrospectively. Such a model also allows us to make predictions about latencies for problem types. For processes corresponding to identical sequences of processes, we can pool latencies and calculate averages.

It is by no means obvious that different subjects will execute the same sequences of cognitive processes on a given task. Two things might cause them to do so. First, analysis of the task may show that only a unique sequence, or a small number of similar sequences, will lead to solution. Hence, behavior may be strongly constrained by the task demands. Second, in many tasks that have been studied (e.g., mathematics and language), subjects have had prior formal and informal training, and may as a result represent the relevant information in highly similar ways. Even in tasks where they have not had previous training, subjects are usually given some preliminary experience during practice trials, when they can search for efficient ways of doing the task.

We turn first to comparisons of latencies between processes of the form A and AB, respectively (i.e., where the longer process is inclusive of the shorter). There are a few studies, although some of them are methodologically flawed, that test such a relation between verbalizations and latencies. May (1917) collected retrospective reports of directed associations (e.g., "clock, part of"), and found that the mean latencies of trials in which subjects reported no intermediate states were shorter than latencies of trials where subjects reported they had rejected inadequate associations or had used images (p. 41). A relation has also been observed by, for example, Metcalf (1917), between uncertainty, hesitations, or conflicts and response latency among subjects copying visually presented figures, and by Heidbreder (1928) in concept formation.

A study by Hamilton and Sanford (1978) on alphabetic order judgments is a particularly nice example of how retrospective reports can be used to understand the underlying process mechanisms. In this task subjects are presented with a pair of letters and asked to respond "yes" if they are in the correct alphabetic order (i.e., P-S), and "no" if they are not, (i.e., O-M). For a wide range of such order judgments involving digits, alphabet, etc., latencies are found to be longer the closer the two items are in the list (the symbolic distance effect) (Hamilton & Sanford, 1978). Beyond recording latencies for alphabetic order judgments Hamilton and Sanford asked for a report of cognitive processes after each trial. A traditional analysis of the relation between latency and the number of separating letters yielded the usual symbolic distance effect.

In their retrospective reports, the subjects either reported that the answer was automatic or that they searched through a sequence of letters before giving the answer. For example, given M-O subjects may not start with the first letter but instead run through LMNO, and for R-P they may retrieve RSTUV. The authors found evidence that the alphabet was often accessed in groups of letters—like (ABCDEFG), (HIJK), (LMNOP), (QRST), (UVW), (XYZ)—in consonance with other studies of the memory organization of the alphabet.

From the retrospective reports, remarkably strong and interesting predictions of latencies were made. For reports of automatic judgments a constant short latency was observed that was independent of separation of the letters. The longer latencies, where sequences of letters were evoked and reported retrospectively, were a linear function of the number of letters reported. The estimated rate for heeding letters was 3 letters/sec, which is consonant with other estimates of search rates. According to this analysis, the symbolic distance effect is a result of the increased probability of search when two letters are located near each other in the alphabet.

In recent analyses of latencies, retrospective reports have rarely been collected. However, in a few cases, we can match retrospective reports from studies where no latencies were collected studies collecting to latencies without retrospective reports. Klahr (1973) discriminated subitizing (direct perception of the number of objects in a set) from counting by analyzing mean latencies of response to sets of different sizes. For a similar task with fixed tachistoscopic presentation of fixed duration, Oberly (1924) had discriminated three types of cognitive processes from the retrospective reports of his subjects. Two of the processes, immediate perception and counting, match directly the processes identified by Klahr, while the third (grouping) may have been determined by the tachistoscopic presentation.

Meudell (1971) found very similar verbal reports and patterns of response latencies, when he asked subjects "How many window panes are there in your living room?" Subjects reported that they rapidly generated a visual image and then counted the number of panes if there were more than about five of them. A regression-analysis of the latencies gave strong support for such a sequence of cognitive processes. The slightly poorer fit to subjects reporting a large number of window panes may be accounted for by multiple image generation of separate windows or longer times for generation of complex images.

If the same cognitive process is executed again and again, as in counting, the latency would be a function of the number of times the process was executed. From verbal reports we can often determine this number directly from the number of reported intermediate states. Akin and Chase (Chase, 1978) collected both reaction times and retrospective reports on how subjects determined the number of blocks in a visually presented block arrangement. The number of configurations or groups of blocks for which the subjects could assess the number of blocks directly was found to be a much more accurate predictor of the reaction time than the actual number of blocks in the arrangement.

In an experiment by Snygg (1935), subjects were asked to cancel those figures on a sheet that corresponded to one or another of five specified shapes. Striking differences in performance time correlated with the subjects' retrospectively reported representation of the cancellation rule (e.g., "cancel all figures with curved lines" versus "cancel three circles and an oval" versus trials on which subjects did not report any encoding of the figures to be canceled). This result would follow from the assumption that search for more patterns requires more tests.

There are a couple of studies containing retrospective reports from subjects in STM and LTM tasks. Anders and Lillyquist (1971) recorded the time to report back digits in digit-span tasks, with instructions to report them back in the presented order (forward recall) or in the reverse order (backward recall). Subjects reported that forward recall involved simple read-out of all of the presented digits, whereas backward recall required recalling the last group of two or three digits (only part of the presented digits) and reading out these digits in backward order, then recalling the next previous group and so on. The much slower recall in backward order was due to the time-consuming recall of digit groups, for the readout of digits in backward order was almost instantaneous.

In a study of memorization and recall of a digit-matrix (5x5 digits), Ericsson and Chase (1982) found a very high correspondence between the reported sequence of recall processes and the latency of recall. Practiced as well as naive subjects reported committing the matrices to memory by forming encodings of all digits in a row and then associating the rows together. During the subsequent recall the subjects were asked the digits in the matrix in several different orders (e.g., by rows (forward and backward), by columns starting at the top or at the bottom). The subjects reported that it was time-consuming to recall a row, but once recalled, the digits could be reported rapidly.

The observed latencies of recall with the different recall instructions confirmed the verbally reported sequence of processes. The forward recall was performed at a steady and rapid rate. When the recall latencies were averaged over subjects and trials, the backward recall was done at a much slower, yet steady, rate. However, when the recall latencies in the backward recall condition were analyzed for a single subject who consistently grouped the incoming digits in pairs, the verbally reported pattern of latencies were found. This subject had long pauses between groups (around a second) and brief pauses between digits within a group (around 1/5 second), the latter corresponding to her rate of recall in the forward condition. Most other subjects were variable in their grouping decisions, yet the particular groups used on an individual trial could mostly be identified on the basis of the longer between-group pauses when a new row had to be retrieved. This relation was equally strong for practiced and novice subjects.

Most of the tasks discussed above are done very rapidly, so that the verbal reports have almost always been gathered retrospectively. Several studies have been concerned with more complex problems, where solutions take longer, yet still exhibit a predictable and invariant sequence of processes for a given problem. Mental multiplication is such a task.

Dansereau and Gregg (1966) instructed a subject to verbalize each step while multiplying two multi-digit numbers mentally. The additional task of verbalizing did not change response latencies as compared with silent performance of the same tasks (for a more complete discussion, see Chapter 2). A simple regression model, based on the number of steps required for doing the same problem with pencil and paper, predicted the response latencies for both the verbalizing and silent conditions.

Using a more detailed model of the multiplication process, Dansereau (1969) was able to predict not only total solution times but also most of the times for intermediate stages for the different kinds of problems. A further important validation of the verbal reports comes from cases where subjects reported using shortcuts to solve the problems.

The latencies of such solutions were predictably different from solutions to the same problems using the "normal" procedure.

Problem Behavior Graphs

In some cases processing models have been specified even in cases where not all subjects use the same sequences of processes, and where the sequence is not uniquely determined by task analysis. Often the sequence actually used is determined by detailed analysis of a small number of TA protocols.

Perhaps the most influential coding technique of this kind is the Problem Behavior Graph (PBG) (Newell, 1966, 1968; Newell & Simon, 1972). The analysis assumes that the subject solves the problem by searching through one or more problem spaces (i.e., sets of alternative states of knowledge). With each transition between states is associated an operator (a process that generates or transforms knowledge). By careful task analysis, a small number of alternative problem spaces can be proposed. Analysis of a subject's protocol, statement by statement, reveals in which of these problem states (if any) he is operating. "The key constraint is that all changes in the knowledge state (as defined for the problem space) that are detectable in the protocol must come about through one of the operators of the problem space." (Newell, 1966, p. 34)

The ambiguity and incompleteness of a protocol may make the determination of the subject's problem space difficult (Newell & Simon, 1972). Nevertheless, protocols have been encoded in terms of PBGs for a wide range of tasks, including propositional logic (Newell & Simon, 1972), cryptarithmetic (Newell & Simon, 1972), chess (Newell & Simon, 1972; Wagner & Scurrah, 1971), Missionaries and Cannibals (Newell, 1966), mental imagery (Baylor, 1973), N-term series problems (Ohlsson, 1980), analysis of financial statements (Bouwman, 1980), and others.

Complementing most of these analyses, computer models were constructed that regenerate more or less well the relevant information in the protocol. These analyses provide strong evidence that verbalized protocols correspond closely with the information that has to be considered for generating problem solutions. They also show that the verbalized information can be mapped onto a process model that is *sufficient* for generating the solution from the presented information. There are many examples of such comparisons between computer models and protocols. In addition to the studies we have mentioned elsewhere, we would like to point to an analysis of human move selection in Chinese checkers by Anzai (1977), an analysis of how job candidates are selected for different jobs, by Smith and Greenlaw (1967), and an analysis of how maladjustment is assessed from MMPI data, by Kleinmuntz (1963).

At the level of detail of the PBG, we can expect to encounter significant interpersonal differences in processing. This makes it difficult to use a single computer model to predict or account for the detail of numbers of different protocols. This doesn't mean, of course, that these models are incorrect, but rather, that at the level of detail they capture, we cannot always generalize across individuals. This is an important finding about behavior and about the forms we can expect psychological laws to take, and it leads us to a closer consideration of the problem of generalization.

GENERALIZATIONS ABOUT COGNITIVE PROCESSES

Stimuli do not determine responses uniquely, independently of context and of the contents of a subject's LTM. If problems admit of alternative solution paths, we will not expect all subjects to follow the same path.

Buswell (1956) asked college and high-school students to compute the answer to problems like the following:

Problem A: If 15 hens lay 5 eggs per week for 4 weeks, what is the
               total value of the eggs at 6 cents each?

Problem B: At 60 cents per hour find the total earnings of 12 boys
               if they worked 8 hours per day for 5 days.

When Buswell recorded the sequences of multiplications 101 high-school students used to generate the answers, he found that 76% selected a particular sequence for problem A, but for problem B, only 21% selected the most popular sequence, and four different sequences were selected with almost equal frequency. Essentially the same results were obtained with a larger sample of 233 college students. For a more complex word problem, Buswell constructed a decision tree corresponding to the different solution paths. Only a few subjects (about 10%) selected the most frequently chosen solution path. A fairly large number of paths was chosen by one or more subject, yet these paths constituted only a small fraction of the possible paths.

Ericsson (1975a) studied subjects solving a sliding block puzzle (the Eight Puzzle). Subjects' solutions were described as ordered sequences of moves. The similarity of move sequences among subjects starting from the same puzzle configuration was no greater than would be predicted by chance. Moreover, the solutions of each individual subject to repetitions of the same problem were no closer than would be predicted by chance. Hence, no single model could be expected to predict the exact sequences. However, when the solutions were analyzed at a more abstract level (in terms of the attainment of certain specified configurations of tiles), most subjects followed the same orderly and predictable sequence. The same special configurations (subgoals) were attained by most subjects for most of the different problems in the same order.

Karat (1982) analyzed consecutive solutions to a 5-disk version of the Tower of Hanoi problem. Subjects who did not find a minimum-path solution exhibited no systematic similarities between their consecutive solutions.

When we present a subject with a complex task description or a picture, we cannot generally predict in detail what the subject will recognize or attend to. Recognition and retrieval processes are determined in part by information in LTM, because the information in STM is not sufficiently specific to determine a unique product of recognition and retrieval. This is especially true when the subject perceives a large number of equally acceptable alternatives, like the alternative moves facing a novice chess player.

From this it follows that we will be more likely to be able to make class predictions than unique predictions. We can often predict that the subsequently heeded information or behavior will be drawn from a specified class, where the classes constitute only a small fraction of logically or theoretically possible behaviors or information. Consider the problems posed by Buswell (1956). Each could be solved by taking up four multiplicands in any order, and performing the multiplications. Hence, there are 4! = 24 admissible sequences, all leading to the same solution, and we might expect almost any of these—but no others—to occur.

When it is impossible to predict each step in a sequence with certainty, it becomes far more difficult, of course, to predict the whole sequence. Hence, in fitting behavioral and verbal data to models, we will usually do well to make *conditional* predictions, that is, predictions of each action as a function of the information in STM just before the action was taken. Even such predictions, as we have seen, may succeed only in a probabilistic sense.

Often, we can discover, and then predict, how stimuli will be represented internally by comparing the verbalizations produced when the stimuli are presented in different formats or with different content. For some classes of problems we may also be able to predict the order in which certain kinds of information will be heeded. In these situations, we can view the verbalizations as the dependent variables. Combining these two kinds of prediction, we can determine the STM structures that mediate between stimulus and response.

Model-Based Coding

When prediction is guided by a model, the model identifies relevant information that will be heeded. No attempt is made to deal with all the verbalizations in the protocol. In a coding system proposed by Ericsson (1975b), the coding categories were selected with a model of the verbalization process in mind, similar to the one that has just been sketched out. The coded statements thus represented internal information structures that (according to the model) were heeded. The coding system distinguished four types of statements:

1. **Intentions.** Information representing goals and future states of the subject, easily recognized by verbs of the type, "shall," "will," "must," "have to," and so on.

2. **Cognitions.** Information based on attention to selected aspects of the current situation, easily recognized by constructions indicating presence and immediacy.

3. **Planning.** Information representing intermediate constructions to explore sequences of possibilities mentally, easily recognized by conditional constructions like, "if X then Y and if Z ..."

4. **Evaluations.** Explicit or implicit comparisons of alternatives, easily identified by key words like "no," "yes," "dammit," "fine," and so on.

In such coding schemes, ambiguity can be handled by omitting ambiguous statements or, alternatively (Ericsson, 1975b), by defining decision procedures for making the assessments in ambiguous situations. Carried to the limit, such procedures could make automatic or semi-automatic coding possible.

In his study of problem solving with the Eight Puzzle (Ericsson, 1975b), subjects' verbalized intentions to attain particular configurations of tiles were encoded as described previously. In general, any given configuration can be achieved via different sequences of moves. The strongest prediction is that the subject will choose his move sequence from this set. The set of admissible (efficient) move sequences was then generated, and the actual move sequence matched against it. The analysis showed that subjects followed admissible sequences with few exceptions. Most of the exceptions occurred when a subject rejected an earlier verbalized intention before the goal was attained, and these rejections were accompanied by verbalizations of new intentions to achieve a different configuration, or by verbalized negative evaluations of the original intention.

In the same study, the verbalized cognitions and intentions were analyzed to determine how goals were characterized, by examining each segment that referred to the relation between two or more tiles. In Figure 4-2, showing the goal-configuration of the Eight Puzzle, we have marked logically useful relations between adjacent tiles. From a task analysis it is clear that relations within a column are as important and useful (i.e., the sequential relations between the 1-4 and 4-7 and 1-4-7) as the corresponding relations within a row (i.e., sequential relation 1-2 and 2-3 and 1-2-3). However, from Figure 4-2 it is clear that subjects only mention a small fraction of the logically conceivable goals and intentions. The relations that were verbalized all belong to the linear sequence 1-2-3-4-5-6-7-8, which was the hypothesized representation of the goal configuration for all subjects. The fact that subjects tried to achieve these sequential relations by putting these corresponding tiles in their final position could be inferred from the actual move sequences of another group of subjects (Ericsson, 1975a).

Montgomery (1977) explored the inconsistency and intransitivity of choices between gambles that had been demonstrated by Tversky (1969). The study was essentially a replication of Tversky's, except that the subjects were instructed to think aloud. Since most of the protocol statements referred to gambles and relations between pairs of gambles, Montgomery proposed a coding scheme with nine categories based on the nature of the comparisons and perceived differences between the gambles, and the dimension (i.e., pay-off or probability) to which the statements referred.

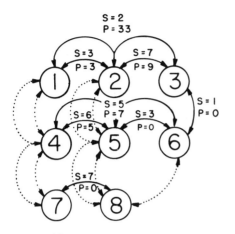

Figure 4-2

The pooled frequencies of expressed intentions to attain certain Seq (X,Y), Seq (X,Y,Z), Place (X,Y), and Place (X,Y,Z) relations are marked on the arcs joining the numbers of the associated tiles, with an S for Seq and a P for Place. Arcs without any recorded occurrences are dotted.

Examples of coding categories were *implicit comparison* ("I'll choose the one with the larger sum of money") and *great difference* ("smaller chance of winning, distinctly"). Two judges, coding all the protocols independently, reached 95% agreement. In matching subjects' actual choices to their verbalized comparisons, simple decision rules emerged, supporting Tversky's hypothesis that subjects choose the gamble with the highest value on the dimension having the greater judged difference between gambles. However, when the differences along the two dimensions were adjudged to be approximately equal, the subjects always selected the gamble with the higher pay-off.

Three studies by Benjafield (1969) sought to identify what aspects of a problem situation determine the choice of a solution process. Each study, with 48 subjects, used a between-group factorial design varying the logical properties of the problem (e.g., specificity of goal, pyramid versus four-sided object, number of inference steps to solution) orthogonally with perceptual properties of the problem-solving material. Selected aspects of the protocol statements were encoded, and separate tallies carried out for subjects making more or less than the median number of errors, respectively. Differences in the protocols were highly correlated with the differences in subject accuracy. For example, in the tetrahedron problem, subjects with fewer errors produced the highest fraction of solutions classified as deductive; while in a pendulum problem, the subject's subgoal identified from the protocol was a better predictor of the type of solution achieved than was the goal presented explicitly to the subject by the experimenter.

From a model of the process of understanding problem instructions, Simon and Hayes (1976) predicted how subjects would represent problems described in different, but isomorphic, forms. The subjective problem representation could be assessed from three different aspects of the verbalized information. The results showed that the subjects acquired the predicted representations almost without exception.

Huesmann and Cheng (1973) proposed a detailed theory to explain how subjects induce mathematical functions to fit observed data. The theory proposes that the induction is achieved by a heuristically directed generate-and-test search of hypotheses, where the order in which hypotheses are generated is mostly independent of the data. The conjecture that hypotheses would be generated in order of complexity was tested by calculating the correlation between the number of operators in a hypothesized function and the order in which it was generated. The rank-order correlations for all subjects but one ranged from .30 to .95, with an average of .65. Two departures from ordering by simplicity were found. In the later stages of their solution efforts, subjects tended to return to simple hypotheses generated earlier. For more difficult problems, not included in the above analysis, subjects sometimes started out with more complex hypotheses, then backed down to see if a simpler one had been missed. Subjects also showed a bias for the operations of addition, subtraction, and multiplication over division and exponentiation, and a bias for proceeding from left to right in proposing hypotheses for parameters labelled a and b, respectively.

Recently, Johnson, Duran, Hassebrock, Moller, Prietala, Feltovich, and Swanson (1981) compared the hypotheses generated by an existing computer simulation program for medical diagnosis with hypotheses verbalized by subjects doing the same diagnosis task. For groups of subjects differing in their level of medical expertise (students, trainees, experts), Johnson et al. (1981) found clear similarities between the *average* number of hypotheses generated by subjects in response to different types of patient data (e.g., results from physical examination, EKG) and the numbers generated by the simulation program, and also between the order in which subjects generated hypotheses and the order used by the program.

It is not surprising that the closest correspondence was found for the expert subjects, as the simulation program was constructed by experts with the goal of expert level performance.

Moreover, Johnson et al. (1981) showed that the less expert subjects' failure to reach the correct diagnosis was due to incorrect interpretation of evidence or failure to link evidence to appropriate disease hypothesis. By withholding certain kinds of patient data from the simulation program, the incorrect diagnoses of less expert subjects could be generated. The idea of degrading various components of a single model to account for individual differences is quite interesting. It has also been used elsewhere, for example, in accounting for errors in arithmetic.

Encoding Strategies

In the examples cited above, individual protocol statements were encoded. Verbalizations can also be encoded on a more global basis, in terms of processing strategies employed. Strategies have often been assessed through directed probes, although the subjects have usually been asked to report their individual applications of the strategies rather than the underlying general rules for them.

Burack (1950), defining nine general "methods of attack" on reasoning problems of three different kinds (inductive, deductive, and a geometrical figure problem), assessed subjects' methods from retrospective reports. For each problem, at least one of the "methods of attack" was found to be closely and significantly related to performance. The generality of the methods defined by Burack has been challenged, because none of them was found to be effective on more than one of the problems. However, this result conforms with other evidence that highly effective problem-solving methods tend to be specialized (Newell & Simon, 1972).

Goldner (1957) used TA protocols as well as other data to classify subjects in terms of their general mode of solving problems. For six different kinds of problems subjects were classified according to whether they considered all information (Whole approach) or concentrated on parts of the information (Part approach) and also in terms of their ability to use a variety of approaches (Flexibility-Rigidity). Each problem was separately analyzed to determine what data would provide evidence for the different modes. For example, in one of the anagram tests generating words with many letters was taken as evidence for the Whole approach whereas production of prefixes and suffixes and partial configurations of letters was evidence for the Part approach. The score of Rigidity was assessed by defining certain behaviors as rigid, like "produces *only* prefixes," "makes the same error," "no manipulation of letters." In other problems the rationale for identifying the different modes is less clear. Goldner (1957) found reliable intercorrelations of the assessed modes with the different types of problems.

Duncan (1964), comparing verbal reports of strategy used with performance on an induction problem, found that subjects who reported using some plan or system solved problems significantly more often than subjects who did not so report. After a memory experiment, Eagle and Leiter (1964) asked their subjects if they used a method or system in memorizing the stimulus words, and if so, what method they used. The subjects reporting that they used a strategy were markedly more successful than the others.

In a recent study Egan and Grimes (1979) used retrospective reports from subjects in three-term series problems to assess how the presented premises (i.e., "a triangle is lighter than a square," "a circle is darker than the square") were represented. The majority of subjects could be unambiguously classified into two groups. "Abstract directional thinkers" arranged the stimulus objects from one end to the other of the described dimension, for example, darkness. Here is a verbal report from such a subject:

> I set up a scale with the lightest on the far right and darkest on the far left and placed the figures on the appropriate spots. (Egan & Grimes, 1979, p. 29)

"Concrete properties thinkers" imagined the objects with their described physical attributes, for example, a fatter square was imagined to be physically larger. Here is a verbal report from such a subject:

> I also drew a picture, and if something was rough I would put craters in it. In my mind smooth was just plain white. (Egan & Grimes, 1979, p. 29)

Not only could Egan and Grimes (1979) show reliable performance differences between the two types of subjects, but they also demonstrated reliable differences in the pattern of errors. A theoretical analysis of the processes led to testable predictions regarding the patterns of errors for each group, and these predictions were validated through regression analysis.

DIRECT ASSESSMENT OF GENERAL PROCESSES

In the previous section we showed how certain types of verbalizations —for example, verbalizations of goals—permit testable predictions to be made about the course of the subsequent process as well as performance. All the assessments we have described require a task analysis to identify the subgoals along efficient solution paths. We have shown that task analysis also permits assessment of selected types of information and mental structures, such as representations, and prediction of the effects upon them of experimental manipulations.

In this section, we explore some attempts to follow a rather different approach, which seeks to capture the truly invariant information in the thinking-aloud protocol directly. This approach is to code the protocols in terms of high-level, and more or less task-independent, theoretical entities. Most theories that fit this description characterize cognitive processes by the types of processes involved, rather than the information heeded. Following such a scheme, we can describe any verbal protocol as a sequence of instantiations of a limited number of *general* processes or processing activities.

Coding Systems

The approach we are about to describe rests on two controversial methodological assumptions, one having to do with the encodability of processes, the other with the segmentation of the protocols.

Encoding processes. Earlier, we argued strongly that information (inputs and outputs to processes, stored in STM) is heeded, and not processes. Hence, the processes themselves cannot be encoded directly from verbalizations, but must be inferred. Let us assume, for the moment, that such inferences can be made reliably. Given a theoretical model of problem solving, we encode a protocol into a sequence of instantiations of a limited number of general processes postulated by that model.

With few exceptions, general theories of this kind are not concerned with the sequential relations among processes, but rather with the typology of processes and their relative frequencies. Predictions might be made, for example, that more skilled subjects would use certain kinds of processes that less skilled subjects would not use. Subjects could then be described in terms of the relative frequency with which they rely on various general processes. In this approach, the extensive original protocol is condensed to a vector of process frequencies, and thus converted into numerical magnitudes that can be analyzed by standard statistical and psychometric methods.

The initial task, in applying this approach, is to explicate how entities (processes) postulated by a theory can be identified in protocols. The usual procedure has been to develop a coding manual and provide practice for coders. Most studies report inter-rater reliabilities, which are generally quite high. Of course reliability does not imply validity of encoding.

Segmenting Protocols. A second methodological problem is that protocols must be divided up so that each segment will constitute one instance of a general process. Segmentation is particularly important if the subsequent analysis makes use of frequencies of processes. There have been many attempts to define criteria for segmentation. Although the usual procedure is to determine segments prior to encoding them, some investigators segment and encode simultaneously (Kilpatrick, 1968).

Under the assumptions of our information processing model, the appropriate cues for segmentation are pauses, intonation, contours, etc., as well as syntactical markers for complete phrases and sentences—the cues for segmentation in ordinary discourse. These are also the cues most often used for segmentation in protocol studies. A slightly different segmentation rule, based on separating *ideas* (Smith, 1971), places more emphasis on the actual content of the verbalizations. Goor and Sommerfeld (1975) segmented by three-second intervals, although it is doubtful that they assessed each interval's verbalization independently of its context.

Many decisions must also be made about aggregating information over problems and over groups of subjects. Since these decisions are mainly determined by the research problems addressed, they will be discussed in the context of the specific studies. Similarly, in the subsequent discussion, we will examine various uses of statistical models.

For several reasons, the dissertation of Kilpatrick (1968) is especially interesting in illustrating the issues associated with this approach. This dissertation represents one of the first attempts to encode a large number of protocols, from several subjects and problems, in terms of the occurrences of general processes. Furthermore, Kilpatrick explored several different sets of categories for describing his protocols, thus demonstrating the possibility of encoding the same protocols from more than a single perspective. Kilpatrick also discusses in some detail a number of methodological issues, and his analyses have been influential on subsequent studies that have used versions of his coding schemes.

The first set of coding categories used by Kilpatrick (1968) tries to capture the general problem solving heuristics proposed by Polya (1957). In a pilot study, Kilpatrick tried to find evidence in think-aloud protocols for heuristics corresponding to Polya's "heuristic questions." In the protocols of his 8th-grade subjects, he couldn't find evidence for more than about half of the Polya heuristics, but, proposing a coding scheme for this subset, he added some additional categories (computational errors, requests of assistance from the experimenter).

The coding assessments were made with access to the complete protocol for the problem (the tape recording). The data used in the analysis were the frequencies of occurrence in the protocol of the coding categories. In Kilpatrick's (1968) main study, the proposed 30 categories were reduced to 15, the others being removed because of skewed distributions or lack of inter-subject generality (categories were retained if the heuristics were used by at least 25% of the subjects for any of the 12 problems.) Applying a strict inter-coder reliability criterion—that codings should be significantly related, and that the difference between coders should be non-significant for each coding variable—the number of coding categories was reduced to eight, of which three could be characterized as indicating the use of heuristics: drawing a figure, using successive approximations, and questioning the existence and uniqueness of a solution.

Kilpatrick's (1968) inability to find empirical support for the remaining theoretically defined heuristics should be, and was, interpreted as partially rejecting the theoretical notions and associated coding specifications, rather than invalidating the verbalizations as data. Two other studies, following Kilpatrick's procedures, but using high-school students (Webb, 1975) and college students (Lucas, 1972) as subjects, were more successful in detecting instances of the use of the heuristics postulated by Polya (1957). The results of their studies will be described later.

A second coding scheme used by Kilpatrick (1968), Lucas (1972), and Webb (1975) employs many distinctions based on activity descriptions. In his initial study, Kilpatrick tried to design a description of the sequence of processes leading to the solution of mathematics problems. An initial coding scheme, using a large number of different categories, was rejected because it made coding too difficult and unreliable. A second and much simpler scheme differentiated between three types of problem-solving activities: preparation, production, and evaluation. Preparation and evaluation use only one coding category each, "reading and trying to understand problem" for preparation, and "checking solution" for evaluation. Production has three categories: "deduction from condition," "setting up equation," and "trial and error." The *result* of a production activity is also coded in one of five categories: incomplete, impasse, intermediate result, incorrect result, and correct result. Some other information was also coded (i.e., errors in understanding, and difficulties in performing activities).

When the coding scheme was tested and its inter-coder reliability evaluated, reliabilities were found to be satisfactory. The coding schemes developed by Lucas (1972) and Webb (1975) were structurally very similar, but employed a larger number of categories. Generally, the encoding is based on local verbalized information, but in assessing "trial and error" and "deduction from conditions," it is less clear how much context is needed to make the correct assessment. Furthermore, our own inspection of examples of coded protocols used in these studies leaves us uncertain as to what constitutes a segment —that is, a single production activity.

Flaherty (1973, 1974) devised a coding procedure for analysing processes used by subjects solving algebra word problems. The coding system, designed and revised with the help of a pilot study, consists of 18 categories, many of them similar to those used by Kilpatrick, Lucas, and Webb. Some of the new categories suggested by Flaherty were "indicates familiarity with type of problem," "notes need for auxiliary information." Flaherty's paper, which makes reference to an un-published doctoral thesis, provides no information about how the assessments were made or whether inter-coder reliabilities were measured.

Applications of the Encodings

There have been several different approaches to applying encoded data of the sorts we have been discussing and to evaluate their validity by predicting problem-solving success or making experimentally testable predictions about subjects with similar processing characteristics.

Kilpatrick's Coding Schemes. Kilpatrick's (1968) study exemplifies the notion of external validation well, and also underlines several methodological problems. His study aimed at finding problem solving patterns of 8th-grade students in mathematics. For 56 subjects, a variety of information was collected: tests to assess systematic styles, to measure cognitive styles, and to measure selected abilities. The protocols from 12 problems were coded according to the two previously described schemas: heuristic strategies, and processes. The performance data for external valuation were times to solution and solution adequacy (scored). A postexperimental questionnaire included items on attitudes towards mathematics, study habits, reflectiveness, plans for the future. Already-existing scores of the subjects on IQ tests and other ability tests were also used. For each subject, the frequencies of coding categories were tabulated and pooled for all 12 problems. These frequences were the only products of the think-aloud data that were retained in the analysis. First, Kilpatrick finds a large number of significant correlations between process-sequence variables, obtained from the protocols, and various problem-solving scores, but discards most of them, either because they have "obvious" interpretations, involve overlap in the encoded information, or reflect artifacts resulting from the structural properties of the coding system. As an example of overlap in encoded information, the correlation between "stops without a solution" and test score is an obvious tautology, and the correlation between "errors in understanding" and score a less obvious one. An example of an artifactual correlation resulting from structural properties of the coding scheme is the relation between total frequency of activities and solution time.

After eliminating all of these more or less spurious relations, one principal relation remains, in Kilpatrick's (1968) data, between the protocol variables and the total test score: a correlation between the use of trial and error and high test scores. A closer analysis of the original protocols shows that, although deduction rather than trial and error was responsible for a majority of problem solutions, trial and error led to fewer incorrect solutions than did deduction (p. 67). The frequency of checking behaviors was also correlated with test scores, but engaging in checking presupposes that a candidate solution has been found, so this relation is also largely artifactual. Both of the relations retained were weak correlations, of .3 and .27, respectively. Since they were identified post hoc from among 45 correlations, significance at the 5 per cent level for the individual correlations is a weak rebuttal of randomness. A search for correlations between the check-list variables (use or non-use of particular heuristics) and the performance variables revealed few significant relations, none of them interpretable.

Likewise, few reliable relations were found between the protocol variables and the other data that were gathered about the subjects. No interpretable correlations were observed between French's systematic styles and the protocol variables. The only significant interpretable relations with check-list variables were between the frequency of drawing figures and some self-report variables (reporting that one's father does not help with mathematics homework, that one draws figures frequently when solving problems, and that drawing figures is helpful). Some process variables showed consistent relations with measures of special and general abilities. The use of equations was found to correlate with general reasoning, word fluency, and mathematical achievement. Structural errors and difficulty with process showed negative correlations with most of the same measures.

Since similar issues were addressed by Webb (1975), we will consider only the differences between her findings and Kilpatrick's (1968). For 40 high school students, pretest scores were collected on mathematical and general ability, and protocols on eight problems were coded, using the previously described coding schemes. Questionnaire data were also obtained. As in Kilpatrick's study, data were pooled over subjects and total test scores were calculated. Because there were so many variables (16 pretest variables, 23 check-list variables, 11 process variables), Webb decided to reduce them by three component analyses, which produced 4, 5, and 4 components, respectively. A stepwise regression was carried out to assess the relative importance for problem solving ability of cognitive ability measures versus information about the use of processes derived from the protocols. Three components accounted for significant independent variance: two components of cognitive abilities (mathematical achievement and verbal reasoning, with 50% and 5%, respectively), and one heuristic component (pictorial representation, with 8%). The process components accounted for less that one per cent. The frequency of use of specific heuristics differed significantly between problems for all but two heuristics—"bright idea" and "derives solution by another method."

In Kilpatrick's (1968) analyses of the relation between categories extracted from the protocols and performance on the math problems, subjects could be differentiated by the frequency of trial and error search. An informal analysis of encoded descriptions of solutions suggested four different groups that showed consistent, but not statistically significant, differences for other recorded variables. One group of subjects was characterized by the use of algebra, and the other three by their relative frequencies of use of trial and error methods.

In Webb's (1975) study, each subject was described in terms of heuristic strategies and types of processes used. Cluster analysis was applied to these scores to identify patterns in the use of heuristics and types of processes by groups of students. The cluster analyses showed that higher-scoring students either used a wide range of heuristic strategies and an average amount of trial and error and equations, or they used a large amount of deduction.

A study by Lucas (1972) was designed to explore the relative effectiveness of heuristically oriented instruction in the calculus as compared with more traditional teaching. In a factorial design, some of the 36 subjects were given a pretest of seven problems, while the others were not; and some subjects were given heuristically oriented instruction, the others were taught more traditionally. All subjects took a posttest of seven problems. Data from coded protocols, using the coding schemes already described, were pooled over the problems in a test session for each subject. The only significant differences that could be unambiguously tied to the experimental manipulation, heuristic versus traditional teaching, was that subjects taught heuristically tended to recall related problems more often.

We have reviewed these experiments in some detail to show how meager are the results that have been obtained from this kind of high-level encoding of protocols. A little later, we will discuss a study by Gimmestad (1976), using the same encoding scheme, that casts some light on the reason for these disappointing outcomes.

Other Coding Schemes. Goor (1974) proposed a seven-category coding system for analyzing think-aloud protocols from problem solving tasks. His categories, designed to be complete and mutually exclusive, could be seen as grouping sets of activities in terms of type and status of information used by them. His first category is *surveying given information*, which we would label a little more broadly from its description as *operating on given or previously generated information*. The remaining categories are: (2) generating new information or hypotheses, (3) developing or working on a hypothesis, (4) unsuccessful solution, (5) changing the conditions of the problem, (6) self-reference or self-criticism, and (7) silence (Goor coded all three-second time segments). Category 6 contains verbalizations that are irrelevant to the task, and Category 5 is limited to proposed changes in the given information. Categories 2, 3, and 4 are structurally related, in that rejecting a hypothesis presupposes that one has been generated.

An interesting property of this coding scheme is that it captures the intuitively important distinction between previously generated (old) information and new information. However, there are two kinds of difficulty in making that assessment. First, the judgment that two hypotheses are the same or different requires a taxonomy of the possible hypotheses for the task. Second, a hypothesis can be assessed as new only after a review of all the hypotheses that have been generated previously (unless the subject makes some comment implying the novelty of the hypothesis, and assuming such subjective remarks are reliable). Goor and Sommerfeld (1975) report that two coders, after working together for seven hours, independently coded 2,400 segments with 94% agreement. No measures of reliability were presented for the individual coding categories.

In another study, Goor (1974) collected protocols on three problems for 26 students with very high test scores on creativity tests, and 26 students with very low scores. Goor calculated the probabilities of each of the processes immediately succeeding each of the others (i.e., treated the data as reflecting a Markov process). There were highly significant differences between the two groups of subjects. The "creative" students spent more time developing and generating new hypotheses, while the "uncreative" students had more intervals of silence. An analysis of conditional probabilities, of one process following after another had occurred, revealed no additional differences between the two groups.

Another possible basis for a coding scheme to classify actions according to very general processes is Guilford's *Structure of Intellect* model, designed to factor intelligence items. In a dissertation by Smith (1971), Guilford's classification system was taken as the basis for representing all the statements in the protocols. Each statement was coded in terms of its content (symbolic, figural, semantic, behavioral), its operation (cognition, memory, production, evaluation), and its product (units, classes, relations, systems, transformations, implications). Some examples are given below from the coding manual:

F P St. "If you draw a line you would come out with three equal squares."

Sy E Cl. "Ratios won't work."

Sy M St. "Let me think back how many trains there would be."

Heeded information should be readily encoded in terms of product categories, but inferences about the content and operation categories will often be problematic and require attention to the context of preceding protocol segments. The coding manual prepared by Smith says explicitly: "the sequence or context is a significant factor in classification" (p. 101), so that the encodings of individual statements cannot be seen as all mutually independent. For three coders with experience in using the code, agreement ranged from 98 to 81 per cent (chance agreement would be less than 25 per cent). However, a previously untrained coder having access only to the training manual attained only about 56 per cent agreement with more experienced coders. Data are not available on reliabilities for individual categories.

Smith's (1971) aim was to distinguish process patterns in problem solving for six groups of subjects differing in vocational interest (two levels) and experience in mathematics (three levels), using a total of 23 subjects. Interpretable patterns distinguishing the groups were found, and the results seemed to be stable over two sets of problems, administered a week apart. However, the variance accounted for was small, and the results lack rigorous statistical support.

A common conceptualization of cognitive processes is to break them down into a sequence of stages, with relative homogeneity of activity within each stage. Havertape (1977) proposed three stages for cognitive processes in problem solving: getting the information, understanding the problem, and solving the problem. Activity during each stage was coded according to its adequacy in achieving the goals of that stage. The code, for example, for "getting the information" was: reads problem correctly, reads problem correctly after several efforts, rereads problem several times, reads only part of the problem, does not read the problem. In carrying out the coding, context external to the stage being coded was used. For example, the sub-categories for "understanding the problem" are explicitly related to the correctness of the subsequent problem solving.

Havertape compared a group of twenty learning-disabled students with a group of "normal" students on 26 problems. When the sub-categories were mapped onto scale values and submitted to a multivariate analysis of variance, there were clear and significant differences between the two groups, distributed over all stages, and indicating a uniform deficiency of the learning-disabled subjects.

From a theory of undirected thought, Klinger (1974) has proposed a set of cognitive processes that must be added to undirected thought to produce directed thinking. Two of these processes, which would fall within our categories of "orally coded self-instructions" and "evaluations" are, according to Klinger, discriminable from think-aloud protocols. The first of Klinger's processes, *control of attention*, was exemplified by verbalizations like, "Let's see," or "Where was I"? The second class of processes, *evaluation of success*, was exemplified by, "Yep," "Dammit," "Now wait," and the like. Many of these coding assessments would require no inferences, being identifiable directly as parts of the protocol segments.

For one type of task, manual puzzles, Klinger (1974) derived intercoder reliabilities by comparing the two coders used in the study with a third coder. Reliabilities were .96 for attention control scores and .82 for evaluation scores. Additional information about the occurrence and context of attention control processes was coded informally. A coder characterized each occurrence in terms of the kind of content that had just preceded it, and in terms of the coder's impression of the subject's goal in controlling his attention at that point. No strictly defined categories were used in this coding, and hence, no intercoder reliabilities calculated.

Klinger had his subjects generate TA protocols under four conditions, selected to contrast undirected with directed thought. Solving manual puzzles and logic problems were selected to illustrate directed thought, and reverie (day-dreaming with eyes open) and a hypnagogic condition (day-dreaming with eyes closed) to illustrate undirected thought. Each subject served in both conditions. Omitting subjects with equal scores in both conditions, 27 of 29 subjects had more evaluative utterances, and 24 of 26 more utterances indicating attention control in the conditions of directed thought, than in the conditions of undirected thought.

To analyze think-aloud protocols for subjects seeking to understand different kinds of problems, Bree (1969, 1975) proposed a coding scheme having over 20 different categories. Each segment of protocol was coded in terms of its locus, for example: what step in the description of the problem solution it referred to, what action was taken by the subject, and what deviations this represented from a straightforward application of the action. The actions were of two types: simple functions (e.g., mentioning a step, rephrasing the step, stating reasons for the step), and planning functions (e.g., deciding to find a certain step, to go through the solution description again, and so on). "Deviations" included difficulties in applying an action and incorrect application of an action. In order to enhance coding reliability, Bree explicitly designed his coding system to make the encoding very simple, based just on the protocol statement being encoded "without the coder (the author) intentionally referring to any previous or later passages in the protocol." (Bree, 1969, p. 16) To guard further against bias, the identity of the subject was unknown to the coder. These encodings were subsequently analysed by computer to infer automatically higher-level and global characteristics of the process.

The subjects studied the description of the solutions to different problems by concentrating on one step of the solution at a time. However, in trying to understand a given step they often went back to previously studied steps. The first task of the computer program was to segment the encodings into episodes that corresponded to all cognitive activity centered around the study of a single step. Once these episodes were identified, the program assessed more complex processes, like *predicting* a step (verbalizing a subsequent step not yet studied), *explaining* a step by interrelating the current step to previously presented premisses (steps), etc.

Only a few studies address explicitly the problem of testing consistency in the pattern of processes used by a particular individual over a period of time on the same or different tasks. Bree attempted such an analysis. The frequencies of five features of the protocol steps were tabulated: explains, predicts steps, reasons or rephrases, requests and studies of presented information. Using the extension of Fisher's exact test to 2x5 frequency matrices, he could calculate the probability that two profiles of these features had the same underlying distributions. Intra-individual profiles showed greater similarity than inter-individual profiles. A detailed analysis showed that the consistency of individuals arose primarily from the "explains" dimension.

Summary

Protocol analysis using general, task-independent process categories has not greatly extended our understanding of cognitive processes. Those relations that have been obtained, and which are not artifactual, are weak, accounting for only a small part of the variability in performance. Predictability is low even when the protocols are collected for the same solutions from which performance measures were derived. Ideally, we would collect protocol data from one set of solution processes and make predictions for the performance of the same individuals on another set of solutions to different problems.

It would be erroneous to conclude from these negative results that there is no useful information to be extracted from the protocols. The methods of analysis used in the studies described in this section are different from those that we advocate. The processes of generating data from the protocols also incorporate numerous assumptions, which may be invalid.

It is possible that the particular sets of general processes assumed in these studies are not the right ones. Alternatively, it is possible that good problem solvers cannot be discriminated from poor ones by differences in such general, task-independent processes. We start with the obvious observation that if someone lacks the knowledge necessary for performing a task, no number of general skills will save the day for him. Expert and excellent performance in one domain does not predict the quality of performance in another, unrelated domain. In mathematics problem solving, Webb (1975) showed that the overwhelmingly important and successful predictor was mathematical knowledge.

A study by Gimmestad (1977), relying essentially on Kilpatrick's coding schemes, provides data that allow us to examine one of the assumptions about task-independent processes. The assumption in question is that the relation between reliance on heuristics and problem-solving performance should be the same for all problems, at least in a given problem environment. Analyzing the relation between the number of instantiated heuristics on individual problems and performance on those problems, she found that different heuristics were differentially useful for specific problems. More important, she found that the use of certain heuristics was *negatively* correlated with success on some problems, and at least one of the negative relations she detected was statistically significant.

In order to evaluate the consistency of subjects' use of heuristics on very similar problems, she constructed two problems that called on the same algebra but had different semantic content. There was no indication that the subjects used the same heuristics on both problems. Although it is clear from other research, for example Hayes and Simon (1976), that isomorphic problems are not necessarily perceived and represented in the same way, this lack of consistency in the use of heuristics raises questions about what is actually captured in these kinds of protocol encodings.

In sum, we believe that at our current level of understanding, an analysis of the heeded information revealed in a protocol, in the context of a task analysis, is a more fruitful approach to protocol analysis of cognitive processes than is an encoding and analysis in terms of task-independent general processes.

VERBAL REPORTS AND THEORIES

Theories in psychology have usually been formulated in highly abstract terms. Many of them make predictions only for aggregated data that are pooled over items and over subjects. Some theories posit mechanisms that specify, on some level, how behavior is generated under different experimental conditions. In this section, we wish to illustrate with a few examples the relevance and import of verbal reports for testing such theories. In the remaining chapters of this book we will be more concerned with how verbal reports can be used to generate and test detailed information processing models of task performance.

When verbal reports contradict theories that are not disconfirmed by other experimental data, it is convenient to disregard the reports as epiphenomenal. But, if we believe that the verbal reports are pertinent, and not epiphenomenal, we should show that a general theory adequately captures the verbal information on some level of abstraction. We will evaluate various ways in which implications of theories can be tested against the detailed sequences of heeded information. We will also point to cases where such tests lead to rejection of the corresponding theory.

Protocol data have been used to support and refute proposed mechanisms underlying various processes. Verbal reports, even from a small number of subjects, can serve as evidence that at least some subjects' cognitive processes conform to a hypothesized model of the sequence and type of information that is heeded. In such situations the verbal reports serve as evidence for the existence of certain cognitive structures and processes, an important first step towards gaining evidence for generality and generalizability. Similarly, evidence of the existence of some cognitive structures in the memories of some subjects can refute the universality of a theory that makes strong predicitions about the nature and range of internal cognitive states.

A second issue is the relation between the information-rich data on the course of cognitive processes, and mathematical models that posit general characteristics of processes. Many assumptions in mathematical models of cognitive processes do not have to be left as assumptions, but can be converted into testable predictions on the level of process data. A third and related issue has to do with ways of understanding, in terms of mediating processes, empirical relations between observed behavior and experimental manipulations.

The first published study using TA protocols was carried out by Watson (1920). He instructed one of his friends to think aloud while trying to identify the function of an unfamiliar physical object. From his analysis of the protocol, Watson made two different theoretical points. First, he showed that the problem solving behavior could *not* be seen as insightful or as a sequence of logically connected steps. The view that problem solving was *always* driven by a rational, deliberative process could thus be rejected. (See also Henry (1934) for a similar observation on geometry theorem proving.) Second, in attempting to identify the structure of the problem solving process, Watson found it to have many elements in common with trial-and-error processes observed in maze learning.

It is when we ask him to think aloud ... that we begin to grasp how relatively crude is the process of thinking. Here we see typified all of the errors made by the rat in the maze: false starts appear; emotional factors show themselves, such as the hanging of the head and possibly even blushing when a false scent is followed up. The subject returns again and again to his starting point as shown by his asking, "You say the given facts are so and so?" The experimenter says, "Yes," and again the subject starts off. (Watson, 1920, p. 91)

However, Watson does not make the mapping to trial-and-error processes any more explicit. For him, the important argument is that the observed structural characteristics of the process are incompatible with a rational cumulative solution process.

In criticism of Hull's (1920) assertion that concept formation is achieved by identifying common elements (in Hull's experiments, identifying common radicals embedded in complex Chinese ideograms), Smoke (1932) carried out two TA studies. From the protocols, he demonstrated that subjects attended to relational attributes—that is, attributes requiring consideration of the whole pattern—rather than local attributes derived from a physically restricted subpart of the stimulus. In support, he presented excerpts of TA protocols displaying such global hypotheses. These protocols were clearly inconsistent with the contemporary S-R theories of concept formation.

Gestalt psychologists have often demonstrated the need for postulating complex subjective structures (Gestalten) to account for subjects' cognitive processes and behavior. Duncker (1926, 1945) provides perhaps the best example of using protocol data to reject other theories and in support of his own account. Duncker presents a logical argument against the sufficiency of associative and S-R theories to account for productive problem solving (problem solving where the subjects cannot rely on memory of experience with identical or similar problems).

Duncker carefully selected his problems so that the situation would not contain common elements with any other problem solving experiences of the subjects. In these situations, problems could not be solved by evoking associations with previous experiences, but required general solution methods that, in turn, would direct the generation of more specific useful solutions.

From his analysis of the TA protocols, Duncker showed that his subjects used such general methods prior to evoking specific solutions. Unfortunately, he does not report the verbatim protocols, but only his own functional encodings of the subjects' verbalizatons. However, the same argument can be made as above: that any theory of productive problem solving would need to account for the subjects' accessing, attending to, and verbalizing general solution methods.

In testing their theory of anagram problem solving against information in TA protocols, Mayzner, Tresselt and Helbock (1964) found that their theory could not account for many of the words heeded, especially words that contained letters not contained among those presented in the anagram. The fact that subjects heeded words, and not just bigrams or trigrams, suggested to the authors that their theory had to be extended to account for the problem solving process in this task.

Grudin (1980) showed that subjects can and do vary their strategies in solving verbal analogies (i.e., A:B::C:?) beyond what was assumed in the existing theories (Sternberg, 1977). Sternberg's (1977) theory assumed that subjects always looked for the relation between A and B, and then applied it to C to find the right answer. However, Grudin (1980) recorded the following think-aloud protocol from a subject solving such anologies.

ITEM: BIRD:FISH:AIR: (BREATHE, SWIM, WATER)
PROTOCOL: "bird is to fish (pause) birds are in air, fish are
             in (pause) water."   (Grudin, 1980, p. 72)

This protocol clearly contradicts the theory, in that the relation between A and C is found and applied to B. In two experiments analyzing latencies, Grudin (1980) demonstrated the general occurrence of such strategies.

Dominowski (1974), searching for the cognitive processes underlying concept formation, collected TA protocols and retrospective reports from a large group of subjects, and found that no single processing model could account for the protocols of all subjects. Although he found some inter-subject similarities, there was overriding evidence for the use of several strategies involving different processes.   Several other investigators have also observed different strategies being used to perform the same task (Gilmartin, 1975; Anzai & Simon, 1979; Bruner et al., 1956). We have already discussed to some extent the problems for theorizing and prediction that arise when processes are not uniform, and we will reopen this discussion later in this section.

In models of problem solving like the General Problem Solver (Newell & Simon, 1972), it is assumed that the subject holds explicitly defined goals and subgoals. These allow differences between the current situation and the target situation to guide the problem solving process through means-ends analysis. According to means-ends analysis, subjects first determine specific differences between the goal and the current situation, and then seek to eliminate one of these differences by selecting an appropriate method. Relying on TA protocols from five high-school students solving geometry problems, Greeno (1976) found that means-ends analysis could not account for all of the observed cognitive processes. For example, the subjects often generated (and verbalized) the goal of proving that two triangles were congruent. Means-ends analysis would predict that the subject would select one of several possible congruency conditions (like side-angle-side correspondence) and evaluate its applicability, and if not successful, then proceed to evaluate another congruency condition, etc. However, Greeno (1976) found that the indefinite goal of proving congruency led subjects to discover the correct congruency condition by direct recognition rather than search. Through an analysis of the protocol, he could show that there was no sequential testing of different possibilities. The assessment that indefinite, rather than definite, explicit subgoals were used was made by three judges who independently coded 24 protocols.

We have selected these samples to illustrate how evidence that subjects heed certain types of information can often be used simply and directly to test theoretical generalizations. The assessment that the information was actually heeded can be made with a minimum of interpretation and without strong prior theoretical assumptions. The heeding of the information constitutes a datum to be accounted for by any theory of the corresponding cognitive process. It would be very difficult for a model to account for the subjects' verbalizing relevant information without concluding that this information was generated en route to the solution of the problem by the corresponding task-directed processes. It is, of course, logically possible that such information is generated in parallel with the actual task-oriented processes and without contact with them, but such an interpretation does not provide a plausible and parsimonious account of the data.

CONCLUSION

Our main concern in this chapter has been to investigate the claim that has frequently been made that thinking-aloud protocols and other verbal reports are epiphenomenal, and cannot be relied upon to provide evidence about the course of ongoing task performance. We have assembled all of the experimental evidence we could find that bears on this issue. With great consistency, this evidence demonstrates that verbal data are not in the least epiphenomenal but instead are highly pertinent to and informative about subjects' cognitive processes and memory structures.

Human subjects are not schizophrenic creatures who produce a stream of words, parallel but irrelevant to the cognitive task they are performing. On the contrary, their thinking aloud protocols and retrospective reports can reveal in remarkable detail what information they are attending to while performing their tasks, and by revealing this information, can provide an orderly picture of the exact way in which the tasks are being performed: the strategies employed, the inferences drawn from information, the accessing of memory by recognition.

As we saw in the final section of the chapter, verbal data often provides a powerful means for testing broad theoretical generalizations, which can sometimes be confirmed or refuted by demonstration of the presence or absence of certain information in subjects' verbalizations. But the real promise of verbal data, a promise already partly realized over the past two or three decades, lies in their use in developing and testing detailed information processing models of cognition, models that can often be formalized in computer programming languages and analyzed by computer simulation. To take advantage of the power of verbal data in carrying out this enterprise, we must develop a methodology for encoding and interpreting these data. The remaining chapters of this book are centrally concerned with this methodology.

5

MODEL OF VERBALIZATION

Up to this point, we have aimed mainly at identifying from verbalizations what information subjects attend to. In this chapter, we will add to our model of verbalization more detail about the underlying processes, as a basis for our subsequent discussion of techniques of protocol analysis. We will not alter our earlier general model, but will strengthen the assumptions on which it is based and add some new assumptions. We will describe first, in summary form, the model for concurrent verbalization.

GENERAL MODEL AND ASSUMPTIONS

The model of Chapter 2 showed the dependence of verbalizations on how information is stored and represented, and showed how verbalizations are coordinated with the ongoing cognitive processes. The model allowed us to predict the existence and locus of effects of instructions for various kinds of verbalizing. In this chapter, we will focus on the *content* of the verbalizations, and the relation of that content to the way in which information is represented internally.

The following assumptions are at the core of the model:

1. The verbalizable cognitions can be described as states that correspond to the contents of STM (i.e., to the information that is in the focus of attention).

2. The information vocalized is a verbal encoding of the information in short-term memory.

In order to be able to discuss in more detail how the contents of STM are verbalized, we need to find some way of describing the information structures it holds. For lack of a better label, we will refer to them as *thoughts*. Since only one thought can be verbalized at a time, we need a mechanism that determines which one. In addition, we want to specify how non-verbal thoughts are translated into verbal form. By understanding this translation process we should be better able to infer the non-verbal representations from the observed vocalizations.

The first additional assumption we require is that thoughts are selected for verbalization as they are heeded.

3. The verbalization processes are initiated as a thought is heeded.

The second assumption relates to structure.

4. The verbalization is a direct encoding of the heeded thought and reflects its structure.

Up to this point, we have used the terms "talk aloud" and "think aloud" interchangeably. In applying our more detailed model, it will sometimes be necessary to distinguish the case where a subject utters thoughts that are already encoded in verbal form from the case where the subject recodes verbally and utters thoughts that may have been held in memory in some other form (e.g., visually). When it is necessary to make the distinction, we will refer to these two forms of utterance as *talking aloud* and *thinking aloud*, respectively.

In providing protocols, subjects will not always distinguish between these two kinds of verbalizations, but to some extent, differences in instructions (see the Appendix to Chapter 7) may influence them to produce the one or the other. The nature of the task will often have even more influence on the verbalizations. When it is not clear which term better describes the verbalizations, we will generally refer to them as "thinking aloud."

Before we discuss the cognitive processes involved in verbalizing under talk-aloud or think-aloud instructions, we need to discuss briefly these cognitive structures that we are calling thoughts.

Characterizing Cognitive Structures ("Thoughts")

We will have little to add to the long-standing argument over whether *all* mental content is verbal, or at least verbalizable (See McKellar (1968) for such a discussion). Holding to our earlier limits, we will only consider heeded information that is relevant for task-directed cognitive processes. This restriction relieves us from considering many of the most controversial kinds of mental content.

The restriction to thoughts that reflect heeded information in STM means that the "stream of thought," discussed by James (1890), will not concern us. According to James' own characterization these peripheral elements are never completely heeded. Likewise, day-dreams and similar thoughts contain imagery that never is heeded directly. We will also exclude feelings from the thoughts we will consider.

Many of the categories of thought we are excluding raise difficult problems of interpretation and analysis. The difficulties are not nearly so great for task-relevant information acquired through verbal instructions and verbal problem stimuli. In Chapter 3 we presented empirical evidence to show that the kinds of thoughts we are considering are generally sufficient to account for the cognitive mechanisms in task performance.

In nearly all linguistic analyses, the sentence is regarded as the verbal realization of a meaningful idea. Task-relevant information to which a subject attends, even if it is sometimes figural rather than verbal, can usually be described at least approximately in terms of propositions that are expressable in sentences. As our discussion of visual imagery in Chapter 2 suggests, however, the encoding of some kinds of stimulus information into sentences may be quite complex and difficult. For the present, we will consider stimuli that do not present this difficulty. How can we use sentence structure to discriminate between different mental contexts in which information can be heeded?

There are many different kinds of verbal information. Some information reflects the current problem situation. It may be an encoding of the stimulus, or information that is true of the task. Verbalizations of this *Current-State* information are often marked by verbs such as "be," "have," etc., in the present tense. Some verbalizations reflect intentions or goals to attain configurations or attributes not true for the current situation. This *Future-State* information is often marked by verbs or verb constructions like "want to have," "like to have," or verbs in the future tense. Finally, some information in verbalizations is modal in character. *Modal-State* information is hypothetical or conjectural, and verbalizations of this type are marked by "if..." constructions or verbs like "assume," "guess," or constructions involving "maybe" or "perhaps." We see that the primary cues for identifying these different kinds of thoughts are the verbs and their tenses. Occasionally finer distinctions in the underlying processes are made: "I remembered that...," "I noticed that...," "I forgot that...." These implicit descriptions of the processes will be discussed in more detail later.

Relation to Research on Language

Thinking aloud and talking aloud can be elicited almost instantaneously by the appropriate instruction from virtually all human adults. This means that the necessary cognitive processes need not be learned, but rather are available and ready for use, suggesting that the verbalization processes must be very closely related to processes used by people in everyday language behavior. Although normal language behavior usually involves social interaction, its processes should not be very different from those that produce TA protocols. In our subsequent specification of the verbalization processes used in concurrent verbal reporting we will draw on the published research on language and speech production. To be able to do this legitimately, we must point out the relation between this research and research using verbalization of thoughts.

Studies of language production have lagged considerably behind research on language and text comprehension. A likely reason is the difficulty of obtaining adequate experimental control over the generation of verbalizations. Moreover, subjects may express thoughts in various syntactical and lexical forms. To combat this variability, researchers in speech production often instruct subjects to generate one sentence as fast as they can. A common design is to show subjects a simple picture and require it to be translated into words, or to display some words that have to be integrated into a full meaningful sentence. Other studies ask subjects to recall previously presented sentences from memory. Yet other studies ask subjects to describe and explain more complex stimuli, like cartoons, recall personal events, or describe well-known environments from memory. What mainly sets these studies apart from studies of concurrent verbalization of thoughts is the instruction to *describe* some externally perceived event or object, often with additional linguistic constraints. We will later discuss research contrasting verbal descriptions generated for other people with verbalizations generated for a subject's own use. In both cases we will argue that the observed verbalization corresponds to a thought, and it is primarily in the selection of the thought and in some aspects of its verbal expression that we would expect differences.

It is even more obvious that research on speech production will be relevant to the specification of verbalization processes. There is now considerable evidence (Danks, 1977) of a close link between parts of sentences pronounced in a single burst (identified by features of articulation, like intonation, stress, pauses, etc.) and their meaning. The original proposal for such units of articulation based on meaning (syntagmas) was made Kozhevnikov and Chistovich (Danks, 1977).

A major step beyond post-hoc evidence for such a link was taken by McNeill (Danks, 1977). He was able to show that articulation units in most cases (around 70%) could be predicted from the underlying conceptual structure. The latter was defined a priori in terms of conceptual relations, like "is an agent of," "at location of." Syntactical boundaries accounted for most of the remaining units. Furthermore, McNeill showed that hesitations and pauses were best predicted by major shifts in the conceptual structure—grammatical structure was not as good a predictor. In a later paper, McNeill (1975) reviewed further evidence for the validity of syntagmas in data on language development and analyses of the coordination of gestures with language in adults. Accepting his analysis we will add the following assumptions to our model of verbalization:

5.   Units of articulation will correspond to integrated cognitive structures.

6.   Pauses and hesitations will be good predictors of shifts in processing of cognitive structures.

The tight coordination between verbalization and thought, even in normal speech, is summarized by McNeill in this way:

"For many speakers, normal speech seems to be uttered *as* it is organized. The conceptual arrangements behind speech can be worked out at nearly the same time the sentence is produced, certainly not always a phrase or sentence in advance." (McNeill, 1975, p. 356)

In a recent study, Chafe (1979) showed that subjects recalled information from a picture in verbalized units that consisted of about 5 words each with a mean duration of less than 2 seconds. Most of the units or segments were single case frames. With the exception of some instances (less than 5%) that were coded by Chafe as "mistakes" of the speaker, the units did not exceed a single clause each.

CONCURRENT VERBALIZATION

Having laid down these six assumptions about verbalization processes, we will now look at talk-aloud and think-aloud processes. Since, according to our definition of talking aloud, the verbalized information is heeded in oral form, no translation is necessary. Hence, we will start our discussion with talk-aloud before turning to a discussion of the more complex processes involved in think-aloud. In the final section, we will compare evidence on these two types of verbalization and also explain how subjects occasionally verbalize cognitive processes and activities.

Talk-Aloud Procedures

The instruction for talk-aloud asks the subjects to say *out loud* whatever they are saying silently to themselves. In Chapter 2 we proposed that subjects frequently attend to phonemic information that can be vocalized directly, and we reviewed the many forms of independent evidence that support this claim, including electrophysiological recordings of the vocal tract, errors, interference from concurrent chanting, and so on.

A fairly wide range of tasks call for cognitive processes operating on orally encoded information. The most obvious are those where subjects maintain large amounts of auditorily presented phonemic information through direct rehearsal. The following protocol from a delayed recall of a sequence of stimulus digits can serve as an example.

Auditorily presented digits	05545550
Protocol	045 4550
	045 55450
	045 45550
	045 45550
	045 45550

Oral information is also used to provide access cues for lexical information (e.g., in ANAGRAM problem solving) and other types of rote information, like addition and multiplication tables.

Solving an Anagram: *SCLIAO*
(Sargent, 1940, pp. 30-31)

SUBJECT 2	SUBJECT 3
S.C (pause)	S.C.I..I.A.O
O-L--	C--(pause)
S.O--C	C.L.I.
Social!	L.I
	L.I.A.S.
	L.I--
	I must break the SCL combination
	S.O.I
	Soil
	S.O.I.L

Soilac
L.O
L.O.S
L.O.S.I.A.C
C.I..O.S.I.A
No
S.O.A
So
Soail
No
C
S.C.I.I.
Selee
S.O.C.I.A.L.
Social!

An example of a protocol of a subject adding visually presented digits is given below.

Visually presented digits	5 2 8 9 7 4 3 6 3 4
Protocol	2 and 8 is 10 and 5 is 15 and 9 will be 24 and 7 is 31 and 4 is 35 and 3 and 6 is 9 makes 44 3 and 4 is 7 makes 51

Finally, we observe that subjects often generate internal speech spontaneously and sometimes vocalize it. This internal speech may contain self instructions, like "Let me see," "Wait a minute," etc., or more extensive self-dialogues.

When heeded information is already encoded orally, we claim that the internal activation associated with attending to this information provides input for a process (VOCALIZE) without additional central processing. In talk-aloud we assume that verbalization begins as soon as the internal activation takes place.

The protocols we have just reproduced clearly satisfy several of the assumptions of our model of verbalization: Assumption 2 (the verbalized information is in STM), 3 (the vocalization is initiated by heeding), 4 (the information is encoded directly). Since the verbalization is necessarily serial, the apparent ease with which subjects talk aloud gives support for the seriality of attention (Assumption 1). In our extensive review in Chapter 2, we found that talking aloud did not even slow down task performance.

The model's assumptions (5 and 6) about the articulatory and temporal structure of TA verbalizations are also supported by empirical evidence. Ericsson, Chase and Faloon (1980) showed that a subject in the digit-span task recalled digits in 3- and 4-digit groups with longer pauses between predictable digit groups. The digit groups were encoded mnemonically. The longer pauses were also shown in experiments to correspond to additional retrieval. The subjects' retrospective reports were the earliest and most powerful evidence for these structures. Other analyses of recall have provided additional support.

Think-Aloud Procedures

In thinking aloud we have verbalization of both orally encoded information and other kinds of thoughts. We would like our model to accommodate all kinds of thoughts—whether simple or complex, and whether perceived, generated through cognitive processes, or recalled from LTM. We also require that the verbalization follow the rapidly changing thought content dynamically. To thread our way through the many issues and the large volume of empirical evidence, we will structure our discussion along the following lines.

First, we will discuss verbalization of simple thoughts occurring without a context of other thoughts. Then we will turn to verbalization of thoughts in context. Verbalization of complex thoughts retrieved (or generated) from LTM will then be discussed. Finally, we will discuss the temporal integration between thoughts and verbalization, and then examine evidence that thinking aloud in some circumstances is incomplete.

Context-free Verbalization. We will limit our discussion to stimuli and STM contents that are readily encoded in words. This limitation does not exclude pictorial stimuli or images, provided that they need not be described at too low a level of detail. With this limitation, thoughts—representational structures—can be described by propositions that denote one or more attributes of an object or conceptual entity, or denote relations among several entities. Although there are many general schemes for representing propositional knowledge, all of which could serve almost equally well for our purposes, we will use the system proposed by Kintsch (1974), which has the advantage of providing a close link between the proposition and the verbalization. Such a representation appears adequate even when the story is presented through pictures (Baggett, 1975).

There is considerable support for propositional representations. In an interesting series of studies, Chafe (1977) showed brief films to 80 people. When these subjects described from memory a film where a banana was transferred from an older boy to a younger boy, almost all of them (76) used a sentence with a verb, an agent, a beneficiary and a patient—like "The older boy handed/gave/passed the younger boy a banana." Hence there was virtually perfect agreement on the relations and entities involved. However, there appears to be more variability in lexical choice and syntax. Chafe (1977) gives an example of a verbal description given by the same speaker after seeing the same brief film 8 weeks apart.

"*First occasion:* He picked up some hay and lifted it over the corral fence and into the corral. All of the animals eagerly went after and began eating the hay. *Second occasion:* He threw some hay over the top rail of the corral fence to the animals inside." (Chafe, 1977, p. 47)

Apart from the omitted information in the second description there is high consistency in the elements of the two descriptions.

To discuss the variability, especially observed between people in surface structure of verbalizations, we will assume that the abstract structure using relations and elements is the preferred description of the thought. To produce a verbalization from a thought, first, lexical items must be selected for each relation and entity; second, a syntactical form or order of verbalization must be selected. Although many investigators have argued that these processes interact, we will initially discuss them independently.

Selection of Lexical Items. We propose two encoding processes, NAME(X) and REFERENCE(X), to generate verbal codes for entities.

NAME(X) simply creates a name for entity X. Many visual and symbolic entities already have unique labels. The experimenter often provides such labels in the task instructions. In many tasks there are established naming conventions known to subjects with even a little task experience. In chess, all the pieces and each square of the chessboard have well-known names. In mathematical and other symbolic systems, the symbols often have conventional names. The common language shared by subjects leads them to apply the same names to ordinary physical objects. In all such cases, the naming of entities and relations in the heeded proposition is unproblematic.

Chafe (1977) proposed that objects vary in terms of their codability, that is, the consistency of the labels assigned by different individuals. In analyzing the film mentioned earlier, he observed remarkable consistency in calling the transferred object a banana. Of the 80 subjects, 72 (90%) called it a "banana." The remaining subjects called it an "object" (6%), "thing" (1%), "something" (1%), and "toy auto" (1%). To what extent the deviations were due to misrecognition of the object or failure to find the label can not be assessed in that study. Much lower agreement was found in subjects' descriptions of an object on which children were seen playing in a play ground. Of the 80 subjects, 73 (91%) did refer to this object. However, the most common labels were "jungle gym" (19%), "object" (14%), and "structure" (11%). In fact, 20 different labels were used. Chafe (1977) found that subjects tended to use more modifiers with the names or labels for the playground object—on the average 2.12 modifiers were used; for the banana, only .16 modifiers were used on the average. We will later describe additional research on verbal descriptions in the section comparing thinking aloud with other forms of verbalization.

Also relevant to the issue of lexical selection is the influential paper by Clark (1974), where he shows subjects' preferences for using unmarked adjectives to describe relations and attributes. For example, subjects prefer "longer" to "shorter" and "bright" to "dark." The unmarked adjective appears to be the one that subjects assess.

Due to the direct access of the names and the fact that most names are established by convention rather than semantically derived, the generation of names will not likely affect the subsequent cognitive processes. By careful design or selection of tasks, reliance on the NAME process can be increased. However, there are many instances when an object or entity cannot be *uniquely* referenced by its name, for example, in cases where several objects have the same label, or where an object lacks a readily elicited name. Then we will postulate an encoding process called REFERENCE(X). An attribute or combination of attributes of the entity can often be used as a unique reference: "the red ball," "the large block," etc. In other cases reference can be made either to spatial location ("left," "furthest down"), or to spatial relations with other reference points ("on the table"). (See Olson (1970) for a discussion of the influence of perceptual context on linguistic form of reference). In still other cases earlier events can be used to refer to the heeded entity, like "the block that used to be on the table."

The REFERENCE process requires cognitive processing beyond that required to NAME. We postulate that subjects, for economy's sake, will tend to use attributes, from among all those logically possible, that are already activated and part of their representation of the current task. However, in cases where the subjective representation doesn't allow easy generation of a verbal referent (e.g., sizes of disks in the Tower of Hanoi with more than 3 disks), we assume that the reference will be based on task-irrelevant salient perceptual cues (e.g., color).

Subjects are free to circumvent the NAME and REFERENCE processes by using pronouns, and experience shows that pronouns are used frequently in think-aloud protocols where the alternative would be to use REFERENCE(X).

Selection of Syntactical Form. Thoughts can be expressed syntactically in many ways. In view of the recent comprehensive review by Bock (1982) of the factors influencing choice of syntax, we will limit our discussion here to a few examples of such factors. There have been only a few studies where subjects have been asked to describe pictorial stimuli. Clark and Chase (1972) had subjects give a sentence describing one of the stimuli below.

(A)   (B)

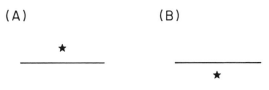

Figure 5-1
Two Examples of the Kind of Stimuli used by Clark and Chase (1974)

In both cases most subjects preferred to start their sentences with "The star." For picture A, 89% of the subjects wrote, "The star is above the line." For picture B, 69% of subjects wrote, "The star is below the line." This lower frequency in the second case can be attributed to a general preference for "above." One possible inference from this study is that the star provides the perspective for describing the scene. The sentence produced is the implicit answer to the question, "Where is the *star?*" Clark and Chase (1972) showed that the preference for this syntax was entirely consistent with other subjects' latencies in a picture-sentence verification task. MacWhinney (1977), exploring the general evidence for the perspective hypothesis, notes that attempts to provide a perceptual context that elicits passives have been rather unsuccessful. Using other experimental manipulations (e.g., eliciting questions), more success has been achieved.

Another major experimental method for studying sentence generation is presenting subjects with sentences and studying their later recall for them. For cued recall there is a considerable effect of the location of the cue word in the sentence. For passive constructions recall is much more often correct if the cue word is the starting point of the stimulus sentence (cf. Bock, 1982; MacWhinney, 1977). In an interesting study by Bock and Irwin (1980) recall of a sentence like, "The rancher sold the horse to the cowboy," could be changed to "The rancher sold the cowboy the horse," by referring to a "cowboy" or to an example of a cowboy, like "Roy Rogers," in the preamble to the recall cue. Bock and Irwin found that giving the lexical item "cowboy" resulted in more change. In her review, Bock (1982) explores how far these syntactical selections can be accounted for by lexical accessibility.

Another series of studies on verbalization of thoughts present subjects with one or more words that are to be made into sentences. In reviewing his own and other investigators' studies of this kind, Danks (1977) shows quite convincingly that a stage model, where the thought is first generated and then translated, cannot account for the data in this experimental situation. In one of his experiments subjects were simply asked to generate ideas containing the stimulus words and signal when this process was completed. Later the same words were presented again and subjects had to verbalize the thought or indicate that they could not remember it. One of the main results was that the thought production latency was related to linguistic variables of the later produced verbalizations. Danks interprets these results to indicate some linguistic encoding of the ideas, even when verbalization is not requested.

Other investigators, like Taylor (1969), did not find that syntactic complexity made a difference in how long it took to *start* to verbalize an idea containing a single abstract or concrete noun. However, Taylor did find a clear difference in this starting latency between abstract and concrete nouns, a difference which can probably be attributed to the great difficulty of generating ideas involving abstract nouns. Danks (1977) argues that the effects of syntactical complexity may have been present, but too small for Taylor's study to find. (A study of Johnson (1966) suggests that the effects may be on the order of less than a tenth of a second).

In a study of very simple sentences or even syntagmas (i.e., noun-verb and noun-verb-object), Lindsley (1975) found evidence that verb selection is initiated but not completed when subjects start verbalizing the sentence with noun and verb. Since the initiation latency was unaffected by asking the subjects to generate an additional object, thought generation and linguistic encoding must go on in some parallel fashion. The generality of these results may be limited by the fact that subjects employ special strategies for generating ideas that contain the visually presented words. However, these studies demonstrate quite nicely the immediacy of verbalization of thoughts.

In sum, verbalization of thoughts relies on processes for lexical and syntactical selection that can be quite variable between individuals in situations where no accepted terminology has been developed and acquired. However, in many situations the verbalization of thoughts is quite immediate and follows closely their generation.

Verbalization of Complex Thoughts. We will make a major distinction between verbalization of newly generated thoughts and verbalization of thoughts recalled from memory. Generating new thoughts, under all kinds of constraints of relevance, is a slow process. Old thoughts are already well integrated with other information in memory. Retelling a story that one has told many times is much easier and fluent than telling a story that is being generated as it is told. In writing letters the constraining feature is not verbalization or writing speed, but the time taken to generate what is to be said or communicated (Gould, 1978, 1982). Bock (1982) reviews some studies showing that planning *what* to say takes much more time than deciding *how* to say it. Deese (1978, 1980) found that when subjects had previously decided what to say—but not how—they were much more fluent than when they made such decisions while speaking. Goldman-Eisler and Cohen (1970) found planned speech to be more varied syntactically than extemporaneous speech. Finally, verbal descriptions of cartoons and events are much more fluent than explanations (Goldman-Eisler, 1968; Levin, Silverman, & Ford, 1967), which require more thinking and analysis.

We will first discuss verbalization of ongoing productive thought and then turn to verbalization of recalled thought or perceptually available information.

Verbalization of Productive Thought. One of the basic assumptions (Assumption 3) in our model of concurrent verbalization is that heeded information is verbalized at the time it enters attention. For processes that use STM for storage of inputs and outputs, Assumption 1 then allows us to generate the following empirically testable hypothesis:

Hypothesis of Sequential Verbalization. Information required as *input* to some process or operation will be verbalized before the *output* of that operation is verbalized.

We can illustrate this hypothesis with a couple of examples and also show that it is not trivial and that alternative outcomes are conceivable. The first example is taken from a mental multiplication task, where one of the component multiplications is 6*4:

TASK: Multiply 26*34

	Input	Output	Input
Prediction from sequential hypothesis	6 times 4 is	24	
Alternative hypothesis		24	Because it's 6 times 4

Without exception, the protocols to be discussed in Chapter 7 support the sequential hypothesis. Although the verbalization in reverse order is a legitimate English utterance, it simply does not occur in this situation. In fact if we alter the experimental situation slightly and show the subjects a card with 6 * 4 = —, they will be most likely respond in agreement with the alternative hypothesis or simply report the output. In this case we are dealing with recognition processes, which do not use STM for their inputs. Before discussing recognition processes we present one more example. Consider the following protocol segment from a subject trying to move tiles in the Eight Puzzle to reach the goal configuration from the current puzzle configuration, where the irrelevant tiles are denoted by X's.

Current puzzle configuration	Goal configuration
1X3	123
X2	456
XXX	78

Observed: I think that if I am to get 2 up there then I have to move
3 down again ... that is what I am thinking about ...
It's that I get so mad about

Possible verbalization reversing the order of goal and action:
I have to move 3 down again because I want to get 2
up there

If the goal is heeded prior to selecting means for obtaining it, then we would expect that it should be verbalized prior to the means. According to our model, it is possible that the action is generated or accessed so quickly that verbalization of the goal is omitted. It is then possible that the subject generates the *because* construction by a subsequent retrieval of the goal from STM. The two forms of verbalization are possible, yet the evidence supports overwhelmingly the sequential hypothesis for nonrecognition processes. In all the protocols mentioned in Chapter 7, we rarely find cases of reversed verbalizations of inputs (premises or constraints) and outputs (conclusions or results).

It is, however, not sufficient to show that in most cases plausible inputs are verbalized prior to plausible outputs. There are cases, where "because" and "since" constructions may be consistent with the order in which the information was actually heeded, and hence, with the sequential hypothesis. In recognition processes the input is not available in STM prior to access of the recognized structure. However, once the structure is recognized and in STM, that structure can be used as input to further tests and evaluations. Let us consider this hypothetical example of somebody seeing someone else passing in the hall at a distance:

Input	Output-recognition	Text of recognition
-----	It must be John,	because he was wearing that funny-looking hat.
-----	It must be Peter,	but I don't think so because he doesn't have a hat like that.

If we assume that the "funny-looking" hat was not distinctive of John, then the test could only be made after the hypothesis of John had been accessed. This is also the case in the second example.

Hayes-Roth and Walker (1979) found subjects who had to verify inferences from previously memorized texts relying frequently on recognition processes, for example (p. 129):

Fragments of memorized text:	Albert Profiro hated King Egbert. King Egbert was a dictator.
Protocol:	True, because King Egbert was a dictator, and Albert Profiro hated all dictators. So it's true.

In work on geometry theorem proving, Greeno (1976) showed that subjects used indefinite subgoals (see Chapter 4). For example, the subgoal of proving that two triangles were congruent appeared to elicit the particular theorem or case by recognition rather than by a serial evaluation of the alternatives. We earlier reported that Greeno did not find any evidence in the protocols for explicit serial evaluation of the possibly applicable theorems. In this case we would expect the recognition processes to produce *because* constructions. Here is the central portion of a protocol from a subject solving the problem stated in Figure 5-2.

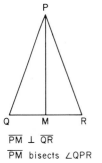

$\overline{PM} \perp \overline{QR}$
$\overline{PM}$ bisects $\angle QPR$
Prove $\triangle PQM \cong \triangle PRM$

Figure 5-2

A Problem of Proving Congruence of Triangles (Greeno, 1976)

S: Well: if I'm going to write down a reason ... well, that's kind of
       given. I'm trying to think if I know a reason. About bisecting.
       But, when ... the definition of a bisector, I guess.

E: That would be fine.

S: Okay, and ... make this three and four. Three is congruent to four
       because of perpendicular lines form right angles; right angles are
       congruent ... And then PM is congruent to PM, because of the
       reflexive property ... And then I have angle-side-angle.
       (Greeno, 1976, p. 482)

In this protocol there are a couple of *because* constructions that
contain the formal test or reason for congruency of sides and angles. A
closer look at these reasons suggest that they can only be applied when a
pair has already been identified and cannot be used for generating congruent pairs.

As the final piece of evidence we will look at the sequential relations between inputs (premises, P) and outputs (conclusions, C) in the
cryptarithmetic task (Newell & Simon, 1972). Our evidence comes from
the intensively analyzed protocol of Subject 3.

In the cryptarithmetic task subjects are shown an addition, where a
unique letter has been substituted for each digit, and are asked to determine the original digits. Subjects solve this problem by using relations
between digits in the addition columns and trial assignments of digits to
letters as premises to generate conclusions about further assignments of
digits to letters. We would predict that the premises would be verbalized

prior to the conclusions, in the form "P implies C." An analysis of the protocol shows the following syntactic constructions.

Form	Frequency
P→C	14 (Total)
P, therefore C	2
P, which will mean that C	1
P, which means that C	2
P means that C	1
P, which will make C	1
P, which leaves C	1
Since P, C	2
P, now C	1
If P, so C	1
Suppose P, then C	1
P, so C	1
C→P	6 (Total)
C because P	5
C, since P	1

The table shows that premises are usually verbalized before the corresponding conclusions. Let us now carry the analysis a little further and determine whether the six reversed verbalizations are violations of the sequential verbalization hypothesis.

The sequential hypothesis is violated if a necessary premise is mentioned after the corresponding inference, when this inference was generated for the first time. The requirement that it has to be the first generation is important, for if the inference had been made earlier, then it could have been retrieved from memory independently of the new inputs. After retrieving an inference from memory it may even be appropriate to *test* its validity against relevant premises. In a couple of cases, the heeded information is obviously a test of the generated inference rather than an input for its generation. In the following instance the conclusion is used as input to a subsequent test:

B66   R is going to be a 7,
B67   then this will be a 7,
B68   and that will be a 7,
B69   and it's the L's that will have to be 3's,
B70   because 3 + 3 is 6
B71   + 1 is 7

If the premise were a reflection of intermediate states towards the generation of the conclusion (i.e., $L = 3$), then the following verbalization would be expected: "7 − 1 is 6 and 6 divided by 2 is 3."

In another case we can see that the subject is clearly testing, as he just previously generated the inference with the same inputs that appear in the *because* construction.

B20   2 L's equal an R....
B21   Of course I'm carrying a 1.
B22   Which will mean that R has to be an odd number.
B23   Because the 2 L's ...
B24   any two numbers added together has to be an even number
B25   and 1 will be an odd number.

In still another case it appears possible that a generated inference ("E is an even number") is retrieved and its validity checked and tested in the *because* construction. Below we will show first the segment giving the initial generation, and then the subsequent segment with the *because* construction.

B91   Let's see....
B92   I have two A's equaling an E.
B93   Therefore, E has to be an even number,
B166   Let's see, E can't be 9 though.
B167   It doesn't look like E can be 9,
B168   because A + A has to equal E.

Observe that the first verbalization of the inference that E cannot be 9 is *not* linked to the *because* construction, which makes it even more unlikely that it was used as input for generation of that inference. In the last type of example, S3 verbalizes information in the *because* construction that is a mere statement of fact, not corresponding to information useful in the generation of the conclusion. It is, however, a reasonable test for the validity of a retrieved inference.

B111   I decided that R had to be greater than 5,
B112   because that was given

Verbalization from Perceptions or Recall. When subjects are recalling thoughts from memory or perceiving information in the environment, thoughts can be heeded much faster than they can possibly be verbalized. We will deal with the resulting incompleteness in a special section in this chapter. Here we will focus on verbalization of more complex thoughts and the effects of context on the form of the verbalizations.

Let us first look at effects of context and perspective. Context can be induced by presenting events in a particular order. Osgood (1971) demonstrated that the form and content of verbalized descriptions of stimulus events reflected the structure of the perceptual situation and the subjects' presuppositions based on events presented previously. The extent to which objects were perceived as new or previously seen was directly linked to the use of indefinite or definite determiners and pronouns. Modifiers like adjectives and adverbs were used when needed to discriminate similar objects and events. The structure of the perceptual situation and the sequence of events is related to the phrase structure of the verbalized sentence. In a controlled experiment, Jeremy (1978) found that whether events occurred at the same or different times, or the same or different locations affected the structure of verbalizations about the events, but the content of the events produced no effect.

In an interesting study of subjects' attempts to comprehend the mechanisms of sewing machines, Miyake (1982) showed that the "mental" points of view of subjects could be assessed from their verbalizations. She showed that there was a relation between shifts in point of view and lack of understanding and that final understanding was associated with a stable point of view. The point of view was assessed through occurrences of verbs, like "go" and "come," and demonstratives, like "this" and "here." A view from above the sewing machine was, for example, inferred from verbalizations describing the needle as "going down" and "comes up." Conversely, a view from below was inferred by describing the needle as "comes down" and "goes up."

Thoughts that are inherently complex must be broken down into their components to generate a verbal code for them. Even though a thought is activated as a unit in LTM, it will appear as a sequence of propositions. The following example is taken from a subject, who is instructed to think aloud while letting his mind wander freely (daydream).

"The Volkswagon is very easy to repair by yourself, since the engine is in the back, and very small, and since there are so few moving parts, it is easy to repair." (Bertini, Lewis, & Witkin, 1964, p. 507).

Another example is taken from a subject selecting a move in chess.

"A King side push of pawns to break up the Black King side would take too long, because we are after all under the necessity of protecting the Queen's Knight pawn." (Newell & Simon, 1972, p. 742).

We postulate that verbalization of complex recalled thoughts is in many ways similar to verbalization of new sequences of thoughts. Because of the limits of STM capacity, complex thoughts are not kept as entities in STM. A complex thought can be heeded as a whole only in the sense that all the subordinate elements are *directly* available for retrieval and subsequent attention. In the same way, a complex scene is not perceived simultaneously in all its detail. Instead the information is accessed piecemeal with the aid of rapid eye movements. (Simon & Barenfeld, 1969). There is thus a continuum from rapid access to simple thoughts and stimuli, to much slower and sequential access to complex memories and complex visual stimuli, to still slower production times for newly generated thoughts.

There are only a few studies where the recall of well-integrated structures has been systematically examined. In analyzing subject's verbal descriptions of the layout of their apartments, Linde and Labov (1975) isolated rules for the generation of the verbal descriptions. For example, they found that major rooms may be introduced in subject noun phrases and with a definite article whereas minor rooms were mentioned in complements. The evidence suggests that the structure of thinking-aloud verbalizations is indicative of subjects' internal representations.

Similar analyses of the long-term memory representation of complex information structures have been made with verbal descriptions of planned meals (Byrne, 1977) and with vebally given road directions (Klein, 1981; Wunderlich & Reinelt, 1981). In a recent study Levelt (1982) has systematically studied verbal descriptions of spatial networks of colored dots and has explored the interesting problems of memory and path-selection involved in generating a sequential linear description of such organized structures.

We recommend using similar tasks for warm-up exercises (see Appendix), for example, asking subjects to think aloud while determining the number of windows in their homes. Here is an example of a concurrent protocol followed by a retrospective report given immediately afterwards.

> **Concurrent: (S16-2)**
> Let's see, there's 3 windows in the living room, 3 windows in my room, 1 in the bathroom, 2 in the sewing room, that's 5 and 3, 6, 7, 8, 13—4 in the kitchen which would make 17; 3, 4 in the TV room which would make 21, 2 in my brother's room, 23; and 1 in the upstairs bathroom, 24; and 3 in my parent's room, 27; and then 1 in the attic, 28.
>
> **Retrospective: (S16-2)**
> The living room 3 windows, my room 3 windows, the bathroom has 1 window which comes up to 7,—the sewing room has 2 windows which is 9 which means I added wrong. The study has 5 which is 14, the kitchen has 4 which makes

18, the TV room has 4 which would make 22, my brother's room has 2 which would make 24, the upstairs bathroom has 1 which would make 25; parent's room has 3 would be 28 and the attic is 1, 29.

Verbal reports have often been collected in research on the retrieval of selected information from memory (Johnson, 1955; Read & Bruce, 1982; Whitten & Leonard, 1981; Williams & Santos-Williams, 1980). These studies show convincingly the dependence of recall upon retrieval cues, and that dependence has strong implications for the nature of the cognitive processes involved, and hence for the verbalizations. Williams and Hollan (1981) discuss a wide range of retrieval cues and structures. The following protocol segment shows how subjects use highly organized information about locations when they are asked to recall as many names as possible of students in their graduating class in high-school.

That's a new name. He lived on Alvian Street. Ah, let me see, on the other side of there, there is Bob. He was a year older and that other girl was a year older. O.K., so there is Margaret Mott and if you come up and around, there is no one right there. Jim Gott lived down there, but I've already named Judy Nicholson and let me see if there is anybody on the cross street. There was a girl that was younger and she had a brother that was a year older than me. Then there was a girl a year younger and there is Gay Masterson. I already named her, and Barbie Tollen. They live on the same street and they have no one else on that street that went to Point Loma with us. If I keep going down Silvergate there is someone who lived on the corner house. It had a purple door... (Williams & Hollan, 1981, p. 104)

In a recent dissertation, Walker (1982) studied free recall of members of different categories (e.g., cars, soups, and detergents) which were selected to reflect different degrees of familiarity to the subjects. As expected, subjects were able to generate more names of the more familiar categories. More interestingly, Walker found that subjects used a greater variety of retrieval cues for the more familiar categories. In only about 5% of the instances were names retrieved without a verbalized retrieval cue. As is shown by the protocol segments below, subjects appeared to use very similar cognitive processes in generating names for both familiar and less familiar categories.

Generation of names of cars:
Just keep on picture where cars are, /parking lot,/ ... a sales lot / ... on the road, / Subaru Brat, / Celica, / ...

picturing cars in the front of my dorm / ... ones I come out
and see all the time / ... Midget / ... I know like no names / ...
Camaro, / my sister got her first Camaro. (Walker, 1982,
p. 42)

> *Generation of names of detergents:*
> S: Okay. If I was a housewife this would probably be a
> lot easier to do. Unfortunately, I'm not. And I don't watch
> too much TV, except football games, and they usually have
> beer on for football games, so it's kind of tough. Unless I
> watch 'General Hospital', of course, then they have laundry
> detergents on, so I'll see what I can come up with from there.
> Umm, think of ALL-TEMPACHEER. There's one. And the
> stuff that I use is FRESH START. That's two. And then,
> umm, I could think of OXYDOL, which is on TV. And
> there's always good old WISK, for ring-around-the-collar.
> There's some pretty silly commercials about that. (Walker,
> 1982, p. 207)

There are also a few studies of the recall or generation of thoughts
rather than names of items. Caccamise (1981) asked subjects to generate
ideas for inclusion in papers on different topics. Using a modified form
of the propositional analysis proposed by Kintsch (1980), she described
the structure and complexity of the thoughts. She found that, on
average, 2.5 propositions were produced for each thought. She also
found that most of the pauses occurred at points where the thought
content changed. (For a more extensive discussion of Walkers' &
Caccamise's work, see van Dijk & Kintsch (1983).) Thought generation
has also been explored as part of the writing process, in extensive studies
by Flower and Hayes (1978).

In sum, there are important communalities between verbalization
of recalled thoughts and concurrent verbalization of *new* sequences of
thoughts. The less well integrated are the thoughts and information in
memory, the more constrained will be the access to further thoughts, and
the more dependent will access be on actively generated retrieval cues.
For both newly generated thoughts and (to a lesser degree) thoughts
recovered from memory, the evidence shows that the sequence of verbalizations parallels closely the sequence of thoughts.

Verbalizing Cognitive Process

In the previous sections of this chapter we were primarily concerned with verbalization of heeded information. This information is both the output of processing and the input to subsequent processing. For our purposes we can view the attention to new information as instantaneous. Since cognitive processes have a nonnegligible duration, our inference that we are attending to them derives from our awareness of a sequence of internal states. The information heeded during the execution of a process is our only source of data about the structure of that process.

In this section our aim is two-fold. First, we will specify how descriptions of cognitive activities can be generated within our model. Second, we will specify under what circumstances such descriptions are verbalized and when they become an obtrusive activity induced by instructions to verbalize.

We would like to discriminate three different sources of information that would allow subjects to report on activities with duration. First, in many situations the cognitive activity has an external counterpart in motor activities, which can either be observed visually or by means of other information available in the sensory stores. Second, due to the limited capacity of STM, information will only reside there for a limited time and it is possible that subjects have information about this time in STM. Third, higher-level activities like reading and writing are made up of numerous subprocesses that use STM for inputs and outputs. Subjects' awareness of these inputs and outputs enables them to report the occurrence and duration of the higher-level activities.

As processes become automated, less and less information becomes available about them. This is particularly true of many motor activities. Tasks involving physical manipulation do not produce detailed verbal traces of the motor activity. What are verbalized in these situations are the higher-level directions for the manipulative attempts (Ruger, 1910) and monitoring evaluations of the sucess of attempts (Klinger, 1974).

Even though this may be the usual case, still the subject can change his processing and describe the activity in detail from his perception of his own visual, kinestetic or tactile input. Examples of this kind of verbalization of motor and perceptual-motor activities are given by McNeill (1975). He asked subjects to describe each movement as they made it in highly automatized activities, like sitting down on the floor and rising to standing, and in other tasks, like assembling an aquarium. By analyzing the videotape recordings, he found a very close temporal correspondence between the movements and the verbal descriptions. In the assembly task the verbal description was initiated after the motor activity was initiated, suggesting that the verbal description was cued by the motor process. In the highly automatic activities there was an almost perfect correspondence between the initiation of the verbal description and the movement, suggesting that the anticipated next movement served as a cue for the verbal description.

Although subjects are able to access and attend to motor processes and also describe them, in most cases this is an additional activity unrelated to the verbalization of the information heeded in the normal course of the process. For many motor skills the verbalization is highly obtrusive.

Although the instruction to "think aloud" clearly asks for verbalization of heeded information, it sometimes evokes descriptions of activities instead. In the following example of activity descriptions one should note the frequency of the present progressive verb tense.

B33	330	I'm just scanning the rules, not in search of anything in particular.
B34		I can't find anything that's going to help me.
B35	360	Now, I'll start back on equation 1 again.
B36	390	Right now, I'm looking at equations 2 and 3 and thinking of applying...
		(pause)
		(Newell & Simon, 1972, p. 511)

This protocol fragment has a predominance of high-level activities, as if the subject were intermittently asking himself, "What am I doing?" As we would expect, subjects who give mainly activity descriptions verbalize at a slow rate. The subject in the example above spoke less than 40 words/minute. We would not be safe in extrapolating to this kind of verbalization the conclusions we have reached about think-aloud protocols that report mainly STM contents. Verbalization of activities may possibly influence the problem solving process, although we are not aware of specific evidence that it does.

Although we consider the process of attention or heeding as essentially instantaneous, it may be possible to determine how long a given piece of information is retained in STM. Information about future states, given premises, goals or subgoals will be kept in STM as long as they actually direct the subjects' processing. It is therefore understandable why subjects use the present progressive in the following type of construction:

"Now I am thinking that I shall get 1 up there" (Ericsson, 1975b, p. 93)

Similarly for modal states in planning:

"And knowing that the two L's add up to some number greater than 10" (Newell & Simon, 1972, p. 264)

These kinds of verbalizations are derived from information that is heeded, but they are generated as responses to a probe, like "What am I thinking about?", and not directly as reports of the information attended to.

Cognitive activities of the third type are organized into skills that are used recurrently. If the skills are highly automated, reportable intermediate states may occur infrequently; otherwise, the attempt to report the activity may compete for processing capacity with verbal encoding processes. Examples of such activities are reading simple text, doing arithmetic, searching visually for displayed information, recalling information from memory, generating combinations by manipulation. When such activities are executed, subjects may refer verbally to the activity and its associated goal at the time the activity is initially heeded (e.g., "Let me see if I can remember how I did it last time."). The activities mentioned can be of high or low level, broad or narrow scope: "I want to solve this problem first," or "I want to find the value of Y first." Items seem most likely to be mentioned when the decision is being reached to take them up next, rather than while the activity is actually under way.

As subjects acquire more skill in a domain through practice, they develop a more sophisticated internal representation and better methods for attaining goals. Subjects may both attend to these procedures and plans, and also verbalize them. Initially a subject may recognize that he can apply a procedure he has used at an earlier time. Later he may simply refer to it as "the procedure for attaining X." Such a report is different from a reference to a procedure as it is heeded. A subject can only report that he has used a procedure previously if he can recall some of the earlier instances. Hence, such a report suffers all of the deficiencies of recall from LTM, and must be interpreted more cautiously than a report of information that is being heeded.

Differences Between Verbal Reports and Descriptions

A few studies address directly the differences between thinking aloud and various kinds of descriptions. To explore the differences between internal representation (inner speech) and communication (external speech), Kaplan (Werner & Kaplan, 1963) compared descriptions of non-figurative drawing and odors that were to be used by the subjects themselves with descriptions that were to be used by some other naive person to identify the original stimuli. External speech was more explicit, consisting of more words per description, and employing relatively conventional references (i.e., to size, shape, location) as opposed to analogies (i.e., "looks like a talking penguin"). Loewenthal (1967) reports that verbal descriptions of colored shapes become less and less explicit, as a function of whether the descriptions were to be used by another naive person, the subjects themselves several weeks later, or the subjects themselves immediately after the experiment.

These studies did not demonstrate the subjects' abilities to use their own or other subjects' verbal descriptions to identify the stimuli. In a study using colors as stimuli (Krauss, Vivekanantham, & Weinheimer, 1968) and a study using abstract drawings (Danks, 1970), subjects could match their own verbal descriptions against the stimuli with more than 75% accuracy after a two week interval. In one condition, subjects were instructed to generate names to be used by themselves (Own), in the other condition, to be used by others (Social). Matching accuracy was essentially the same in both conditions. However, rarer words were used by subjects in the Own condition, and their vocabularies varied more between descriptions (Krauss et al., 1968). Danks (1970) included an additional group, instructed to generate their *first* associations to the figures. The matching was slightly (ten per cent) slower for these immediate associations, indicating that in the Own condition subjects did not use just their first associations.

In a study by Dickson, Miyake, and Muto (1977), Japanese students described 16 abstract figures in two different ways. One of the descriptions was to be analytical (e.g., "a crooked triangle whose bottom part is missing"), the other metaphorical (e.g., "the upper part of a rose viewed from above"). A subset of descriptions was selected that Japanese students could identify correctly about 50% of the time. These descriptions were translated literally into English. When groups of American and Japanese students were asked to identify the objects from the verbal descriptions, the average accuracy was about 50% for both the analytic and metaphoric descriptions, with the Japanese group only slightly better than the American. Only a few items showed reliable differences between the two groups, and many of these differences could be ascribed to cultural differences. For us, the main result is that these verbal descriptions remained valid even after translation, and for subjects with a radically different cultural background.

In a study designed to inquire whether "think aloud" should be seen as a form of introspection, Benjafield (1969) instructed one group of subjects to think aloud, and interrupted the other group of subjects every minute to make "introspective" retrospective reports. More words were recorded in the think aloud condition. In addition, Benjafield found differences with respect to immediacy and reference. More verbs were in the present tense in the think aloud condition, and more in the past tense in the retrospective reports. As would be predicted from our previous discussion, pronouns and fragmentary utterances occurred more frequently in the think aloud condition.

Ohlsson (1980) coded TA protocols to distinguish between heeded thoughts, on the one hand, and introspections, retrospective reports, and communications to the experimenter, on the other. Three criteria were used to identify introspections, which are difficult to characterize. Reports were classified as introspections if the grammatical subject was the speaker (e.g., "I," "my head"); if the verb was epistemic (e.g., "remember," "feel," "know") and if the verbalization did not contain specific information about the current problem. In the protocols of 10 subjects, each solving six problems, only 3.5% of the verbalizations were introspections, retrospective reports, or communications to the experimenter. Over 96% were verbalizations of currently heeded thoughts. From many other studies we can derive estimates that suggest similar proportions of the two kinds of verbalizations in TA in other problem domains.

INCOMPLETE VERBALIZATION OF INFORMATION IN STM

We return now to the issue of the completeness of verbalizations, first discussed in Chapter 3. The central problem is that thought in non-oral form can proceed much faster than speech. The major empirical evidence for the incompleteness of information in think-aloud protocols is twofold: (1) inconsistency in how much is reported on repetitions of essentially the same process, and (2) comparisons of think-aloud protocols with retrospective reports.

When a thought structure comes into attention, it serves at the same time as the input to the processes for verbalization. The oral code has to be retrieved and generated, and at the same time vocalized. Earlier, we reviewed the evidence that these processes overlap in time. However direct the processes, they operate on semantic structures of nonnegligible size (syntagmas). Hence, even in the case where an oral code for the structure is directly retrievable, substantial time will elapse before the vocalization can begin, and more before it is complete. We illustrate these temporal relations in Figure 5-3.

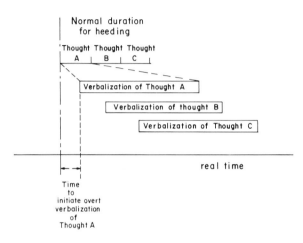

Figure 5-3

An Illustration of the Temporal Relation between Heeding a Thought and its Overt Verbalization, and the Impossibility of Direct Verbalization of a Complete Series of Rapidly Occurring Thoughts

As can be seen from the figure, the time required for heeding a structure during task performance may be only a fraction of the time required to complete its vocalization. This can be shown by asking subjects to think aloud while carrying out a relatively simple task (e.g., mental paper-folding, sentence-picture verification). Attention to task information moves too rapidly to allow the corresponding oral code to be generated and vocalized.

One might imagine a subject pausing when each new structure enters attention to provide a verbal report before continuing his work on the task. Many thinking-aloud instructions (See Chapter 2) explicitly instruct the subjects to slow down their thought processes in order to permit this. Where the task is an unfamiliar one, the problem may not arise, since new information comes into attention at a slow pace. We will focus on situations where experience and skill in the task permit information to be acquired rapidly. In these situations, a number of difficulties arise in trying to slow down the cognitive processes without changing them.

First, it is hard to control the very rapid processes that acquire new information by recognition. When, for example, a subject is scanning a visual stimulus for information and recognizes something, it may be impossible for him to prevent himself from recognizing additional structures before he has reported the first one—unless the visual stimulus can be removed at the moment of the initial recognition. This difficulty is likely to arise, for example, for subjects in the anagram task who adopt the simple strategy of acquiring information by recognition until sufficient cues have been obtained to elicit the word from memory.

Second, some cognitive processes can only be executed under time constraints. There are many cases, especially in the motor domain, where processes cannot be slowed down without drastically changing outcome and accuracy. Examples of such activities are juggling and riding a bicycle. There are also activities where the rapid decay of sensory stores imposes bounds on the time during which the information in those stores can be accessed. Interruption and suppression of rehearsal lead to a rapid loss of information from STM. Hence, we would expect that prolonged attention to items in STM to allow verbalization will be disruptive of tasks that impose high loads on STM.

To assess how serious these problems of verbalization are, we need to examine the relevant empirical evidence. Our review will be carried out in three parts. First, we will examine some general implications of our model for individual differences and for rate of verbalization. Second, we will analyze cases where concurrent verbalization has been alleged to be incomplete. Finally, we will discuss techniques, like slowing subjects down or using verbal probes to keep them talking, that have been proposed to increase verbalization.

Implications of Real-Time Assumption.

Complete verbalization of heeded thoughts, as de Groot (1965) notes, takes time and effort, thus "slowing down the thinking itself." De Groot observes that describing perceptually available objects, like men on a chessboard, requires naming and references to location (e.g., "Rook on c4."). Some tasks, like chess, have a precise language for communicating about board configurations and moves. Other tasks, like tying knots and other motor activites, do not usually have a shared common vocabulary.

Speech in a foreign language illustrates how encoding processes that are not automatic slow processes down. Persons fluent in a second language can usually think aloud in that language even while thinking internally in the oral code of their native language or in non-oral code. In this case, there is nearly a one-to-one mapping between structures in the oral code of the first language and the code of the second language that is used for vocalizaton. How much the thinking is slowed down will then be a function of the subject's skill in the second language.

Individual differences. Individual differences in facility in thinking aloud are wholly consistent with our model. Some people are certainly better able than others to vocalize their thoughts in normal social contexts. The marked variety in spontaneity and richness among the protocols recorded by de Groot (1965) and Claparède (1934) may be attributed to such differences.

Ease in verbalizing thoughts and private experiences of a nonverbal type, like day-dreams, fantasies, and transitional imagery states, depends on possessing vocabulary and efficient encoding processes for doing so. In fact, Klinger (1971) observed that only highly verbal female subjects were able to give rich and fluent verbalizations in a reverie condition containing mostly visual images.

Some individual differences in concurrent verbalization of thoughts observed by Johnson (1964) can also be accounted for within the framework of our assumptions. Some of his subjects followed a "think-then-summarize" procedure, encoding and verbalizing after the completion of a sequence of thoughts. A subject requiring more time for encoding than was available in the course of thought would be predicted to behave in this way.

Individual differences may also be due to style or convenience. We can reduce such differences by giving subjects warm-up tasks with oral information (e.g. mental multiplication, anagrams) where *all* subjects should be able to produce concurrent protocols. (See the Appendix for further information about the warm-up procedure.)

Rate of verbalization. When a subject attends to a steady stream of non-oral information, our model would predict a rather steady verbalization, at a rate close to relaxed normal conversation, or about a hundred words per minute. It appears unreasonable that subjects would verbalize at a faster rate than normal conversation in experiments lasting from five minutes to several hours. We will first review evidence from protocols that approach this upper bound. Then we will discuss some situations where the observed rates of verbalization are slower.

According to our model, several words correspond to each thought. Some authors have attempted to estimate the total numbers of thoughts that receive attention, others have estimated the numbers of thoughts or structures of particular types. Thus, we may try to report the rate of verbalization (words/minute), the "rate of thinking" (thoughts/minute), or the rate of language production (phrases and speech bursts/minute). Only a few studies report one or more of these measures.

There is not much variance among studies of TA in the average rates of verbalization. Roughly, normal relaxed continuous talking produces about 150-200 words/minute. Thinking-aloud protocols vary from about 50 to 110 words/minute for 10 subjects in Ohlsson's study (1980) of series problems and the 11 subjects in Biggs' (1978) study of portfolio selection. Roth (1965) reported that his subjects talked 30 to 50 per cent of the time, which is consistent with the ratio of conversational rates to protocol rates cited above.

Over the 19 physics problems in the study of Simon and Simon (1978) the novice had a verbalization rate of 69.3 words/minute, but the expert verbalized at an average rate of 153.7 words/minute. Somewhat lower rates of verbalization can be inferred from Sargent's (1940) anagram-solving study and Montgomery and Allwood's (1978) study of problem-solving in statistics. Deffner (1983) reports rates of verbalization in terms of letters per 4 seconds, but these can easily be converted into words/minute if we assume 5 letters in a word on the average. Except for anagrams, he found average verbalization rates for 5 different tasks between 40 to 72 words/minute, and also no systematic difference in rate of verbalization for easy and difficult problems of each type. The rate of verbalization with anagrams was 25-30 words/minute with a reliable decrease of rate of verbalization for difficult anagrams.

Ohlsson's (1980) study shows little variation in verbalization rates from one problem to another, and little reduction in rate of verbalization during the course of an experimental session. Simon and Simon (1978) also found that verbalization did not vary with problem. Roth (1966) found that subjects verbalized only 30% of the time when solving matchstick problems, but around 50% of the time when solving water-jug and river-crossing problems.

Words/minute is a poor measure for comparing amounts of verbalization from one task to another. In a protocol from the anagram-solving task, a word corresponds to a complete thought, whereas in many other domains, a thought may be expressed in five to ten words. The available evidence suggests that thoughts/minute are more nearly comparable between tasks than words/minute. Sargent (1940) estimates that subjects generate hypotheses at rates ranging from 2 to 9 per minute.

In the portfolio selection task, Biggs' (1978) subject generated new operators at rates ranging from 3.5 to 10 per minute. Protocols on such widely varying tasks as logic, chess, and cryptarithmetic showed new knowledge states being generated at rates between 8 and 11 per minute (Newell and Simon, 1972).

From the evidence we have reviewed, several general conclusions may be drawn. The rate of verbalization under think-aloud instructions is a little lower, on average, than the normal rate of speech. The limiting factor may be the rate at which new thoughts are heeded. In only one case, the expert subject in Simon and Simon (1978) did the verbalization rate (over 150 words/minute) even approach the upper limits of human vocalization abilities. Analysis of the protocol in that case suggests that the expert did very little problem solving but relied on recognition and recall of solution methods from memory.

Incomplete Concurrent Reporting. Cases in the literature where the evidence points to serious incompleteness in thinking-aloud protocols fall into a few categories.

1. Subjects reading text or attempting to understand written problem descriptions sometimes give rather scanty and uninformative thinking-aloud protocols (Hayes & Simon, 1974; Bree, 1969).

2. In situations where intense cognitive activity can be inferred, protocols become sparse. Johnson (1964) found that subjects pause during verbalizing when they experience difficulties in solving the problem. Durkin (1937) found that subjects were silent when they were reorganizing their perceptions of the problem.

3. Mediating steps leading directly to the solution are often not verbalized (Duncker, 1945). Comparisons between thinking-aloud protocols and retrospective reports of the "solution trace" collected for the same solutions by Durkin (1937) and Sargent (1940) confirm this kind of incompleteness.

Duncker (1945) notes that subjects often transform the original representation of the problem to a more constrained one without verbalizing or, for that matter, being aware of the shift. However, this does not constitute incomplete reporting of the information heeded by the subject. A subject may verbalize a series of representations, yet not compare them or notice the differences. A person may transform the equation $x(x - 3) = 5x$ to $x - 3 = 5$ without being aware that a solution of the original problem has been eliminated. Yet the two representations may be reported accurately. Our model implies that only the information in attention is verbalized. In general, the fact that something has left STM is not itself information stored in STM, hence is not usually reported.

Techniques for Increasing Verbalization

Several experimental techniques may be used to increase concurrent verbalization. In terms of our model, we can describe these techniques as being aimed at slowing down the task-directed processes. An alternative is to substitute retrospective for concurrent reports. The primary cause for a flow of heeded information that is too rapid to report completely are recognition processes elicited by information that is perceptually available.

We have found studies using at least four different techniques to secure more complete reporting:

1. Perceptual access to the stimulus may be denied. Then subjects have to generate new states internally, and cannot rely on rapid recognition of changing stimulus characteristics. We have already discussed studies using this technique (Benjafield, 1971; Durkin, 1937). A more extreme method is to replace the external stimulus by information that must be held internally (e.g., mental multiplication, addition, and paper-folding tasks).

2. Stimuli may be segmented into smaller pieces of information that are presented at a slower rate. Well-known examples are the use of information-displays in decision-making, where the subjects are shown a matrix of information with alternatives and attributes as dimensions. The values are not perceptually available, but can be accessed either by turning over cards or by requesting the information from the experimenter. (For a review and discussion of such methodology, see Lehmann & Moore (1980) and Payne, Braunstein, & Carroll (1978).)

Below we will discuss in more detail some examples from reading studies where the text is broken up into a sequence of physically separated sentences to break the flow of perceptually based recognition.

3. Ongoing skilled activities may be interrupted with a signal to give a report of the contents of attention. In many skilled activities, like piano-playing, typing, and other skills where real-time performance is an integral part of the skill, attempts to slow down the cognitive processes may alter them greatly. In his extensive study of typing, Book (1925) instructed his subjects to type at their normal speed, and then interrupted them at unpredictable moments in time, at which points they reported

the information they were heeding. He noted very interesting differences between subjects that could be related to amount of practice and could be validated against detailed analysis of the rates of typing individual letters and of typing errors. Chase and Ericsson (1981) also used this method to study the contents of attention in an exceptional subject, whose digit-span was over 80 digits. While digits were read at the rate of 1 digit per second, the subject was interrupted at an unpredictable moment and asked to report all information in attention. The reports were systematic over trials and consistent with other analyses of performance.

4. Reminders may be given during silent periods to keep verbalizing. In Chapter 2, we discussed the rather widespread practice of reminding subjects to think aloud when they had been silent for some specified number of seconds. Below we will discuss some hypotheses about the causes of such silence and review a study comparing the information verbalized spontaneously with that verbalized in response to reminders to keep talking.

We have selected two topics for fuller discussion: thinking aloud while reading, and reminders to verbalize.

Thinking-Aloud While Reading. Earlier, we cited studies reporting that when subjects think aloud while reading, little more than the text itself is vocalized. One possible reason for this is that the internal representation (and hence the vocalization) simply mimics the text. However, most models of reading postulate that during reading with comprehension information must be accessed in LTM to generate a coherent representation of the text's meaning. A protocol that simply follows the text omits this kind of information.

Several investigators have modified the reading task to slow it down and permit more complete verbalization. Sentences were displayed separately with several lines between instead of in paragraph form, and the subjects were encouraged to "try to express every thought that comes into your mind while reading each sentence" (Waern, 1979, p. 4). A similar procedure was developed independently by Guindon (1980, 1981). According to Waern (1979), this procedure did not change the content of the verbalizations but only increased the total amount of verbalization.

However, Waern's (1979) method of analyzing the protocols did not permit prediction of what information would be heeded, hence does not allow an evaluation of how completely the subjects reported the heeded information. That the amount of verbalization increased markedly under the slow-down procedure is suggestive. Moreover, when

Waern coded the protocol statements into broad categories, she found significant differences between protocols produced by subjects instructed to read with the explicit purpose of applying the information to a task and those produced by subjects simply asked to read. Hence, the additional verbalization was not simply a regurgitation of the text.

Guindon (1980, 1981), while comparing different models of story comprehension, obtained data that casts light on the completeness of protocols produced while reading. She was particularly interested in how subjects made inferences in order to achieve a coherent representation of the story. From a formal analysis of the stories, she was able to specify what inferences were essential. Subjects were either instructed to think aloud, or were asked to give a retrospective report after they finished reading. Subjects in both conditions indicated that the verbalization did not interfere with their performance of the task. No differences were found in level of comprehension for the two reporting conditions, nor were there differences in the numbers of inferences generated under the two conditions.

Guindon (1980) found a fairly high degree of verbalization of the inferences in the TA condition and only a slightly lower degree in the retrospective condition. In a finer analysis (Guindon, 1981), she showed that most of the omitted inferences were those that could be made by automatic recognition processes: for example, disambiguation of pronoun references, and role attributions. For example, in the following text segment, the co-reference of the pronoun *he* has to be inferred:

> ... The driver, visibly nervous, gets underneath the truck. Twenty minutes later, just as the police arrives, *he* emerges.

In the protocol that assesment is only given implicitly:

> The driver emerges from underneath the truck and tells the police ...

Guindon's analysis (Guindon, 1981) showed that inferences about plans, causes, and scripts were verbalized in 65% of the cases, whereas pronoun references and role attributions in only 11%.

A valuable study relating verbalizing while reading to reading time has been carried out by Olson, Mack, and Duffy (1981). Their subjects read two kinds of texts (stories and essays) in two conditions. In the silent condition, subjects were shown one sentence at a time on a CRT, and selected a new sentence when they were ready by pressing a key. In the TA condition, subjects read the same text, sentence by sentence, while verbalizing. When the protocols were segmented and coded into eight categories (e.g., predictions, inferences, general knowledge, associations), there was great similarity in the nature of the thoughts elicited from different subjects. Here are four protocols from sentence 18 in the story on "Lentil."

Subject	Comments
24	I expect the plot will succeed in getting the Colonel to hear Lentil playing his harmonica. The Colonel will be impressed and Lentil will be rewarded somehow.
17	Maybe a celebration is planned (parade, etc.) and Lentil will win the day with a rousing welcoming song.
07	Expect to read that Colonel Carter will have some kind of of role in what's going on with Alto and his music and Old Sneep. Expect to hear something about Colonel Carter's reaction to Lentil.
23	We expect to see some interaction between Colonel Carter, Old Sneep, and Lentil. Probably a great celebration. Suspect that Lentil will probably be asked to play for him. (Olson, Mack & Duffy, 1981, p. 300)

The authors were able to predict the average silent reading times of individual sentences from the number of inferences, predictions, and so on, in the protocols for these sentences. This relation was only observed for stories, where subjects could successfully predict the continued story development, and not for essays, which were processed retrospectively rather than through anticipation.

Several other studies have used protocol analysis successfully to reveal basic processes in comprehension of text (Collins, Brown, & Larkin, 1980) and official documents (Flower, Hayes & Swarts, 1980). Some applied studies have used protocol data to improve the comprehension process.

Reminders to Think Aloud. When subjects think aloud they are doing something more than they normally do while thinking. They are, at least, overtly vocalizing their verbal thoughts and, in addition, encoding non-verbal thoughts into verbal form. Although subjects require very little instruction to enable them to think aloud, most people's normal mode of thinking is silent. Even after tens of hours of producing protocols, subjects never complain that they are unable to revert to their customary silent thinking. In order to account for the subjects' ability to think aloud in experiments, we have to assume that TA processes are controlled by a marker in STM.

For tasks involving non-verbal information, task-relevant information can be accessed faster than it can be encoded and vocalized.

When task-relevant processes require a lot of STM capacity, subjects often stop verbalizing (Duncker, 1945; Johnson, 1964) and remain silent. However, even a brief reminder from the experimenter will start them speaking again. These reminders may take many forms like, "Please, tell me what you are thinking," "Please, think aloud," "Keep talking," etc. We would recommend "Keep talking" because it is the least directive and does not require any direct answer to the experimenter.

Our interpretation of these phenomena is that the marker in STM directing the verbalization of thoughts may disappear when task-relevant information is being accessed rapidly. The simple reminder reinstates the marker. In fact, the reminder does not have to be verbal, for tones appear to serve just as well. In support of the view that, during intervals of silence, thoughts are heeded but not verbalized, we find that subjects will almost invariably resume reporting in response to reminders to think-aloud (Ericsson, 1975b). Occasionally, however, subjects will report that they are not attending to any thoughts and that their minds are "blank."

In our experience it is important to have subjects do warm-up tasks with oral information (See Appendix.). This appears to eliminate silence due to misunderstanding of the instruction to think aloud. It gives subjects practice in expressing thoughts directly without explaining or interrelating the information.

According to our model the information reported in response to a reminder should be the same as the information reported spontaneously, with one important difference. When subjects are verbalizing concurrently, they will verbalize the information as it is heeded. However, when subjects have been reminded to think aloud, they will verbalize the information in STM. But not all information resides in STM for the same length of time. Almost any model of the cognitive processes would predict that goals will be kept in STM longer (usually, until they are satisfied) than intermediate results, which can be discarded as soon as they have been used as imputs for subsequent processing. Thus, our model would predict a relatively high frequency of reports of goals in response to reminders. In a study by Ericsson (1975b), the verbalized information was sorted into several general categories, that are described in Chapter 4. Immediately after reminders, goals and intentions were verbalized relatively more frequently, as compared with recognitions of relations and evaluations, than in other portions of the protocols.

IMPLICATIONS FOR PROTOCOL ANALYSIS

The basic assumption of our model is that the information in focal attention is vocalized directly (in the case of an oral encoding) or vocalized
after an initial encoding into oral verbal code. The obvious implication
of this for analyzing recorded verbalizations is that the originally heeded
information should be recovered by decoding the "encoded" verbalizations (i.e. those not originally in oral form). The first step in such an
analysis is to identify the verbalization units (segments) that correspond
to units of heeded information. If verbalizations reflect the internal
representation, we can use syntactic information as well as pauses in
articulation, phonemic intonation contours, and stress to uncover these
units.

The second implication of the model is that each segment is verbalized independently of those that precede and follow it; hence that each
can be encoded independently, without attention to context.

This independence of protocol segments from context is incomplete in several respects. First of all, pronouns and descriptive phrases
can often only be interpreted in the context of the preceding verbalizations. In most cases, the referenced entity can be easily identified and
substituted in a pre-coding stage. There will, of course, be more difficult
cases, where information is heirarchically organized, and the structure of
contexts complex.

A third implication of our model is that verbalizations should be
encoded in terms of the heeded information they express. Thinking
aloud protocols consist almost entirely of verbalizations of heeded information. At the current state of our knowledge, other types of verbalizations contained in them (e.g., descriptions of process) present a more
complex coding task. For example:

"I remembered that last time I tried to substitute ...." *Fictional*

An appropriate inference from this segment is that the subject is
attending to his *memory* for earlier goal-driven activities that he *now*
recalls performing. Because of the possibility of error in recall from
LTM, it is incorrect to infer that he *actually* performed them earlier.

This last point is very important, and highlights a difference between some common practices of protocol analysis and the practices our
model would recommend. Many procedures attempt to encode the
processes that generate heeded information, rather than the information
itself. But the processes can only be implied from the information in
STM, which does not, as we have seen, usually include information

about process. Information can be brought to the attention of the subject in many different ways. It can be retrieved from LTM, or it can simply be recognized and detected as part of the perceptually available stimulus display. Or it can be the product of some process, inferential or other. Currently, we don't know enough about the structure and form of verbalizations to be certain that they contain cues that would enable us to distinguish different histories of generation. Encoding the occurrence of a specific process on the basis of protocol data requires assumptions about the underlying mechanisms. Hence it is more in the nature of a theoretical explanation than a simple encoding of data. In a later chapter, we will discuss the relations among raw data, interpreted data, and theory.

6

METHODS FOR PROTOCOL ANALYSIS

Having developed and examined in detail a model of the way in which verbal reports are generated, we are now ready to discuss specific techniques for deriving valid data from them. First we will describe a number of specific methods of analysis that have been used, and then we will examine them in the light of the methodological principles that should govern the encoding of verbal protocols.

EARLY PROTOCOL ANALYSIS

In early work, protocols of subjects thinking aloud consisted of the experimenters' notes summarizing the vocalizations rather than direct transcriptions of the subjects' actual words. Until tape recorders became available (about 1945), there were no practicable means to record verbalizations. The investigator was forced to select and interpret the subject's speech in real time, without any chance of going back to reinterpret or reevaluate the initial records and encodings.

The earliest documented analysis of a think-aloud protocol of which we are aware was made by Watson (1920). As we saw in Chapter 4, he used the protocol to illustrate some general characteristics of cognitive process in problem solving, presenting his own interpretation and description of the protocol with little or no effort to provide systematic evidence in support of his views. Subsequent research using protocol analysis attempted to take down the ideas more closely as they were generated by the subject. Duncker (1926) analyzed a number of protocols for over 20 problems in search of the mechanisms that generated the solutions. His analysis (Duncker, 1926, 1945) was a meta-level description of the solution attempts and theoretical mechanisms that could generate the transitions to new ideas for possible solutions. Several studies (Bulbrook, 1932; Durkin, 1937) set out to find the nature of insights and the conditions under which they occur. From their analyses of protocols, they contended that the observed processes did not imply any special phenomenon of insight but could be described in terms of other kinds of cognitive processes.

De Groot (1965) recorded extensive TA protocols of chess players selecting moves in games, and used the theoretical framework proposed by Otto Selz (1913) to encode the processes he found expressed in them. While the protocols were recorded by hand, and hence certainly incomplete, they contained enough information to allow de Groot to draw a rather detailed picture of the problem-solving processes of novice and expert chess players. He was generally able to reconstruct the subjects' search trees, and provide examples from the protocols of the processes postulated by Selz.

The outstanding feature of most of this early work is its exploratory nature. The main aim was to generate concepts and potential mechanisms rather than to address questions of validation and generality. The contact between the protocols and the theoretical ideas was through the investigators' descriptions and interpretations of the protocols, which had to be generated in real time. There could be little explicit, detailed comparison between theory and the protocol record. Many methodological issues simply could not be addressed when the subjects' original verbalizations could not be preserved in their raw form.

With the introduction of tape recorders after World War II, the situation changed markedly, for it was now possible to analyze the verbalizations without any real time constraints. The practice of transcribing the tapes literally into typewritten form developed rapidly. From written transcripts, the investigator could obtain almost instant access to all the verbalizations corresponding to a given process. Issues of coding reliability could also be addressed by presenting several coders with the same raw transcript of the verbalizations.

With the emergence of computer simulation of cognitive processes (Newell & Simon, 1956; Newell & Shaw, 1957) models were proposed that made explicit claims as to what information was processed by subjects, hence could become part of the verbal protocol. Intensive analysis was made of a small number of verbal protocols for a task, sometimes a single protocol, to demonstrate that the information in the protocol could be regenerated, approximately, by the simulation model operating on the same task. We will have a good deal to say about this approach in this chapter.

In Chapter 4, we have already discussed another stream of literature, in which information in verbal protocols has been encoded at a very abstract level with the aim of uncovering generalizable aspects of cognitive processes. As we saw there, the majority of these studies did not test specific hypotheses or models of the cognitive processes but sought to induce and identify regularities and patterns in the recorded data. In many of these studies, the protocol data were encoded into very general categories, and these categories were related only weakly to any process description of cognitive processes capable of performing the tasks. The link between protocol and encoding was often not explicit, and it was often not clear on what basis the encoding decisions were reached. We will not pay much further attention to these methods in this chapter.

INTRODUCTION TO TECHNIQUES OF PROTOCOL ANALYSIS

In this section we describe some forms of protocol analysis that are especially useful for comparing sequences of verbal behavior with the behavior predicted by models expressed as computer programs. These methods retain, as fully as possible, the content of the protocol (low-level encoding), so as to permit very detailed matching of the encodings with the trace of the program.

Basic Assumptions

The methods to be described are not theoretically neutral; they rest on a set of assumptions about the general structure of problem-solving processes, and about the verbal reporting process itself. The major theoretical assumptions that underlie these methods are:

1. The subject's behavior can be viewed as a search through a problem space, accumulating knowledge (not always correct) about the problem situation as he goes. This gradual, step-by-step accumulation of knowledge can be represented by a *problem behavior graph*, the kth node of which represents the subject's knowledge after k steps of search.

2. Each step in the search involves the application of an operator, selected from a relatively small set of task-relevant operators, to knowledge held by the subject in STM. Application of the operator brings new knowledge into STM, moving the subject to a new point in the problem space.

3. The verbalizations of the subject correspond to some part of the information he is currently holding in STM, and usually to information that has recently been acquired.

4. The information in STM, and reported by the subject, consists primarily of knowledge required as inputs to the operators, new knowledge produced by operators, and symbols representing active goals and subgoals that are driving the activity. A goal may take the form of an intent to apply an operator; in which case the protocol may contain explicit evidence for the application of operators.

The first two of these four assumptions can be viewed as weak postulates about the problem-solving process (weak because a wide range of alternative processes can be represented as searches). The third and fourth assumptions do little more than summarize the postulates about verbalization that we have been using throughout this book. Therefore, they do not introduce important new assumptions into the protocol analysis process.

Encoding Vocabulary

As a preliminary to the encoding process, the task and the protocol are analyzed to extract the vocabulary of objects and relations needed to define the problem space and operators. For example, in the Tower of Hanoi task, a subject might refer in his protocol to "disks" and "pegs," and to "moving Disk X from Peg Y to Peg Z," essentially using the language of the problem instructions. (See the protocol reproduced as an appendix to Anzai and Simon, 1979.) The subject may identify the disks by numbers (Disk 1 for the smallest, say), and the pegs by letters (A, B, C, from left to right). The labels may be borrowed from the problem instructions, or devised by the subject. To describe problem situations, the subject may use relations like "larger" and "smaller," and more complex relational naming devices like, "the next smallest disk to Disk 2 on Peg A."

Protocols almost always also contain information that reveals the subject's control and evaluative processes and goals. For example, the protocol mentioned above contains such statements as: "Oh it's getting there," "this time it's easy," "I don't know for sure," "wrong," "5 will have to go to C," "I will move the remaining four from B to C." (The latter two statements represent goals because the indicated actions require multiple moves.)

Synonyms. At this point, certain equivalents may be defined, to permit the protocol to be encoded in a simpler, canonical form. For example, "smallest disk" may be defined as synonymous with Disk 1, so that the former name may always be replaced by the latter in the encoded protocol. Provided that synonymity is not judged too lightly (and that anaphoric reference is not prejudged), this kind of stylization raises few problems of coding reliability. Nevertheless, replacing terms by synonyms, even through reliably, may lose semantic content. The phrase "smallest disk" may provide information about the subject's perceptual encoding that is lost by translation to "Disk 1." Whether the translation should be made or not in the process of encoding will depend on whether the distinction makes a difference in terms of the theoretical models under study.

The cryptarithmetic protocol of Subject 3, analyzed in detail by Newell and Simon (1972), provides many examples of the possibilities of canonical recoding. For instance, in about twenty instances where S3 draws an inference from the known numbers associated with a column in the problem to those still unknown, he gives a reason of the form "Premise (P) implies Conclusion (C)." These reasons are actually verbalized as "P, therefore C" (2 instances), "P, which will mean that C," "P, which means that C" (2 instances), "P means that C," "P, which will make C," "P, which leaves C," "Since P, C" (2 instances), "C because P" (5 instances), "P, now C," "If P, so C," "Suppose P, then C," "P, so C," and "C, since P." For all except very special purposes, all of these expressions could be coded "(P → C)," or in some other appropriate standard notation.

Completeness of Vocabulary. The protocol may now be scanned to discover what statements cannot be coded in the language thus far defined. Additional terms (e.g., goal expressions) may be added to the list until as much of the protocol language as desired has been accounted for. Experience shows that, for relatively well-structured problem solving tasks, a small vocabulary (in the dozens and hundreds, not thousands) of terms, relations, and statement forms is sufficient to code more than ninety per cent of the language of a protocol. For example, the Tower of Hanoi protocol we have mentioned is about 2,000 words in length, but contains a vocabulary of only about 165 different words. A good rule of thumb for protocols of any considerable length is that the number of different words will be between five and ten per cent of the length of the text. Usually the different words will be distributed by frequency in a highly skewed way, following the rank-frequency law of

Zipf (1949) and Yule (1924). This has the unfortunate consequence that about one-half of all the words that occur will occur only once in the text—a serious impediment to parsimonious encoding.

Newell and Simon (1972) provide other examples of encodings for tasks like cryptarithmetic, chess, and logic problems, Ericsson (1975b) for the Eight Puzzle. See Chapter 4 for additional references.

Segmenting and Encoding Processes

For the actual encoding, the protocol is segmented, each segment corresponding to a statement. If oral prose were completely grammatical, a statement would essentially be a clause or a sentence, but in normal speech, statements are often abbreviated to phrases—even to single words. Nevertheless, segmentation is not usually difficult, and can be carried out with high reliability.

Coding the Segments. Each segment is then encoded. To the extent possible, it is coded from the information contained in the segment itself. When the segment is fragmentary, or contains anaphoric reference (e.g., pronouns, naming by description, and so on), context—preceding and following segments—may need to be consulted to remove ambiguity, but for reasons that we will discuss later, the range of context used is kept as narrow as possible. Again, it has been found that coders who understand the task can code segments, using context, with reliabilities of .8 or .9. (Later in this chapter, inter-coder agreement will be discussed further.)

Usually the encodings of segments can be somewhat formalized by using functional notation: $R(x,y,...)$, where the R's are relations, and the x, y, etc., arguments. In fact, the whole apparatus, including quantifiers, of the first order predicate calculus can sometimes be used to good advantage. The relations in such an encoding are generally derived from the verbs, prepositions, and adjectives of the protocol, while their arguments often take the form of nouns and noun phrases. Thus, a statement like, "I'll place 3 from A to C," might be encoded as "Move(Disk 3; from A, to C)," or more briefly, "Move(3;A,C)."

The amount of context that must be considered when encoding a statement is a function of both the protocol and of the depth of the encoding. Figure 6-1 shows a small segment of the Tower of Hanoi protocol mentioned above, encoded at a relatively shallow level, and with slight use of context. The statement, "29. I'll place 3 from A to C," simply becomes "Move(3;A,C)," no context being used to code this particular sentence. But 32.2 contains an implicit reference to 30, while 33 and 34, although containing four clauses, have to be encoded as a unit: "Because {Goal(4 on B) & [Move(1;B,C) implies (Move(4 to B) impossible)]}, Move(1;B,A)."

29.	I'll place 3 from A to C.	Move(3;A,C)
30.	And so I'll place 1 from B... to C.	Move(1;B,C)
31.	Oh, yeah! I have to place it on C,	Goal(2 on C)
32.	Disk 2.	
32.1.	No, not 2	contradiction, because
32.2.	But I placed 1 from B to C... Right?	Move(1;B,C)
33.	Oh, I'll place 1 from B to A	Because {Goal(4 on B)&
34.	Because... I want 4 on B,	[Move(1;B,C)implies
	and if I had placed 1 on C from B	Move(4 to B) impossible]}
	it wouldn't have been able to move.	→ Move(1;B,A)

Figure 6-1

Encoding of Portion of Tower of Hanoi Protocol

Prior Assumptions in Encoding. In encoding protocols of students solving thermodynamic fluid flow problems, Bhaskar and Simon (1977) made stronger assumptions, and encoded the protocol at a correspondingly deeper level. They assumed that all protocol statements could be encoded as one of a small list of actions, like: choose system, notice keyword, write energy equation, revise equation, find value of variable, solve energy equation, check units. Any statement in the protocol that could not be encoded in terms of one of these actions was retained as a comment. The actions, which were derived from a detailed task analysis and preliminary examination of the protocols, generally accounted for two-thirds or more of the protocol segments in these rather highly structured tasks.

A third variant form of encoding is illustrated by the detailed analysis in Newell and Simon (1972), pages 165-183, of a segment of a protocol. (A sample of this encoding is shown in Figure 6-2, below.)

These authors postulate the form of the subject's production system, and seek to reveal in their encoding not only the succession of knowledge states, but also the productions that were executed to move from one knowledge state to the next. For example, "each D is 5; therefore, T is zero" is encoded as "P1: (D ← 5), and Find-column (containing D) [col. 1], and Process-column(1) yields T=0." (For readability, we depart here from the actual compact notation used by the authors.)

B5.	Therefore, I can, looking at the two D's ...	P1:	D←─5─→FC(D)(⇒col.1); PC[col.1](⇒T=0 new)
B6.	each D is 5;		
B7.	therefore, T is zero.	P11:	T=0─→TD(T,0)(⇒+)
B8.	So I think I'll start by writing that problem here.		
B9.	I'll write 5, 5 is zero.		
B10.	Now, do I have any other T's?	P1:	T=0─→FC(T)(⇒fail)
B11.	No.		
B12.	But I have another D.	P1:	D←─5─→FC(D)(⇒col.6) (no PC)[col.6]
B13.	That means I have a 5 over the other side.		
B14.	Now I have 2 A's	P9:	get all-letters FL(all-letters)(⇒R); get R
B15.	and 2 L's		
B16.	that are each ...		
B17.	somewhere ...		
B18.	and this R ...		
B19.	3 R's ...		
B20.	2 L's equal an R ...	P2:	get R─→FC(R)(⇒col.2); PC[col.2 for R](⇒R odd new)

Figure 6-2

Encoding of Portion of Cryptarithmetic Protocol

In this kind of encoding, the entire postulated production system is taken as context for encoding each statement or short segment of statements. The way in which encoding inferences can be made and justified is discussed by the authors at length.

The Use of Context. The use of context in coding protocols involves a tradeoff. On the one hand, interpreting protocol statements in terms of context permits a much larger part of the semantic content of the protocol to be retained than if context is ignored. On the other hand, when context is used in interpretation, the evidence provided by each statement is no longer wholly independent of the evidence drawn from other statements (used to interpret the former). We will have more to say about this issue presently.

The extent to which a particular mode of coding requires consideration of context can also be illustrated by the protocol on the Tower of Hanoi problem reported by Anzai and Simon (1979). The subject was making the actual moves in the problem on a large wooden Tower of Hanoi. She verbalized every move, without exception, and in relatively uniform language. She also verbalized some of her goals, and some of the planning calculations that derived the next move from the current goal. A particularly clear passage from the beginning of her third trial of the problem is this one:

110. If it were five, of course, 5 will have to go to C, right?
111. So, 4 will be at B.
112. 3 will be at C.
113. 2 will be at B.
114. So 1 will go from A to C.

This is the beginning of a new trial, where Disk 5 cannot legally be moved. The situation, and the language (the conditional "if it were" and the "will have to") allow us to interpret statement 110 as describing a goal (G), and to encode it: (G:5 → C).

Since Disks 4, 3, and 2 also cannot be moved in this situation, and because of the "so" in 111, statements 111-113 are to be interpreted as a plan (P) for moves preparatory to moving Disk 5. They can be coded: (P:4→B), (P:3→C), (P:2→B). Now, with another "so," the subject deduces that the next move should be: 114. (M:1→C), and actually makes this move.

The protocol at the corresponding point in the fourth trial reads as follows:

164. first 1 will go from A to C.
165. Because 5, at the end, will go to C, so,
166. So, 4 will go to B.
167. And then, 3 will go to C.
168. And then, 2 will go to B.
169. So, 1 will go from A to C.

Here the subject announces immediately the result of her means-ends analysis to determine her first move, and then explains her reasoning ("because"). Statements 165-169 correspond in one-one fashion to 110-114. Note that the "and then" of the planning statements is not to be interpreted temporally, but as meaning "and therefore"; the actual moves will be made in the opposite temporal order.

As already remarked, the planning statements can be distinguished from the moves because the former do not refer to legal moves. However, the coding is much easier (and unequivocal) if we consider the context of the whole brief episode at once, instead of encoding the individual statements ignoring that context.

In the 52 statements that cover the third trial in this protocol, 31 can be encoded as moves, 6 as goals, 10 as subgoals or plans, and 5 remain to be encoded in some other way (mainly as evaluations). In the 56 statements made during the fourth trial, 31 report moves, 5 goals, 8 plans, and there are 12 statements of other kinds. The statements of the first trial were less highly stylized (and correspondingly harder to encode) than those of the later trials. There were more evaluative statements during the first trial, and more retrospective statements of reasons for moves (the latter perhaps being partly a consequence of an early prompt from the experimenter, "If you can, tell me why you placed it there.") Fifteen of the first 24 statements were evaluations or gave retrospective reasons for moves.

Automation of Encoding

To increase the reliability and validity of encoding, various efforts can be made to automate the encoding process. We will mention two such systems here, PAS and SAPA. Both will be discussed in more detail later in the chapter.

The most ambitious steps in this direction were taken by Newell and Waterman (1971, 1973) with the PAS-I and PAS-II systems. A less ambitious attempt at moving toward automation of coding is the SAPA (semi-automated protocol analysis) system of Bhaskar and Simon (1977). While the PAS systems, after the problem space has been defined and the protocol segmented manually, analyze the protocol automatically, to produce a problem behavior graph, SAPA is an interactive program, specially tailored to each task environment, that supports the human coder in analyzing successive protocol segments.

A major advantage of automatic encoding is that it requires all of the underlying assumptions, the vocabulary and the inference rules, to be defined explicitly and applied consistently. Hence, it makes clear exactly what assumptions have entered into the encoding. Reliability is perfect (given the same protocol, the system will always reach the same interpretation), and the robustness of the encoding to changes in the underlying vocabulary and rules can be tested directly.

The loop is completed by testing the encoded protocol against the trace of a computer program that purports to provide a theory of the subject's behavior. Trace and protocol can be expressed in precisely the same formal language, so that there is nothing problematic about the comparison. Notice that the test is really simultaneously a test of the mutual consistency of the problem space definitions, the inference rules for encoding, *and* the theory of the subject's behavior. Misfits between protocol and trace may be attributable to any of these sources. This is exactly the situation we encounter in any theory testing, where a failure of data to fit theory perfectly may be due to errors of observation, of instrument calibration, of approximation (if we leave "unimportant" variables out of the theory), of incorrect auxiliary hypotheses (e.g., incorrect hypotheses about the operation of instruments), or of the theory itself. What we are always testing, when we confront a theory with data, is the mutual consistency of all of the presuppositions (including the theory itself) that underlie the comparison.

Semi-automated protocol analysis does not remove all of the elements of subjectivity that a completely automated procedure does. However, experiments with semi-automatic protocol analysis using SAPA shows: (a) that it enhances the reliability with which coding can be carried out; (b) that at least in tasks having fairly definite structure imposed by the task environment, the assumptions built into the program do not significantly distort the encoding; and (c) that it makes the task considerably easier for the human coder. Readers who have had actual experience in encoding verbal protocols will not underestimate the importance of this last point. In particular, by focussing the coder's attention on individual segments, one at a time, and cueing possible interpretations, an interactive system for protocol analysis permits sustained attention to the coding task over much longer stretches of time than are tolerable without it.

Level of Analysis

The kind of statement-by-statement encoding we have been discussing so far retains most of the semantic content of the protocol. For many purposes this is desirable, or even indispensable. For example, if the goal is to compare the protocol with a detailed computer simulation of the behavior, than as detailed a matching as possible between program trace and protocol may be desired.

On the other hand, the full protocol also retains all of the idiosyncracies of individual behavior. If the aim is to test theory more globally—the commonalities of behavior, say, shared by a whole group of subjects—then it may be desired to encode the protocol at a more aggregate level. What are some of the ways in which such aggregation can be accomplished?

Aggregation by Episodes. For the description of problem-solving protocols at an aggregate level, Newell and Simon (1972) introduced the notion of problem-solving *episodes*. Certain steps in solving a particular problem may be "obvious," other steps problematic. For example, solving a problem in physics may involve writing down the appropriate algebraic equation, then solving it. If the equation is simple and the subject skilled in algebra, solving the equation, once discovered, may be non-problematic, to be summarized as a single step in the problem behavior graph. The detail of the solution may be of no particular interest from a problem solving standpoint beyond demonstrating that the subject has mastered the basic algorithms of algebra.

Generalizing from this example, a subject often organizes his problem solving efforts in terms of a hierarchy of subgoals. Once this hierarchy has been identified, the protocol can be condensed, working in bottom-up fashion, by collapsing into a single step the segment of the protocol that relates to the achievement of a non-problematic subgoal—one that is reached by use of a well-practiced procedure. The process that achieves the goal may be regarded as a macro-operator. For example, a subject skilled in algebra may have a well-practiced procedure for solving linear algebraic equations in one unknown, so that the details of his solution process afford him no difficulty and are of no psychological interest. In that case, "solve linear equation" can be encoded as a single macro-operator that takes the subject to the new knowledge state containing the solution of the equation.

An application of the episoding technique to the analysis of cryptarithmetic protocols at a relatively abstract level may be found in Newell and Simon (1972), pp. 282-309. Here the aggregated protocols revealed very clearly the differences among the problem spaces in which different subjects were working, and how these differences in problem spaces affected the way in which subjects accumulated knowledge as they worked through the problem behavior graph. The episodes also revealed clearly the common means-ends analysis heuristic that almost all of the subjects were using to organize their efforts.

Aggregation by Solution Steps. In a study comparing the problem-solving processes of experts and novices solving kinematics problems in physics, a similar summarizing technique was used to contrast the working-forward solution paths of the experts with the working-backward solution paths of the novices (Simon & Simon, 1978). This difference could be extracted objectively and reliably from the protocols by recording as an equation each evocation of a principle of physics and its instantiation in terms of the data of the problem.

For example, "If the average speed was 200 meters per second, and the barrel is half a meter, ... then it would have to be 1/400 of a second," could be coded as:

$$L/V^* = T \ (.5/200 = 1/400)$$

where L is length, V^* is average velocity, and T is time.

Then each protocol can be encoded in terms of the sequence of equations each subject evoked and instantiated, and these sequences can be compared between subjects.

Aggregation by Processes. Sometimes a number of consecutive protocol segments refer to the execution of a single major process by the subject, and this whole set can be given a single encoding. For example, a major process in the cryptarithmetic task is to process a column, taking known information and substituting it for letters in the column in order to derive information about other letters. "Each D is 5; therefore, T is zero" —obtained by processing the column that reads: $D+D=T$. The principal information that is verbalized by subjects when processing a column is the identity of the column being processed, the information already available about it (input information), and the new information derived (output information). This information could be encoded in some such form as: $PC(1;5+5=T) \rightarrow T=0, c(2)=1$, where $c(2)$ designates the carry to column 2.

Newell and Simon's Subject 3 is very consistent in providing in each case of processing a column most of the information indicated above. In 36 segments each of which was an instance of PC, the number of the column being attended to was mentioned 34 times. Some 37 input quantities were mentioned, and 21 omitted; 43 output quantities were mentioned, and 5 omitted. In four cases where a contradiction was encountered, neither input nor output quantities were mentioned. Of the 21 unmentioned inputs, 8 were carries (of 1 or 0) and 10 were values of the letters D, R, or E, all of which had remained constant for some time. Of the 5 unmentioned outputs, 4 were carries. Hence, by coding each instance of PC as a single segment, and without using any context outside that segment, almost complete information could be obtained from the protocol about the information to which the subject had to attend in order to carry out the process and use its result.

Individual Differences. As the examples cited show, aggregating protocols is an effective technique for studying individual differences different subjects. It also suggests a comment on the common complaint that descriptions of problem solving gleaned from protocols cannot be generalized.

The difficulties of generalizing about problem solving from data obtained from individual protocols are not to be regarded simply as annoyances associated with the method of protocol analysis. The variety in problem-solving processes is a psychological fact: Human beings differ widely in the knowledge they possess and the knowledge they evoke and apply in particular problem-solving situations. "Smearing over" these genuine individual differences by aggregating data does not destroy their reality; what it destroys is a large part of the information contained in the original data. If human beings use different strategies in solving the same problem, we cannot validate laws of behavior that assume the strategies to be all the same. Psychological invariants must be consistent with, and not dismissive of, this variety in human behavior.

METHODOLOGICAL ISSUES

In scientific work we would like to separate "facts" from the theories that might be generated to explain or account for them. The term *data* is usually used to denote the factual information employed for testing theories. According to the conventional wisdom, data, properly gathered, must be accepted by all scientists; theories need not be, for the same data might be explained in several different ways. But matters are not quite so simple. We have already seen that various sorts of theoretical commitments must be made in the process of gathering and recording data, and all data are consequently tainted by theory. For example, theory-based decisions must be made as to what kinds of data are relevant, hence worth gathering. Observations are made with instruments, which are designed on the basis of theory. In these and other ways, theory creeps into the gathering and recording of data.

Still, we wish to preserve the greatest possible distance between data and theory, so that data can be used to test theories with a minimum of bias, pro or con, from preconceptions. What we must strive for is a kind of bootstrap operation. In designing our data-gathering schemes, we make minimal essential theoretical commitments, then try to use the data to test stronger theories. In fact, that is the strategy we have followed in this volume with respect to our theory of protocol analysis. On the basis of weak assumptions about short-term memory, we were able to interpret the available experimental data on verbalization, to check whether these weak assumptions are tenable, and to strengthen them into a more complete theory of the verbalization process.

Translating Behavior Into Data

Coombs (1964) has discussed the interdependence of theory and data in an illuminating way, and has analyzed how the observable aspects of psychological phenomena can be converted into data. The sequence of operations he describes for deriving data from traditional psychological measurements is fully parallel to the sequence for deriving data from recordings of verbal behavior. Coombs (1964) starts the cycle with a theory that already exists prior to any collection of observations. The theory delimits which aspects of of potential observations should be recorded and become available for further processing. Potential observations outside the limits will simply be ignored.

Coombs describes what might be called theory-driven science. Scientific inquiry may also be driven by data. Theory should not preclude the scientist from searching for new phenomena, or from paying serious attention to phenomena he hits on adventitiously. Many important scientific discoveries have been made in this way, with little prior guidance or discipline from theory. As a second step, the observations that have been recorded are mapped onto the language of the theory. If the theory is sufficiently weak, it will allow the expression of alternative hypotheses (alternative strong subtheories). We will use the term "data" to refer to the result of this mapping process, which encodes raw observations in the language of theory.

It is not hard to describe the corresponding steps in analyzing verbalizations. When a tape recorder or video recorder is used to capture behavior, a great deal of information about the subject is irretrievably lost (e.g., his blood pressure, EEG pattern, and many other potentially observable phenomena). Transcribing recorded tapes involves a further selection of information, for the voice inflections, for example, are usually ignored, or imperfectly encoded in punctuation. The more difficult problems arise, however, in encoding the transcripts into the language of theory. Roughly, we can describe the encoding process as follows:

Input → Encoding → Output

The input, given explicitly, corresponds to one or more units of the transcript. These units can be individual words, sequences of words separated by pauses, phrases, sentences, or even complete protocols.

The output must belong to an *a priori*, explicitly given, set of alternative encodings. To minimize the contamination of data by ad hoc theory, the alternatives should be explicated prior to accepting input for encoding. Encoding decisions are based on some specific body of knowledge and procedures held by the encoder, whether man or machine. In the ideal case, the encoding would be done by a computer program, for then we would know exactly what knowledge and procedures were being used, and with what theoretical entailments. In the case of the human coder, too, it would be highly desirable to be able to specify what inferences and knowledge are used to reach the encoding decisions. The definition of the encoding categories should be clear and explicit. The theoretic and practical problems of using natural language definitions in science is discussed in depth by Mandler and Kessen (1959). As we have already shown earlier in this chapter, it is possible (and, of course, desirable) to base the encoding categories on a formal task-analysis in terms of a space of knowledge states and a set of operators. Among their many advantages, such explicit and formal definitions of encoding categories will help increase coding reliability.

Context-Free Encoding

The entanglement of data with theory is reduced and simplified to the extent that each output is independent of those that precede and follow it. In order to secure complete independence the encoding operations for each output would have to be distinct, and would not refer to the same recorded observations. When the encoding is done by humans, such independence is almost impossible to attain, for coders may recall information from previous inputs to bias their encodings of subsequent inputs. We have already adverted to this problem above and will discuss it in more detail later in this chapter. These rather general and abstract remarks can usefully be illustrated by a few examples.

Memory-span Task. In the memory-span task, subjects are instructed to repeat back a series of verbal symbols (e.g., digits) in exactly the order in which they were presented. If a complete match is attained, the output is "correct," else "incorrect." The encoding operation is the result of a sequential match between the input string and the recorded verbalized response string.

Free Recall of Lists. Free recall of lists (e.g., lists of words) requires a slightly more complex encoding operation. The recorded verbalizations may be of three kinds: (1) words on the stimulus list; (2) incorrect "guesses" of words thought to be on the list; and (3) other verbalizations, like, "let me see," "I am pretty sure there was an animal name on the list," or the like.

Nobody seriously questions that distinctions among these three kinds of verbalizations can be encoded reliably and veridically by people. Yet a computer program capable of discriminating between the second and third categories would be distinctly non-trivial.

Story Recall. Encoding of verbalizations becomes still more complex if the task is to recall texts or stories. The meaning of a text is not captured uniquely in a specific string of words, but can be expressed, at least approximately, in a large number of different ways. For purposes of encoding, it is necessary to have a theoretical framework within which the semantics of the text can be characterized.

Suppose that the meaning of the text is represented by propositions (Kintsch, 1974). Prior to encoding, the stimulus text is analyzed into a set of propositions that convey its meaning. Then, during encoding, the verbalizations of the subject are converted into propositions, and these are compared for semantic equivalence with the propositions previously derived from the text by the experimenter. In most applications of this coding method, the number of propositions successfully identified as matching text meanings is counted, and propositions that cannot be matched are not evaluated.

Other Issues

From our discussion to this point, we can identify a number of issues that should be discussed in more depth. First, there is the selection of the information that is to be included in the raw data, and the further winnowing of this information in the preparation of the transcript. At the same time, the information must be segmented, to determine the units that are to be input to the encoding process. These issues will be discussed in the next section.

That discussion will be followed by a consideration of how protocol analysis must be designed to preserve, as far as possible, the degrees of freedom in the raw data from contamination by theory and expectations generated from the same data. In the next main section of the chapter, we will discuss potential biases of the encoding processes themselves.

Selection of Information for Coding

There are many characteristics that are desired in a transcript. The transcript should be usable by investigators with different theories and research foci. Hence, transcription should not rely on theoretical assumptions that are controversial or not generally shared by the relevant investigators. All information that is important to subsequent encoding into the language of different theories should be preserved in the transcript.

Our discussion here is limited to situations where a single person is performing a task, and does not include those where two or more persons are working together, as in reaching a decision (Payne, 1976). We also ignore the influence of the experimenter on the subject. Two-person interaction, each person providing stimuli for the other, presents many additional problems we do not wish to deal with here. (See Ochs (1979) for a discussion of parent-child interactions.)

Even though most cognitive tasks elicit relatively simple behavior and occur in rather static perceptual environments, not all of the relevant information can be retained if the transcription task is to be manageable. Through an analysis of the task itself, the information about behavior and environment that is relevant to task performance can usually be defined fairly well. Information about the physical environment, especially if the stimulus is partly or wholly visual, is important and sometimes difficult to capture adequately. It is important because it is part of the definition of the stimulus. It is difficult to capture because such visual stimuli are often not easy to describe verbally, and because the subject's references to these stimuli are often not easy to disambiguate without a rather complete record of the information that is perceptually available.

Cognitive tasks vary widely in the amount of task-relevant information that is available perceptually and in the stability or change of this information while the task is being performed. Many tasks (chess, Tower of Hanoi) employ boards or other physical devices that are altered by the subject's moves. Other tasks, like mathematics and physics problems, are presented visually and allow the subject to use paper and pencil. For those problems that use a static display of information it is not necessary to record changes in the environment in the transcription of behavior. Purely mental problems, like mental multiplication with oral presentation of the problem, force the subject to keep the necessary information in memory. Similarly, for retrospective reports, since the original stimulus will no longer be available, the problem as presented should usually provide a sufficient context for interpreting the transcriptions.

The verbalizations of adults can generally be transcribed into ordinary words. Dictionary words may not adequately describe the verbalizations of young children (Ochs, 1979). However, even in adult speech several aspects of the recorded verbalizations, such as intonation patterns and pauses, are not easily transcribed. Furthermore, encoding the stress and duration of each word and pause is tremendously time-consuming and costly. Hence, it is important to make a theoretically sound and uncontroversial abstraction from the raw protocol that allows reliable coding and captures the relevant information for subsequent coding operations.

A rather similar problem is encountered in describing eye movements. The direction of the gaze can be recorded continuously, so that it becomes important to find a time interval over which to integrate, in order to make the data manageable. Because, for static displays, the eyes move by sudden discrete saccades, the sequence of directions of gaze between saccades and the duration of each of the intervals can be taken as the basic measurements (Winikoff, 1967).

In our model of the production of verbalizations, we earlier proposed that they should also be unitized by speech bursts. Only the durations of longer pauses need be recorded, since these may indicate periods when the subject is not obeying the instructions to verbalize. Speech bursts provide only a partial solution to the encoding problem, however, for they are not always large enough units for encoding and assessing theoretical terms. Encoding may therefore have to be based on larger, syntactic or even semantic, units.

"Contamination" of Data by Theory

Beauty may lie in the eye of the beholder, but it is a major goal of scientific method that truth should lie in the data — should be objective rather than subjective. As applied to verbal data, what does this requirement of objectivity mean?

It cannot mean that data are collected and encoded without regard to existing theory. We have already seen why that cannot and should not be done. A single verbal protocol is not an island to itself, but a link in a whole chain of evidence, stretching far into the past and the future, that gradually develops, molds, and modifies our scientific theories. It needs to be processed with full attention to these linkages.

The process must be viewed as a repeated cycle (or helix, if we believe there is constant progress along the axis). At any given time certain concepts and propositions are given credence as providing more or less plausible accounts of a body of phenomena. These concepts and propositions may constitute a single theory, or a collection of competing theories, or even a hierarchy of theories, from very general (but weak) to very specific (but strong), and from highly probable to barely plausible. In the limiting, but not infrequent, case, data may exist that exhibit clear regularities without any current theory to describe or explain them. Such regularities often lead to the induction of new theories (Simon, Langley, & Bradshaw, 1981).

The existing theories suggest new observations and experiments to be made, either with the aim of choosing between alternative hypotheses, or of strengthening (or weakening) the credibility of a specific theory when there are no competitors, or of improving and extending an existing theory. If existing theories explain only part of the phenomena, with a good deal of residual "error variance" or "noise," as is almost always the case, then the new observations may introduce new variables and measurements, sometimes depending on new instrumentation, in an effort to account for the unexplained variance.

Power and Parsimony. The "quality" of a particular theory in the face of a body of evidence must be judged by the relation between the amount of variance the theory explains and the number of degrees of freedom (parameters) required to fit the data. Exactly what figure of merit, what function of variance explained and degrees of freedom employed, should be used to evaluate theories is a deep problem in the modern theory of statistics, and there is at present no consensus on the precise answer. But everyone does agree that "power" and "parsimony" are the important characteristics of a successful theory, and that there is some tradeoff between these two measures. If the power of a theory is enhanced by adding new variables or parameters, its parsimony is decreased; if it is simplified to increase parsimony, power will usually be lost.

The best we can aspire to, in scientific inquiry, are large increases in power in exchange for very small losses in parsimony. On rare occasions, new formulations are found in some domain that greatly increase power without loss of parsimony. These are the true "scientific revolutions" of which so much has been written in recent years.

In the literature of statistics, most attention has been paid to the situation where two theories are competing to explain the same body of data. If the two theories are equally parsimonious, have the same numbers of degrees of freedom, then obviously the most powerful is to be preferred. If one is more parsimonious than the other, then some tradeoff ratio can be used to make the choice. The more complex, and we believe, the more common case is one in which only *one* theory has been put forth, and the task is to evaluate it in the light of new evidence. To see how this might be done, we must make an excursion into Bayes' Theorem.

A Bayesian Framework. Even though we seldom have available adequate data to apply it numerically, Bayes' Theorem provides us with a framework within which we can examine more closely the issues of power and parsimony. We will not try to attach a spurious quantification to our argument, but simply use Bayes' Theorem as a qualitative guide.

The credence we place in a hypothesis, say H_i, on the basis of all of our previous knowledge and evidence is called, in Bayesian theory, its *a priori probability*, which we will denote by $P_0(H_i)$. When we analyze new data and throw it into the balance, revising this initial probability for each of the hypotheses we are entertaining, we calculate a new probability, the *posterior probability*, for each hypothesis. We will call this $P_1(H_i)$. Bayes' Theorem provides a rule for calculating these latter probabilities.

To make this calculation, we must also know the probability that each hypothesis would produce the data actually observed. This probability, called the *productive probability* of the hypothesis for the data, will be denoted by $P_p(D;H_i)$.

Consider two urns (hypotheses) containing four balls each. The first has three white and one black ball; the second one white and three black balls. Matters are arranged so that it is equally likely that we will draw a ball from either urn. (The *a priori* probability of each hypothesis is 1/2.) We draw a ball, and find that it is white. What is the posterior probability that it was drawn from the first urn? Since, in this simple case, the probability of drawing each of the balls is exactly the same, and since there are three white balls in the first urn and only one in the second, the answer is obviously 3/4. More generally, and for less simple cases, Bayes' Theorem gives the posterior probability that the ball came from the first urn (H_1 was correct) as:

$$P_1(H_1;W) = [P_p(W;H_1)P_0(H_1)] / [P_p(W;H_1)P_0(H_1) + P_p(W;H_2)P_0(H_2)]$$

$$= [3/4 \times 1/2] / [3/4 \times 1/2 + 1/4 \times 1/2] = 3/4$$

Of course the formula can be generalized to an arbitrary set of hypotheses. Then the denominator simply becomes the sum, over all of the hypotheses, of the products of their productive probabilities for the observed data by their prior probabilities.

When we are dealt a hand of thirteen spades in bridge, we have to choose between the hypothesis that the deck has been well shuffled, and the hypothesis that the dealer has played a trick on us. The productive probability of the first hypothesis (the hypothesis that a well-shuffled deck will produce a deal of thirteen spades to one player) is very low, but the prior probability—since we have known our friend, the dealer, as an honest person — is quite high. On the other hand, the productive probability of the second hypothesis (that a trickster will deal out a hand all of one suit) is quite high, although its prior probability is low. Bayes' Theorem tells us what credence to put in our friend's honesty after the deal, on the basis of these probabilities. The productive probabilities can be computed from the theory of combinations, but the prior probabilities must be based on our previous experience with human nature in general and our friend in particular.

Implications of Bayes' Theorem for Coding. What does Bayes' Theorem have to tell us about the problems of recording, encoding, and interpreting verbal data? First, it has something important to say about the venerable problem of prediction versus postdiction. What difference does it make whether we announce a hypothesis first, then gather and analyze data to test it, or whether we gather the data and induce the hypothesis from it? The received wisdom is that the hypothesis is to be given greater credence in the first case than in the second. But is this correct?

We can apply Bayes' Theorem thus. Before we gathered the new data, the hypothesis in question (whether enunciated or not) had a certain prior probability. The hypothesis also has a definite productive probability for the new data. The same may be said for any other hypotheses that had been or could have been generated. Hence we can calculate the posterior probability of our hypothesis in the usual way, and the time when it was generated simply does not enter into the calculation (Simon, 1977).

But the common wisdom on this matter is not wholly indefensible. Assume that hypotheses are constructed by some process, which we will refer to as the generator. The generator will produce hypotheses on the basis of the information available to it, and presumably will be so designed as to produce hypotheses with high prior probabilities (in the light of this information) before it produces hypotheses with low probabilities. If the generator has produced a particular hypothesis before certain new data were available, then it is reasonable to suppose that the prior probability of that hypothesis was substantial. If, however, the generator is given the new data as well, and allowed to run until it produces a hypothesis compatible with these data, it may put forward candidates that would have been assigned low priors before the new data were gathered. Hence, we cannot really assume equal prior probabilities in the two cases. This is presumably the basis for our greater confidence in a hypothesis that has made successful predictions, than in one that has been constructed with the data it has to fit already in view. The former generally comes to the new data with a higher prior probability than the latter.

This does not in any way imply, however, that data gathered prior to the formulation of a hypothesis has no probative value for the hypothesis. Even though we had not considered the possibility that our friend was a trickster before we picked up our hand of thirteen spades, and only formulated the hypothesis at that moment, the fact that we were dealt that hand markedly increases the probability of the hypothesis from its previous level, and its posterior may now be quite large as a result of this evidence, and even in the face of a very low prior. The common view that hypotheses must be formulated before experiments are run in order for the data to have value as evidence is simply false. However, *how much* credence we should place in them on the basis of the evidence may depend on whether or not they were thought of first.

In the use of protocol data, it is a common practice, and often a necessary one, to extract the coding categories and procedures from a study of the protocol itself. The model of the process that we wish to test may be constructed after examination of the same data. These procedures obviously consume some of the degrees of freedom of the data, but if the coding categories and procedures are relatively simple and highly objective, and if the model to be tested is parsimonious in relation to the volume of data to be explained, then there is nothing circular about proceding in this way. A good fit of model to data still contributes to the posterior probability of the model, and the more parsimonious the model and procedures, and the more voluminous the data, the greater the increment in the credibility of the model.

In the same way, it is often necessary, when coding protocol segments, to take into account a wider or narrower context of each segment. Again, this practice reduces the degrees of freedom in the data, but does not, in any absolute sense, compromise the coding procedure as a way of testing models of the data.

Necessity should not be made a virtue. Data cannot be used twice as evidence in Bayes' formula—first in calculating the prior probability, and again in calculating the productive probability of the hypothesis being tested. Hence, when degrees of freedom in the data are absorbed by their use prior to testing, their absorption should be taken into account in the testing process. In general, formal statistical methods for doing this are not available, but conceptually, the case is clear.

Moreover, a given body of data will provide stronger evidence for or against a model if the coding categories and procedures have already been constructed from analysis of the task domain, or from previously gathered protocols of other subjects, and if the model has also been formulated on the basis of other evidence.

Let us now return to the situation, introduced in the previous section, where we are not choosing between alternative hypotheses, but have *at most* one theory to fit our data. Without alternative hypotheses, we can not apply Bayes' formula; but we can imagine a surrogate hypothesis, with very low prior and productive probabilities for the data, to represent all of these unknown alternatives. Suppose that the hypothesis we are considering (whether invented before or after we saw the data) explains the data very successfully and parsimoniously. Then its productive probability for the data will be high. Examining Bayes' formula, we see that since the remaining terms in the denominator will be close to zero, numerator and denominator will be nearly equal, with the consequence that the posterior probability of our hypothesis will be close to unity.

We do not wish to push this conclusion too far. But it does illustrate how data can provide credibility to a single hypothesis, even in the absence of explicit alternatives with which to compare it. Moreover, the argument again does not depend on whether the hypothesis was generated before or after the data were produced.

Disconfirmation of Theories. Contrary to the doctrine of the Popperians, there is no "sudden death" of theories. Since observations have to be encoded and interpreted, using existing theoretical knowledge for that purpose, before they can confront theories, the failure of a theory to fit observations precisely does not mean that it has to be rejected outright. Perhaps the fault does not lie in the theory, but in some of the auxiliary, methodological, and theoretical assumptions that have been made in the fitting process. Classical Newtonian mechanics was not rejected simply because some planets deviated from the expected Newtonian paths. Instead, the implicit assumption in the calculations, that there were no unobserved planets, was tentatively rejected, and a search undertaken for bodies that might account for the deviations. Twice the theory was saved in this way (by the discoveries of Neptune and Uranus); on the third occasion (explanation of the precession of the perihelion of Mercury), it gave way to a competing theory, General Relativity, that explained the phenomenon without postulating a new planet.

The case of the overthrow of a theory by a completely new one is dramatic, but comparatively rare. More often, unexplained variance is dealt with by seeking new variables (as in the Newtonian case) to account for it. Hence the argument for a theory, that it explains a good deal of variance parsimoniously, is usually more important than the argument against it, that it leaves much variance unexplained—unless, of course, there is a competing theory that does a better job. The practice of science exemplifies the practical wisdom of politics that "you can't beat something with nothing."

General Lessons for Methodology. The parsimony of a theory is as hard to evaluate as its power. Degrees of freedom are used up not only in estimating the parameters of the model from empirical data, but also in the process of encoding and interpreting the data. Even in a simple physical case, the measurement of temperature, say, a great many degrees of freedom lurk in the procedures for calibrating the thermometers and recording the temperature in the experimental situation. Since the contemporary experimentalist does his work against an enormous background of heat measurement and instrument calibration by his predecessors, he is provided with a standardized environment, and does not "consume" degrees of freedom in fashioning his own instruments.

The case is quite different in analyzing protocols for a new cognitive task, one that has not been studied extensively in the laboratory. Large numbers of degrees of freedom may be used up in the early steps

of data recording and data encoding, with the result that the final interpretation of the data and its matching against the theory may appear to
reflect mainly hindsight — pulling out of the data the hypotheses that
have been implicitly hidden in it by the data interpretation process. This
is the core of validity in the criticisms sometimes leveled against computer simulation of thinking, although it hardly justifies the extravagant
and usually false claim that "If you are given a verbal protocol, you can
always write a computer program that will simulate it."

How can the problem of parsimony be solved? The answer for
verbal protocols seems to be exactly the same as the answer for any other
kind of data. It has several components.

1. In choosing data for transcription, and in transcribing and encoding
   them, the theoretical commitments that are made should be kept as
   small and weak as possible. We have already emphasized this principle throughout our discussion.

2. The theoretical assumptions and presuppositions underlying the
   data analysis should be made explicit. This is easy when the
   analysis is done automatically; difficult when it is done by humans.

3. The data analysis process should be not only objective and
   reproducible, but it should remain constant from one protocol to
   another. In this way, the degrees of freedom that are used by these
   procedures are absorbed by a constantly growing body of data.
   This can be done by dividing the protocol material into two parts,
   developing the data anlysis scheme on one half, and testing it
   against the other half.

4. Convergent procedures should be used wherever possible. For example, as much as possible of the encoding language and concepts
   should be derived from an analysis of the task environment, independent of the problem spaces defined by the subjects.

5. Constant and invariant data analysis procedures should be used
   over large bodies of data. It is much easier to build a consistent *ad
   hoc* theory to explain a protocol of 11 segments than one of 200
   segments.

6. Even where different theories are needed to explain behavior in
   different tasks, the theories should share as many common elements and components as possible, so that a (weaker) general
   theory can be abstracted from the specific ones.

7. Even where different theories are needed to explain the behavior of
   different subjects in a given task, the theories should also share as

many common elements and components as possible, so that a theory of the "representative subject" (the American college sophomore?) can be constructed.

Examples as Evidence. Protocol analysis sometimes consists largely of extracting examples of concepts or processes from the verbalization as evidence for theories that predict them. As Bayes' Theorem shows us, the contribution of such examples to the credibility of a theory depends on what alternative explanations are available. The recent methodological dispute about language acquisition in apes is an interesting case in point. Much of the important evidence for apes' ability to combine signs creatively into novel constructs comes from anecdotes (Seidenberg & Petitto, 1979). For example, the chimpanzee Washoe combined the signs for "water" and "bird" to refer to a duck, and the gorilla Koko combined the signs for "cookie" and "rock" for a stale cookie. Out of context, these episodes seem to yield rather strong evidence for the creative use of language by apes. However, Seidenberg and Petitto (1979, p. 182) point out that the *water bird* example is less persuasive if the ape also combined *water* and *bird* with other signs (e.g., *water shoe, water banana, cookie bird,* etc.). A chimpanzee named Nim (Terrace et al., 1978) combined signs into many such permutations. Although the combinations are not all idiomatic, there is no way to tell whether they were meaningful to the animal; they may have been random.

RELIABILITY AND VALIDITY OF ENCODING

A central task in using verbally reported information is to make the encoding process as objective as possible. Without appropriate safeguards, the encoder, exposed to a series of ambiguous verbal statements, may encode them with a bias toward his own preferred interpretation.

Context provides a principal source of disambiguation of verbal information. Suppose a concept-formation experiment in which a subject verbalizes a hypothesis like:

a dark ball

Without context, a coder might have great difficulty in deciding what objects should be regarded as instances of the concept defined by this phrase. However, in the context of a particular experiment, where all possible stimuli are colored shapes (dark blue, yellow, or white;

square, triangle, rectangle, or circle), the same hypothesis is relatively unambiguous, for it is synonymous with "blue circle."

As a second example, in a problem-solving experiment, a subject says:

I want to get 1 to its place.

If the experimenter knows the task the subject is performing, a coder can convert this verbal statement into an explicit goal. In the Eight Puzzle, for example, the subject is instructed to slide square tiles from a given configuration, like the one shown in Figure 6-3 below, to a specified goal configuration.

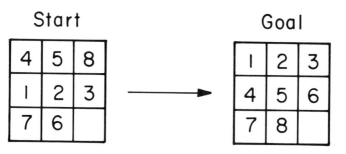

Figure 6-3

Example of a Configuration for the Eight Puzzle (left); this is to be Transformed into a Goal Configuration (right)

In this context, the verbal statement is readily encoded as the goal of getting the tile with the number 1 to the upper left-hand corner of the frame.

In these two examples, the disambiguation does not even require that other parts of the protocols be examined, but can be achieved by careful task analysis prior to the coding of the protocols. The task analysis can identify, in the first case, a space of possible concepts; in the second, a set of problem configurations and goals. Mapping the subjects' verbalizations on these may then be quite objective and unproblematic.

Many of the same issues are involved in assuring the objectivity of encoding as we discussed in connection with the objectivity of the verbal reports themselves. Consider, for example, two encoding situations. In both situations the encoder knows that he is encoding verbalizations taken from a think-aloud protocol from a concept attainment experiment. In the first situation, the encoder is asked if a verbalization is a statement of the correct hypothesis (e.g., "blue and round"). The output from the encoding decision is "yes" or "no." In the second situation, the encoder is asked to encode any hypothesis that can be stated as a combination of one of the three colors and one of the four shapes that occur in the task environment. Now the encoding can proceed in a quite definite way from the information in the protocol.

A computer program called HEARSAY (Reddy & Newell, 1974), developed for automatic recognition of continuous human speech, provides a useful metaphor for thinking about the encoding problem. The speech HEARSAY recognized consisted of instructions to make moves in a chess game. In order to identify what the speaker said, HEARSAY used various types of information that were averaged together to determine the most likely utterance.

One type of information came from the speech signal. Another type of information came from HEARSAY's chess knowledge of what moves were likely (e.g., plausible moves) in the given chess position. If HEARSAY attached too much weight to its expectation of what move would be made, it would simply "hear" what it believed the subject *should* have said. If HEARSAY attended only to the speech signal, then, because of the variability of speech sounds, it might believe (falsely) that the subject had chosen a highly implausible move. The use of context has both the potential to improve the encoding of verbal protocols by resolving ambiguities, and the potential to bias the encoding by relying too heavily on prior expectations. Effective encoding finds a middle pathway between these two extremes.

Encoding Process and Encoders

Encoding is often evaluated by tests of reliability—agreement between different persons encoding independently of each other. But reliability is not enough. In this section we will discuss some problems and issues that arise even when high inter-coder agreement is achieved. We will be concerned with biases toward the confirmation of hypotheses that have been put forward, inferences of what the subject must have said, rather than what he did say, and problems of restricting the influence of previous encoded information on subsequent coding decisions.

Independence of Encoding Judgments. After a protocol is divided into separate segments, one or more encodings must be generated for each segment. We are interested in ways for eliminating or greatly reducing the dependence among encodings of different segments so as not to lose degrees of freedom in the data.

The problem arises because human coders remember their previous encodings, and other information about earlier segments. Traditionally, coding judgments are made about segments in the order they were verbalized. It is not uncommon for a subject to verbalize an intention, like "I want to get the first row in order," or a concept like, "I think it must be small red squares," and then make later reference to it, like, "I still think it is that," or "I am thinking about the same hypothesis." It would be incorrect to regard these subsequent verbalizations as wholly independent evidence that the subject was heeding the hypothesis of "small, red squares." The later verbalization is evidence that he is heeding the same hypothesis as before, but doesn't provide new evidence of what that hypothesis was. Not all instances of such cross reference are as explicit as this one, but they all pose essentially the same problem.

A possible solution to this problem involves two things. During the segmentation, units should be defined that are large enough that all information for making an encoding decision is contained in a single segment. For certain encoding decisions, like assessing strategies, this may mean that the entire protocol is a unit. Later, we will propose an alternative approach of establishing encoding categories that can be assessed from smaller segments.

Second, segments should be encoded in random order, thus eliminating the possibility that the encoder will rely on information in preceding segments to make subsequent decisions. A computer-based support system for making such encodings is described in the next section.

Bias and Inference. Two types of bias are of particular interest and concern. The first results from the encoders having prior knowledge of the hypotheses being tested. The second results from the encoders assuming that subjects will think in the same ways that they do.

With respect to the first, the best situation is one in which the coders are naive with respect to the experimental design and the hypotheses. Of course this is unimportant when the protocol information is very explicit and clear, as it is in many problem-solving protocols. But for ambiguous and brief protocol segments, the danger of bias may be serious, and inter-coder agreement does not measure coding validity. In some recent studies (cf. Waern, 1979) explicit steps were taken to keep the coders from knowing the design or the hypotheses.

The second type of bias arises because encoding often requires at least simple inferences, and assumes that the subjects made the same inferences. In general, this is a quite valid assumption, useful and even necessary for understanding other people's thought processes. Again, it becomes problematic when the coder is faced with an ambiguous or schematic statement. With information about the task, the encoder (as in our HEARSAY analogy above) may attribute to the subject the action or thought he regards as most reasonable under the circumstances. Several coders with similar backgrounds, yet different from the background of the subject, could give the same incorrect interpretations. Even if the inference is "correct," it is not determined by the recorded verbalization. In the next section we will discuss some methods for restricting the inferential activity of the encoder.

Mini Protocol Analysis System (MPAS)

This section describes an interactive computer program for encoding protocol segments. While the computer is not a necessary component of the scheme, it facilitates presenting the protocol segments to the coder, and also makes the encodings directly available for further analysis on the computer.

The core idea of the scheme is to control the information used to encode each protocol segment. There are two types of control. One aims at meeting the criterion of independence of encodings, and reduces the possibility of the coder relying on information from earlier protocol segments. The other exerts control over the extent to which the coder can infer plausible encodings from previous knowledge, rather than relying on the explicit protocol information.

MPAS presents to the coder segments from a number of different protocols, sampled in a random order. When the pool of segments to be sampled is sufficiently large, the coder is unable to infer any relation between the current segment and those presented previously. In Figure 6-4, the simple structure of MPAS data organization is shown, together with an example of the coder-computer interaction. MPAS samples one of the stored segments and presents it at the computer terminal. Often, the segment can be coded directly as presented, but if it is too small to provide sufficient information for encoding, options in MPAS permit the just preceding and succeeding segments to be generated. Thus the context can be gradually widened as necessary, but information can be retained as to how much context was used in encoding.

An earlier section mentioned three types of knowledge that might lead a coder to infer what the subject might or must have been thinking instead of coding the explicit information in the protocol sentence. One such type of knowledge, information about the situational context, is removed by the randomization procedure just described.

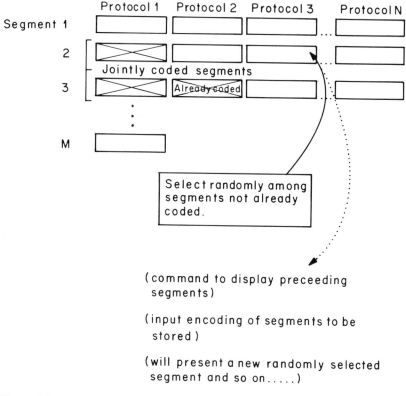

Figure 6-4

The Memory Structure of the Mini Protocol Analysis System

Another type of knowledge, information about the task, is largely contained in the coding categories, which of course must be available to the coders. Hence this source of bias cannot be removed. However, a third type of knowledge, information about the subject's immediate goals, need not be provided to the coders, and generally should not be.

Let us consider how presenting or not presenting the last two types of information affects the inferences that can be made by the coders. We use as our examples some protocols collected from subjects trained on solving the 4-disk version of Tower of Hanoi (Neves, 1977; Neves, D., 1979, personal communication).

	Current Situation			Goal Situation		
Pegs	A	B	C	A	B	C
Disks	(43	1	2)	(-	-	4321)

The 4 has to go to the 3[C] But the 3 is in the way. So you have to move the 3 to the 2[B] post. The 1 is in the way there. So you move the 1 to the 3[C].

If he knew only the current situation, and not the goal, the coder could only test whether the verbalized operations are feasible and do not violate any rules or physical constraints. If he knew also the goal situation, he could discriminate plausible from implausible sequences of thoughts, with the possible introduction of bias into the encoding.

If the goal situation is always the same, so that the coders know it, bias might be controlled by replacing pertinent semantic information with nonsense labels. This can be done automatically by the MPAS program. Thus, the protocol segment shown above could be converted to:

The $\langle X1 \rangle$ has to go to the $\langle X2 \rangle$. But the $\langle X3 \rangle$ is in the way. So you have to move the $\langle X3 \rangle$ to the $\langle X4 \rangle$ post. The $\langle X5 \rangle$ is in the way there. So you move the $\langle X5 \rangle$ to the $\langle X2 \rangle$.

Encoding Reliability

We turn now to methods for ensuring that the mapping of input to coding categories is reliable and does not vary among encoders. In statistical terms, we wish to show that inter-coder agreement is better than chance, and also that the differences between encoders are not systematic.

Ordinarily, in tests of coding reliability, coding categories are determined in advance. We are aware of only one exception, a study by Rasmussen and Jensen (1974), where the coders of protocols of subjects who were troubleshooting electronic equipment developed their own coding categories. The two coders, who came to the task with agreed-upon goals and a common theoretic viewpoint, generated quite similar categories. (There is no easy way to quantify the degree of similarity.) There are also striking similarities in the codes that different investigators have proposed for the same tasks (see Bettman & Park, 1979). Hence, it would seem that coding categories might be induced reliably from the protocols themselves. Nevertheless, the studies discussed here all consider reliability in the context of fixed, predetermined coding categories.

At least three variables play an important role in determining the consistency and reliability of encoders' judgments. The first is the extent to which the encoder must make inferences. (For example, encoding a heeded thought requires fewer inferences than encoding the process that brought the thought to attention.) The second is the extent to which each encoding is independent of the others. Coding should be more reliable when each segment is coded in terms of its own content than when relations among segments are taken into account. We will first consider the latter, more complicated, situations and then turn to the coding of individual segments.

Encoding Complete Process Descriptions. The goal of protocol analysis has often been to generate a complete model of the problem-solving process. (See Newell, Shaw, & Simon (1958) analysis of GPS model and protocol.) Alternatively, protocols have been encoded into sequences of interconnected states in a Problem Behavior Graph (PBG). In these analyses, theoretical assumptions must be used to make inferences, supply missing information, and abstract protocol statements to general rules. There are few studies where inter-coder reliability has been assessed systematically for this kind of encoding. The coding is extremely costly in time, and it is difficult to find volunteers who are willing to duplicate it.

Haines (1974) made an ambitious attempt to evaluate the reliability of complete process descriptions derived from protocols. The thinking-aloud protocols were collected from subjects deciding to make purchases (e.g., personal clothing). One of the protocols is reproduced as Figure 6-5. Haines used a decision tree to describe the cognitive processes. The decision tree model, commonly used in research on consumer decision making, assumes that the subjects makes ordered series of tests on the alternatives, which usually have outcomes of "yes" or "no." Depending on the test outcome, the subject performs further tests, rejects the item, or decides to purchase it.

Second Subject—Women's Suits

INT: Just go ahead and talk.

SUB: Well another question would be if a salesgirl
            wants to help me or something and I don't usually
            like to have help until I have picked out the
            items I want—now can I tell her this
            there or do you care in any way
            or can I just go ahead and do whatever I want?

First shopping trip

DATE: May 23rd

Shopping companion—Zenna Z

SUB: Casual Corner looking at suits now. Here we are.
            Ummm. I guess all this is size 10s. Ohh I
            don't think the color pink, too frilly looking,
            straight skirt. White is impractical. Pink
            again, straight skirt, bows, not much—I don't
            like sleeveless things. The color's nice, a
            greenish color. An orangey yellow knit, sleeveless.
            Impractical too. White again—same thing.
            Uhh light blue kind of attractive knit suit but
            straight skirt—no good. Exact same style as the
            blue, but straight skirt. A pink straight skirt
            same style. Oh a print. I like the print color.
            It's a pinky reddish color. A-line skirt. Very
            attractive $14.99—I can't afford it. Yellow is
            very similar to the pink and blue. Knit straight
            skirt. I am not interested in straight skirts.
            Ohh, here is one like the print of the reddish
            color. It is a greenish color—A-line
            skirt—almost the exact same thing—
            box jacket. Also $15 about. Very attractive. I'll
            try it on too. That's just like the suit I have on
            isn't it? A yellow. It's a jersey knit sleeveless
            —sort of a very tiny top. Not at all
            practical for school. Oh, here is a sort of beige,
            well very light eggshell suit with sort of leather
            piping very attractive. Box jacket effect. I
            like the light color. I like the A-line skirt.
            I like the piping a lot. I'll try that on too.
            Let me check the price first.

INT: It's on the back.

SUB: Size 10. $22.99. That's $23. That's still
            all right Uhh. Sort of a flowery green and
            purple and pinky thing. Too loud-looking for
            school and I am interested in school clothes.
            A plaid sort of muddy-colored kind of drab
            looking but is the style I like. AAA, a box
            jacket suit again, A-line skirt sort of a muddy
            color almost but I think it is kind of attractive.
            I'd like to try this on too. It's not frilly.

It's tailor cut. Here is the green suit again
—like I saw before. Here is a print
suit but not as attractive as the other one in
sort of a bluey color and I think I prefer—.
Let me just look at this green one again. Ahh,
well maybe I like the blue Umm, let me see I
have a green dress suit at home. So maybe I'll
take the blue and leave the green here. You
poor thing. Ha. Ha.

INT: It's all right.

SUB: Right, here we go. I'll take the bluish
         color one.

Figure 6-5

Protocol of a Subject Making a Purchase Decision

Haines asked students in a computer science class to derive decision trees for these protocols independently. A couple of the students' decision trees are shown in Figure 6-6.

From visual inspection, we can see that there are considerable differences between the trees. Using a quantitative method developed by Bettman (1970), Haines (1974) derived a measure of similarity. The decision trees were compared for encoders analyzing the same protocol, and for a single encoder analyzing different protocols. Haines found that only about half the time was there greater consistency among encoders of a single protocol than among encodings of different protocols by a single encoder. He concluded that authors should not publish decision trees without reporting the protocols from which they were derived, since the trees cannot be derived reliably from the protocols.

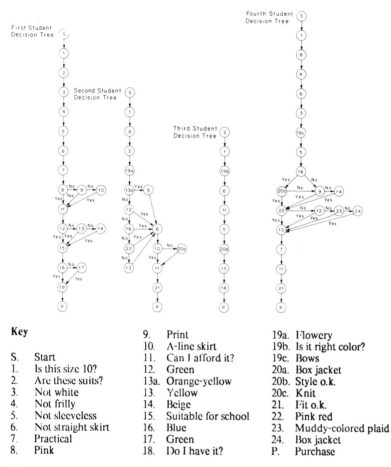

Key

S. Start
1. Is this size 10?
2. Are these suits?
3. Not white
4. Not frilly
5. Not sleeveless
6. Not straight skirt
7. Practical
8. Pink

9. Print
10. A-line skirt
11. Can I afford it?
12. Green
13a. Orange-yellow
13. Yellow
14. Beige
15. Suitable for school
16. Blue
17. Green
18. Do I have it?

19a. Flowery
19b. Is it right color?
19c. Bows
20a. Box jacket
20b. Style o.k.
20c. Knit
21. Fit o.k.
22. Pink red
23. Muddy-colored plaid
24. Box jacket
P. Purchase

Figure 6-6

Decision Trees Induced from Student Protocols

Haines' (1974) assumption that a single decision tree underlies a subject's decision processes is questionable. Later in this chapter we show how different encoding procedures as well as different theoretical ideas produce very high inter-rater agreement. First we wish to describe some studies that have tried to capture the entire cognitive process by encoding instances of complex subprocesses.

Encodings Based on Complete Protocols. In many studies only selected features of protocols are encoded. An example is a protocol obtained by Kilpatrick (1968) on the solution of an algebra word problem, reported in the study by Kilpatrick that was discussed earlier. From the protocols, Kilpatrick assessed instances where the general heuristics proposed by Polya (1957) were used. In the following protocol Kilpatrick found, among other things, an instance of "successive approximation."

> **Subject P-10:** "A barrel of honey weighs 50 pounds. The same barrel with kerosene in it weighs 35 pounds. If honey is twice as heavy as kerosene, how much does the empty barrel weigh?" Well, ... first you have to ah, find out what ah, kerosene weighs, and the honey weighs, if it's twice that. And so, I have to find ah, one number to find the weight of the barrel. So, say ... I take some amount from both of them and this number would be half of that. So take, let's see ... (What are you thinking of?) Well, I'm trying to figure out a number that'd be, that you'd take away from both numbers and this would be half of, of this number. (What are you trying?) Well, first I'd probably try the even numbers like 5, 10, 15, and so forth. It couldn't be 5, because that'd make that, ah, 30. And, this, and you multiply 30 times 30 and you get 60, and that's more than the total weight already. So, then it'd have to be somethin', ah, down by, like 20, or something like, some—, a, a number even lower. So you take about, probably, oh, 25, something like that..... And, not 25, a little, let's say, 20. That'd be 15. And 20 from that would make that 30. So 15 times 15 is 30. So that'd makes the, ah, ba-, the barrel weigh 20 pounds.

In Kilpatrick's (1968) procedure, there is no guarantee that two or more encodings may not be extracted from the same protocol segment. Nor can one determine precisely what information was used to make a particular encoding. Because he analyzed a large number of protocol segments, Kilpatrick could address the methodological issues statistically. He computed the frequency of occurrence of each heuristic in each subjects' protocols over eight problems. He then evaluated these frequencies, and eliminated data and encoding categories for which inter-rater reliabilities were low. An advantage of his procedures is that the encodings can be made directly from the tape recordings without transcription. There seems to be no objection in principle to this kind of encoding as long as the information is aggregated for each problem.

Encoding Segments or Phrases. Many of the difficulties encountered in earlier coding methods can be eliminated by coding individual segments of protocols. It is easy to compare the encodings of different raters and to report percentage agreement among them as an aggregate measure of reliability. Later, we will discuss some problems with such an aggregate measure.

In his study of choices between pairs of gambles, Montgomery (1977) used nine different encoding categories. Each category, coding a single statement, reflected a particular kind of comparison For example, "it is only 2:50 [Swedish crowns] more" was coded as a small difference (SD), and "the chances of winning seem to be equally large" as equality (EQ). Over 1,000 statements were encoded by two raters with overall agreement in 95% of the encodings.

Svenson (1974) asked subjects to select, for hypothetical purchase, among descriptions of houses. The houses could be described by values on a set of attributes. Each utterance was encoded that evaluated an attribute of a house or compared an attribute of different houses. About 90% agreement was reached by two coders in identifying attributes and values in 1,000 statements. Nearly half (48%) of the disagreements related to evaluations that subjects made with explicit hesitations.

In an even more extensive analysis, Bettman and Park (1979) took TA protocols from 68 subjects selecting among fifteen different microwave ovens, which were described by values on nine attributes. Bettman and Park used seventy coding categories, largely derived from earlier coding schemes (Montgomery, 1977; Payne & Ragsdale, 1978; Svenson, 1974). For two raters (who were allowed sometimes to assign multiple encodings), the average agreement was nearly 80% (78.3%) for about 2,000 encodings.

These studies show both that high inter-coder reliabilities can be obtained for TA protocols of decision processes and, by comparison, that decision nets do not provide a very good representation for these processes.

We should not generally be satisfied, however, with a single aggregate measure of coding reliability. Such a measure will mainly reflect the very frequent coding categories, and the encodings of infrequent categories may be much less—or more — reliable than the average. Reliability of coding individual categories can and should be tested separately.

There is a tradeoff between fineness of encoding and reliability, and substantial advantages in retaining reliability even at the expense of fine-grain resolution. First, automation of encoding decisions is difficult if reliability is low. Second, low reliability implies uncertainty as to what information in the verbalization provides the evidence for the encoding, hence uncertainty about the process of verbalizing the heeded information.

Automatic and Semi-Automatic Protocol Analysis

It would be highly desirable to automate, wholly or partially, the encoding of protocols. In this section, we describe two research efforts, mentioned earlier, that were aimed at developing such encoding programs: the PAS-I and PAS-II research of Waterman and Newell, and the work on SAPA by Bhaskar and Simon.

We will focus on PAS-I for several reasons. It was designed to be a completely automatic system, and thus to confront the entire range of encoding problems and to propose methods for dealing with them. Furthermore, the performance of PAS-I was evaluated in detail, the evaluation providing a helpful source of information about problems of protocol analysis.

Since the SAPA program was designed to be used interactively by a human coder, it did not have to address all of these problems. Each program was tested on only a single task — SAPA on problems in thermodynamics and PAS-I on cryptarithmetic problems. However, the principles of design underlying the systems have broad applicability.

PAS-I. The PAS-I program was designed to produce Problem Behavior Graphs directly from segmented protocols. The program was so structured that information peculiar to the given task could be separated from general information. In a subsequent version, PAS-II, rules special to a given application could be read into the program. However, we will mainly describe PAS-I, which was programmed to analyze cryptarithmetic protocols.

The final product of PAS-I is the Problem Behavior Graph (PBG), which incorporates several theoretical assumptions that constrain its generation. However, since PAS-I proceeds with its analysis in stages, we can look at the intermediate products also, and see where the theoretical assumptions affect the coding process.

Before PAS-1 goes to work on a protocol, a problem space is defined manually, by examination of the task and the protocol. This problem space delimits the kinds of encodings that can be derived from the protocol statements. The protocol is also segmented by hand in preparation for the automatic encoding. The encoding aimed at by the PAS systems was essentially that which Newell and Simon (1972) had previously specified in their manual encodings of protocols—that is, it was to produce a PBG showing the successive states of knowledge attained by the subject and the productions that were executed in proceeding from each state to the next.

We will first describe the basic sequence of processing in PAS-1. Next, we will describe some important components in detail. Finally, we will raise some methodological issues and discuss the results of actual runs with PAS-1 and the sources of its errors.

Basic Structure. PAS-1 is organized in three separate programs, the latter two operating on the outputs of their predecessors. The segments of the protocol are first analyzed by the *linguistic processor*, which encodes the segments into propositions. The output from the linguistic processor is the input to the *semantic processor*, which recodes the propositions into smaller sets of primitives, and groups the propositional information as inputs and outputs of possible information processes. Finally, the output of the semantic processor is the input of the *problem behavior graph generator*, which generates a PBG for the protocol.

Each protocol segment is encoded by the linguistic processor independently of the others (cf. the local encoding by MPAS). Moreover, all further processing is done from the output of this encoding, without reference to the raw protocol. Let us consider how a propositional encoding ("semantic elements" in the terminology of Waterman & Newell) can be generated from protocol segments.

Waterman and Newell use a keyword grammar to map the protocol segments on propositional elements. This grammar can be seen as a formal specification of the set of linguistic patterns that should be mapped on a given propositional relation. For example, in the cryptarithmetic task, the subject is seeking to assign a given letter (say, D) to its proper number. A protocol segment of the form "D equals 2" or "Change D to 2" is judged propositionally equivalent to "D = 2" or "(Eq D 2)," and is so encoded. All protocol segments that should be mapped onto "(Eq ⟨letter⟩ ⟨digit⟩)" are specified formally by the linguistic processor. Waterman and Newell (1971) provide the following example:

> \<letter\> directly followed by \<prep1\> and then \<digit\>
>
> Start segment with "Change" directly followed by \<letter\> and the \<digit\>
> or \<letter\> directly followed by "equals" and the \<digit\>.

where \<letter\> denotes one of the letters relevant to the task, and where \<prep1\> refers to a preposition. "Change" is a keyword that has to appear literally in the text.

This template would recognize and encode the following segments:

> D for the 2
> Use D as the number 2
> Change R to 2
> Each D is 5
> Each D equals 5

In the following figure, taken from Waterman and Newell (1971), we can see how the last sentence above is mapped, as well as some more complete structures.

This type of template grammar thus provides a flexible link between the propositional elements identified in the task analysis and a large number of different possible protocol segments.

Waterman and Newell (1972) argue against a full-fledged linguistic and semantic analysis of protocol segments, for several reasons. The most obvious is that such an analysis would be difficult and call for a much more complex program than PAS-I. Furthermore, since protocol segments are often incomplete sentences and not fully grammatical, syntactic information would have limited use. They argue that the PAS program should be more interactive, expectations being generated by the earlier parts of the analysis, and used to guide the linguistic analysis on the basis of assumptions of reasonable continuation. However, the current program analyses each segment locally and independently of previous ones— incidentally providing us with useful information about the feasibility of local encoding.

Evaluation of PAS-I. PAS-I was evaluated by analyzing its performance on one protocol from each of two subjects. Since a portion of one of the protocols was used in building the program, the other protocol provides the best test of its generality.

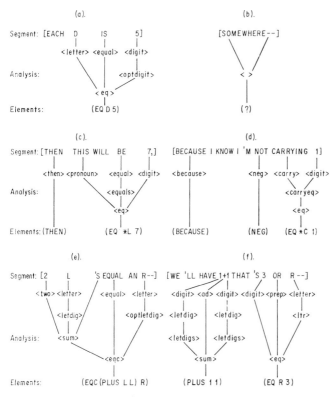

Figure 6-7

Examples of Linguistic Processor operation.

This is particularly important, for it is tempting to construct patterns in the keyword grammar that use the specific structures that appear in an individual protocol.

The output of PAS-I was compared to the encoding of the same protocol by an expert human coder. Mismatches were analyzed to identify the program elements responsible for them. For both protocols, the linguistic processor was rarely responsible for the mismatches, which speaks well for the feasibility of encoding protocols locally. It should be noted that a few changes were made in the keyword grammar before the second protocol was analyzed.

We turn now to a more detailed analysis of the failures of the linguistic processor. Most failures resulted from the absence in the processor of appropriate categories. For example, the absence of a category corresponding to the notion of "in front of" produced the following failure:

B50.   It's not possible that there could be another letter in front of this R, is it?

(NEG) (PEQ *L *D) (LETTER R) (QUES)

A similar shortcoming is illustrated by the following segments, which contain an abstract idea.

B72.   Now, it doesn't matter anywhere what the L's are equal to —
B73.   So I'm independent of L when I get past the second column here.

In this case, the processor detects the letter L and the negation in B72, and the letter L and the column reference in B73, producing:

B72.   (NEG) (EQ L *D)
B73.   (THEREFORE) (LETTER L) (PLACE SECOND)

The idea is missed completely, and the corresponding information lost irrevocably.

Another example from protocol 1, part 2, shows a sequence that PAS-I cannot handle.

B106. Rather—
B107. Let's see, how did I arrive at the point of that
B108. This is going to be a little confusing to start trying to trace back here.
B109. What's the reasoning here

Other failures of PAS-I are linked to missing clues for inferences:

B98.   If E has got to be an ...

PAS-I encodes this segment as (EQ E *D), where *D corresponds to some digit. The human encoder notices the article "an" and infers "E is even" (EVEN E).

Seldom does the linguistic processor fail to extract information connecting references across segments. However, in the following case it did.

B24.   Any two numbers added together has to be an even number.
B25.   And 1 will be an odd number.

(ODD (PLUS *X 1))

Table 6-1

Performance of the Linguistic Processor on Portion of Protocol 1

Total Segments		100
No Output (correct)		4
Correct Output		86
Complete	58	
Incomplete	28	
Incorrect Output		10

PAS-1 is a highly promising system for automatic protocol analysis. More developmental effort will be required, however, before it becomes a finished system that can be put to routine use in encoding protocols.

SAPA. In their analysis of problem solving in thermodynamics, Bhaskar and Simon (1977) proposed a semi-automatic system for protocol analysis realized as a computer program (SAPA). The program incorporates a prediction (predicted problem space and strategy) of the problem solving process in this task domain. Both the sequence in which information will be addressed, and the decisions that will be reached are predicted. Figure 6-8 shows the main components of the problem solving process incorporated in SAPA and the order in which they are predicted to occur.

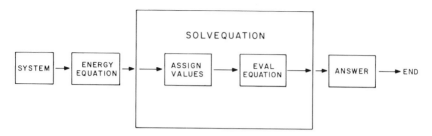

Figure 6-8
Flow diagram of SAPA program

SAPA embodies a rough preliminary model of the subject's problem solving strategy. As each new segment is taken up, it prompts the coder by predicting the operation the subject will apply next. If the prediction is correct (the operation expressed or implied by the segment corresponds to that predicted by SAPA), the human coder merely provides, from the protocol, the operator's arguments. If the prediction is incorrect, the human coder executes a "break" in the SAPA strategy, which puts the program back on the right track again and then inserts a paraphrase of the uncoded segment as a "comment." For the protocol shown below (Tables 6-2 and 6-3), SAPA does a very good job of anticipating its contents and the order in which they will appear.

The SAPA scheme for these thermodynamics problems rests on the task-dependent assumption (empirically valid for these subjects) that the solution process will be built around the equation of conservation of energy, and the special form this equation takes in each particular problem. The "logic" of the solution process consists in trying to solve successively for the remaining unknowns in this equation, after it has been specialized to fit the particular conditions of the problem.

Problem 2

Nitrogen flows along a constant area duct. It enters at 40 F and 200 psi. It leaves at atmospheric pressure and at a temperature of −210 F. Assuming that the flow rate is 100 lb/min, determine how much heat will be transferred to the surroundings.

Protocol

1. OK, the first thing I'm going to do is pick a system,
2. that is, the system will be the duct.
3. OK, I draw that like this.
4. and I'm going to write the first law on this duct,
5. as Q plus Ws will equal m times $h2$ minus $h1$,
6. where I'm ignoring the changes in kinetic and potential energy.
7. And this is probably a pretty good assumption.
8. OK, I'm asked to determine how much heat will be transferred to the surroundings.
9. OK, that will be the Q term here.
10. Since we just have a duct here, there will be no shaft work,
11. so Ws will equal zero.
12. Q then will simply equal m times $h2$ minus $h1$.
13. OK, m I know as 100 lb/min,
14. and $h2$ minus $h1$.
15. in order to determine that, I will need some physical properties for nitrogen.
16. So let me look these up.
17. Found these.
18. OK, so let me put m is 100 lb/min.
19. OK, $h2$, 2 is downstream,
20. so $h2$ is the enthalpy at one atmosphere and −210 F.
21. So let me look that up.
22. −210°. OK, this is in degrees Rankine, −210°, ah . . .
23. OK, is 250 degrees Rankine, this is $T2$.
24. While I'm at it, I'll just note that $T1$ will be 500°R.
25. OK, so 14.7 lbf/cu. in.,
26. at a temperature of 250 degrees Rankine.
27. I read h as 126.443 BTU/lbm, that's $h2$.
28. Now as $h1$ I have 200 psia and 500 degrees Rankine.
29. Let me look that up,
30. and I read $h1$ as 187.408 BTU/lbm.
31. OK, I'm simply going to do the calculation.
32. I see that the pound masses cancel as they should,
33. and my final answer will be in BTUs/min,
34. which is what I'd expect.
35. Let me do the calculation now.
36. 126.443 − 187.408
37. and when I multiply that by 100 and I get −6096.5,
38. the negative sign is as it should be,
39. because it indicates that heat is being transferred out of the system.
40. That's it.

Table 6-2
Protocol for Problem 2

CHOOSE SYSTEM.
  The system is: (2) the system will be the duct.
  EQUATION: (5) $Q + Ws = m(h2 - h1)$.
  The variables are; Q Ws m $h2$ $h1$
  COMMENT: (6–7) I'm ignoring the changes in kinetic and potential energy.
  FIND Q.
    VALUE Q: (8–9) unknown, dependent variable
    COMMENT: (10) Since it is a duct, there is no shaft work
  FIND Ws
    VALUE Ws: (11) 0
    COMMENT: (12) now $Q = m(h2 - h1)$
  FIND m.
    VALUE m: (13) 100 lb/min
  FIND $h2$.
    READ TABLE.
    nitrogen tables: (16–17,19–23,25–27) 126.443 BTU/lbm
    VALUE $h2$: (16–17,19–23,25–27) 126.443 BTU/lbm
  FIND $h1$.
    READ TABLE.
    nitrogen tables: (24,28–30) 187.408 BTU/lbm
    VALUE $h1$: (24,28–30) 187.408 BTU/lbm
  SOLVE: (5) $Q + Ws = m(h2 - h1)$
  CHECK UNITS.
  SOLVE: (5) $Q + Ws = m(h2 - h1)$
    SOLUTION: (35–37) – 6096.5
  END

Table 6-3

Encoded Protocol for Problem 2

Bhaskar and Simon (1977) view the SAPA predictions as a zeroeth order approximation of the problem solving process in the domain of problems to which it applies. "SAPA's predictions can be seen as a reference point for identifying differences that would lead to better and more detailed descriptions of the problem-solving processes in thermodynamics." In their analysis of two other protocols from the same subject, they use SAPA in exactly this way.

Analyses of the thermodynamics protocols could be made with the same approach as we have used earlier. Encodings, which could be made identical with those required by SAPA's prompts, would be made of the protocol segments. SAPA's predictions about the order in which these categories should occur could then easily be evaluated against the order in which the encoding assessments appear.

SAPA-like systems for other task domains can be built with modest effort. Of course, no a priori judgement can be reached as to how well they will capture protocol contents in those domains. That depends on how regular the problem solving process turns out to be, and how much similarity there is among the protocols of different subjects. However, semi-automatic protocol analysis appears to be a useful tool for problem domains that have a reasonable amount of structure.

EFFECTIVE PROTOCOL ANALYSIS PROCEDURES

In this concluding section, we will sum up our discussion by making suggestions as to which approaches to protocol analysis appear to have the highest potential of success. We have identified a number of problems, and suggested solutions for some of them. We will now try to show how these solutions follow from (or are at least consist with) our theoretical model of the processes of verbalization.

Matching Coding Categories to Verbalizations

Our model asserts that verbalization is a reflection of the heeded information. If that is so, then the more directly an encoding scheme can capture the units and structure of the verbalizations, the better—for several reasons. First, the closer the match between encoding categories and verbalizations, the easier it will be to encode them, and the more reliable will be the encoding. Automating the encoding will also be easier. Second, the closer the match, the less will be the need to use non-local context to make encoding decisions. Third, the closer the match, the larger will be the fraction of the information in the verbalization that can be encoded. In the ideal case, one should be able to regenerate the actual verbalizations from the information contained in the encoding, using a simple grammar. We have argued earlier that local encoding will usually be adequate. However, new data may show that some internal states can only be assessed by using a much larger context than we have been considering.

We see two substantial objections to the approach we have been describing and advocating, and a third objection that we consider wholly invalid. Let us start with the latter. It is still the case that protocols are often collected and analysed in the absence of a cognitive model defining what verbalizations would constitute evidence for each coding category. We believe that this procedure will be used less and less as the need for a theoretical base for encoding is understood.

Of the other two objections against our approach, the most serious is that it is exceedingly time-consuming. Especially when only selected aspects of the cognitive process are of interest, it may require inordinate effort to analyze all protocol segments in detail. We will show later how selected aspects can be extracted from a protocol at the segment level without requiring a full-blown analysis of the entire protocol.

Another objection is that we may want to abstract or extract generalizable entities, like representations, rules, strategies, and so on, instead of encoding segment by segment. Evidence about such entities may be scattered through the protocol, so that their assessment requires simultaneous consideration of the entire cognitive processing activity. It may be methodologically admissible to make such global assessments, but we would argue against it on theoretical grounds. We will argue that the protocol contains more reliable basic information that can be used as data for the assessment at the more general level.

In Chapter 7, we will provide several examples to show how goals, intermediate results and generated problem-configurations can be encoded separately and how an analysis of a large number of such encodings can support a general representation. We will also discuss briefly the use of experimental methods to increase the probability that all subjects will heed a wide range of stimulus instances. When subjects all attend to the same information, their responses allow us to evaluate the generalizability of the proposed representations and strategies.

Verbalization of General Knowledge and Rules

Generalized entities, like representations and procedures, are directly verbalized only under extraordinary circumstances. A subject will not usually say, "I will consider all logically possible combinations of variables X and Y that have feature Z." More often, subjects explore specific instances that we can describe as being combinations of X and Y with feature Z. It is also only rarely that subjects state explicit that a new knowledge structure they have generated is an instance of a general process or procedure with such and such characteristics. Protocols provide many instances of knowledge structures, but the generality and scope of the processes that generated them must be inferred, and is seldom indicated explicitly in the protocols.

It is quite possible, of course, for subjects to use abstract concepts, relations, knowledge, and rules that are general and generalizable in the sense that they apply to many situations and contexts. An obvious example is the verbalization of an hypothesis in a concept learning experiment. Verbalized knowledge elements are also general. In cryptarithmetic, Subject S3 of Newell and Simon verbalized the following relation:

"Since D + D = G, G must be even."

an inference that applies in several situations in this and other cryptarithmetic problems.

An indirect verbalization of a rule can be identified in the following verbal report on mental multiplication, "First I will put the largest number on top," and the verbalization of a goal, "Have largest number on top." It is often easy and tempting to encode information logically. However, it is psychologically possible and even plausible that a concept like "largest" will not be generated or heeded unless the number exceeds some limit of magnitude. The preconditions of this rule will not be met by numbers differing by only a small amount, contradicting the logical interpretation. Hence, abstract or general statements cannot be translated into a formal representation without careful consideration of the context. Thus, in the context that this rule and goal was generated and verbalized, one of the numbers was noted as being the largest. Yet, under what circumstances this verbalization will occur requires further specification.

Knowledge and rules reside in LTM. In order to be heeded and to influence the cognitive process, they need to be accessed by appropriate retrieval cues. Even though we have been able to identify them in a protocol on one problem, we cannot be certain that they will be accessed and used on other problems.

Meta-comments are another source of general statements about the cognitive processes. A description of a general procedure for dealing with a class of problems is not a meta-comment, for it draws on previously stored information. A clear case of a meta-comment is a subject's attempt to verbalize regularities in his own cognitive processes. We argued earlier that these verbalizations are often of limited value, and are clearly abstractions, influenced by the episodic information that the subject can retrieve at the time.

The best single test for distinguishing meta-comments from verbalizations of current processes derives from their role in subsequent processes. A verbalized procedure, like a recipe, will be accessed each time the corresponding cognitive process is executed. It corresponds to the representation of the relevant knowledge. A meta-comment will most likely not be accessed and used to direct subsequent behavior.

Conclusion

In this chapter we have shown how the information heeded during a cognitive process can be identified by an analysis of the corresponding verbalizations. In protocol analysis, we are trying to infer what information was heeded as input for the observed verbalization. Through a careful task analysis it is possible to define a priori a space of possible encodings representing the information relevant to the task. Then, encoding protocols involves finding the category that expresses the same information as the verbalization.

In the earlier chapters, especially Chapter 5, we argued that TA verbalizations closely match the flow of attention to information. By locating language production units and linguistic structures, the sequence of heeded information can be uncovered. Although the majority of encoding schemes define their categories so that individual protocol segments can be encoded, many schemes do not attempt to uncover the heeded information, but seek to infer directly the processes that generated the heeded information. We argue that, whenever possible, the original encoding should reflect as closely as possible the verbalized information, and should preferably be derived by automatic or semi-automatic means. Once verbalizations are converted to formal encodings, theoretical proposals for representations, processes and strategies can be introduced to provide parsimonious accounts for the protocol data.

7

TECHNIQUES OF PROTOCOL ANALYSIS

EXAMPLES

In the previous chapter we developed a general framework for considering the encoding and analysis of protocols. We raised and discussed a number of theoretical issues, and illustrated various forms of protocol analysis. In this chapter, we will examine a substantial number of concrete examples of protocol analysis to illuminate the more general questions that have been raised, and to provide further illustrations of techniques and issues. We begin with a discussion of informal methods of analysis. Then we discuss methods for inferring theoretical entities from protocols. Finally we will review studies exploring the reliability, validity and generalizability of protocol data, and discuss future direction of these kinds of analyses.

INFORMAL PROTOCOL ANALYSIS

In order to construct a theoretical framework and coding scheme for a set of protocols, pilot work will be necessary to develop the coding categories. Even during these preliminary and exploratory phases of analysis there exist general methods that are useful both for understanding the cognitive processes reflected in the protocols and for approaching the definition of coding categories.

Verbalizations cannot convey more information than was available to the process that produced them. Protocol analysis may involve categorizing the verbalizations according to the processes that could have generated them. We wish to provide some guidelines for making this classification uniquely and unambiguously. We assume a hierarchy of processes, the simplest being operations like *Copy*, which transfer information that is available from the senses or in memory. At the first step, we encode each verbalization in terms of the simplest process that could account for it.

A verbalization may be a *literal copy* of information that is presented or has been memorized previously. In this case, the verbalization may or may not be generated without being processed semantically. It will seldom be possible to infer with certainty whether it was understood or parroted. As a second possibility, paraphrasing, a verbalization may copy the *semantic content* of information that is presented or remembered, rather than copying literal verbal strings. In this case, the source information may or may not have been in oral form; if not, it has to be recoded for production. As a third possibility, inference, a verbalization may not be a copy, literal or semantic, of available information, but may be *generated* in various ways from such information. As a fourth possibility, information that was heeded at an early time may be *recalled* or *retrieved*.

Example: Protocol from a Series Task

To explore these distinctions, we will now examine a protocol collected and transcribed by Ohlsson (1980). In his study, the subject was given a complex variant of the 3-term series task. The subject, having been presented with information about the relative order of pairs of objects, must integrate this information to construct a unique ordering of a whole set of objects. The actual physical objects are not presented, so the task has to be carried out mentally, and without written notes. The task is difficult enough to require considerable cognitive processing. The information given the subject consists of seven segments (information units), as follows:

> I.O1. A child puts blocks of different colors on top of each other.
> I.O2. A black block is between a red and a green block.
> I.O3. A yellow block is higher up than the red one.
> I.O4. A green block is bottommost but one.
> I.O5. A blue block is immediately below the yellow one.
> I.O6. A white block is further down than the black one.
> I.O7. What block is immediately below the blue one?

Major Processes

Let us see how we can encode the verbalizations in this protocol in terms of the processes that produced them. We will employ a sequential decision process, first trying to account for each verbalization as a literal copy, then as a semantic copy, and finally, by default, as newly generated. Although the classification can be done locally segment by segment, we will report the results here by type of process.

In this situation, the primary process for literal copying is reading the information that was presented. If the subject's verbalization literally matches the text, we will infer that it was read. The inference might be further confirmed from records of eye movements, but eye-movement data were not collected for this protocol. What deviations from an exact literal match will we accept as "reading"? In the protocol (see below), we classified 17 segments as produced by reading. In one of these 17 cases, the subject prefixed the literal text with an "and," in two others, there was an omission of one or two words, for example:

PI.8. [a] black block is between a red and a green [block]

Thus, the **Read** process accounts for almost a third of the protocol segments, 17 out of 56.

We placed in the second class (semantic copying) segments that express the content of one of the seven lines of information that were presented, but paraphrase and do not literally copy them. We can further classify these segments by the way in which they deviate from literal copying. To comply with customary rules of reference in English, definite articles are sometimes interchanged with indefinite articles—"[P15] the yellow one is higher up than the red one"—just after the yellow one has been mentioned. In all but one of seven occurrences of this transformation, the same object has been referred to in one of the two just preceding protocol segments. The one exception is associated with a verb in the past tense (the only such verb in the protocol)—"[PL48-49] and then we had *the* blue one which is immediately below the yellow."

In four other cases, all involving LO5, the subject varies syntactical or lexical constructions while retaining the information content.

PI.16. and immediately below the yellow one comes the blue one
PI.24. below the yellow one is a blue block
PI.52. the yellow one
PI.53. and the blue one is immediately below
PL55. *which one* [what block] is *then* immediately below the blue one

Processes of the second kind, **Paraphrase**, account for 11 segments. Together with those accounted for by the Read process, they make up one half of the protocol.

Of verbalizations in the protocol that provide information about the arrangement of the blocks, 11 would seem to have required generating processes (i.e., **Inference** processes) for their production. The nature of the inferences can be seen from the list of these segments:

PI.16. and immediately below the yellow one comes the blue one
PI.17. then comes a red one
PI.18. I'd say
PI.26. below the yellow is then also a red
PI.27. a blue and a red are below the yellow one
PI.29. a blue and a red are under the yellow block
PI.40. white, red, black, green
PI.41. I'll say then
PI.43. then I'll say
PI.44. white, green, black, red
PI.45. instead
PI.46. then the white one is bottommost
PI.47. then the white one is bottommost
PI.51. then it is topmost so far
PI.54. then it comes topmost but one
PI.56. immediately below the blue one is then the red one

It is interesting to note that PI.29 is identical with PI.27 except that the relation "below" has been renamed "under," and "one" has become "block," a semantic but not literal equivalence.

Since the three-way classification of segments was made on the basis of the information expressed, it is interesting to look for verbal tags of features that may distinguish generated from copied information. In 8 of 11 instances of generated segments, the subject includes the word "then." The three exceptions can be accounted for by the fact that the same information has been generated previously. (PI.27 and PI.29 contain the same information as PI.26; PI.47 is almost equivalent to PL44; PL25-26 is almost equivalent to PI.16-17.) From the fact that PI.27 and PI.29 are identical in meaning, but slightly different in syntax, we would infer that these oral expressions were produced separately from one internal representation.

Protocol Interpretation

What does the protocol below tell us about the inference processes that produced the generated information?

Pl.1. a child puts blocks in different colors on top of each other
Pl.2. a black block is between a red and a green block
Pl.3. a yellow block is higher up than the red one
Pl.4. a green block is bottommost but one
Pl.5. a blue block is immediately below the yellow one
Pl.6. a white block is further down than the black one
Pl.7. what block is immediately below the blue one
Pl.8. black block is between a red one and a green
Pl.9. block
Pl.10. well that does not mean that it must be exactly between
Pl.11. could be something else between also
Pl.12. a yellow block is higher up than the red one
Pl.13. a green block is bottommost but one
Pl.14. a blue block is immediately below the yellow one
Pl.15. the yellow one is higher up than the red one
Pl.16. and immediately below the yellow one comes the blue one
Pl.17. then comes a red one
Pl.18. I'd say
Pl.19. well
Pl.20. a
Pl.21. a yellow block is higher up than the red one
Pl.22. a green block is bottommost but one
Pl.23. a blue block is immediately below the yellow one
Pl.24. below the yellow one is a blue block
Pl.25. and a yellow block is higher up than the red
Pl.26. below the yellow is then also a red
Pl.27. a blue and a red are below the yellow one
Pl.28. and a
Pl.29. a blue and a red are under the yellow block
Pl.30. and a green block is bottommost but one
Pl.31. a black block is between the red and the green
Pl.32. a black block
Pl.33. a black block is between the red and the green block
Pl.34. a white block is further down than the black one
Pl.35. then there is a white
Pl.36. and then we have a
Pl.37. oh how difficult
Pl.38. a white block is further down than the black one
Pl.39. and the black one is between the red and the green
Pl.40. white, red, black, green
Pl.41. I'll say then
Pl.42. but the green one is bottommost but one
Pl.43. then I'll say
Pl.44. white, green, black, red
Pl.45. instead
Pl.46. then the white one is bottommost
Pl.47. white, green, black, and red
Pl.48. and then we had the
Pl.49. blue one which is immediately below the yellow
Pl.50. the yellow is higher up than the red
Pl.51. then it is topmost so far
Pl.52. the yellow one
Pl.53. and the blue one is immediately below
Pl.54. then it comes topmost but one
Pl.55. which one is then immediately below the blue one
Pl.56. immediately below the blue one is then the red one

We will consider here a number of examples of the process of protocol interpretation. The first example involves the segment from Pl.12 through Pl.18. Pl.14 through Pl.16 are concerned with the relations of the yellow block with those below it. Pl.12-Pl.14 are paraphrased from l.O3-l.O5, respectively; then Pl.15 picks up Pl.12 again, and Pl.16 paraphrases Pl.14. The "and" in Pl.16 makes it plausible that Pl.15-Pl.16 are being considered in conjunction with each other. This produces the inference, prefaced by "then," in Pl.17. Pl.18 may mark the previous statement as a hypothesis.

Pl.23-29 provide a second example of the use of "and" to mark the conjunction of propositions for an inference process. Here, Pl.24 and Pl.25, conjoined by "and," suffice to generate the information in Pl.26-29.

Pl.38-41 provide a third example of the same thing. Pl.40 is derived from Pl.38-39, which are conjoined by "and." Pl.41 indicates that Pl.40 is held only as a hypothesis, and indeed, it is revised in Pl.42-45, where Pl.42, prefaced with "but," is introduced as a new premise that requires a reordering. The interruption of Pl.41 by Pl.42 suggests that at Pl.39, the subject was aware that the "between" was symmetric, allowing two interpretations, of which only one was verbalized in Pl.40. There is no indication of how Pl.42 is evoked at this particular moment, but having been evoked, it causes the interpretation of "between" to be revised, to select the other hypothesis.

There is no clear indication as to how the inference in Pl.46 was arrived at. It follows logically, of course, from Pl.42 and Pl.44, but the subject may have inferred it in some other way. Any account of this inference must be hypothetical.

The inference from Pl.47-51 also goes from an "and" to a "then," but is slightly more complex, for the past tense in Pl.48 suggests a backward memory reference to Pl.25-27.

Pl.51-54 is a rather straightforward inference of the type, "X and Y, then Z." This is followed by Pl.55-56, where two new assertions are made without explicit premises. Here we would infer that the inferences are derived directly from an internal model of the sequential ordering of the blocks.

If we are correct in our assumption about the general structure of the "and/then" process, and believe that the heeded information is verbalized concurrently with awareness, then the subject will not be aware of the inference at the time he is verbalizing the premises and the "and."

In fact, there are a couple of instances where "and" is verbalized without a new inference being drawn. In Pl.29-31, for example, the third statement is not inferred from the first two, but merely represents another fact about blocks mentioned in the first two. Note the use of the definite article in Pl.31 for the objects that have been mentioned in the two previous statements. Again, in Pl.33-37, there is a failure to draw an inference from conjoined premises, followed by a recovery in Pl.38-40. Note how Pl.33-34 are reordered in Pl.38-39.

In our analysis of this protocol, we have shown how statements can be rather unambiguously classified as reading, paraphrasing, or interpreting. Furthermore, it appears that these assessments can generally be made locally, that is, by evaluating a single segment consisting of just a few statements independently of the broader context. We have also illustrated how we can use this analysis, in many cases, to account for the inference processes that produced the newly generated information. Of course a careful distinction should be maintained between such theoretical interpretations of the mechanisms that may have produced the protocol statements and the encoding and classification of the statements themselves. In our discussion of the examples, we suggested some organizations of processes that would have produced the statements that appeared in the actual protocol. With some additional analysis, we could construct a formal coding scheme that would define the kinds of information that the subject might become aware of and heed. The theoretical interpretation could then be specified in terms of sequences of protocol statements drawn from this set, and could be evaluated against other hypotheses. In his dissertation Ohlsson (1980) analyzed this and other protocols in unusual depth, using a complete process model and problem-behavior graph.

USING A THEORY FOR PROTOCOL PREDICTION

Where a theory of the cognitive processes under investigation has already been postulated, several kinds of predictions can be made about the information that subjects will attend to and report orally. On the one hand, a theory can yield weak predictions of the kinds of information that will be heeded in performing the task, without predicting the sequence in which information will be attended to. On the other hand, a theory can permit inferences about the sequences of processes required to reach a correct solution of the task, and thereby yield strong predictions that only those sequences of processes would appear in subjects' protocols.

To make these predictions as precise as possible, the theory of task performance needs to be complemented by a theory of verbalization, so that we know what part of the information that is heeded has a high probability of being verbalized, and what part has a low probability. We have tried in the earlier chapters of this book to provide such a complementary theory.

To test a hypothesis of the first, or weaker type, we need to compare the set of statements implied by that hypothesis with the statements implied by competing processes. The union of these sets defines the totality of coding categories that needs to be considered in encoding the protocols in a manner that is both comprehensive and neutral among the hypotheses.

A hypothesis of the second, or stronger, type predicts either a unique sequence of verbalizations or a set of acceptable sequences. Such a sequence or set can also be represented as a transition network, a representation that may be attractive for some purposes. The two representations, as set of sequences or network, are of course logically equivalent. Alternative hypotheses can be explicated in the same way as sets of sequences of verbalizations, and the actual sequences can readily be compared with those predicted by the different hypotheses.

To make these considerations concrete, we will carry through in some detail analyses of two kinds of examples. First, we will show how an analysis of identified instances of generated information can allow us to derive and evaluate hypotheses regarding the representation of information. Then we will show, by means of examples, how hypotheses about processes and strategies can be used to predict the order in which information is verbalized.

CHARACTERISTICS OF GENERATED INFORMATION: REPRESENTATIONS

Determining what representation a subject is using in a problem solving task is often a difficult and subtle matter. In this section, we will describe two studies that used protocols as data to infer subjects' representations. First, we will explore different methods for characterizing heeded information using the Eight Puzzle as our example. Then we will show how representations of the Tower of Hanoi can be inferred from protocols.

The Eight Puzzle

First, we need to describe the Eight Puzzle and say something about the experiment that produced the protocols (Ericsson, 1975b). In the Eight Puzzle, subjects are presented with a 3x3 matrix of numbered square tiles (Figure 7-1a). By sliding one of the directly adjacent tiles into the empty space, the arrangement of tiles can be changed. Subjects are instructed to achieve the goal arrangement (Figure 7-1b). In this experiment, subjects were given different starting configurations, but all asked to achieve the particular goal configuration shown in the figure.

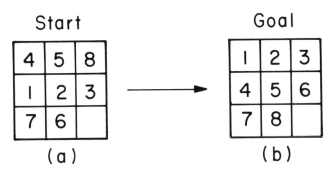

Figure 7-1

Example of a configuration for the Eight Puzzle (left); this is to be transformed into a goal configuration (right), the one shown here being used throughout the present experiment.

The Eight Puzzle is solved by deriving information relevant to choosing moves from a comparison of the current puzzle configuration (PC) with the goal configuration (GC). PC and GC can be represented internally and compared with each other in many ways. For example, the subject can measure or estimate the qualitative similarity of PC to GC, or a numerical "distance" of the one from the other. Most artificial intelligence programs for solving the Eight Puzzle use some kind of distance measure that takes into account considerable information about PC (Nilsson, 1971; Pohl, 1969). On the other hand, a program along the lines of the General Problem Solver (Newell, Shaw, & Simon, 1958), would consider the "major difference" (i.e., a feature like a particular tile not in its final position) between PC and GC, and would ignore most of the other information about PC. These two general approaches make quite different predictions about what we might expect to find in subjects' protocols.

The protocols of the subjects were categorized on the basis of mainly syntactic information (Ericsson, 1975b). Two categories, *intentions* and *cognitions*, have major relevance to the form of representation the subjects were using. Intentions are verbalized goals, defining the attributes of configurations subjects are seeking to achieve (e.g., "I want to get 3 in its correct place"). Cognitions are verbalized characterizations of the current PC (e.g., "I see that 7 is in its correct place").

We will present our analysis of these two categories separately, a procedure that will permit us to evaluate, or at least comment on, the generality of the representation. Our analysis employs 274 protocol segments coded as intentions, and 132 encoded as cognitions, pooled from the protocols of ten subjects. We start by discussing intentions.

The most striking finding about intentions is that subjects define goals in terms of only a few tiles (or one). In 162 cases (59%) the goal involved positioning a single tile; a pair of tiles in 61 cases (22%). Properties of three tiles were mentioned in 49 cases (18%), four tiles in two cases (1%). In no case did a subject mention a goal of positioning more than four tiles. The majority (75%) of intentions involving single tiles expressed the goal of putting them in their "correct" position in the GC. Some examples of such verbalizations are given in Table 7-1.

These are exactly the kinds of goals that a GPS-like model would predict. In the remaining cases, subjects verbalized "getting the tile closer to its goal" or "getting tile in its correct row," or "getting the tile to a location different from that in GC," or "getting rid of a blocking tile."

Verbalized intentions involving two tiles are of two kinds (Ericsson, 1975b, discusses five exceptions). The tiles are either to be placed in their correct positions, or in correct sequential order independently of absolute location. It might be thought that these goals would involve all pairs of tiles adjacent in the GC. In actual fact, with one exception, all such goals involved pairs of tiles with adjacent ordinal numbers (e.g., 1-2, 4-5, etc.). This suggests an internal representation of the GC as shown in Figure 7-2.

When we turn to intentions involving three or four tiles, the same pattern emerges. All but five instances (47) involve the correct placement or correct sequential order of the tiles in the first or the second row of GC, that is, 1-2-3 or 4-5-6. The five other cases, which are not true exceptions, are analyzed by Ericsson (1975b).

Table 7-1

Examples of Verbalizations to Attain Correct Placement of Tile 1

I'm going to try	to get 1	at the very top
I must	get 1 up there	
I shall try	to get 1	here
first	get 1	there instead of 4
as usual	get 1 up	
	get 1 up there	
	get 1	(so I can follow after with 2 and 3)
shall be empty so that	1	can go up to its correct location
	get 1	in its correct location
	get 1 at the top	
want to	get 1 up	
now I must	have 1	in the left corner
must try to	get 1 up too	
I shall	have 1 up	
I want to	have the 1 up there	
	move 1 up where it should be	
thinking of moving	1 up at once	
that I shall	get 1	here
	to get 1 up (and get 2 there, first 1 up)	
in any case	get 1	in place first and foremost
now I want to	have 1 up right from the beginning	
try to get them in order to start with	1 upmost to the left and get it in	
I'm going to try	to get 1 back up there	
no I thought I must		
try to	get 1 down there in between so I can get it up in its place	
now I'm thinking if I can in any smart way	get 1 up in the left corner where it should be without any greater arrangements	
then I shall try to	get 1 up there	
now I'm thinking that I shall	get 1 up there again	
well I thought of trying to get 1 up		
because I must get that one again -(E)-		
I want to	have 1	in place
to	place 1	in some manner
and now I shall try with	1 furthest to the left	
I shall try to	get 1 up	

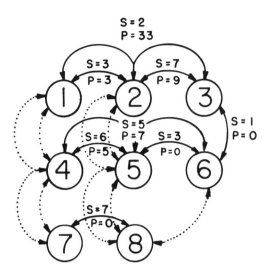

Figure 7-2

The pooled frequencies of expressed intentions to attain certain Seq (X,Y), Seq (X,Y,Z), Place (X,Y), and Place (X,Y,Z) relations are marked on the arcs joining the numbers of the associated tiles, with an S for Seq and a P for Place. Arcs without any recorded occurrences are dotted.

The subjects' verbal intentions that appear in these protocols can thus be described almost completely as simple differences falling out from a comparison of PC with GC.

Analysis of cognitions, verbal descriptions of the PC, yields very similar results. Of the 132 protocol segments encoded as cognitions, 54 (41%) involved the attributes of a single tile, while 52 (39%) involved the attributes of a pair of tiles, and 18 (14%), three tiles. Three instances involved noticing that tiles 1-2-3-4-5 and 1-2-3-4-5-6-7-8 followed each other in numerical order, or that 8-7-6-5-4 were in reverse numeric order.

The cognitions about single tiles correspond with those for intentions. In 24 segments, the subject observed that a tile had reached its correct location or its correct row, or was closer than before to the goal. In 24 cases, subjects observed that a tile's location was incorrect, thus making explicit mention of a difference between PC and GC. The remaining six segments referred to tiles obstructing the placement of other tiles.

In more than ninety per cent of the cases referring to two tiles, they are reported to have the right locations, or the correct sequential order, or the reversed sequential order. The mentions of sequential order are consistent with the hypothesized representation of the GC.

In the case of three tiles, correct placement or sequential order are mentioned. With only three exceptions (Ericsson, 1975b), the members of the triad belong in a single row of GC.

In these protocols, we find a great consistency in subject behavior (between subjects as well as for single subjects), permitting us to determine with considerable assurance what features of the situations they are attending to, and how they are representing it.

Isomorphic Problems

Hayes and Simon (1974) proposed a model describing how subjects comprehend written problem instructions and construct an internal representation of problem information. The model was able to generate problem representations for the Tea Ceremony problem, a formal isomorph of the Tower of Hanoi. Thinking-aloud protocols were gathered from subjects presented with this problem, but the protocols proved to be rather sketchy for the interval during which subjects were formulating the problem and devising a representation of it. It was difficult, from these protocols, to determine what representations subjects had constructed. However, as we shall see, protocols taken during the interval when subjects were solving the problem disclosed these representations clearly.

In a subsequent study, Simon and Hayes (1976) used problem isomorphs that, their model predicted, would cause subjects to adopt distinctly different problem representations. We will consider here two of these isomorphs, a move problem and a change problem, respectively.

In its usual form, the Tower of Hanoi involves moving of transferring disks among three pegs. Only one disk can be moved at a time, and a larger disk cannot be placed on a peg on which there is already a smaller disk. In this form, the Tower of Hanoi is a move problem. The starting and goal configurations of disks and pegs are shown in Figure 7-3. Here the pegs are labeled "A, B, C" and the disks are labeled "1 = small," "2 = medium," "3 = large," and will be referred to by these names in all the isomorphic problems.

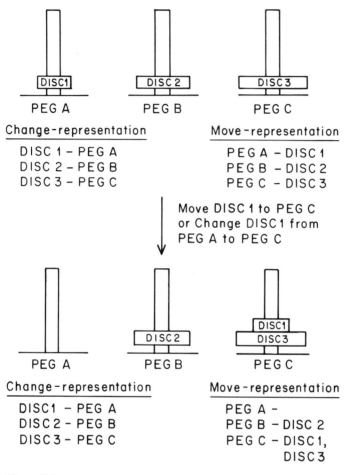

Figure 7-3

Illustration of Different Representations in the Tower of Hanoi Problem with 3 Disks

In the Tower of Hanoi, the disks retain their physical identities; only their locations (the pegs on which they are placed) change. Symbolically, we can describe any disk configuration as a list of three locations (corresponding to the three pegs), and lists of the appropriate disks associated with each location, (as shown in Figure 7-3). We will call this symbolic representation a *move* representation.

Alternatively, we could represent exactly the same information symbolically by a list of the three disks, and with each member of the list, an indication of the peg with which it is associated. We will call this a *change* representation.

When a move representation is used, then an alteration in the problem situation is recorded by removing the name of one of the disks from its peg list and placing it on the list of a different peg. When a change representation is used, then an alteration in the problem situation is recorded by altering the name of the peg with which some particular disk is associated. Thus, the same move in the Tower of Hanoi is represented by different symbol-manipulating processes in the two different symbolic representations of the task. (See Figure 7-4.)

Isomorphs of the Tower of Hanoi can be constructed by substituting other kinds of objects for disks and pegs, and the legal transformations with these objects can be described in terms of moves or changes. Below, we give examples of problems in which the objects are "monsters" and "globes," and the transformations involve either moving a globe from one monster to another, or changing the size of the globe.

Since these two problem descriptions are logically equivalent (that is, isomorphic with respect to states and moves), it is logically possible that a subject would use either the change or move representation when faced with *either* of the problems. The UNDERSTAND model of Simon and Hayes (1976) made explicit predictions as to whether subjects would represent particular problem statements as move or change problems. In particular, it predicted for the examples presented here that the first would be represented as a move problem, and the second as a change problem. That is to say, if the problems were described to subjects as involving an object moving from one location to another, the subjects would represent it symbolically in just that way; while if it were described to them in terms of objects changing their sizes or other properties, the subjects would represent it symbolically in that other way.

To provide evidence of the representations that the subjects used, two different kinds of protocol statements were analyzed for subjects presented with these problem isomorphs. The statements of the first kind were verbalized descriptions of moves, statements of the second kind were verbalized descriptions of current problem states and configurations.

Three five-handed extraterrestial monsters were holding three crystal globes. Because of the quantum-mechanical peculiarities of their neighborhood, both monsters and globes come in exactly three sizes with no others permitted: small, medium, and large. The medium-sized monster was holding the small globe, the small monster was holding the large globe, and the large monster was holding the medium-sized globe. Since this situation offended their keenly developed sense of symmetry, they proceeded to transfer globes from one monster to another so that each monster would have a globe proportionate to his own size. Monster etiquette complicated the solution of the problem since it requires:

1.   that only one globe may be transferred at a time;
2.   that if a monster is holding two globes, only the larger
      of the two may be transferred; and
3.   that a globe may not be transferred to a monster who is
      holding a larger globe.

By what sequence of transfers could the monsters have solved this problem?

Three five-handed extraterrestial monsters were holding three crystal globes. Because of the quantum-mechanical peculiarities of their neighborhood, both monsters and globes come in exactly three sizes with no others permitted: small, medium, and large. The medium-sized monster was holding the small globe, the small monster was holding the large globe, and the large monster was holding the medium-sized globe. Since this situation offended their keenly developed sense of symmetry, they proceeded to shrink and expand the globes from one monster to another so that each monster would have a globe proportionate to his own size. Monster etiquette complicated the solution of the problem since it requires:

1.   that only one globe may be shrunk or expanded at a time;
2.   that if a monster is holding two globes, only the larger
      of the two may be shrunk or expanded; and
3.   that a globe may not be transferred to a monster who is
      holding a larger globe.

By what sequence of transfers could the monsters have solved this problem?

Figure 7-4

Isomorphic Forms of the Monster Problem

Descriptions of moves. Most of the protocol statements describing moves provide substantial evidence for assessing the underlying representation, as the following examples show:

> So the small globe goes over to the guy with the medium-sized globe.

This statement implies a list of monsters, but that globes are being transferred from one to another.

> The medium-sized monster changes his into a small globe.

This statement implies a list of monsters, but that properties (sizes) of the globes are being changed by their owners.

> I will move the monster which is on the medium-sized globe to the large globe.

This protocol statement implies a list of globes, and that monsters are being moved from one globe to another. From the information in these kinds of statements, two encoders independently assessed the representation used by the subject for the entire solution attempt, and assessed whether the representation was changed or modified during the solution process.

Descriptions of states. Aspects of the representation can also be identified easily when subjects are describing the current state of the problem. Consider the following two examples of protocol segments:

> The small monster has the large, the medium has the small, the large has the medium.

> A small monster is holding a small globe, a large monster holding a medium-size globe, a medium-size monster holding a large globe.

The two segments clearly refer to a list of monsters with globes of different sizes rather than vice versa.

In one of the many problem isomorphs that were studied, the monsters transferred their names, and a monster could have more than one name at a time, or none. The following segment gives evidence, for this isomorph, of representation in terms of a list of monsters:

> The guy with long name now has a long name and medium-size name.

The UNDERSTAND model predicted the representations used by subjects in all cases but one. The analyses of moves and of states always yielded the same representation, and there were no disagreements between the two encoders. The UNDERSTAND model also predicted correctly in all cases which type of object (monster or globe) would constitute the main list.

From some informal analyses of protocols in Newell and Simon (1972), we are convinced that the representations underlying the Problem

Behavior Graph in the crypt-arithmetic and logic problems could have been inferred or confirmed through similar methods of analysis. It is clear that any hypothesis about representation of information will, at least implicity, involve assumptions about the processes that generate the information.

SEQUENCES OF HEEDED INFORMATION

We now turn to a series of examples where hypotheses about processes and strategies are used to predict sequences of heeded information. The first two examples show how the adequacy of strategies can be evaluated by comparing predictions of heeded information with information verbalized in the protocol. Such evaluation is quite powerful even when information is incompletely verbalized. The next pair of examples show how a complete process model including a model of verbalization, can be constructed and evaluated. Lastly, we present an example that illustrates the many possible realizations of cognitive processes. The examples deal with tasks that are quite familiar and whose processes are uncontroversial. We will present two analyses of mental addition, an analysis of the Tower of Hanoi problem and one of mental multiplication.

Mental Addition of Digit Sequences

Subjects were shown a card on which was printed a line of digits, and were instructed to find the sum of the digits while thinking aloud.

Task analysis. Digits can be added together in a large number of ways to obtain the correct sum. Here we will consider, as hypotheses, only two of these ways. The first hypothesis is that the subjects form a single partial sum, adding the digits to it cumulatively, from left to right. This model of the process, simple as it is, contains several implicit assumptions. First, it assumes that each successive addition is carried out in a single step (the subject is aware of only the final result, and there are no heeded intermediate states). Second, it assumes that finding the next digit to be added is also an automatic process without intermediate steps.

The model is powerful enough to predict the exact sequence in which information will be heeded, but it can be weakened to predict only the order in which the partial sums will be heeded (and presumably verbalized). Consider the following example, where the upper line displays the digits, and the lower line the corresponding successive partial sums:

5	2	8	9	7	4	3	6	3	4
7	15	24	31	35	38	44	47	51

Ignoring sequence (the weakest model, H2), it can be predicted that all the verbalized two-digit numbers will belong to the following set:

III = { 15,24,31,35,38,44,47,51 }

(Note that we omit 7, which is not a two-digit number.)

Consider, now, the alternative hypothesis (H2) that the subject adds the digits from right to left, instead of from left to right:

4	3	6	3	4	7	9	8	2	5
7	13	16	20	27	36	44	46	51

Model H2 makes the quite different predictions that the verbalized two-digit numbers will belong to the following set:

H2 = { 13,16,20,27,36,44,46,51 }

This set has only one member in common with H1 (44).

We will now encode three protocols, comparing the encodings with H1 and H2. Our coding alternatives will be the space of all two-digit numbers, 10-99. All other information in the protocols will be ignored.

Protocol 1		Protocol 2		Protocol 3	
Protocol	Encoding	Protocol	Encoding	Protocol	Encoding
7		2 and 8 is 10	10	5 plus 2 is 7	
15	15	and 5 is 15	15	plus 8 is 15	15
24	24	and 9 is 24	24	plus 9 is 24	24
31	31	and 7 is 31	31	plus 7 is	
35	35	and 4 is 35	35	what—31	31
38	38	3 and 6 is 9		plus 4 is 34	34
44	44	makes 44	44	plus 3 is 37	37
47	47	3 and 4 is 7		plus 6 is 43	43
51	51	makes 51	51	plus 4 is, see	36
				36 plus 4 is 40	40

The protocols shown above were selected to make certain points in the discussion that follows. A more representative sample would contain more protocols like Protocol 1, but with fuller verbalization about the addends.

Evaluation of hypotheses. Before matching against the numbers predicted by the weak hypotheses, we would want to eliminate duplicates from the reported partial sums, and also the final result (51), which is implied by any model that generates the correct answer.

For Protocol 1, the verbalized partial results all correspond to those postulated by H1, and none correspond with the predictions of H2. The chances that such a close match with H1 could be produced by chance are less than one in a trillion. Even if the random generator was constrained to produce a succession of two-digit numbers, each not more than 9 larger than its predecessor and all of them less than the correct sum, the probability would be less than one in a million. H1 clearly describes Protocol 1 better than H2 does.

In the case of Protocol 2, the verbalized partial sums match those predicted by H1 in six cases, but fail to match in one. Again, they do not match at all with the predictions of H2. The superior fit of the protocol to H1 as compared to H2 cannot be attributed to chance. Nevertheless, the failure to achieve a perfect fit suggests that H1 could be extended or modified to provide a more satisfactory explanation of the protocol. We will come back to this point later.

Turning now to Protocol 3, there are only three matches with H1, and six failures to match. For the alternative model, H2, there are two matches and seven failures. In this case, neither model can be preferred over a random model. Nevertheless, informal analysis of the protocol suggests that H1 might describe the verbalizations if some assumptions about errors in the addition process were introduced. Again, we will return to this issue later. We mention it here mainly to indicate the damaging effect of errors on direct predictions when a single error may change the whole succeeding stream of verbalizations.

Concluding remarks. This simple example shows how information verbalized by a subject while thinking aloud can sometimes be predicted in a straightforward manner. For the protocols of subjects who got the correct answer, H1 makes accurate predictions, and clearly conforms to the evidence better than H2. The fact that the two models make quite different predictions facilitated the choice between them.

One of the attractive features of making the test in this form is that incomplete verbalization does not then create a serious problem it simply decreases the power of the test in choosing between alternative hypotheses. Moreover, with the weak hypotheses, very specific predictions can be made without having to make explicit assumptions of the sequential order of processes. The example in the next section brings out this last feature more clearly.

Strategies for the Tower of Hanoi

How can we predict verbalizations of subjects using different strategies to solve the same problem? In particular, can the strategies be identified reliably from protocols? The data are derived from a study by Neves (1977), in which he trained subjects to use different strategies to solve the Tower of Hanoi puzzle, and then asked them to think aloud during the solution process.

First, we will summarize the theoretical analysis of Simon (1975), describing several different strategies that all lead to correct solutions of the puzzle. The analysis makes explicit what information enters and is retained in STM at all times. From the theoretical models we derive the sequence of heeded information for a number of puzzle configurations, and use these to predict what information would be verbalized with each strategy. We then encode protocols from subjects trained in using these strategies, and match them against the predictions. The Tower of Hanoi puzzle has already been described earlier. We will be concerned with the 4-disk version. At the start of the probolem, the disks are all on Peg 1; the task is to move them to Peg 3.

Task Analysis. The theoretical models of the solution process are expressed in the form of *production systems.* This formalism is described by Simon (1975, pp. 274-275) as follows:

> A production system (Newell & Simon, 1972) is simply an ordered set of processes called productions. Each production has two parts: a condition (C), and an action (A), which are usually written with an arrow connecting them: $C \rightarrow A$.

The reader will not mislead himself badly if he equates the arrow in a production with the link in a special kind of S-R structure. The productions fall into two classes: a general class and a special class called perceptual tests. The condition of a production belonging to the general class is a test usually for the presence of absence of a particular kind of symbol on the contents of STM. The test is either satisfied or not. Whenever the test in the condition part of a general production is satisfied, and only them, the action part is executed. The action may be a motor act, the performing of a perceptual test, an act of retrieving information from long-term memory, or an act of changing the contents of short-term memory. The condition part of a production may involve a conjunction of several elementary tests, and the action part may involve a sequence of elementary actions. A simple example of a general production is:

"Problem-solved" → **Halt**

The condition side of this production calls for a test whether the symbol, "Problem-solved," has been stored in STM. The action taken in this case is to halt the entire process. If the symbol is not found in STM, no action is taken.

The production subsystem representing perceptual tests is activated by executing a Test action in one of the general productions. The condition of a perceptual test is a perceivable feature of the task environment, or a conjunction of such features. If the feature or conjunction of features is present, and only then, the action part of the perceptual test is executed. The only action of a perceptual test is to change the contents of STM. Execution of a perceptual test makes the system "aware" of some perceivable feature of its environment by storing information about that feature in STM.

The production system and the perceptual subsystem are each assumed to operate serially only one production may be activated at a time. If the conditions for more than one production are satisfied simultaneously, only the first of these on the list of productions is activated. Hence, the order of productions on the list is an integral part of the definition of the program; changing the order could (and usually will) cause significant changes in the system's behavior.

The advantages of production systems as programming formalisms, and the reasons for thinking that strategies stored in the human central nervous system may be organized as production systems are discussed in Newell and Simon (1972, pp. 803-806), and in Newell (1973). The particular kind of production system we are using here has two advantages worth mentioning. First, it makes explicit exactly what information is held in short-term memory, so that processing assumptions that would place unrealistic demands on STM are immediately detectable. Second, the system makes equally explicit what assumptions are being made about perceptual capabilities. Features of the environment can only be taken into account by means of specific perceptual tests, and these tests can lead directly only to knowledge, not to action.

Simon (1975) describes a number of different strategies, among which we will consider here only the goal-recursive strategy. The move-pattern strategy is so different from these that it can be trivially distinguished from the other two with protocol data (Neves, 1977).

The *goal-recursive* strategy applies recursively a procedure that allows the correct move to be generated for any configuration of the disks on the pegs. Basic to the procedure is the concept of a pyramid of K disks (i.e., the pyramid consisting of all disks of size K and smaller). The goal of moving Pyramid (K) to a given peg can be attained by recursive application of the following procedure:

Try to move disk K to Peg (X):

If such a move has already been made, create the goal
of moving Pyramid (K—1) to Peg (X).

If such a move can legally be made, make it.

If such a move cannot be made, create the goal of
moving Pyramid (K—1) to the Other peg (i.e., the
peg that is neither X nor the one on which disk
K stands).

To see why this strategy works, consider an example. First, if all the disks are in the starting position, the strategy first generates the goal of moving the pyramid of four disks to the goal peg. Since the largest disk cannot legally be moved, the goal is generated of moving all the remaining disks to the other peg. Since the largest of these remaining disks (Disk 3) also cannot be moved, the goal is generated of moving the pyramid of the two smallest disks to the goal peg. This also fails, so the goal is now created of moving the smallest disk to the other peg. This move is made successfully. The goal-recursive strategy is sufficiently powerful to generate the correct move in any configuration of disks on the pegs. The production system implementing the goal-recursive strategy is shown in Figure 7-5, reproduced from Simon (1975).

P1.   State = Problem-solved → Halt

P2.   State = Done,Goal = Move(Pyramid(k),A)
      → Delete(STM), Goal ← Move(Pyramid(k—1),A)

P3.   State = Can,Goal = Move(Pyramid(k),A)
      → Delete(STM), Move(k,P(k),A)

P4.   State = Can't,Goal = Move(Pyramid(k),A)
      → Delete(STM), Goal ← Move(Pyramid(k—1),O(P(k),A))

P5.   Goal = Move(Pyramid(k),A) → Test(Move(k,P(k),A))

P6.   else → Goal ← Move(Pyramid(n),Goal-peg)

Figure 7-5

Production System for Goal Recursion Strategy

The *perceptual* strategy can be viewed as a modification of the goal-recursive strategy (Simon, 1975). By using more sophisticated perceptual predicates and tests, the need for goals of moving pyramids of disks can be eliminated. The perceptual strategy identifies the *biggest* disk blocking a given move. The observation that a move can't be made because of Disk J is denoted Can't(J). Further, it is assumed that the largest disk not yet on the goal peg can be identified perceptually. We will denote this disk by Biggest(J).

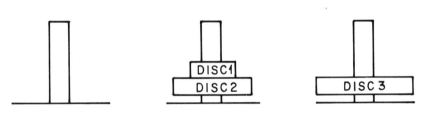

Figure 7-6

A Disk Configuration in the Tower of Hanoi Problem

The logic underlying the perceptual strategy can be illustrated with the disk configuration shown in Figure 7-6. The subject first notes that the largest disk not yet on the goal peg is Disk 2 (Biggest(2)), and generates the goal of moving this disk to the goal peg. In testing the legality of this desired move, the subject notices that it can't be made, and that Disk 1 is the largest disk blocking it (Can't(1)). The subject then generates the goal of moving Disk 1 to the peg that is neither the one where Disk 2 is located nor the one to which Disk 2 is to be moved. This move can now be executed.

The production system representation of the perceptual strategy, from Simon (1975) is shown in Figure 7-7.

P1'.   State = Problem-solved → Halt

P2'.   State = Done,Goal = Move(k,P(k),A)
        → Delete(State), Delete(Goal)

P3'.   State = Can,Goal = Move(k,P(k),A)
        → Delete(State), Move(k,P(k),A)

P4'.   State = Can't(J), Goal = Move(k,P(k),A)
        → Delete(STM), Goal ← Move(J,P(J),O(P(k),A))

P5'.   Goal = Move(k,P(k),A) → Test(Move(k,P(k),A))

P6'.   State = Biggest(J) → Goal ← Move(J,P(J),Goal-peg)

P7'.   else → Test(Biggest-remaining)

Figure 7-7
Production System for Perceptual Strategy

We can predict what information will be heeded, successively, by subjects using either of these two models in a particular puzzle configuration. To show how this is done, we will examine in detail a few examples. To facilitate comparison between model predictions and protocol data, the two will be presented side by side for each example.

Encoding Categories for Verbalizations. Neves (1977) wished to encode verbalizations mentioning goals and subjects' evaluations of the feasibility of attaining the goals in the current situation. There are three possible outcomes for such an evaluation or test (T):

(1) The goal is already attained or done (D);

(2) The goal can be attained in a single move from the current disk configuration (C);

(3) The goal cannot be attained directly from the current configuration (N).

Any goal can be described as aiming to get a given disk (N) on a particular peg (X): G(N,X).

This notation does not provide for goals of moving whole pyramids rather than individual disks. In what follows, we will not encode such goals or predict their verbalization. With respect to the perceptual strategy, we need to encode also verbalized reasons why a goal can't be attained: "can't because of Disk K." We will encode this at T(N(K)). The biggest disk not yet on the goal peg (K) will be encoded as B(K). In situations where the protocol doesn't allow all aspects of the encoding to be assessed, the missing information is coded by the symbol "%." The following two examples show how protocol segments will be encoded according to these rules. (Note that numbers are used to designate both disks and pegs.)

> The 4 has to go to the 3 [peg], but the 3 [disk] is in the way.
> G(4,3), T(N(3))

> The 4 has to go over, but there is something in the way.
> *Fictitious*   G(4,%), T(N(%))

Empirical Evaluation of Predictions. Taking as our example the disk configuration that we used above to describe the two strategies, we will provide an explicit trace of all information entering STM for each of the strategies, and the corresponding predictions of protocol segments. First, we will give the trace for the goal-recursive strategy:

> {Goal = Move(Pyramid(4),3)}
> Test(Move(4,3,3)), State = Done   G(4,3), T(D)
> {Goal = Move(Pyramid(3),3)}
> Test(Move(3,3,3)), State = Done   G(3,3), T(D)
> {Goal = Move(Pyramid(2),3)}
> Test(Move(2,1,3)), State = Can't   G(2,1), T(N(%))
> {Goal = Move(Pyramid(1),2)}
> Test(Move(1,1,2)), State = Can   G(1,2), T(C)

The goals of moving pyramids have been put in brackets, because they are not predicted by the model (see previous discussion). Tests of desired moves are interpreted as expressions of goals to make those moves.

For the same puzzle configuration, the information entering STM with the perceptual strategy is the following:

> Biggest(2)   B(2)
> Goal = Move(2,1,3)   G(2,3)
> State = Can't(1)   T(N(1))
> Goal = Move(1,1,2)   G(1,2)
> State = Can   T(C)

Let us look now at the thinking-aloud protocols collected for subjects trained to use one of the two strategies we are considering. First, we exhibit the protocol of a subject trained to use the goal-recursive strategy for the same puzzle configuration.

I'm looking at Peg 3, at the largest, which is already done.	G(4,3), T(D)
So I move to the next to the largest, which is the 3, which is already done.	G(3,%), T(D)
So I try to move the 2, which is on Peg 1.	G(2,%)
Which I can't move because a smaller one is above it.	T(N(1))
So I move to Peg 2, which is the next to the smallest, which is the 1, which I can move. So my move is 1 to 2.	G(1,2), T(C)

Note that the encodings use only verbalized information and not information about the disk configuration. If such information were consulted, it would be obvious that the undetermined target in the second goal is Peg 3. The peg for the third goal cannot be determined simply to looking at the actual configuration. To argue that Peg 3 must have been intended would be to go well beyond the information given. Although Disk 1 is not mentioned explicity in the fourth segment, it can be inferred since it is the only disk smaller than Disk 2. For some idiosyncractic reason this subject consistently says "next to the smallest" when he means "the next smaller." In this protocol, this inconsistency can be resolved by taking the most specific reference as the correct reference. In subsequent protocols, we will interpret "next to the smallest" literally.

We look next at the protocol given by a subject trained to use the perceptual strategy.

The 4 and 3 are in place.	
The 2 has to go over.	G(2,%)
So you have to move the 1 to the middle one, first.	T(N(1)), G(1,2)

The first statement is problematic, as it could be argued that it reflects an intermediate state towards identifying the biggest disk not yet on the goal peg. However, one could also argue that it implies that the goals of getting Disks 3 and 4 on the goal peg have already been attained. Since it does not reflect the sequence of goal followed by test, it is not coded. The construction "goal so you have to do X first" is readily seen as an elimination of an obstacle, corresponding closely to the idea behind T(N(X)).

For the goal-recursive strategy, the protocol encodings can be mapped directly onto the model predictions. There are only three minor mismatches. On two occasions it was impossible to assess toward which peg the disk is to be moved. In both cases the goal is verbalized, and it would be more accurate to refer to these omissions as lack of explicitness rather than incomplete verbalization. The third mismatch is the ver-bε..ization of the disk blocking the goal of moving Disk 2. A closer look at the corresponding protocol segment shows that although the subject describes the blocking disk, he does not use this information to generate the next goal. Thus, there is no violation of the basic structure of the goal-recursive strategy.

The protocol can also be mapped against the model for the perceptual strategy. Many of the verbalizations predicted by the model are absent from the protocol: for example, the assessment of the biggest disk not yet on the goal peg, and the two evaluations of the goals that are generated. Hence, the fact that the subject was instructed to use, and apparently did use, the recursive strategy is strongly supported by comparison of the protocol with the models.

The next protocols and model predictions are generated for the disk configuration shown in Figure 7-8.

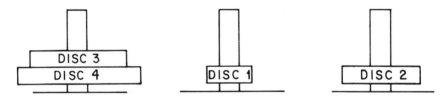

Figure 7-8
Disk Configuration for Tower of Hanoi Protocol

For the goal-recursive strategy the predictions of the models are as follows:

Trace	Predicted encoding
{Goal = Move(Pyramid(4),3)}	
Test(Move(4,1,3)), State = Can't	G(4,3), T(N(%))
{Goal = Move(Pyramid(3),2)}	
Test(Move(3,1,2)), State = Can't	G(3,2), T(N(%))
{Goal = Move(Pyramid(2),3)}	
Test(Move(2,3,3)), State = Done	G(2,3), T(D)
{Goal = Move(Pyramid(1),3)}	
Test(Move(1,2,3)), State = Can	G(1,3), T(C)

These predictions can now be compared directly with the protocol of the subject instructed to use the goal-recursive strategy, and the encoding of that protocol.

Protocol	Encodings
I'm looking at Peg 3, which has 2 at the bottom, which is not the largest. Peg 1 has it, and can't be moved because the smaller one is on top.	G(4,3), T(N(%))
Got to peg 2 and try to move the next to the smallest, which is the 3. I cannot move it, because something smaller will be below it.	G(3,2), T(N(%))·
Go back to Peg 3 and try to move the next to the largest, which is already done, which was the 2.	G(2,3), T(D)
Look for the next to the smallest, which is the 1, that is on Peg 2, but can be moved. My move is therefore, 1 to 3.	G(1,3), T(C)

Here the protocol and the predictions of the model are in perfect agreement.

The perceptual strategy gives the following predictions of verbalized information for this disk configuration:

Trace	Predictions
State = Biggest(4)	B(4)
Goal = Move(4,1,3)	G(4,3)
State = Can't(3)	T(N(3))
Goal = Move(3,1,2)	G(3,2)
State = Can't(1)	T(N(1))
Goal = Move(1,2,3)	G(1,3)
State = Can	T(C)

The corresponding protocol for the subject isntructed to use the perceptual strategy and its encodings are given below.

Protocol	Encodings
The 4 has to go to the 3.	G(4,3)
But the 3 is in the way.	T(N(3))
So you have to move the 3 to the 2 post.	G(3,2)
The 1 is in the way there.	T(N(1))
So you move the 1 to the 3.	G(1,3), T(C)

Except for the subject not mentioning that the biggest disk was not yet on the goal peg, there is complete correspondence between the encodings of the human protocol and the predictions of the model.

Our examples demonstrate the range in completeness of verbalizations. Even when they are quite incomplete, the subjects' strategies can be determined with some certainty for individual disk configurations, and determining which model fits best for a number of disk configurations, the strategy can be assessed with high validity. If the disk configurations presented to subjects are selected carefully, so that different models will make different predictions for these configurations, then the assessment of strategies can be made from just a few configurations.

Mental Multiplication

There are several reasons why mental multiplication of two-digit numbers is an attractive task for intensive analysis. Earlier work (Dansereau, 1969; Dansereau & Gregg, 1967; Hitch, 1978) have shown that subjects display a very orderly sequence of cognitive processes in this task. This orderliness allows us to make very strong predictions about the order in which information is heeded, and hence, verbalized. In the Appendix, we will argue that this kind of task is particularly useful for warming up subjects. We can use it to calibrate the subjects' verbalization processes, and use this calibration in analyzing individual differences in performing less stereotyped tasks.

The models we shall examine are aimed simply at identifying the information the subject needs in finding the intermediate and final results of the multiplication. They leave open more fundamental issues of how the numbers are represented by the subject. The multiplication may be segmented into three major parts, to make the description easier to follow. The three major stages in multiplying $d1d2*d3d4$ (where each d is a digit from 0 to 9) are:

(1) $d1d2*d4 = S1$
(2) $d1d2*d3d0 = S2 \, (d0 = 0)$
(3) $S1 + S2 = ST \, (\text{solution})$

Our model may be described in terms of a transition net for each of these stages. We will indicate the predicted verbalizations associated with each for the multiplication of $d1d2*d3d4$, and in particular, for the example 36 x 24.

Stage 1: Multiplication of d1d2*d4. In Figure 7-9, we show the transition net for this multiplication. Since it is almost self-explanatory, we will simply comment on some critical points.

First the subject has to retrieve d1d2 from memory, then the result of d2*d4. If the result of this multiplication is a two-digit number, it has to be broken up into a digit (Sd), and a carry (Sc). Next d1*d4 (S") is retrieved from memory. If there is a carry, it must be added to S" (Sc + S" = S'). Finally, Sd and S' must be merged as S'Sd.

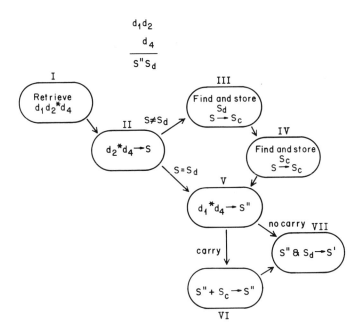

Figure 7-9

Transition Net for Multiplication of d1d2*d4

If this is the process some subjects use for the first step, what can we predict about their verbalizations? Let us consider three possible degrees of completeness of verbalization. In a model for complete verbalization (M-C) we assume that inputs, outputs, and operation are verbalized at each substep. In an intermediate model (M-I) we assume that information is verbalized at the time it enters attention and STM, but not when it is already in STM and reused immediately as input to the next process. In a model for a low level of verbalization (M-L) we assume that only information that is newly generated will be verbalized. We would expect the following output for the three models in the first stage of multiplying 36 x 24:

Model C	Model I	Model L
36*4	36*4	
6*4 = 24	6*4 = 24	24
24 4	4	4
24—C:2	C:2	C:2
3*4 = 12	3*4 = 12	12
12+2 = 14	+2 = 14	14
14 – 4 – 144	4 – 144	144

In this example, we denote the carry by C: #, and use the hyphen to separate information verbalized sequentially.

Stage 2: Multiplying d1d2*d3d0. In Figure 7-10, we show the transition net for the second stage. First, the multiplication is converted into a multiplication of d1d2*d3, with a 0 in the 1's column of the answer. Then the multiplication process of Stage 1 is repeated. Finally the result of d1d2*d3 is merged with the 0.

The protocols predicted by the three verbalization models are these:

Model C	Model I	Model L
0	0	
2*36	2x36	
2x6 = 12	2x6 = 12	12
12 – 2	2	2
12 – C:1	C:1	C:1
2x3 = 6	2*3 = 6	6
6+1 = 7	+1 = 7	7
7 – 2 – 72	2 – 72	72
72 – 0 – 720	0 – 720	720

Stage 3: Adding S1 + S2 = ST. The partial sums resulting from the two 2x1 multiplications are brought back into STM. The addition proceeds from right to left. Addition of corresponding digits continues until all digits in the sum have been generated. These digits are then merged by a two-stage operation into a single number representing the answer (see Figure 7-11 for corresponding transition net).

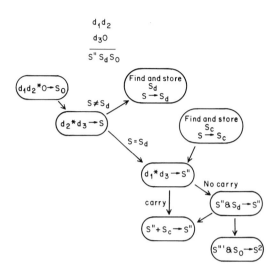

Figure 7-10

Transition Net for Multiplication of d1d2*d3d0

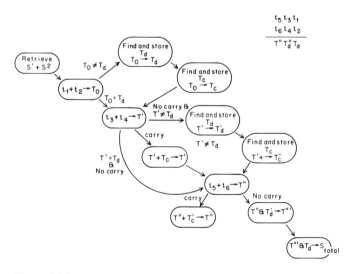

Figure 7-11

Transition Net for Addition

The three models of verbalization would predict these protocols:

Model C	Model I	Model L
720 + 144	+ 144	
4 + 0 = 4	4 + 0 = 4	4
4 + 2 = 6	4 + 2 = 6	6
1 + 7 = 8	1 + 7 = 8	8
8 − 6 − 86	6 − 86	86
86 − 4 − 864	4 − 864	864

Encoding the Protocols. The differences among the predicted protocols do not relate to the postulated cognitive processes, but are differences in what is verbalized. All predicted verbalizations can be expressed as either:

1. A number; $\langle N \rangle$

2. A number being carried; $C:\langle N \rangle$

3. Two numbers being added; (a) $\langle N \rangle + \langle M \rangle = \langle L \rangle$
   (b) $\langle N \rangle + \langle M \rangle$

4. Two numbers being multiplied; (a) $\langle N \rangle * \langle M \rangle = \langle L \rangle$
   (b) $\langle N \rangle * \langle M \rangle$

Encodings in this format could usually be made automatically by a computer program, and could certainly be made with reliability by a human coder considering only individual segments, without context.

We exhibit, next, two protocols collected for the same subject more than a week apart. Between the time the two protocols were collected, the subject had done several other mental multiplications.

PROTOCOL 1

Protocol	Encoding
OK	
36 times 24	36*24
um	
4 times 6 is 24	4*6 = 24
4	4
carry the 2	C:2
4 times 3 is 12	4*3 = 12
14	14
144	144
0	0
2 times 6 is 12	2*6 = 12
2	2
carry the 1	C:1
2 times 3 is 6	2*3 = 6
7	7

```
720              720
720              720
144 plus 720     144 + 720
so it would be 4  4
6                6
864              864
```

PROTOCOL 2

Protocol	Encoding
36 times 24	36*24
4	4
carry the—no wait	
4	4
carry the 2	C:2
14	14
144	144
0	0
36 times 2 is	36*2 =
12	12
6	6
72	72
720 plus 144	720 + 144
4	4
uh, uh	
6	6
8	8
uh	
864	864

Evaluation of Predictions. A visual inspection of the predictions and the encoded protocols shows that both Model-1 and Model-L fit the data quite well. The comparison could, of course, be made mechanically, looking for a mapping function between the sequence of encoded segments and the sequence of predictions that yields the highest degree of correspondence. Below, we have carried out that mapping by hand for Model-L's predictions and the two protocols:

Model L	Protocol 1	Protocol 2
	36*24	36*24
24	4*6 = 24	
4	4	(4)
C:2	C:2	C:2
12	4*3 = 12	
14	14	14
144	144	144
	(0)	(0)
		(36*2)
12	2*6 = 12	12

```
2                 2
C:1               C:1
6                 2x3=6           6
7                 7
72                                72
720               720             720
                  (720)
                  (144+720)       (+144)
4                 4               4
6                 6               6
8                                 8
86
864               864             864
```

With only a slight modification of Model-I., its printed verbalizations would always correspond to verbalizations in Protocol 1. The required modification is that the result of the multiplications and additions
are merged into a single number in one step.

Although mental multiplication is a task that makes especially
simple the encoding of protocols and the comparison of protocols with
predictions derived from processing models, it is a very useful one for
illustrating what is involved in such encoding and comparison. The same
principles apply to more complex protocols, although it will not always
be as easy to apply them.

PROCESSES WITH ALTERNATIVE REALIZATIONS

In many cognitive tasks, the exact verbalizations of a subject are not
determined uniquely by the task, or even by the subject's strategy. Under such circumstances, assessing whether a protocol fits the predictions
of a model is a little like judging whether a sentence is grammatical.
Linguistics has traditionally relied on native informants for making judgments of grammaticality. Only very recently has it been possible to
attempt such assessments automatically with the aid of computers.

In the same way, most analyses of protocol data are carried out by
investigators who have had extensive experience with the cognitive
processes and their verbalization for the task under study. Comparing a
verbal protocol with the predictions of an information processing model
involves a judgment not dissimilar to the judgment of grammaticality. Its
validity depends at least partly on the consensus of the judges.

There are also some structural similarities between utterances and
cognitive processes that are worth noting. It is not uncommon for people

to start to say something and then to stop and begin a new sentence that is completed. People also stop midway in sentences, and then restart by repeating some words and then completing the sentence. Similar interruptions and restarts occur in cognitive processes like those we have already examined in this chapter, especially processes like mental multiplication and addition that gradually cumulate information. In verbal reports, such interruptions or repetitions are marked by intonation or explicit comment. As far as possible, such occurrences should be identified when the verbal transcript is being preprocessed.

Addition of Digits

Returning to the addition task that was considered in an earlier section, we now go beyond the original analysis, which was limited to reports of intermediate inputs and results, and undertake a more complete examination of the full protocols. We shall see how this additional information can be used to constrain the possible models of the cognitive process. Here are two protocols from the addition task:

3 plus 0 is 3	2 and 8 is 10
plus 8 is (uh) 11	and 5 is 15
plus 1 is 12	and 9 will be 24
plus 2 is 14	and 7 is 31
plus 4 is 18	and 4 is 35
plus 9 is 27	and 3 and 6 is 9 makes 44
plus 0 is 27	3 and 4 is 7 makes 51
plus 6 is (uh) 33	
plus 7 is 40	
plus 3 is 33	
no 43	

Formal task analysis. M digits can be added together in many ways that form partial sums, and at last the final sum. At the most general level, the task can be described by a sequence of internal states, each containing the set of digits not yet added and the partial sum just computed. The initial state would be the set of digits to be added, and the final state the sum of the whole set of digits. The sequence of partial sums will be defined uniquely if each contains all the digits already summed. However, a subject might retain several partial sums for subsets of digits, these to be added together subsequently.

The formal task analysis does not provide more than hints as to how the subject might represent the task information internally. There are two kinds of information the subject needs to know at all times: (1) which digits have not yet been processed (the digits are available in a visually accessible row), and (2) the partial sums that have not yet been incorporated in the total.

Each partial sum can be represented by a one- or two-digit number. We know that normal subjects, without extensive practice, can retain only a few numbers in memory. Partial sums are particularly difficult to retain, for they are modified and changed frequently. From studies of short-term memory, Waugh and Norman (1965) showed that only 4 digits could be kept readily accessible in short-term memory while a task was being performed. From these findings we would predict that subjects will use only a small number of different partial sums (probably one, or possibly two) when they are trying to add sets of digits rapidly.

Assume that the subject remembers the digits to be added in terms of their location on the stimulus card. After more than four or five digits have been processed and added, a non-trivial amount of information is needed to keep track of the processed and unprocessed digits. How much information is needed depends on the order in which the digits are cumulated. Consider a random ordering, and an ordering from left to right, respectively (There is an X below each processed digit.):

Random case:

```
3   0   8   1   2   4   9   0   6   7   3
        X       X       X           X   X
```

Preferred case:

```
3   0   8   1   2   4   9   0   6   7   3
X   X   X   X
```

In the random case, the identities of the five processed digits or the six unprocessed digits have to be remembered, a substantial memory load. In the ordered case, the subject need only keep note of the last processed digit, or the one to be processed next. After a digit has been processed, attention moves to the one immediately to its right. We can use this large difference in STM requirements, together with our knowledge of the capacity of STM, to predict that subjects will, in fact, process the digits in sequential order and not in random order.

Following Newell and Simon (1972), a similar argument can be made that limits on the processes available are the principal constraints on the processing strategy that will be used. If it is assumed that the only available addition process combines two numbers into their sum, then the operations combining the stimulus digits and previously generated partial results, will be of three kinds:

I.   Adding two digits to form a partial sum
       $M + N = L$

II.   Adding one digit to a partial sum
       $L1 + N = L2$

III.   Adding two partial sums
       $L1 + L2 = L3$

It is reasonable to assume that most subjects will add pairs of digits by recognition that is, by "table lookup" in the sums table that is already stored in LTM. However, when a two-digit number is added to a one-digit number, several steps may be required, and intermediate states may be heeded in STM. (For children, there is good evidence for intermediate states even in addition of single digits (Groen & Parkman, 1972; Svenson, 1975).) Assuming that fast recognition processes will be used when available in memory, the task of adding six digits may require various strategies, three of which are illustrated in the next Figure (Figure 7-12).

4   2   6   3   5   9

Strategy 1: add single digits to partial results.

$4+2=6$ $6+6=12$ $12+3=15$ $15+5=20$ $20+9=29$

Strategy 2: add single digits together before adding onto partial results.

$4+2=6$ $6+3=9$ $6+9=15$ $5+9=14$ $14+15=29$

Strategy 3: combination strategy avoids 2-digit + 2-digit additions (except for the number 10).

$4+2=6$ $6+3=9$ $6+9=15$ $15+5=20$ $20+9=29$

Figure 7-12

Comparison of Three Strategies for Addition

These different strategies impose different loads on STM. With Strategy 1, subjects need only move their gaze one place to the right after each addition. With the other strategies, subjects would have to look further ahead and keep track of several partial results. If we assume that errors are frequently associated with losing the correct positions of "pointers," then the errors that subjects make will be associated with the strategies they use, and can be used as data to identify those strategies.

What verbalizations will be expect in these addition processes? For Type I additions (M + N = L), we might postulate:

$$M \quad N \qquad = L$$
$$5 \; + \; 3 \qquad = 8$$

M	N	= L
5 + 3		= 8
INPUT FOR recognition process		accessed from memory

For Type II additions (L1 + N = L2), not all of the inputs may be verbalized. The stimulus digit may be encoded directly without verbalization, and the intermediate sum may have been verbalized previously as output of the previous step, and hence not verbalized again.

L1	+	N	= L2
15	+	4	= 19
previously verbalized		may not be verbalized	newly generated intermediate result

We would not expect verbalization of the processes involved in selecting the next digit to be added, nor information about the "pointer" locations. These processes are likely to be very rapid, and to operate on information that is not represented verbally. Even in this simple addition task, the verbalizations often span several processes in sequence. For example, there are often references to several additions and their intermediate results, like: 6 and 3 is 9, which makes 31.

Here, the first addition (6 + 3) yields a result (9), which is added to the current intermediate result (evidently, 22) to give the result (31), a Type III addition.

Advantages of Local Encoding. We have now outlined a space of possible verbalizations of cognitive processes in the addition task, and have analyzed the STM limits on the strategies available to subjects in performing the task. We have shown how protocols can be encoded to reveal the steps taken and the information heeded. From these encodings, we can draw many inferences about the organization and structure of the cognitive processes for solving the complete problems. This "bottom up" approach to encoding, in which each verbalization is encoded nearly independently of its context, seems to us to have advantages, where it is feasible, over more global approaches. We wish to consider these advantages in a little more detail.

In Chapter 6, we discussed at some length how to evaluate the evidential support for a given description of a protocol. A human encoder who uses a global approach will argue that the mechanisms postulated in his description are plausible, and will hope that other investigators will find his account persuasive. One kind of argument that is frequently used is to show that the proposed interpretation satisfies the constraints that are known to apply to the human information processing system.

Additional empirical support for an interpretation can be derived from a local encoding approach. The strength of local encoding is that each segment is encoded independently (or nearly independently) of context. If the pattern of each, or many, segments can be predicted from a model, each segment provides an independent data point for the model. Consider, by way of example, the following protocol:

(Stimulus digits are 5   2   8   9   7   4   3   6   3   4)

Segment	Encoding
2 and 8 is 10	$2+8=10$
and 5 is 15	$X+5=15$
and 9 will be 24	$X+9=24$
and 7 is 31	$X+7=31$
and 4 is 35	$X+4=35$
and 3 and 6 is 9 makes 44	$X+(3+6=9)=44$
3 and 4 is 7 makes 51	$X+(3+4=7)=51$

If we postulate that this subject retains only one intermediate sum between segments, we can test this hypothesis by comparing the partial sums that are verbalized as outputs of the additions (e.g., 24, 31) with the unverbalized input to the subsequent addition (e.g., $35-4 = 31, 31-7 = 24$). The probability that all seven intermediate products would correspond in this way as a matter of chance is less than 10^{-6}. The independence of the encodings provides us with uncontaminated data for testing many hypotheses about the structure of the process.

In some analyses of protocols, the process has been described in such detail that computer programs can be constructed to retrace the exact sequence of steps. It should not be supposed that protocols are sufficiently informative to allow such programs to be derived by purely

deductive processes. As with all induction of theories from finite bodies of data, alternative descriptions may be possible of the same data. For example, if a subject adds the digits {3 6 3 4} into a sum, we cannot, from the protocol alone, determine that the order is from left to right. For suppose the protocol is: $3 + 6 = 9$; $9 + 3 = 12$; $12 + 4 = 16$.
The alternatives are:

```
    3     6     3     4    or     3     6     3     4
       9                             9           9
          12                          12
                16                              16
```

Local encoding is helpful in revealing the alternative models that may be consistent with the protocol data. If the process of mapping the encodings on models is automated, possible interpretations may be revealed that would be hard for a human encoder to conceive of.

Error analysis. In our earlier analysis of the arithmetic task, we suggested that three types of errors are particularly likely to occur. The first two have to do with the generation and retention of intermediate results. The last has to do with keeping track of the digits not yet added. In most protocols for the simple addition task, each segment contains at least one of the stimulus numbers and the partial result of an addition. This means that we can infer the partial sum before and after each addition. If we find a mismatch between the intermediate sums in successive segments, an error in generating or retaining the sum is implied. In the following protocol, two such mismatches are identified.

5 plus 2 is 7	$5 + 2 = 7$
plus 8 is 15	$X + 8 = 15$
plus 9 is 24	$+ 9 = 24$
plus 7 is what 31	$+ 7 = 31$
plus 4 is 34	$+ 4 = 34$
plus 3 is 37	$+ 3 = 37$
plus 6 is 43	$+ 6 = 43$
plus 3 is 46	$+ 3 = 46$
plus 4 is	$(+ 4)$
see 36 plus 4 is 40	$36 + 4 = 40$

The first error $(31 + 4 = 34)$ is most likely an error in generating the sum. The second (replacement of 46 as partial sum by 36) is most likely a memory error. In the protocol above, we can find a one-one mapping between the digits presented in the stimulus and those added, which precludes error in the selection of the successive digits for addition. It seems clear (though it hasn't been done) that a computer program could detect and diagnose errors of the kinds present in this protocol.

Inferring process models. A number of issues arise in using protocol data to infer process models. We will consider three of them here: First, what generalizable inferences can be drawn from protocols; Second, how can the stability and instability of cognitive processes be studied using protocols; Third, what can we learn from retrospective reports about the addition task?

The information reported by subjects in the addition task consists almost exclusively of intermediate sums and stimulus digits. One may conclude from the absence of other information that selection rules to choose the next digits for addition and other strategic rules in the performance strategy are highly "automated" and governed in considerable part by recognition processes. There may, of course, be some differences in these processes from one subject to another. Insofar as they lead to different orderings of the processes, hence to different sequences of digits, they can be inferred from the protocols. Examination of a large number of protocols enables us to define the space of possible strategies, and to arrive at conclusions about which strategies are common, and which ones rare in the population of subjects.

Buswell (1928) cites many interesting examples of deviant rules for adding and subtracting numbers, inferred from studies of school children. Below, we exhibit a couple of examples of unusual processing rules that would be highly difficult to anticipate in advance and accommodate in a coding scheme.

Task: $86-4=$
Protocol: 6 and 4 are 10   10 and 8 are 18   turn it the other way makes 81.

Task: $42-36=$
Protocol: 32 to 42 is 10 and 4 were (32 to 36) is 14.

Task: $42-36=$
Protocol: 6 from 2 is nothing   3 from 4 is 1.

In our laboratory, we have collected protocols from the same subject performing the same task (as a warm-up task) on different days (Ericsson, Chase, & Faloon, 1980). We present four of these protocols here, with a few comments, to illustrate the degree of stability of strategy that is exhibited by a single subject over repetitions of a task.

Day 1	Day 2	Day 3	Day 5
4 and 4 is 8	4 and 4 is 8	4 and 4 is 8	8
5 and 5 is 10	5 and 5 is 10	5 and 5 is 10	
18	18	18	18
21	21	21	21
27	27	27	27
32	32	32	32
35	um, 35	35	35
40	40	40	40
		42	
49	49	49	49
um, 53	ah, 53	53	53
	3 and 4 is 7	3 and 4 is 7	7
7 and 6 is 13	6 is 13	and 6 is 13	13
and 9 is 22	and 9 is 22	and 9 is 22	22
23	23	23	23
um, 24	24	24	
um, 30	um, 30	30	30
	32	32	
33, ah, 33	33	33	33
35	ah, 35	35	35
41	41	41	41
45	45	45	45

The protocols for the first three days are virtually identical. The protocol for Day 5 is structurally the same, although the verbalization of some steps has disappeared. This particular subject, at least, was very consistent over the period of a week in his organization of his cognitive processes while performing this task.

Since we do not have retrospective reports for this task, we can only hypothesize what they will contain. We would expect that we would obtain little information from them beyond what is obtainable from the concurrent protocols. The prediction stems from the hypothesis that information not reported in the concurrent protocols was not heeded during the process (e.g., information about the digit selection strategy), hence is not available in LTM for the retrospective report.

RELIABILITY OF VERBAL REPORTS

The reproducibility of data on repeated test occasions is critical to its interpretation. An obvious approach to showing reproducibility is to give the same subjects the same tasks on several occasions, and then compare the verbal reports. In Chapter 3, we have already discussed the complex issues involved in reproducing cognitive processes experimentally. Systematic differences might arise from one reproduction to the next because of specific memory for the previous solution to the task, gradually acquired skill in the task, and generalized learning of skills applicable to the task domain. Even in a single session, cognitive processes in the same task may show considerable variation. Thus it is hard to produce identity in cognitive processes on two successive occasions.

In one particular kind of situation we are assured that successive verbal reports reflect, accurately or not, the same cognitive process. This is when we obtain concurrent and retrospective reports from the same subject for the same task performance. In Chapter 5, we discussed some general differences between concurrent and retrospective reports that are predicted by our model. The retrospective report may, in particular, be expected to be less complete than the concurrent one, but they should agree on the information they both contain. In this section, we will review some evidence for this prediction of consistency.

There are only a few studies of the reliability and consistency of verbal reports. We will review most of the studies we are acquainted with together with some of our own data. We will organize our presentation around several studies that have addressed both the issues of reliability and consistency. Our discussion will make extensive use of individual protocols, to give the reader some feeling for the kinds of behavior that may be encountered. Because of the limited availability of data, we will draw only very tentative generalizations from them.

Protocols for Anagrams

In this first example, we compare a concurrent protocol on an anagram problem with the same subject's retrospective report. We will carry out the comparison with local encoding of the protocols, and will show that the resulting evaluation could be carried out automatically, without the intervention of subjective human judgment.

At the core of an anagram-solving procedure, we assume, is a generate-and-test process, where alternatives are generated under constraints. The constraints are imposed by the subject's judgment that certain combinations of letters are "likely" building blocks for words. In the protocols we will encode these constraints together with the alternative words the subject generates as possible solutions. To formalize matters, we will encode the constraints as:

C:XYZ...,

where XYZ... represent a sequential letter combination that the subject is testing, and the alternatives as:

A:<Word>.

We exhibit first the concurrent protocol, then the retrospective one.

Table 7-2

Concurrent Protocol for CEPART

OK, uhm	
it's not—it's not much to talk about now	
it's just	
E: Just	
I am just looking at part forms of words	
E: If you could just verbalize them	
Ok, part forms of words I am trying to	
Uhm I am just trying to rearrange the letters	
and I—it's not an easy thing to do when you talk	
uhm	
E: Would you consider a combination like RT	
Ok well I am considering T as	
the first letter in the combination	C:TR
uhm R generally—many times follows T	
so I am considering that	
uhm TRAP forms a word	
but I don't know how to bring C and E into that	C:TRAP
uhm Let's see	
I'm really not—Let's see—uhm—TRAP	A:TRAP
I have given up on trying TR—I am trying the R now	C:PR
I am trying I don't know—I am trying the R now	
R with a—well—I will try the P and R	
so I will	
well—Let's see—I see a PRACTICE without the I	
so that doesn't work	A:PRACTICE
Let's see	
Let's I am trying PAR again	C:PAR
I am trying CAR	C:CAR
OK I have got it it is CARPET	

Table 7-3
Retrospective Protocol

The first thing I remembered was	
that PART formed a word immediately	C:PART
but I decided—I immediately tried to form a word	
using C and E and PART as a unit	
and that didn't work out so I started	
with a smaller unit and I started	
with the TR since that's a common unit	C:TR
ah that didn't work—I tried a different combination	
of that that I didn't verbalize	C:PR
and Uhm then I tried the PR and came up with PRACTICE	
without the I	A:PRACTICE
so that didn't work	
Uhm I couldn't think of anything else so then I just ...	
zeroed in on CAR	C:CAR
and just tried the other combinations around CAR	
and it worked ... so	

Clearly, these encodings use only local information. To compare them, we arrange them linearly, one above the other:

$$P = \langle C:TR, C:TRAP, A:TRAP, C:PR, A:PRACTICE, C:PAR, C:CAR\rangle$$
$$P = \langle C:PART, C:TR, C:PR, A:PRACTICE, C:CAR\rangle$$

In this particular case, it would be easy to map the concurrent protocol on the retrospective one automatically. Four of the five elements of the latter are matched by unique elements of the former. Only one new element appears in the retrospective protocol; it mostly differs from the concurrent one by omission, as predicted. Since there are 1,230 logically possible constraints that the subject could use, the odds against agreement between two randomly generated constraints are about $1:10^6$.

Series Problems

Hagert (1980a, 1980b) has collected protocols from a subject solving five-term series problems (an extension of 3-term series problems). His findings relate both to the relation between concurrent and retrospective reports for the same solution, and the relation between three solutions to the same problem generated at one-year intervals.

At the first session the subject was asked to solve two five-term series problems while thinking aloud, and was then asked to give retrospective reports for his solution to the first problem and then his solution to the second problem. Although the two problems described different situations (people with different names in different situations), and used different primitives (i.e., "leftmost" and "rightmost," instead of "left" and "right"), the two problems were logical isomorphs. The names of the people in the two problems were the same and the solutions identical.

In the retrospective reports from the first occasion, Hagert found that the subject was able to remember almost nothing from the solution.

1. no it feels rather empty
2. yes it does it's completely gone
3. I don't even remember the names
4. I remember Carl
5. were there five names?

On the other hand, the subject's retrospective report from the solution to the second (last) problem was remarkably complete:

1. yes I started with Ann
2. she stood rightmost
3. and then there were
4. there were three persons
5. where someone stood in between
6. it was Ann who stood between Bob and Carl
7. and then I got
8. Eve who stood to the left of these three
9. and David ... who stood immediately to the right
10. of David
11. and so I got
12. Ann Bob Carl David Eve
13. and the question was who stood immediately to the right of David
14. and that was Carl
15. I remember that

The subject recalls veridically the order in which the given premises were combined, and recalls also the correct answer. Hagert notices that the premises are not recalled perfectly, and that the memory appears to reflect generated structures of sublists of ordered items rather than the original premises. Below, we reproduce the concurrent protocol for this same problem:

Instructions

Several people are standing in a row. Ann is standing
rightmost. Eve is standing to the left of Carl. Bob is standing
between Ann and Carl. David is standing immediately to the right
of Eve. Who is standing immediately to the right of David?

Protocol

F 1	yeah these are nice examples
F 2	Ann is standing rightmost
F 3	Eve is standing to the left of Carl
F 4	Bob is standing between Ann and Carl
F 5	Ann
F 6	it should then be
F 7	could be C B A here on the end
F 8	try the same strategy here see if it's okay
F 9	it should then be C B A
F10	C B A in any case
F11	C B A
F12	Eve is sitting to the left of Carl
F13	then it should be
F14	E C B A
F15	E C B A
F16	David is standing immediately to the right of Eve
F17	what did I say
F18	have to start again
F19	it's easiest to begin somewhere in the middle here I think
F20	Bob is standing between Ann and Carl
F21	that was then
F22	C B A yes
F23	Eve is standing to the left of Carl
F24	that is
F25	E C B A
F26	E C B A
F27	David is standing immediately to the right of Eve
F28	that should be
F29	D E C B
F30	no
F31	E C B A yes
F32	D E
F33	C B A
F34	who is standing immediately to the right of David
F35	damned
F36	Ann is standing wait
F37	Ann is standing rightmost yes
F38	Bob
F39	yes that's right
F40	that's wait
F41	C B A yes
F42	Eve is standing to the left there
F43	And David is standing
F44	I make it to be Eve (no)
F45	it was wrong (yes)
F46	Carl

```
F47    Bob Ann
F48    Carl Bob Ann
F49    Eve
F50    Carl Bob Ann
F51    Eve Carl Bob Ann
F52    Eve Carl Bob Ann
F53    David is standing immediately to the right of Eve
F54    yes that's right
F55    I turned it
F56    I thought the opposite
F57    it should be
F58    Eve
F59    I have to take it from the beginning
F60    David Eve
F61    yes that's right
F62    it should be the one who stands
F63    Bob is standing between
F64    Carl Bob Ann
F65    David is standing immediately to
F66    it is David
       (yes)
```

The retrospective and concurrent reports differ most strikingly in the presence of several unsuccessful solution attempts in the latter. The instructions given to the subjects may account for their absence from the retrospective reports. The subjects were asked: "Did you remember anything from the second problem? Is there any information left over in which steps you built the series?" (Hagert, 1980a, p. 43) There were marked differences in the information reported for the two solutions. (Remember that the first solution was recalled first.) From these results Hagert infers that the information was stored temporarily in a working memory of intermediate duration, although other interpretations are certainly possible. The suppression of information from the first solution can be labeled, although not explained, as "retroactive inhibition."

In Hagert's (1980b) analysis of the three successive protocols for the first problem, taken at one-year intervals, he notes that the protocols are not by any means identical. Even the solution paths are different. On the first occasion, the subject's first proposed solution is incorrect, but the second one, correct. A year later, the first proposed solution is also incorrect, although different from the one a year earlier, while the second is again correct. On the final occasion, the subject generated the correct solution directly.

Hagert built a computer model, in the form of a production system, that predicted quite accurately the information in 98% of the protocol segments from the first occasion. However, the model could account for less than half of the fragments from the other two protocols. But with local and minor changes, the model could account for up to 90% of the segments in these protocols. The protocol from the second occasion could be described accurately if two processing errors were allowed when premises involving "right of" or "left of" were converted into sequential orderings. Modifying a single rule involved in checking the correctness of the tentative orderings improved the description of the third protocol. Although these modifications were post hoc changes, with the benefit of hindsight, still the analysis indicates that the subject's cognitive processes remained substantially the same at a strategic level through three problem-solving sessions extending over two years.

Concept Formation

In a study of concept attainment, Johnson (1962, 1964) gave some of his subjects the same problem twice (the same sequences of instances and non-instances of the concept). In no case did the subjects' verbalizations indicate that they recognized the problem the second time. Given our earlier discussion of subjects' poor memory for sequences of instances in concept learning, their failure to recognize the problems is quite plausible.

Of three students who each solved the same problem twice, one solved Problem 5 in two different ways, "although her basic approaches were about the same." (Johnson, 1962, p. 38) Another subject solved Problem 2 twice "in identical ways, even down to making the same type of comment at the same point in both solutions." (Johnson, 1962, p. 38) A third subject failed to find the solution of Problem 4 twice, "both times in a manner characteristic of all her failures." (Johnson, 1962, p. 38) Johnson concludes that the method and strategy component of cognitive processes remains constant but that lower-level detail may vary from trial to trial.

Johnson published the protocols only for the third problem. To make the discussions of the protocols meaningful, we need to describe some of the details of the experiment. Subjects were presented with a sheet of patterns arranged in order. (The same sheet was used for all problems.) The subjects were told that each pattern could be classified uniquely according to some rule into two categories labeled by "red" and "green." The subjects were asked to come up with the rule by predicting the color for each successive pattern with feedback from the experimenter. The subjects had to write down the correct color for each instance, hence at all times had available perceptually the information about all instances that had so far been presented. Each pattern consisted of five circles, which were either white or black, a total of 32 different possibilities.

Because the protocols are very lengthy, we will reproduce only the initial portions, and show how they were encoded by Johnson. We will then discuss his encoding of the remaining portions.

Pattern	Correct Response	Occasion I	Occasion II
XOOOO	G	E: Number 1 is a green.	E: Number 1 is a green.
OOXOO	G	S: 2 red? E: 2 is a green.	S: 2 is green? E: Right. For a reason or a guess? S. Well, two possible reasons—the old hypothesis of four blank in each and, also, only one darkened dot.
OOXXO	G	S: 3 green? E: 3 green.	S: 3 would be red? E: For which reason now? S: Well, another reason. These two might be green because the last two on the end are left light. E: In this case, 3 is still green.
OOXOX	R	S: 4 red? E: 4 is red ... What are you working on?	S: Uh-hmm...4 is green? E: Now for what reason? S: Because there are two light dots together as there have been all along. E: 4 is really red.
XXOXO	R	S: The color at the end dot which would make 5 a green on my hypothesis.	S: ... Well so far in all of these it has been the 1st two light and the last light. When it was the 1st two light but the 2nd to the last light, it changed color so that might have

			something to do with it ... Is 5 green? E: Uh ... 5 is really red.
XXXOX	G	S: ... It has nothing to do with the color of any particular dot, or the side of the center the dots are on, more than one, two or the number of dots ... Could be a splitting. 6 red?	S: ... 6 is red? E: For what reason? S: It might have something to do with the groupings of twos and threes. If they are together and they are dark they are red.
	E:	6 is green.	E: Uh-hmm. 6 is really green.

Although the protocols are obviously different, there are some similarities in the hypotheses generated. For example, at Trial 3, the subject appears, from both protocols, to notice the positional relevance of the last circles. Whether similar consistency would appear in protocols from other subjects we cannot tell. Let us, instead, look at Johnson's encoding of the protocol, including the later portions not reproduced here.

In the next table, we have translated Johnson's codes into English without comment. Johnson only specifically encoded hypotheses that used features of the pattern. Hypotheses mentioning the sequence of reds and greens are simply called *sequential.* Predictions based on similarities with previously presented instances with known color associations are called *actuarial.* The most striking similarity in the table between the behavior in the two sessions is the subject's tendency to begin with positional attributes and patterns and end up with actuarial predictions. Unfortunately, we have little data from which to judge to what extent the same similarity appears in comparisons between subjects.

Table 7-4

Encodings of Two Successive Protocols for Same Problem

	Occasion I	Occasion II
2		G::NB:1
3	G::5:w Green if 5th circle white	G::(4:w).(5:w) Green if 4th and 5th circle white
4		G::LW:2 Green if longest run of white is 2
5		*Sequential hypothesis
6	R::AB:s Red if black circles are adjacent	G::LB:2v3 Green if longest run of black is 2 or 3
7	Sequential hypothesis	Actuarial prediction
8	Color hypothesis	*RR::L:2
10	Actuarial hypothesis	
12	*Sequential hypothesis	
13		Actuarial prediction
14	Actuarial prediction	Actuarial prediction

*Not valid, given the already presented instances.

Johnson was able to simulate the hypothesis generating process for all his subjects using a single computer program and only varying a small number of parameters. In the discussion of the simulation, Johnson notes that the subject whose protocol is given above never generated hypotheses of the type required for Problem 4 (i.e., "green if 2nd and 5th circles have the same color"), and for the same reason failed to solve three other problems. Johnson concluded, and we would concur, that the similarities in processes between sessions reflect consistencies in subject's strategies and representations over time, rather than reproduction of explicit processing sequences.

A Memory Task

Ericsson and Polson (in preparation) studied a waiter who could memorize dinner orders from more than 16 people without external memory aids. When we are looking at a highly skilled and rapid performance of this kind, we would expect high reliability in the content and structure of the cognitive processing. Ericsson and Polson created an experimental analogue to the restaurant situation by selecting a subset of items (8 different steaks, 5 durations of cooking, 5 salad dressings, and 3 different starches). A computer generated a random combination of these items for simulated diners (represented by photographs). The experimenter read the complete order (4 items) as the subject (the expert waiter) pointed to the corresponding face. The subject was encouraged to take all the orders as rapidly as possible without making errors in the subsequent recall.

The waiter did *not* recall the orders as presented, but instead recalled them by category, that is, first all the salad dressings, then the steaks, etc. For items within a category, he formed groups or chunks of four items. To remember these items, he relied on various mnemonic encodings, for example, remembering the first letter for salad dressings. The four letters for the dressings could often be recoded as an English word. The experimenters, to study the specificity of the memory skill, substituted items from other domains for dinner items, as shown in Table 7-5:

Table 7-5
Experiment of Analogy for Dinner-order Recall Problem

Item Structure	Dinner	Experimental
belong to the same category	8 steaks	8 names of animals
ordered items within a category	5 temperatures rare → well done	5 time units second → week
belong to the same category	5 salad dressings	5 names of flowers
belong to the same category	3 starches	3 names of metals

The subject used the same or similar encodings for the corresponding items in the "dinner" and "experimental" conditions. For example, he used letter recodings for the flowers and salad dressings, order information for time units and temperatures, and patterns for metals and starches.

The consistency of encodings was studying by giving the subject the same list of experimental items on two occasions a week apart. He was instructed to think aloud, but not to take more time than when he did the task without thinking aloud. The two protocols are reproduced below:

Occasion I

1. S: All right. Go.
    E: Order 1. Cow, minute, tulip, steel.
    S: Cow, minute, tulip, steel.

2. E: Order 2. Elephant, day, violet, steel.
    S: Elephant, day, V, 2 the same. T, V, elephant, day, T, V.

3. E: Order 3. Elephant, week, rose, steel.
    S: T, V, R, elephant, week, next.

4. E: Order 4. Cat, day, tulip, iron.
    S: T, V, R, T, different metal T, V, R, T, cat, day. Okay. Minute, day, week, day, cow, elephant, elephant, cat, T, V, R, T. Next.

5. E: Order 5. Horse, week, daisy.
    S: Horse, week, daisy, iron, horse, week, D, 2, D, next.

Occasion II

S: Alright (knock). Go.
E: Cow, minute, tulip, steel.
S: Okay. Cow, minute, tulip, steel. Cow, minute, tulip, it's a T, system, and steel is the usual, and to refresh myself I've also got iron and copper to think about in the future there. Cow, minute, T, next (knock).

E: Elephant, day, violet, steel.
S: T, V, two steels in a row, elephant, day, T, V, next (knock).

E: Elephant, week, rose, steel.
S: T, V, R, elephant, week, (knock) next.

E: Cat, day, tulip, iron.
S: T, V, R, T, cat, day, T, V, R, T, cat, elephant, cow, two days, one week, T, V, R, T, (knock) next.

E: Horse, week, daisy, iron.
S: Horse, week, D, (knock) next.

6. E: Order 6. Horse, hour, daisy,
       copper.
    S: Horse, hour, daisy, copper.
       D, D, horse, hour. Okay.
       Horse, hour, week, hour, D,
       D, next.

    E: Horse, hour, daisy, copper.

    S: D, T, D, D, I think I'm
       going to need to check
       something. Metal in
       number 4?
    E: Iron.
    S: Okay, iron, iron, copper,
       D, D, (knock) next.

7. E: Order 7. Tiger, hour, daisy,
       steel.
    S: Want to say it again please?
    E: Tiger, hour, daisy, steel.
    S: Tiger, hour, daisy, steel.
       3 metals. D, D, D, tiger, hour,
       horse, hour, next.

    E: The next one is tiger,
       hour, daisy, steel.
    S: D, D, D, three metals
       in a row, tiger, hour,
       (knock), next.

8. E: Elephant, day, violet, hour.
    S: Elephant, day, violet, iron.
       D, D, D, V, iron, copper,
       steel, iron, elephant, day.
       Ah, flower?
    E: Violet.
    S: Violet—iron, D, D, V. Done.

    E: Elephant, day, violet, hour.
    S: Elephant, day, violet, iron.
       D, D, D, V, T, V, R, T,
       flower?
    E: Violet.
    S: Elephant, excuse me,
       animal?
    E: Elephant.
    S: Time?
    E: Day.
    S: Metal?
    E: Iron.

Recall

E: Just give a—thinking aloud
   while you're recalling.
S: Let's see, let's start with
   flowers. They're easy. That's
   a basically easy table.
   Flowers. T, V, R, T—tulip,
   violet, rose, tulip. Flowers
   over here. All right, D, D, V,
   daisy, daisy, violet. Animals.
   All right, cow, elephant, elephant,
   cat, horse, horse, tiger, elephant.
   Metals. All real easy. Steel, steel,
   steel, iron, iron, copper,
   steel, iron. Times are the
   toughest. Minute, day, week,
   day, week, hour, hour, and
   day and that's it, I believe.
E: What's your certainty?
S: 5.

E: Okay.
S: Recall?
E: Uh, huh. And please think
   out loud while you're
   recalling.
S: All right. Flowers first of
   all—first thing that
   comes to mind, T, V, R, T, D,
   D, D, V. That's daisy, daisy,
   daisy, violet. Metals—
   steel, steel, steel, iron,
   iron, copper, steel, iron.
   Animals—cow, elephant,
   elephant, cat, horse, horse,
   tiger, elephant. Times—minute,
   day, week, day, week, day,
   hour, day. Confidence level?
S: 4. I am unsure of the times
   at 2 and 7. 2 and 7.

Retrospective Report

Occasion I	Occasion II

E: Okay, so please now give us the retrospective report. Going back to the beginning. Try to say how much you can remember about your thinking from the very beginning and then just go back and give us as much as you can.

S: Okay, I started off with the cow. It seemed like it was just very hard to just get that started because the first one's always the hardest to just get going with. And then it started to create some patterns and the first easy pattern was the steels. After the first man was locked in well, then the patterns of the metal started to develop and three in a row just is —seems very easy. Then I can concentrate on the rest of the other three variables per person. What was some other interesting points for these first three? There were two elephants there. Okay, well that was nice. The times were in my system good quote, unquote, times, because they were all in a bunch. Minute, week and day— or minute, day, week are all at the—pretty close to the far end of the scale. I didn't have anything bouncing around too badly. I could have a worse pattern than that, really. That wasn't really the worst pattern for times in the world. And times were the most difficult to get down out of this whole table. But I didn't know that at this time. I was just on these first three. Then, man number 4 had a—had iron for a metal and that was no problem either— especially when order number 5 came in and it was also an iron and suddenly I've

E: Okay, I think it was— why don't you give me a retrospective report before I give you a feedback.

S: Okay.

E: But basically, do what you're thinking and you generally do by starting off at the beginning and just tracing back.

S: All right. Cow, minute, tulip, steel. And then the next thing I associated was the elephant, day, and minute and day were my— that's where I ran into my first problem in my recall, was that day didn't seem to be right when I quoted it on recall. However, it does fit my pattern of association, or I associated on either side of the hour mark, the hour being the center analogy or the medium analogy in my little graph that I drew for you. So I had them on either side of me, or the hour part, and then the next one was week, I'm fairly sure of that. It was elephant, week, and that T, R, V. No, T, V, R. Tulip, violet, rose. And I had 3 steels in a row, so there was an case of metals presented immediately. And the first strange metal came up on number 4, and that was iron and that was cat, day. I had a day associated with number 2 and number 4. Cat, day, tulip. I had to associate a line from 4 to 1, and iron was the metal. Number 5, horse, week, daisy, iron, I had an iron drawn to number 4 and the horse, week, just seems easier to remember, so I had a horse, week, doesn't—weeks tend to fit my mind

got just 2 things to
remember on the steel, or
on the metal pattern, and
that is steel and iron. All
I had to do is know where
to draw the line on dividing
those.

better for some reason.
I make easier associations
and iron was the metal
there—horse, week,
daisy, iron.

As expected, the two concurrent protocols are remarkably similar. The differences relate to very local processes and not to the basic structure of the skill. The retrospective reports resemble each other as closely or more closely than they do the corresponding concurrent protocols. The protocol study, while only a single example of verbalized data from highly skilled performance, should demonstrate the feasibility of examining the stability and adaptation of processes under varying conditions. There have been similar findings of reliability in other research on mnemonic encodings (Chase and Ericsson, 1981, 1982) and medical diagnosis (Wortman, 1966).

Summary

The comparisons of concurrent and retrospective reports in this chapter and Chapter 5 are in substantial agreement in showing that the reports are mutually consistent, the retrospective reports often omitting information contained in the concurrent reports. Comparison of thinking-aloud protocols for the same task on successive occasions shows greater variability. For some highly practiced skills, like mental addition and the memorization of our skilled waiter, there is remarkable consistency from one occasion to another. In the case of protocols where subjects had only a little experience with the task, there is little evidence that subjects reused specific information from a previous solution or acquired generalized knowledge or skill for the task domain (Hagert's subject on the third occasion may be a partial exception to this last claim). The variability observed in the protocols may be viewed as "local" (low-level) variability in the cognitive processes.

More important than the fact that there is some variability is the equally prominent fact that there is great stability of the successive protocols in terms of strategies and representations.

CONCLUDING REMARKS AND FUTURE DIRECTIONS

In the beginning of this book we proposed that cognitive processes could be described as sequences of heeded information and cognitive structures and that verbal reports corresponded to this heeded information. The examples discussed in this chapter illustrate how verbalizations can be encoded and matched against hypotheses about the structure and sequence of the heeded information. The rather extensive literature using protocols as data has, for the most part, relied on methods and encoding schemes that are similar to those described here, which we view mainly as extensions and explications of previous studies.

In the beginning of this book we argued that verbal reports should be seen as one of many sources of data about cognitive processes and structures, and that models and methods accounting for verbal data should not be different, in principle, from accounts of other types of data. It is essential that the methodology for using verbal reports be wholly integrated with the main stream of experimental psychology and other areas of cognitive science. Many of the most recent studies have quite successfully embedded the collection of verbal reports within experimental designs and have addressed issues of generalizability. However, we need many more studies of this kind to provide models for verbal reports analysis.

Considerable progress has also been made toward integrating the more detailed analyses and models of verbal reports with existing theories and models. Maybe the greatest challenge is presented by the mathematical models of performance of groups of subjects. We need to be able to identify the structural and process characteristics that give rise to these confirmed regularities of performance. In Chapter 4 we made a first attempt to show how such a mapping can be carried out between general characteristics of heeded information and regularities of performance. We also want to point to Einhorn, Kleinmuntz, and Kleinmuntz's (1979) analysis showing the consistency between process models derived from verbal reports and the more traditional mathematical regression models. However, much more theoretical and analytical work is required to achieve a complete integration of these different bodies of data and theory.

In the beginning of Psychology, many influential psychologists viewed verbal reports, and more precisely introspection, as the *only* valid method for data-collection in psychology. At a later period, during the reign of behaviorism, verbal reports were almost totally rejected as data.

It is now time for verbal reports to reassume their position as a rich source of data, combinable with other data, that can be of the greatest value in providing an integrated and full account of cognitive processes and structures.

APPENDIX

In this appendix we will give some practical advice and information on how to elicit various types of verbal reports under standard conditions. Tasks and situations that require variations of the standard procedure are discussed in Chapter 5. We will distinguish three types of verbal reports, namely talk-aloud, think-aloud and retrospective reports. Apart from discussing the verbal reports individually we will also describe the recommended procedure, where both think-aloud *and* retrospective reports are elicited for the same process. We should point out that the suggestions expressed here are based on our experience and intuitions, rather than experimental studies. We hope such systematic studies will be made in the future.

First, we will briefly comment on some variables relating to the experimental situation, then we will describe instructions and warm up procedures for the two different types of verbalizing procedures.

In many studies we want to collect verbal reports for cognitive processes that are no different from those occurring in traditional experiments. Apart from the instruction to verbalize and the production of the verbalization, the only differences are the presence of the monitoring experimenters and of the tape recorder.

After a short time subjects become accustomed to both the experimenter and tape-recorder. In many tasks, especially problem-solving tasks, subjects get so involved in the task that little notice is taken of the environment, and situational factors have no real effect. For other cases, we have found it better to keep the tape-recorder and the experimenter outside the view of the subject. Most high quality tape-recorders are able to adapt their sensitivity automatically and thus give good recording quality even when placed slightly behind the subject. The experimenter can also be seated behind the subject. Evidence from verbalization of free associations in clinical situations suggest that it is better to have the analyst outside the view of the subject, like behind the coach (Havens, 1973; Freud, 1963, pp. 135-156). If reminders, like "keep talking", are used, the subject will not feel obliged to address the experimenter or turn around to answer him. The number of verbalizations that are social and directed to the experimenter may be used to evaluate how much the experimenter has intruded (cf. Ohlsson, 1980).

TALK-ALOUD

When we are interested in preserving the temporal properties of the cognitive process we may ask our subjects to talk aloud. Of course, it is only for tasks where we can assume subjects rely on oral codes that we can expect to get much verbalization with such an instruction. The procedure we use contains a general instruction and a couple of warm-up tasks. The warm-up tasks are selected to be particularly easy to use "talk-aloud" with and one's for which the cognitive processes are well understood. Here is a sample instruction for talk-aloud.

INSTRUCTION:

In this experiment we are interested in what you say to yourself as you perform some tasks that we give you. In order to do this we will ask you to TALK ALOUD as you work on the problems. What I mean by talk aloud is that I want you to say out loud *everything* that you say to yourself silently. Just act as if you are alone in the room speaking to yourself. If you are silent for any length of time I will remind you to keep talking aloud. Do you understand what I want you to do?

Good, before we turn to the real experiment, we will start with a couple of practice problems. I want you to talk aloud while you do these problems. First, I will ask you to multiply two numbers in your head.

So *talk aloud* while you multiply 24 times 34!

Good!

Now I would like you to solve an anagram. I will show you a card with scrambled letters. It is your task to find an English word that consists of all the presented letters. For example, if the scrambled letters are KORO, you may see that these letters spell the word ROOK. Any questions? Please "talk aloud" while you solve the following anagram!

<NPEPHA = HAPPEN>

Good!

These warm-up exercises have several purposes. First, we want subjects to begin talk aloud under circumstances where it is comparatively easy. Second, we want to make certain that all subjects talk aloud. If particular subjects appear not to verbalize as much as normal subjects, one can give them more practice problems. Furthermore, one can ask them for a retrospective report after they complete the task. Either the subject will notice the discrepancy between talk-aloud protocol and retrospection, or the experimenter will see that the subject did talk aloud. In our experience it is very rare that subjects do not spontaneously verbalize in a normal fashion after a couple of practice problems. It also happens that subjects occasionally "think aloud" rather than "talk aloud". In this case subjects will verbally describe the spatial arrangement of numbers in a mental multiplication and refer to them by their spatial location. Subjects can then be asked to do the corresponding task silently to realize that they take much longer while verbalizing, or the experimenter can ask "Did you say X to yourself silently?" Simply recording the time often leads subjects to the more rapid "talk aloud".

Selecting tasks for warm-up exercises is not easy. Sometimes mental multiplications are too difficult and embarrass the subject. For such subjects mental addition of 2- or 3-digit numbers may be more appropriate. Other possible tasks are, "Find as many words as possible that rhyme with 'beef'," "Generate as many words as possible using the letters like 'ONDTERH!'."

THINK-ALOUD WITH RETROSPECTIVE REPORTS

Rather than considering think-aloud and retrospective reports separately, we will discuss them as parts of a more general procedure, which we recommend be used whether think-aloud or retrospective reports or both be given for the same cognitive process. The main reason for combining them in a common warm-up procedure is that for cognitive processes of intermediate duration we expect the "think aloud" protocol and the retrospective report to contain basically the same information. Hence by having the subject give both reports for the same cognitive process we are in a position to assess completeness of the think-aloud protocol and assure that the retrospective report contains an actual record of the cognitive process. A general instruction with warm-up examples is given below.

In this experiment we are interested in what you think about when you find answers to some questions that I am going to ask you to answer. In order to do this I am going to ask you to THINK ALOUD as you work on the problem given. What I mean by think aloud is that I want you to tell me EVERYTHING you are thinking from the time you first see the question until you give an answer. I would like you to talk aloud CONSTANTLY from the time I present each problem until you have given your final answer to the question. I don't want you to try to plan out what you say or try to explain to me what you are saying. Just act as if you are alone in the room speaking to yourself. It is most important that you keep talking. If you are silent for any long period of time I will ask you to talk. Do you understand what I want you to do?

Good, now we will begin with some practice problems. First, I want you to multiply these two numbers in your head and tell me what you are thinking as you get an answer.

"What is the result of multiplying 24 x 36"

Good, now I want to see how much you can remember about what you were thinking from the time you read the question until you gave the answer. We are interested in what you actually can REMEMBER rather than what you think you must have thought. If possible I would like you to tell about your memories in the sequence in which they occurred while working on the question. Please tell me if you are uncertain about any of your memories. I don't want you to work on solving the problm again, just report all that you can remember thinking about when answering the question. Now tell me what you remember.

Good. Now I will give you two more practice problems before we proceed with the main experiment. I want you to do the same thing for each of these problems. I want you to think aloud as before as you think about the question, and after you have answered it I will ask you to report all that you can remember about your thinking. Any questions? Here is your next problem.

"How many windows are there in your parent's house?"

Now tell me all that you can remember about your thinking.

Good, now here is another practice problem. Please think aloud as you try to answer it. There is no need to keep count, I will keep track for you.

"Name 20 animals".

Now tell me all that you can remember about your thinking.

This warm-up procedure is based on the observation that it helps subjects verbalize oral information concurrently. More importantly, the easy and direct verbalization of such information makes it clear to the subject that think-aloud involves concurrent verbalization of heeded thoughts rather a retrospective and explanatory report, which subjects may be more familiar with. Hence, the first task, or more if that is required, is the same as used to elicit talk-aloud verbalization. The only difference is that with think-aloud instruction we admit or even encourage verbalization of information that was encoded in non-verbal form. The over-all idea is to present the subject with warm-up tasks until he or she is comfortable in thinking aloud and provides reports of the same information in both retrospective and concurrent reports. Occasionally the experimenter may be required to point out differences between information reported during think-aloud and retrospectively reported information. Also, subjects may use a more retrospective mode of reporting during think-aloud, or during the retrospective report engage in analysis of why they thought in a certain way, especially if they recognize making errors. (For a more detailed discussion of deviation from think-aloud and retrospective report, see Chapter 5, 6, and 7). Most of these deviations can be set straight by simply repeating key phrases of the general instruction. Some subjects may be benefitted by interspersing silent trials, for which the solution time is recorded, to assure that they are not changing their mode of thought to accomodate verbalization.

During the actual experiment we recommend that both think-aloud and retrospective reports be recorded. Even for cognitive processes of long duration, where we know that the retrospective report will be incomplete, it will be quite useful. In this case, it will more clearly convey the general structure of the process, as most of the detailed information will not be retrieved, and retrieval will use the higher-level organizational cues, like subgoals, or recall cues.

BIBLIOGRAPHY

Ajzen, I., & Fishbein, M. Attitude-behavior relations: A theoretical analysis and review of empirical research. *Psychological Bulletin*, 1977, *84*, 888-918.

Allwood, C.M. Use of knowledge and error detection in statistical problem solving. *Goteborg Psychological Reports*, 1982, *12*(1).

Allwood, C.M., & Montgomery, H. Knowledge and technique in statistical problem solving. *European Journal of Science Education*, 1981, *3*, 431-450.

Allwood, C.M., & Montgomery, H. Detection of errors in statistical problem solving. *Scandinavian Journal of Psychology*, 1982, *23*, 131-140.

Anders, T. R. Retrospective reports of retrieval from short-term memory. *Journal of Experimental Psychology*, 1971, *90*, 251-257.

Anders, T. R. A high-speed self-terminating search of short-term memory. *Journal of Experimental Psychology*, 1973, *97*, 34-40.

Anders, T. R., & Lillyquist, T. D. Retrieval time in forward and backward recall. *Psychonomic Science*, 1971, *22*, 205-206.

Anderson, J.R. FRAN: A simulation model of free recall. In G.H. Bower (Ed.), *The psychology of learning and motivation (Vol. 5)*. New York: Academic Press, 1972.

Anderson, J. R. *Language, memory, and thought*. Hillsdale, NJ: Lawrence Erlbaum Associates, 1976.

Anderson, J. R., & Bower, G. H. *Human associative memory*. Washington, D. C.: V.H. Winston, 1973.

Angell, J. R. Methods for the determination of mental imagery. *Psychological Review Monographs Supplements*, 1910, *13*(53), 61-107.

Anzai, Y. Recognition of coalition by computer in a three-person game. *Behavioral Science*, 1977, *22*, 403-422.

Anzai, Y., & Simon, H.A. The theory of learning by doing. *Psychological Review*, 1979, *86*, 124-140.

Atkinson, R.C., & Shiffrin, R. Human memory: A proposed system and its control processes. In K. Spence & J. Spence (Eds.), *The psychology of learning and motivation (Vol. 2)*. New York: Academic Press, 1968.

Baddeley, A.D., Thomson, N., & Buchanan, M. Word length and the structure of short-term memory. *Journal of Verbal Learning and Verbal Behavior*, 1975, *14*, 575-589.

Baggett, P. Memory for explicit and implicit information in picture stories. *Journal of Verbal Learning and Verbal Behavior*, 1975, *14*, 538-548.

Baranowski, T. *Clinical judgment as a cognitive process: A comparison of linear regression and decision net models.* Unpublished paper, University of Kansas, 1975.

Bartel, H. Uber diee Abhangigkeit spontaner Reproductionen von Feldbedingungen. *Psychologische Forschung,* 1937, *22,* 1-25.

Bartlett, F.C. *Remembering: A study in experimental and social psychology.* Cambridge: The University Press, 1932.

Baylor, G.W. Modeling the mind's eye. In A. Elithorn & D. Jones (Eds.), *Artificial and Human Thinking.* Amsterdam: Elsevier, 1973, 283-297.

Bem, D.J., & McConnell, H.K. Testing the self-perception explanation of dissonance phenomena: On the salience of premanipulation attitudes. *Journal of Personality and Social Psychology,* 1970, *14,* 23-31.

Benjafield, J.G. The effects of the representation of the goal and the problem materials on the problem solving process (Doctoral dissertation, Brandeis University, 1968). *Dissertations Abstracts International,* 1969, *29,* 3099B. (University Microfilms No. 69-2046)

Benjafield, J. Logical and empirical thinking in a problem solving task. *Psychonomic Science,* 1969, *14,* 285-286. (a)

Benjafield, J. Evidence that thinking aloud constitutes an externalization of inner speech. *Psychonomic Science,* 1969, *15,* 83-84. (b)

Benjafield, J. Evidence for a two-process theory of problem solving. *Psychonomic Science,* 1971, *23,* 397-399.

Bernbach, H.A. Stimulus learning and recognition in paired-associate learning. *Journal of Experimental Psychology,* 1967, *75,* 513-519.

Bertini, M., Lewis, H. B., & Witkin, H. A. Some preliminary observations with an experimental procedure for the study of hypnagogic and related phenomena. *Archivo di Psicologia, Neurologia e Psichiatria,* 1964, *6,* 493-534.

Best, C.T., Morrongiello, B., & Robson, R. Perceptual equivalence of acoustic cues in speech and nonspeech perception. *Perception & Psychophysics,* 1981, *29,* 191-211.

Bettman, J.R. Information processing models of consumer behaviour. *Journal of Marketing Research,* 1970, *7,* 370-376.

Bettman, J.R., & Park, C.W. *Implications of a constructive view of choice for analysis of protocol data: A coding scheme for elements of choice processes* (Working Paper No. 75). Los Angeles: Center for Marketing Studies, University of California, 1979.

Bhaskar, R., & Simon, H.A. Problem solving in semantically rich domains: An example from engineering thermodynamics. *Cognitive Science,* 1977, *1,* 193-215.

Biderman, A.D. Surveys of population samples for estimating crime incidence. *The Annals of the American Academy of Political and Social Science,* 1967, *4374,* 16-33.

Biggs, S.F. *An investigation of decision process models of individual financial statement users.* Unpublished report, Graduate School of Business, University of Wisconsin-Madison, 1978.

Binet, A. From sensation to intelligence. In R. H. Pollack & M. J. Brenner (Eds.), *The experimental psychology of Alfred Binet: Selected papers.* New York: Springer, 1969.

Bishop, G.F., Oldendick, R.W., & Tuchfarber, A.J. Political information processing: Question order and context effects. *Political Behavior, 1982, 4,* 177-200.

Bjork, R.A. The updating of human memory. In G.H. Bower (Ed.), *The psychology of learning and motivation: Vol. 12.* New York: Academic Press, 1978.

Blake, M. Prediction of recognition when recall fails: Exploring the Feeling-of-Knowing phenomena. *Journal of Verbal Learning and Verbal Behavior, 1973, 12,* 311-319.

Bloom, B.S., & Broder, L.J. *Problem-solving processes of college students.* Chicago, IL: University of Chicago Press, 1950.

Bock, J.K., & Irwin, D.E. Syntactic effects of information availability in sentence production. *Journal of Verbal Learning and Verbal Behavior, 1980, 19,* 467-484.

Bock, J.K. Toward a cognitive psychology of syntex: Information processing contributions to sentence formulation. *Psychological Review, 1982, 89,* 1-47.

Boersma, F. J., Conklin, R. C., & Carlson, J. E. Effects of reporting associative strategies on the retention of paired-associates. *Psychonomic Science, 1966, 5,* 463-464.

Book, W.F. *The psychology of skill.* New York: Gregg, 1925.

Boring, E.G. A history of introspection. *Psychological Bulletin, 1953, 50,* 169-189.

Bourne, L.E., Jr., Goldstein, S., & Link, W.E. Concept learning as a function of availability of previously presented information. *Journal of Experimental Psychology, 1964, 67,* 439-448.

Bouwman, M.J. *The use of accounting information: Expert versus novice behavior.* Unpublished manuscript, University of Oregon, 1980.

Bower, A.C., & King, W.L. The effect of number of irrelevant stimulus dimensions, verbalization, and sex on learning bi-conditional classification rules. *Psychonomic Science, 1967, 8,* 453-454.

Bower, G. H. Representing knowledge development. In R. S. Siegler (Ed.), *Children's thinking: What develops?* Hillsdale, NJ: Lawrence Erlbaum Associates, 1978, 349-362.

Bower, G.H., & Hilgard, E.R. *Theories of learning (5th ed.).* Englewood Cliffs, NJ: Prentice-Hall, 1981.

Bower, G.H. & Winzenz, D. Group structure, coding, memory for digit series. *Journal of Experimental Psychology Monograph, 1969, 80(2).*

Bree, D.S. The understanding process as seen in geometry theorems and the missionaries and cannibals problem (Doctoral dissertation, Carnegie-Mellon University, 1969). *Dissertation Abstracts International, 1969, 30,* 1675-A. (University Microfilms No. 69-18588)

Bree, D.S. Understanding of structured problem solutions. *Instructional Science, 1975, 3,* 327-350.

384   Protocol Analysis

Brehmer, B. Hypotheses about relations between scaled variables in the learning of probabilistic inference tasks. *Organizational Behavior and Human Performance*, 1974, *11*, 1-27.

Brehmer, B., Kuylenstierna, J., & Liljegren, J. E. Effects of functional form and cue validity on the subjects' hypotheses in probabilistic inference tasks. *Organizational Behavior and Human Performance*, 1974, *11*, 338-354.

Brehmer, B., Kuylenstierna, J., & Liljegren, J. E. Effects of information about the probabilistic nature of the task on learning of uncertain inference tasks. *Umea Psychological Report* (No. 90). Sweden: Department of Psychology, University of Umea, 1975.

Brelsford, J.W., & Atkinson, R.C. Recall of paired-associates as a function of overt and covert rehearsal procedures. *Journal of Verbal Learning and Verbal Behavior*, 1968, *7*, 730-736.

Brewer, W. F. There is no convincing evidence for operant or classical conditioning in adult humans. In W. B. Weimer & D. S. Palermo (Eds.), *Cognition and symbolic processes*. Hillsdale, NJ: Lawrence Erlbaum Associates, 1974.

Bricker, P.D., & Chapanis, A. Do incorrectly perceived tachistoscopic stimuli convey some information? *Psychological Review*, 1953, *60*, 181-188.

Broadbent, D.E. *Perception and communication*. New York: Pergamon Press, 1958.

Broadbent, D. E. Levels, hierarchies and the locus of control. *Quarterly Journal of Experimental Psychology*, 1977, *29*, 181-201.

Brodie, D.A. Free recall measures of short-term store: Are rehearsal and order of recall data necessary? *Memory and Cognition*, 1975, *3*, 653-662.

Brodie, D.A., & Murdock, B.B. Effects of presentation time on nominal and functional serial-position curves of free recall. *Journal of Verbal Learning and Verbal Behavior*, 1977, *16*, 185-200.

Brooks, L.R. Spatial and verbal components of the act of recall. *Canadian Journal of Psychology*, 1968, *22*, 349-368.

Brotsky, S. J., & Linton, M. L. The test-retest reliability of free association norms. *Psychonomic Science*, 19, 8, 425-426.

Brown, R., & McNeill, D. The "tip of the tongue" phenomenon. *Journal of Verbal Learning and Verbal Behavior*, 1966, *5*, 325-337.

Bruner, J.S., Busiek, R.D., & Minturn, A.L. Assimilation in the immediate reproduction of visually perceived figures. *Journal of Experimental Psychology*, 1952, *44*, 151-155.

Bruner, J.S., & Postman, L. On the perception of incongruity: A paradigm. *Journal of Personality*, 1949, *18*, 206-223.

Brunk, L., Collister, G., Swift, C., & Stayton, S. A correlation study of two reasoning problems. *Journal of Experimental Psychology*, 1958, *55*, 236-241.

Brunswik, E. *Perception and the representative design of psychological experiments*. Berkeley, CA: University of California Press, 1956.

Brunswik, E., & Herma, H. Probability learning of perceptual cues in the establishment of a weight illusion. *Journal of Experimental Psychology*, 1951, *41*, 281-290.

Bugelski, B.R. Presentation time, total time, mediation in paired-associate learning. *Journal of Experimental Psychology*, 1962, *63*, 409-412.

Bugelski, B. R., & Scharlock, D. P. An experimental demonstration of unconscious mediated association. *Journal of Experimental Psychology*, 1952, *44*, 334-338.

Buhler, K. Tatsachen und Probleme zu einer Psychologie der Deukvorgange: II. Ueber Gedankenzusammenhange. *Archiv fur die gesamte Psychologie*, 1908, *12*, 1-23. (a)

Buhler, K. Tatsachen und Probleme zu einer Psychologie der Dankvorgange: III. Ueber Gedankenerrinerungen. *Archiv fur die gesamte Psychologie*, 1908, *12*, 24-92. (b)

Bulbrook, M. E. An experimental inquiry into the existence and nature of "insight". *American Journal of Psychology*, 1932, *44*, 409-453.

Burack, B. The nature and efficacy of methods of attack on reasoning problems. *Psychological Monographs*, 1950, *64* (7, Whole No. 313).

Buswell, G.T. Diagnostic studies in arithmetic. *Supplementary Educational Monographs*, 1928, *30*.

Buswell, G.T. Patterns of thinking in solving problems. *University of California Publications in Education*, 1956, *12*, 63-148.

Byrne, R. Planning meals: Problem-solving on a real data-base. *Cognition*, 1977, *5*, 287-332.

Caccamise, D.J. *Cognitive processes in writing: Idea generation and integration.* Unpublished doctoral dissertation, University of Colorado at Boulder, 1981.

Cacioppo, J.T., & Petty, R.E. Social psychological procedures for cognitive response assessment: The thought-listing procedure. In T.V. Merluzzi, C.R. Glass & M. Genest, (Eds.), *Cognitive assessment.* New York: Guildford Press, 1981.

Cady, H.M. On the psychology of testimony. *American Journal of Psychology*, 1924, *35*, 110-112.

Cahill, H.E., & Hovland, C.I. The role of memory in the acquisition of concepts. *Journal of Experimental Psychology*, 1960, *59*, 137-144.

Calder, B.J., & Ross, M. *Attitudes and behavior.* Morristown: General Learning Press, 1973.

Campbell, D.T., & Fiske, D.W. Convergent and discriminant validation by the multitrait-multimethod matrix. *Psychological Bulletin*, 1959, *56*, 81-105.

Cannell, C.F., & Kahn, R.L. Interviewing. In G. Lindzey & E. Aronson (Eds.), *The handbook of social psychology (Vol. 2).* Reading, MA: Addison-Wesley, 1968, 526-595.

Carlson, V. R. Instructions and perceptual constancy judgments. In W. Epstein (Ed.), *Stability and constancy in visual perception: Mechanisms and processes.* New York: Wiley, 1977.

Carmean, S.L., & Weir, M.W. Effects of verbalizations on discrimination learning and retention. *Journal of Verbal Learning and Verbal Behavior,* 1967, *6,* 545-550.

Carmichael, L., Hogan, H.P., & Walter, A.A. An experimental study of the effect of language on the reproduction of visually perceived forms. *Journal of Experimental Psychology,* 1932, *15,* 73-86.

Carpenter, P.A., & Just, M.A. Sentence comprehension: A psycholinguistic processing model of verification. *Psychological Review,* 1975, *82,* 45-73.

Carroll, J. S., & Payne, J. M. Judgements about crime and the criminal: A model and a method for investigating parole decisions. In B. D. Sales (Ed.), *Perspectives in law and psychology: The criminal justice system (Vol. 1).* New York: Plenum, 1977.

Chafe, W.L. Creativity in verbalization and its implications for the nature of stored knowledge. In R.O. Freedle (Ed.), *Discourse production and comprehension (Vol. 1).* Norwood, NJ: Ablex, 1977.

Chafe, W.L. The flow of thought and the flow of language. *Syntax and Semantics,* 1979, *12,* 159-181.

Chapman, D.W. Relative effects of determinate and indeterminate "Aufgaben." *American Journal of Psychology,* 1932, *44,* 163-174.

Chase, W.G. Does memory scanning involve implicit speech? In S. Dornic (Ed.), *Attention and Performance VI.* London: Academic Press, 1977.

Chase, W. G. Elementary information processes. In W. K. Estes (Ed.), *Handbook of learning and cognitive processes (Vol. 5).* Hillsdale, NJ: Lawrence Erlbaum Associates, 1978.

Chase, W.G., & Ericsson, K.A. Skilled memory. In J.R. Anderson (Ed.), *Cognitive skills and their acquisition.* Hillsdale, NJ: Lawrence Erlbaum Associates, 1981.

Chase, W.G., & Ericsson, K.A. Skill and working memory. In G.H. Bower (Ed.), *The psychology of learning and motivation (Vol. 16).* New York: Academic Press, 1982.

Claparède, E. Genèse de l'hypothèses. *Archives de Psychologie,* 1934, *24,* 1-155.

Clark, H.H. Semantics and comprehension. In T.A. Sebeok (Ed.), *Current trends in linguistics (Vol. 12).* The Hague: Mouton, 1974, 1291-1428.

Clark, H.H., & Chase, W.G. On the process of comparing sentences against pictures. *Cognitive Psychology,* 1972, *3,* 472-517.

Clark, H.H., & Chase, W.G. Perceptual coding strategies in the formation and verification of description. *Memory and Cognition,* 1974, *2,* 101-111.

Clarkson, G. *Portfolio selection - A simulation of trust investment.* Englewood Cliffs, NJ: Prentice-Hall, 1962.

Cole, R.A. Listening for mispronunciations: A measure of what we hear during speech. *Perception and Psychophysics,* 1973, *14,* 153-156.

Cole, R.A., & Young, M. Effect of subvocalization on memory for speech sounds. *Journal of Experimental Psychology: Human Learning and Memory*, 1975, *1*, 772-779.

Colle, H.A., & Welsh, A. Acoustic masking in primary memory. *Journal of Verbal Learning and Verbal Behavior*, 1976, *15*, 17-31.

Collins, A., Brown, J.S., & Larkin, K.M. Inference in text understanding. In R.J. Spiro, B.C. Bruce & W.F. Brewer (Eds.), *Theoretical issues in reading comprehension*. Hillsdale, NJ: Lawrence Erlbaum Associates, 1980.

Coltheart, V. Memory for stimuli and memory for hypotheses in concept identification. *Journal of Experimental Psychology*, 1971, *89*, 102-108.

Comstock, C. On the relevancy of imagery to the processes of thought. *American Journal of Psychology*, 1921, *32*, 196-230.

Conrad, R. Interference or decay over short retention intervals? *Journal of Verbal Learning and Verbal Behavior*, 1967, *6*, 49-54.

Conrad, R., & Hull, A.J. Input modality and the serial position curve in short-term memory. *Psychonomic Science*, 1968, *10*, 135-136.

Coombs, C.H. *A theory of data*. New York: Wiley, 1964.

Cox, C. M., Comparative behavior in solving a series of maze problems of varying difficulty. *Journal of Experimental Psychology*, 1928, *11*, 202-218.

Cox, J. W. *Manual skill—its organization and development*. Cambridge: Cambridge University Press, 1934.

Crovitz, H.F. *Galton's walk*. New York: Harper & Row, 1970.

Crowder, R.G. The role of one's own voice in immediate memory. *Cognitive Psychology*, 1970, *1*, 157-178.

Crowder, R.G. Representation of speech sounds in precategorical acoustic storage. *Journal of Experimental Psychology*, 1973, *98*, 14-24.

Danks, J.H. Encoding of novel figures for communication and memory. *Cognitive Psychology*, 1970, *1*, 179-191.

Danks, J.H. Producing ideas and sentences. In R.O. Freedle (Ed.), *Discourse production and comprehension (Vol. 1)*. Norwood, NJ: Ablex, 1977.

Dansereau, D.F. An information processing model of mental multiplication (Doctoral dissertation, Carnegie-Mellon University, 1969). *Dissertation Abstracts International*, 1969, *30*, 1916-B. (University Microfilms No. 69-15746)

Dansereau, D., & Gregg, L.W. An information processing analysis of mental multiplication. *Psychonomic Science*, 1966, *6*, 71-72.

Davies, F. C. The functional significance of imagery differences. *Journal of Experimental Psychology*, 1932, *15*, 630-661.

Davis, J.H., Carey, M.H., Foxman, P.N., & Tarr, D.B. Verbalization, experimenter presence, and problem solving. *Journal of Personality and Social Psychology*, 1968, *8*, 299-302.

Dean, S.J., & Martin, R.B. Reported mediation as a function of degree of learning. *Psychonomic Science*, 1966, *4*, 231-232.

Deese, J. Thought into speech. *American Scientist,* 1978, *66,* 314-321.

Deese, J. Pauses, prosody, and the demands of production in language. In W. Dechert & M. Raupach (Eds.), *Temporal variables in speech: Studies in honor of Frieda Goldman-Eisler.* The Hague: Mouton, 1980.

Deffenbacher, K.A. Eyewitness accuracy and confidence. *Law and Human Behavior,* 1980, *4,* 243-260.

Deffner, G. *Lautes Denken-Untersuchung zur Qualitet eines Dateerhebungsuerfahrens.* Unpublished doctoral dissertation, University of Hamburg, West Germany, 1983.

de Groot, A.D. *Thought and choice in chess.* The Hague: Mouton, 1965.

DeNike, L. D. The temporal relationship between awareness and performance in verbal conditioning. *Journal of Experimental Psychology,* 1964, *68,* 521-529.

Dickson, W.P., Miyake, N., & Muto, T. Referential relativity: Culture-boundedness of analytic and metaphoric communication. *Cognition,* 1977, *5,* 215-233.

Dominowski, R.L. How do people discover concepts? In R.L. Solso (Ed.), *Theories in cognitive psychology: The Loyola Symposium.* Potomac, MD: Lawrence Erlbaum Associates, 1974, 257-288.

Dulany, D. E. The place of hypotheses and intentions: An analysis of verbal control in verbal conditioning. In C. W. Eriksen (Ed.), *Behavior and awareness.* Durham, NC: Duke University Press, 1962.

Dulany, D.E., Carlson, R.A., & Dewey, G.I. *A case of syntactical learning and judgment: How conscious and how abstract?* Unpublished paper, Department of Psychology, University Illinois, Urbana-Champaign, 1983.

Dulany, D.E., & O'Connell, D.C. Does partial reinforcement dissociate verbal rules and the behavior they might be presumed to control? *Journal of Verbal Learning and Verbal Behavior,* 1963, *2,* 361-372.

Duncan, C.P. Effects of instructions and information on problem solving. *Journal of Experimental Psychology,* 1963, *65,* 321-327.

Duncan, C.P. Induction of a principle. *Quarterly Journal of Experimental Psychology,* 1964, *16,* 373-377.

Duncker, K. A qualitative (experimental and theoretical) study of productive thinking (solving of comprehensible problems). *Pedagogical Seminary,* 1926, *33,* 642-708.

Duncker, K. On problem solving. *Psychological Monographs,* 1945, *58*(5, Whole No. 270).

Durkin, H. E. Trial-and-error, gradual analysis and sudden reorganization: An experimental study of problem solving. *Archives of Psychology,* 1937, 210.

Eagle, M., & Leiter, E. Recall and recognition in intentional and incidental learning. *Journal of Experimental Psychology,* 1964, *68,* 58-63.

Egan, D.E., & Grimes, D.D. *Differences in mental representations spontaneously adopted for reasoning.* Paper presented at Annual Meeting, Psychonomics Society, Phoenix, Arizona, November 1979.

Eindhoven, J.E., & Vinacke, W.E. Creative processes in painting. *Journal of General Psychology*, 1952, *47*, 139-164.

Einhorn, H.J., Kleinmuntz, D.N., & Kleinmuntz, B. Linear regression and process-tracing models of judgment. *Psychological Review*, 1979, *86*, 465-485.

Einstein, G.O., Pellegrino, J.W., Mondani, M.S., & Battig, W.F. Free recall performance as a function of overt rehearsal frequency. *Journal of Experimental Psychology*, 1974, *103*, 440-449.

Ellis, H.D., Shepard, J.W., & Davies, G.M. Identification of familiar and unfamiliar faces from internal and external features: Some implication for theories of face recognition. *Perception*, 1979, *8*, 431-439.

Ellis, N.R. Evidence for two storage processes in short-term memory. *Journal of Experimental Psychology*, 1969, *80*, 390-391.

English, H.B. In aid of introspection. *American Journal of Psychology*, 1921, *32*, 404-414.

Epstein, W., & Broota, K. D. Attitude of judgment and reaction time in estimation of size at a distance. *Perception & Psychophysics*, 1975, *18*, 201-204.

Ericsson, K.A. Problem-solving behaviour with the Eight Puzzle IV: Process in terms of sequences of moves (No. 448). *Reports from the Department of Psychology*. Stockholm: University of Stockholm, 1975. (a)

Ericsson, K.A. Instruction to verbalize as a means to study problem solving processes with the Eight Puzzle: A preliminary study (No. 458). *Reports from the Department of Psychology*. Stockholm: University of Stockholm, 1975. (b)

Ericsson, K.A., & Chase, W.G. Exceptional memory. *American Scientist*, 1982, *70*, 607-615.

Ericsson, K.A., & Chase, W.G., & Faloon, S. Acquisition of a memory skill. *Science*, 1980, *208*, 1181-1182.

Ericsson, K.A., & Faivre, I. *Acquiring "absolute pitch" for colors*. Paper presented at the Annual Meeting, Psychonomics Society, Minneapolis, Minnesota, November 1982.

Ericsson, K.A., & Polson, P.G. *An analysis of a memory skill for dinner orders*. Manuscript in preparation.

Ericsson, K.A., & Simon, H.A. Verbal reports as data. *Psychological Review*, 1980, *87*, 215-251.

Ericsson, K.A., & Simon, H.A. Sources of evidence on cognition: A historical overview. In T.V. Merluzzi, C.R. Glass & M. Genest (Eds.), *Cognitive assessment*. New York: Guilford Press, 1981, 16-51.

Eriksen, C.W. Subception: Fact or artifact. *Psychological Review*, 1956, *63*, 79-80.

Eriksen, C. W. Discrimination and learning without awareness: A methodological survey and evaluation. *Psychological Review*, 1960, *67*, 279-300.

Estes, W.K. Phonemic coding and rehearsal in short-term memory for letter strings. *Journal of Verbal Learning and Verbal Behavior*, 1973, *12*, 360-372.

Evans, J. St. B.T.   On interpreting reasoning data: A reply to Van Duyne. *Cognition*, 1975, *3*, 387-390.

Evans, J. St. B.T.   *The psychology of deductive reasoning.* London: Routledge & Kegan Paul, 1982.

Evans, J. St. B.T., & Wason, P.C.   Rationalization in a reasoning task. *British Journal of Psychology*, 1976, *67*, 479-486.

Farley, A.M.   *VIPS: A visual imagery and perception system—the result of a protocol analysis.* Unpublished doctoral dissertation, Carnegie-Mellon University, 1974.

Fazio, R.H., & Zanna, M.P.   Attitudinal qualities relating to the strength of the attitude-behavior relationship. *Journal of Experimental Social Psychology*, 1978, *14*, 398-408.

Fehrer, E.V.   An investigation of the learning of visually perceived forms. *American Journal of Psychology*, 1935, *47*, 187-221.

Feigenbaum, E.A.   The simulation of verbal learning behavior. In E.A. Feigenbaum & J. Feldman (Eds.), *Computers and thought.* New York: McGraw-Hill, 1963.

Feldman, J.   *An analysis of predictive behavior in a two-choice situation.* Unpublished doctoral dissertation, Carnegie Institute of Technology, 1959.

Fernald, M.R.   The diagnosis of mental imagery. *Psychological Monographs*, 1912, *14*(Whole No. 58).

Fidler, E.J.   *The reliability and validity of concurrent and retrospective verbal reports for studying decision making behavior* (Working paper No. 683). Vancouver: Faculty of Commerce, University of British Columbia, 1979.

Finkenbinder, E.O.   The remembrance of problems and of their solutions: A study in logical memory. *American Journal of Psychology*, 1914, *25*, 32-81.

Fischhoff, B.   Hindsight = Foresight: The effect of outcome knowledge on judgement under uncertainty. *Journal of Experimental Psychology: Human Perception and Performance*, 1975, *1*, 288-299.

Fischhoff, B.   Perceived informativeness of facts. *Journal of Experimental Psychology: Human Perception and Performance*, 1977, *3*, 349-358.

Fischler, I., Rundus, D., & Atkinson, R.C.   Effects of overt procedures on free recall. *Psychonomic Science*, 1970, *19*, 249-250.

Fiske, D.W.   *Strategies for personality research: The observation versus interpretation of behavior.* San Francisco, CA: Jossey-Bass, 1978.

Flaherty, E.G.   Cognitive processes used in solving mathematical problems (Doctoral dissertation, Boston University, 1973). *Dissertation Abstracts International*, 1973, *34*(4), 1767A. (University Microfilms No. 73-23562)

Flaherty, E.G.   The thinking aloud technique and problem solving ability. *Journal of Educational Research*, 1974, *68*, 223-225.

Flanagan, J. C.   The critical incident technique. *Psychological Bulletin*, 1954, *51*, 327-358.

Flower, L.S., & Hayes, J.R.   The dynamics of composing: Making plans and juggling constraints.   In L. Gregg & I. Steinberg (Eds.), *Cognitive processes in writing*.   Hillsdale, NJ: Lawrence Erlbaum Associates, 1978, 31-50.

Flower, L.S., Hayes, J.R., & Swarts, H. *Revising functional documents: The scenario principle* (Tech. Rep. No. 10).   Pittsburgh, PA: Carnegie-Mellon University, 1980.

Frankel, F., Levine, M., & Karpf, D. Human discrimination learning: A test of the blank-trials assumption.   *Journal of Experimental Psychology*, 1970, *85*, 342-398.

Freud, S. *Therapy and technique.* New York: Macmillan, 1963.

Fryer, D.H.   Articulation in automatic mental work.   *American Journal of Psychology*, 1941, *54*, 504-517.

Gagné, R. H., & Smith, E. C.   A study of the effects of verbalization on problem solving. *Journal of Experimental Psychology*, 1962, *63*, 12-18.

Geiselman, R.E., & Bellezza, F.S.   Eye-movements and overt rehearsal in word recall. *Journal of Experimental Psychology: Human Learning and Memory*, 1977, *3*, 305-315.

Gekoski, W.L., & Riegel, K.F. A study of the one-year stability of the Michigan Free and Restricted Association Norms. *Psychonomic Science*, 1967, *8*, 427-428.

Genest, M., & Turk, D.C.   Think-aloud approaches to cognitive assessment.   In T.V. Merluzzi, C.R. Glass & M. Genest (Eds.), *Cognitive Assessment*.   New York: Guildford Press, 1981.

Ghatala, E.S., Levin, J.R., & Subkoviak, M.J.   Rehearsal strategy effects in children's discrimination learning: Confronting the crucible. *Journal of Verbal Learning and Verbal Behavior*, 1975, *14*, 398-407.

Ghiselin, B. *The creative process.* New York: Mentor, 1952.

Gibson, E.J. *Principles of perceptual learning and development.*   Englewood Cliffs, NJ: Prentice-Hall, 1969.

Gibson, E.J., & Levin, H. *The psychology of reading.* Cambridge, MA: MIT Press, 1975.

Gilmartin, K.J.   An information-processing model of short-term memory. (Doctoral dissertation, Carnegie-Mellon University, 1975).   (University Microfilms No. 75-09082)

Gimmestad, B.J. An exploratory study of the processes used by community college students in mathematics problem solving (Doctoral dissertation, University of Colorado at Boulder, 1976). *Dissertation Abstracts International*, 1977, *37*, 7590A. (University Microfilms No. 77-11300)

Glanzer, M., & Clark, W.H.   Accuracy of perceptual recall: An analysis of organization. *Journal of Verbal Learning and Verbal Behavior*, 1963, *1*, 289-299. (a)

Glanzer, M., & Clark, W. H.   The verbal loop hypothesis: Binary numbers. *Journal of Verbal Learning and Verbal Behavior*, 1963, *2*, 301-309. (b)

Glanzer, M., & Clark, W. H.   The verbal loop hypothesis: Conventional figures. *American Journal of Psychology*, 1964, *77*, 621-626.

Glanzer, M., & Meinzer, A. The effects of intralist activity on free recall. *Journal of Verbal Learning and Verbal Behavior,* 1967, *6,* 928-935.

Glaser, W.R., & Dolt, M.O. A functional model to localize the conflict underlying the Stroop phenomenon. *Psychological Research,* 1977, *39,* 287-310.

Goldman-Eisler, F. *Psycholinguistics: Experiments in spontaneous speech.* New York: Academic Press, 1968.

Goldman-Eisler, F., & Cohen, M. Is N, P, and PN difficulty a valid criterion of transformational operations? *Journal of Verbal Learning and Verbal Behavior,* 1970, *9,* 161-166.

Goldner, R.H. Individual differences in whole-part approach and flexibility-rigidity in problem solving. *Psychological Monographs,* 1957, *71*(20, Whole No. 450).

Goodwin, R.Q., & Wason, P.C. Degrees of insight. *British Journal of Psychology,* 1972, *63,* 205-212.

Goor, A. Problem solving processes of creative and non-creative students (Doctoral dissertation, University of North Carolina, 1974). *Dissertation Abstracts International,* 1974, *35,* 3517A. (University Microfilms No. 74-26878)

Goor, A., & Sommerfeld, R.E. A comparison of problem-solving processes of creative students and non-creative students. *Journal of Educational Psychology,* 1975, *67,* 495-505.

Gould, J.D. How experts dictate. *Journal of Experimental Psychology: Human Perception and Performance,* 1978, *4,* 648-661.

Gould, J.D. Writing and speaking letters and messages. *International Journal of Man-Machine Studies,* 1982, *16,* 147-171.

Greeno, J.G. Indefinite goals in well-structured problems. *Psychological Review,* 1976, *83,* 479-491.

Greenspoon, J. The reinforcing effect of two spoken sounds on the frequency of two responses. *American Journal of Psychology,* 1955, *68,* 409-416.

Groen, G.J., & Parkman, J.M. A chronometric analysis of simple addition. *Psychological Review,* 1972, *79,* 329-343.

Groninger, L.D. Natural language mediation and covert rehearsal in short-term memory. *Psychonomic Science,* 1966, *5,* 135-136.

Grudin, J. Processes in verbal analogy solution. *Journal of Experimental Psychology: Human Perception and Performance,* 1980, *6,* 67-74.

Guindon, R. *Inferences in story comprehension.* Unpublished M.Sc. thesis, University of Toronto, 1980.

Guindon, R. *Use of verbal reports to study inferences in text comprehension.* Paper presented at the Cognitive Science Conference, University of California at Berkeley, 1981.

Hafner, J. Influence of verbalization on problem solving. *Psychological Reports,* 1957, *3,* 360.

Hagert, G. *Cognitive processing in a spatial series task: A cognitive simulation study* (Working paper No. 7). Stockholm: The Cognitive Seminar, University of Stockholm, 1980. (a)

Hagert, G. Stability and change of strategies: Three simulations of one subject with one-year intervals. *Proceedings of the AISB-80 Conference on Artificial Intelligence*, Amsterdam, July 1980. (b)

Haines, G.H. Process models of consumer decision making. In G.D. Hughes & M.L. Ray (Eds.), *Buyer/consumer information processing*. Chapel Hill: University of North Carolina Press, 1974.

Hamilton, J.M.E., & Sanford, A.J. The symbolic distance effect for alphabetic order judgements: A subjective report and reaction time analysis. *Quarterly Journal of Experimental Psychology*, 1978, *30*, 33-43.

Hamilton, P., Hockey, R., & Rejman, M. The place of the concept of activation in human information processing theory: An integrative approach. In S. Dornic (Ed.), *Attention and performance VI*. London: Academic Press, 1977.

Hanawalt, N.G. Memory trace for figures in recall and recognition. *Archives of Psychology*, 1937, 216, 1-89.

Hanawalt, N.G., & Demarest, I.H. The effect of verbal suggstion in the recall period upon the reproduction of visually perceived forms. *Journal of Experimental Psychology*, 1939, *25*, 159-174.

Hanfmann, E. A study of personal patterns in an intellectual performance. *Character and Personality*, 1941, *9*, 315-325.

Hanfmann, E., & Kasanin, J. A method for the study of concept formation. *Journal of Psychology*, 1937, *3*, 521-540.

Hardyck, C.D., & Petrinovich, C.F. Subvocal speech and comprehension level as a function of the difficulty level of reading material. *Journal of Verbal Learning and Verbal Behavior*, 1970, *9*, 647-652.

Hart, J.T. Memory and the Feeling-of-Knowing experience. *Journal of Educational Psychology*, 1965, *56*, 208-216.

Hart, J.T. Memory and the memory-monotoring process. *Journal of Verbal Learning and Verbal Behavior*, 1967, *6*, 685-688.

Havens, L.L. *Approaches to the mind*. Boston, MA: Little & Brown, 1973.

Havertape, J.F. The communication function in learning disabled adolescents: A study of verbalized self-instruction (Doctoral dissertation, University of Arizona, 1976). *Dissertation Abstracts International*, 1977, *37*, 1489A. (University Microfilms No. 76-19726)

Hayes, J.R., & Simon, H.A. Understanding written problem instructions. In L.W. Gregg (Ed.), *Knowledge and cognition*. Potomac, MD: Lawrence Erlbaum Associates, 1974.

Hayes-Roth, B., & Walker, C. Configural effects in human memory: The superiority of memory over external information sources as a basis for inference verification. *Cognitive Science*, 1979, *3*, 119-140.

Hayes-Roth, F., Klahr, P., & Mostow, D.J. Advice taking and knowledge refinement: An iterative view of skill acquisition. In J.A. Anderson (Ed.), *Cognitive skills and their acquisition*. Hillsdale, NJ: Lawrence Erlbaum Associates, 1981.

Heidbreder, E. An experimental study of thinking. *Archives of Psychology*, 1924, 73.

Heidbreder, E. Problem solving in children and adults. *Journal of Genetic Psychology*, 1928, *35*, 522-545.

Heidbreder, E. A study of the evolution of concepts. *Psychological Bulletin*, 1934, *31*, 673. (Abstract)

Heidbreder, E. Language and concepts. *Psychological Bulletin*, 1936, *33*, 724. (Abstract)

Helson, H. *Adaptation-level theory*. New York: Harper & Row, 1964.

Hendrix, G. A new clue to transfer of training. *Elementary School Journal*, 1947, *48*, 197-208.

Henry, L. K. The role of insight in the analytic thinking of adolescents. *Studies in Education, University of Iowa Studies*, 1934, *9*, 65-102.

Herman, D.T., Lawless, R.H., & Marshall, R.W. Variables in the effect of language on the reproduction of visually perceived forms. *Perceptual and Motor Skills*, 1957, *7*, 171-186.

Hess, R.K. The role of pupil size in communication. *Scientific American*, 1975, *5*, 110-118.

Hilgard, E.R. *Theories of learning*. New York: Appleton-Century-Crofts, 1948.

Hintzman, D.L. Classification and annual coding in short-term memory. *Psychonomic Science*, 1965, *3*, 161-162.

Hitch, G.J. The role of short-term working memory in mental arithmetic. *Cognitive Psychology*, 1978, *10*, 302-323.

Horton, D. L. The effects of meaningfulness, awareness and type of design in verbal mediation. *Journal of Verbal Learning and Verbal Behavior*, 1964, *3*, 187-194.

Horton, D.L., & Kjeldergaard, P.K. An experimental analysis of associative factors in mediated generalizations. *Psychological Monographs*, 1961, *75*(11, Whole No. 515).

Horton, K.D. Phonemic similarity, overt rehearsal, and short-term store. *Journal of Experimental Psychology: Human Learning and Memory*, 1976, *2*, 244-251.

Howard, G.S. Response-shift bias: A problem in evaluating interventions with pre/post self-reports. *Evaluation Review*, 1980, *4*, 93-106.

Howard, G.S., & Dailey, P.R. Response-shift bias: A source of contamination of self-report measures. *Journal of Applied Psychology*, 1979, *64*, 144-150.

Howard, G.S., Ralph, K.M., Gulanick, N.A., Maxwell, S.E., Nance, D.W., & Gerber, S.K. Internal invalidity in pretest-posttest self-report evaluation and a re-evaluation of retrospective pretests. *Applied Psychological Measurement*, 1979, *3*, 1-23.

Huesmann, L.R., & Cheng, C.M. A theory for the induction of mathematical functions. *Psychological Review*, 1973, *80*, 126-138.

Hull, C.L. Quantitative aspects of the evolution of concepts: An experimental study. *Psychological Monographs*, 1920, *28*(Whole No. 123).

Humphrey, G. *Thinking: An introduction to its experimental psychology.* London: Methuen & Co., 1951.

Husband, R. W. Human learning on a four-section elevated finger maze. *Journal of General Psychology,* 1928, *1,* 15-28.

Husband, R. W. Analysis of methods in human maze learning. *Journal of Genetic Psychology,* 1931, *39,* 258-277.

Irwin, F.W., Kaufman, K., Prior, G., & Weaver, H.B. On 'learning without awareness of what is being learned'. *Journal of Experimental Psychology,* 1934, *17,* 823-827.

Jacoby, L.L. Encoding processes, rehearsal and recall requirements. *Journal of Verbal Learning and Verbal Behavior,* 1973, *12,* 302-10.

James, W. *The principles of psychology.* New York: Holt, 1890.

Jensen, J. On the "Einstellung" effect in problem solving. *Scandinavian Journal of Psychology,* 1960, *1,* 163-168.

Jeremy, R.J. Use of coordinate sentences with the conjunction *and* for describing temporal and locative relations between events. *Journal of Psycholinguistic Research,* 1978, *7,* 135-150.

Johnson, D.M. *The psychology of thought and judgement.* New York: Harper & Row, 1955.

Johnson, E.J., & Russo, J.E. *What is remembered after a purchase decision?* (C.I.P. Working Paper No. 379). Pittsburgh, PA: Carnegie-Mellon University, 1978.

Johnson, E.S. *The simulation of human problem solving from an empirically derived model* (Doctoral dissertation, University of North Carolina at Chapel Hill, 1962). *Dissertation Abstracts International,* 1962, *24,* 3435P. (University Microfilms No. 63-3497)

Johnson, E. S. An information processing model of one kind of problem solving. *Psychological Monographs,* 1964, *78*(4, Whole No. 581).

Johnson, N.F. On the relationship between sentence structure and the latency in generating a sentence. *Journal of Verbal Learning and Verbal Behavior,* 1966, *5,* 375-380.

Johnson, N.F. On the function of letters in word identification: Some data and a preliminary model. *Journal of Verbal Learning and Verbal Behavior,* 1975, *14,* 17-29.

Johnson, P.E., Duran, A.S., Hassebrock, F., Moller, J., Prietula, M., Feltovich, P.J., & Swanson, D.B. Expertice and error in diagnostic reasoning. *Cognitive Science,* 1981, *5,* 235-283.

Johnson-Laird, P.N., & Wason, P.C. A theoretical analysis of insight into a reasoning task. *Cognitive Psychology,* 1970, *1*(2), 134-148.

Kahneman, D. *Attention and effort.* Englewood Cliffs, NJ: Prentice-Hall, 1973.

Kantowski, E.L. Processes involved in mathematical problem solving (Doctoral dissertation, University of Georgia, 1974). *Dissertation Abstracts International,* 1974, *36,* 2734A. (University Microfilm No. 75-23764)

Kaplan, I.T., & Schoenfeld, W.N. Oculomotor patterns during the solution of visually displayed anagrams. *Journal of Experimental Psychology*, 1966, *72*, 447-451.

Karat, J. A model of problem solving with incomplete constraint knowledge. *Cognitive Psychology*, 1982, *14*, 538-559.

Karat, J. *Modeling learning and transfer in a problem solving task.* Unpublished doctoral thesis, Department of Psychology, University of Colorado at Boulder, 1983.

Karlton, G., & Schuman, H. *The effect of the question on survey responses: A review.* Unpublished paper, Survey Research Center, University of Michigan, 1980.

Karpf, D.A. Thinking aloud in human discrimination learning (Doctoral dissertation, State University of New York at Stony Brook, 1972). *Dissertation Abstracts International*, 1973, *33*, 6111-B. (University Microfilms No. 73-13625)

Karpf, D., & Levine, M. Blank-trial probes and introtacts in human discrimination learning. *Journal of Experimental Psychology*, 1971, *90*, 51-55.

Katona, G. *Organizing and memory.* New York: Columbia University Press, 1940.

Katona, G. *Psychological economics.* New York: Elsevier, 1975.

Katona, G. Toward a macro psychology. *American Psychologist*, 1979, *34*(2), 118-126.

Kazdin, A. E. Assessment of imagery during covert modeling of assertive behavior. *Journal of Behavior Therapy and Experimental Psychiatry*, 1976, *7*, 213-219.

Keele, S.W. *Attention and human performance.* Pacific Palisades: Goodyear Publishing, 1973.

Kellas, G., McCauley, C., & McFarland, C.E. Reexamination of externalized rehearsal. *Journal of Experimental Psychology: Human Learning and Memory*, 1975, *104*, 84-90.

Kendall, P.C., & Hollon, S.D. *Assessment strategies for cognitive-behavioral inventions.* New York: Academic Press, 1981.

Kendall, P.C., & Korgeski, G.P. Assessment and cognitive-behavioral intervention. *Cognition Therapy and Research*, 1979, *3*, 1-21.

Kennedy, G., Eliot, J., & Krulee, G. Error patterns in problem solving formulations. *Psychology in the Schools*, 1970, *7*, 93-99.

Kennedy, T. D. Verbal conditioning without awareness: The use of programmed reinforcement and recurring assessment of awareness. *Journal of Experimental Psychology*, 1970, *84*, 487-494.

Kennedy, T. D. Reinforcement frequency, task characteristics and interval of awareness assessment as factors in verbal conditioning without awareness. *Journal of Experimental Psychology*, 1971, *88*, 103-112.

Kersh, B.Y., & Wittrock, M.C. Learning by discovery. *Teacher Education*, 1962, *13*, 461-468.

Kilpatrick, J. Analyzing the solution of word problems in mathematics: An exploratory study (Doctoral dissertation, Stanford University, 1967). *Dissertation Abstracts International,* 1968, *28,* 4380-A. (University Microfilms No. 68-6442)

Kintsch, W. *The representation of meaning in memory.* Hillsdale, NJ: Lawrence Erlbaum Associates, 1974.

Kintsch, W. *Psychological processes in discourse production* (Tech. Rep. No. 99). Boulder: Institute of Cognitive Science, University of Colorado, 1980.

Kintsch, W., & Polson, P.G. On nominal and functional serial position curves: Implications for short-term memory models. *Psychological Review,* 1979, *86,* 407-413.

Klahr, D. Quantification processes. In W. G. Chase (Ed.), *Visual information processing,* New York: Academic Press, 1973, 3-34.

Klein, G.S. Semantic power measured through interference of words with color-naming. *American Journal of Psychology,* 1964, *17,* 576-588.

Klein, W. Some aspects of route directions. In R.J. Jarvella & W. Klein (Eds.), *Speech, place, action: Studies of language in context,* Chichester: Wiley, 1981.

Kleinmuntz, B. MMPI decision rules for the identification of college maladjustment: A digital computer approach. *Psychological Monographs,* 1963, *77*(14, Whole No. 577).

Klinger, E. *Structure and functions of fantasy.* New York: Wiley, 1971.

Klinger, E. Utterances to evaluate steps and control attention distinguish operant from respondent thought while thinking out loud. *Bulletin of the Psychonomic Society,* 1974, *4,* 44-45.

Kohler, W. *The mentality of apes.* New York: Harcourt Brace, 1925.

Kohler, W., & Restorff, H. von. Analyse von Vorgangen im Spurenfeld. *Psychologische Forschung,* 1935, *21,* 56-112.

Koriat, A., & Lieblich, I. What does a person in a "TOT" state know that a person in a "don't know" state doesn't know. *Memory and Cognition,* 1974, *2*(4), 647-655.

Koriat, A., Lichtenstein, S., & Fischhoff, B. Reasons for confidence. *Journal of Experimental Psychology: Human Learning and Memory,* 1980, *6,* 107-118.

Krauss, R.M., Vivekananthan, P.S., & Weinheimer, S. "Inner speech" and "external speech": Characteristics and communication effectiveness of socially and nonsocially encoded messages. *Journal of Personality and Social Psychology,* 1968, *9,* 295-300.

Krutetskii, V.A. *The psychology of mathematical problem solving.* Chicago, IL: University of Chicago Press, 1976.

Kubovy, M. Response availability and the apparent spontaneity of numerical choices. *Journal of Experimental Psychology: Human Perception and Performance,* 1977, *3,* 359-364.

Kubovy, M., & Psotka, J. The predominance of seven and the apparent spontaneity of numerical choices. *Journal of Experimental Psychology: Human Perception and Performance,* 1976, *2,* 291-294.

Kulhavy, R. W. Natural language mediators and paired-associate learning in college students. *Psychological Reports,* 1970, *26,* 658.

Kuncel, R.B. Response processes and relative location of subject and item. *Educational and Psychological Measurement,* 1973, *33,* 545-563.

Kurtz, K.H., & Hovland, C.I. The effect of verbalization during observation of stimulus objects upon accuracy of recognition and recall. *Journal of Experimental Psychology,* 1953, *45,* 157-164.

Kutner, B., Wilkins, C., & Yarrow, P.R. Verbal attitudes and overt behavior involving racial predjudice. *Journal of Abnormal Social Psychology,* 1952, *47,* 649-652.

Lakatos, I. *Proofs and refutations.* Cambridge; New York: Cambridge University Press, 1976.

Landauer, T.K. Rate of implicit speech. *Perceptual and Motor Skills,* 1962, *15,* 646.

LaPiere, R.T. Attitudes vs. actions. *Social Forces,* 1934, *13,* 230-237.

Larkin, J.H., McDermott, J., Simon, D.P., & Simon, H.A. Models of competence in solving physics problems. *Cognitive Science,* 1980, *4,* 317-345.

Lashley, K. S. The behavioristic interpretation of consciousness II. *Psychological Review,* 1923, *30,* 329-353.

Laughery, K.R., & Gregg, L.W. Simulation of human problem-solving behavior. *Psychometrika,* 1962, *27,* 265-282.

Lazarsfeld, P.F. The art of asking WHY in marketing research. *The National Marketing Review,* 1935, *1,* 26-38.

Lazarus, R.S., & McCleary, R.A. Autonomic discrimination without awareness: A study of subception. *Psychological Review,* 1951, *58,* 113-122.

Leeper, R. Cognitive processes. In S.S. Stevens (Ed.), *Handbook of Experimental Psychology.* New York: Wiley, 1951, 730-757.

Lehmann, D.R., & Moore, W.L. Validity of information display boards: An assessment using longitudinal data. *Journal of Marketing Research.* 1980, *17,* 450-459.

Levelt, W.J.M. Linearization in describing spatial networks. In S. Peters & E. Saarinen (Eds.), *Processes, beliefs and questions.* Boston, MA: D. Reidel Publishing, 1982.

Levin, H., Silverman, I., & Ford, B. Hesitations in children's speech during explanation and description. *Journal of Verbal Learning and Verbal Behavior,* 1967, *6,* 560-564.

Levy, B.A. Role of articulation in auditory and visual short-term memory. *Journal of Verbal Learning and Verbal Behavior,* 1971, *10,* 123-132.

Levy, B.A. Vocalization and suppression effects in sentence memory. *Journal of Verbal Learning and Verbal Behavior,* 1975, *14,* 304-316.

Levy, B.A. Reading: Speech and meaning processes. *Journal of Verbal Learning and Verbal Behavior,* 1977, *16,* 623-638.

Linde, C., & Labov, W. Spatial networks as a site for the study of language and thought. *Language*, 1975, *51*, 924-939.

Lindley, E.H. A study of puzzles with special reference to the psychology of mental adaptation. *American Journal of Psychology*, 1897, *8*, 431-493.

Lindsley, J.R. Producing simple utterances: How far ahead do we plan? *Cognitive Psychology*, 1975, *7*, 1-19.

Loftus, E.F. Leading questions and the eyewitness report. *Cognitive Psychology*, 1975, *7*, 560-572.

Loftus, E.F. *Eyewitness testimony*. Cambridge, MA: Harvard University Press, 1979.

Loftus, G. R. Eye fixations and recognition memory for pictures. *Cognitive Psychology*, 1972, *3*, 525-551.

Loftus, G. R., & Bell, S. M. Two types of information in picture memory. *Journal of Experimental Psychology: Human Learning and Memory*, 1975, *104*, 103-113.

Lowenthal, K. The development of codes in public and private language. *Psychonomic Science*, 1967, *8*, 449-450.

Lowes, J.L. *The road to Xanadu*. Boston, MA: Houghton-Mifflin Co., 1927.

Lucas, J.F. An exploratory study on the diagnostic teaching of heuristic problem-solving strategies in calculus (Doctoral dissertation, University of Wisconsin, 1972). *Dissertation Abstracts International*, 1972, *32*, 6825A. (University Microfilms No. 72-15368)

Luchins, A.S. Mechanization in problem solving. The effect of Einstellung. *Psychological Monographs*, 1940, *54*(248).

Luchins, A.S., & Luchins, E.H. *Rigidity of behavior: a variational approach to the effect of Einstellung*. Eugene, OR: University of Oregon Books, 1959.

Machotka, O. *The unconscious in social relations*. New York: Philosophical Library, 1964.

Mackworth, J.F. Auditory short-term memory. *Canadian Journal of Psychology*, 1964, *18*, 292-303.

MacWhinney, B. Starting points. *Language*, 1977, *53*, 152-168.

Maier, N. R. F. Reasoning in humans II. The solution of a problem and its appearance in consciousness. *Journal of Comparative Psychology*, 1931, *21*, 181-194.

Mandler, G., & Kessen, W. *The language of psychology*. New York: Wiley, 1959.

Marks, M.R. Problem solving as a function of the situation. *Journal of Experimental Psychology*, 1951, *41*, 74-80.

Martin, C. J., Boersma, F. J., & Cox, D. L. A classification of associative strategies in paired-associate learning. *Psychonomic Science*, 1965, *3*, 455-456.

Martin, E. Stimulus recognition in aural paired-associate learning. *Journal of Verbal Learning and Verbal Behavior*, 1967, *6*, 272-276.

Marx, M.H., & Hillix, W.A. *Systems and theories in psychology*. New York: McGraw-Hill, 1973.

Massaro, D.W. *Experimetal psychology and information processing.* Chicago, IL: Rand-McNally, 1975.

Max, L.W. An experimental study of the motor theory of consciousness I. Critique of earlier studies. *Journal of General Psychology,* 1934, *11*, 112-125.

May, M. A. The mechanism of controlled association. *Archives of Psychology,* 1917, *39*.

Mayzner, M.S., Tressell, M.E., & Helbock, H. An exploratory study of mediational responses in anagram problem solving. *Journal of Psychology,* 1964, *57*, 263-274.

McGuigan, F.J. Covert oral behavior during the silent performance of language tasks. *Psychological Bulletin,* 1970, *74*, 309-326.

McKellar, P. *Experience and behavior.* Harmondsworth: Penguin Books, 1968.

McNeill, D. Semiotic extension. In R.J. Solso (Ed.), *Information processing and cognition.* Hillsdale: Lawrence Erlbaum Associates, 1975.

Mechanic, A. The responses involved in the rote learning of verbal materials. *Journal of Verbal Learning and Verbal Behavior,* 1964, *3*, 30-36.

Merluzzi, T.V., Glass, C.R., & Genest, M. *Cognitive assessment.* New York: Guilford Press, 1981.

Merz, F. Der Einfluss des Verbalisierens auf die Leistung bei Intelligenzaufgaben. *Zeitschrift fur experimentelle und angewandte Psychologie,* 1969, *16*, 114-137.

Metcalf, J. T. An experimental study of the conscious attitudes of certainity and uncertainty. *Psychological Monographs,* 1917, *13*.

Meudell, P.R. Retrieval and representations in long-term memory. *Psychonomic Science,* 1971, *23*, 295-296.

Miller, G.A. The magical number seven, plus or minus two. *Psychological Review,* 1956, *63*, 81-97.

Miller, G.A. *Psychology, the science of mental life.* New York: Harper & Row, 1962.

Mischel, W. *Personality and assessment.* New York: Wiley, 1968.

Miyake, N. *Constructive interaction* (CHIP Report No. 113). La Jolla, CA: University of California, 1982.

Montague, W. E. Elaborative strategies in verbal learning and memory. In G. Bower (Ed.), *The psychology of learning and motivation (Vol. 6).* New York: Academic Press, 1972.

Montague, W.E., Adams, J.A., & Kiess, H.O. Forgetting and natural language mediation. *Journal of Experimental Psychology,* 1966, *72*, 829-833.

Montague, W. E., & Kiess, H. O. The associability of CVC pairs. *Journal of Experimental Psychology Monograph,* 1968, *78*(2, Pt. 2).

Montague, W.E., & Wearing, A. The complexity of natural language mediators and its relation to paired-associate learning. *Psychonomic Science,* 1967, *7*, 135-136.

Montgomery, H. A study of intransitive preferences using a think aloud procedure. In H. Jungermann & G. de Zeeuw (Eds.), *Decision making and change in human affairs*. Dordrecht: D. Reidel Publishing, 1977.

Montgomery, H., & Allwood, C.M. On the subjective representation of statistical problems. *Scandinavian Journal of Educational Research*, 1978, *22*, 107-127.

Morgan, C. L. Characteristics of problem-solving behavior of adults. *Studies in Education, University of Iowa Studies*, 1934, *9*, 105-143.

Morgan, J.B. The overcoming of distraction and other resistances. *Archives of Psychology*, 1916, *5*(35).

Morton, J. The effects of context on the visual duration threshold for words. *British Journal of Psychology*, 1964, *55*, 165-180.

Mueller, G.E. Zur Analyse der Gedachtnistatigkeit und Vorstellungsverlaufes: Teil I. *Zeitschrift fur Psychologie*, 1911, *5*.

Murray, D.J. Vocalization-at-presentation and immediate recall, with varying presentation rates. *Quarterly Journal of Experimental Psychology*, 1965, *17*, 47-56.

Murray, D.J. Overt versus covert rehearsal in short-term memory. *Psychonomic Science*, 1967, *7*, 363-364.

Natsoulas, T. Concerning introspective "knowledge". *Psychological Bulletin*, 1970, *73*(2), 89-111.

Neisser, U. *Cognitive psychology*. Englewood Cliffs, NJ: Prentice-Hall, 1967.

Neves, D. *An experimental analysis of strategies of the Tower of Hanoi puzzle* (C.I.P. Working Paper No. 362). Unpublished manuscript, Carnegie-Mellon University, 1977.

Newell, A. *On the analysis of human problem solving protocols*. Report from Carnegie Institute of Technology, 1966.

Newell, A. On the analysis of human problem solving protocols. In J.C. Gardin & B. Jaulin (Eds.), *Calcul et formalisation dans les sciences de l'homme*. Paris: Centre National de la Recherche Scientific, 1968, 146-185.

Newell, A. Production systems: Models of control structures. In W.G. Chase (Ed.), *Visual information processing*. New York: Academic Press, 1973.

Newell, A. *Duncker on thinking: An inquiry into progress in cognition*. Paper presented at Annual Meeting, American Psychological Association, New York, 1979.

Newell, A., & Shaw, J.C. Programming the logic theory machine. *Proceedings of the Western Joint Computer Conference (WJCC)*, 1957, 230-240.

Newell, A., Shaw, J.C., & Simon, H.A. Elements of a theory of human problem solving. *Psychological Review*, 1958, *65*, 151-166.

Newell, A., & Simon, H.A. The logic theory machine. *IRE Transactions on Information Theory*, 1956, IT-*2*(3), 61-79.

Newell, A., & Simon, H. A. *Human problem solving*. Englewood Cliffs, NJ: Prentice-Hall, 1972.

Newhall, S.M., & Rodnick, E.H. The influence of the reporting-response upon report. *American Journal of Psychology*, 1936, *48*, 316-325.

Newsted, P.R. *Toward a process-oriented theory of concept identification*. Unpublished doctoral dissertation, Graduate School of Industrial Administration, Carnegie-Mellon University, 1971.

Nilsson, N.J. *Problem-solving methods in artificial intelligence*. New York: McGraw-Hill, 1971.

Nisbett, R.E., & Ross, L. *Human inference: Strategies and shortcomings of social judgment*. Englewood Cliffs, NJ: Prentice-Hall, 1980.

Nisbett, R. E., & Wilson, T. D. Telling more than we can know: Verbal reports on mental processes. *Psychological Review*, 1977, *84*, 231-259.

Norman, D.A., & Bobrow, D.G. Descriptions: An intermediate stage in memory retrieval. *Cognitive Psychology*, 1979, *11*, 107-123.

Norman, D.A., & Rumelhart, D.E. Memory and knowledge. In D.A. Norman, D.E. Rumelhart & LNR Research Group (Eds.), *Explorations in cognition*. San Francisco, CA: W.H. Freeman, 1975.

Oberly, H. S. The range for visual attention, cognition and apprehension. *American Journal of Psychology*, 1924, *35*, 332-352.

Ochs, E. Transcription as theory. In E. Ochs & B.B. Schieffelin (Eds.), *Developmental pragmatics*. New York: Academic Press, 1979.

O'Connell, D. C. Concept learning and verbal control under partial reinforcement and subsequent reversal or nonreversal shift. *Journal of Experimental Psychology*, 1965, *69*, 144-151.

Ohlsson, S. *Competence and strategy in reasoning with common spatial concepts* (Report No. 6). Stockholm: The Cognitive Seminar, University of Stockholm, 1980.

Olson, D.R. Language and thought: Aspects of a cognitive theory of semantics. *Psychological Review*, 1970, *77*, 257-273.

Olson, G.M., Mack, R.L., & Duffy, S.A. Cognitive aspects of genre. *Poetics*, 1981, *10*, 283-315.

Olson, S.R. *Ideas and data: The process and practice of social research*. Homewood, IL: Dorsey Press, 1976.

Osgood, C.E. Where do sentences come from? In D.D. Steinberg & L.A. Jakobovits (Eds.), *Semantics: An interdisciplinary reader in philosophy, linguistics, and psychology*. Cambridge: Cambridge University Press, 1971.

Paige, J.M., & Simon, H.A. Cognitive processes in solving algebra word problems. In B. Kleinmuntz (Ed.), *Problem solving*. New York: Wiley, 1966.

Parry, H.J., & Crossley, H.M. Validity of responses to survey questions. *Public Opinion Quarterly*, 1950, *14*, 61-80.

Patrick, C. Creative thought in poets. *Archives of Psychology*, 1935, 178.

Patrick, C. Creative thought in artists. *Journal of Psychology*, 1937, *4*, 35-73.

Patton, E. F. The problem of insightful behavior. *Psychological Monographs*, 1939, *44*(1).

Payne, J.W. Task complexity and continient processing in decision making: An information search and protocol analysis. *Organizational Behavior and Human Performance*, 1976, *16*, 366-387.

Payne, J.W., Braunstein, M.L., & Carroll, J.S. Exploring predecisional behavior: An alternative approach to decision research. *Organizational Behavior and Human Performance*, 1978, *22*, 17-44.

Payne, J.W., & Ragsdale, E.K.E. Verbal protocols and direct observation of supermarket shopping behavior: Some findings and a discussion of methods. In H.K. Hunt (Ed.), *Advances in consumer research (Vol. 5)*. Chicago, IL: Association for Consumer Research, 1978, 571-577.

Penney, C.G. Modality effects in short-term verbal memory. *Psychological Bulletin*, 1975, *82*, 68-84.

Perky, C.W. An experimental study of imagination. *American Journal of Psychology*, 1910, *21*, 422-452.

Perrin, F. A. C. An experimental and introspective study of human learning process in the maze. *Psychological Monographs*, 1914, *16*(70).

Peters, H. Untersuchung zur Codierung eines Problems im Verlauf des Losungsprozesses. *Zeitschrift fur experimentelle und angewandte Psychologie*, 1974, *21*, 409-429.

Peterson, L.R. Concurrent verbal activity. *Psychological Review*, 1969, *76*, 376-386.

Phelan, J. G. A replication of a study on the effects of attempts to verbalize on the process of concept attainment. *Journal of Psychology*, 1965, *59*, 283-293.

Pillsbury, W.B. A study in apperception. *American Journal of Psychology*, 1897, *8*, 315-393.

Pintner, R. Inner speech during silent reading. *Psychological Review*, 1913, *20*, 129-153.

Pohl, I. *Bi-directional and heuristic search in path problems* (Report No. 104). Stanford, CA: Stanford Linear Accelerator Center, 1969.

Poincaré, H. Mathematical creation. In B. Ghiselin (Ed.), *The creative process*. Berkeley and Los Angeles: University of California Press, 1952.

Polanyi, M. *Knowing and being*. Chicago, IL: University of Chicago Press, 1969.

Polya, G. *How to solve it*. Garden City, NY: Doubleday-Anchor, 1957.

Postman, L., Bruner, J.S., & Walk, R.D. The perception of error. *British Journal of Psychology*, 1951, *42*, 1-10.

Postman, L., & Jarrett, R.F. An experimental analysis of learning without awareness. *American Journal of Psychology*, 1952, *65*, 244-255.

Poulton, E.C. Continuous intense noise masks auditory feedback and inner speech. *Psychological Bulletin*, 1977, *84*, 977-1001.

Prentice, W.C.H. Continuity in human learning. *Journal of Experimental Psychology*, 1949, *39*, 187-194.

Prentice, W.C. Visual recognition of verbally labeled figures. *American Journal of Psychology*, 1954, *67*, 315-320.

Prytulak, L. S. Natural language mediation. *Cognitive Psychology*, 1971, *2*, 1-56.

Quillian, M.R. Semantic memory. In M. Minsky (Ed.), *Semantic information processing.* Cambridge, MA: MIT Press, 1968.

Quinton, G., & Fellows, B. J. "Perceptual" strategies in the solving of three-term series problems. *British Journal of Psychology*, 1975, *66*, 69-78.

Rasmussen, J., & Jensen, A. Mental procedures in real-life tasks: A case study of electronic trouble shooting. *Ergonomics*, 1974, *17*, 293-307.

Ray, W.S. Verbal compared with manipulative solution of an apparatus problem. *American Journal of Psychology*, 1957, *77*, 289-290.

Read, J.D., & Bruce, D. Longitudinal tracking of difficult memory retrievals. *Cognitive Psychology*, 1982, *14*, 280-300.

Reber, A.S., & Allen, R. Analogic and abstraction strategies in synthetic grammar learning: A functionalist interpretation. *Cognition*, 1978, *6*, 189-221.

Reber, A.S., & Lewis, S. Implicit learning: An analysis of the form and structure of a body of tacit knowledge. *Cognition*, 1977, *5*, 333-361.

Reddy, R., & Newell, A. Knowledge and its representation in a speech understanding system. In L.W. Gregg (Ed.), *Knowledge and cognition.* Potomac, MD: Lawrence Erlbaum Associates, 1974, 253-285.

Reed, S.K., & Johnsen, J.A. Memory for problem solutions. In. G. Bower (Ed.), *The psychology of learning and motivation (Vol. 11).* New York: Academic Press, 1977.

Rees, H. J., & Israel, H. E. An investigation of the establishment and operation of mental sets. *Psychological Monographs*, 1935, *46*(6).

Riley, D.A. Memory for form. In L. Postman (Ed.), *Psychology in the making.* New York: Knopf, 1962.

Roberts, L. E., & Marlin, R. G. Some comments on the self-description and discrimination of visceral states. In N. Birbaumer & H. D. Kimmel (Eds.), *Biofeedback and self-regulation.* Hillsdale, NJ: Lawrence Erlbaum Associates, 1979.

Roberts, L. E., Marlin, R. G., Keleher, B., & Williams, R. J. Visceral learning as problem solving. In E. Richter-Heinrich & N. E. Miller (Eds.), *Biofeedback: Basic problems and clinical applications.* Amsterdam: North-Holland, 1982.

Roenker, D.L. Role of rehearsal in long-term retention. *Journal of Experimental Psychology*, 1974, *103*, 368-371.

Rogers, S.P., & Haygood, R.C. Hypothesis behavior in a concept-learning task with probabilistic feedback. *Journal of Experimental Psychology*, 1968, *76*, 160-165.

Rommetveit, R. Stages in concept formation and levels of cognitive functioning. *Scandinavian Journal of Psychology*, 1960, *1*, 115-124.

Rommetveit, R. Stages of concept formation II. Effects of an extra intention to verbalize the concept and stimulus predifferentiation. *Scandinavian Journal of Psychology*, 1965, *6*, 59-64.

Rommetveit, R., & Kvale, S. Stages in concept formation III. Further inquiries into the effects of an extra intention to verbalize. *Scandinavian Journal of Psychology*, 1965, *6*, 65-74. (a)

Rommetveit, R., & Kvale, S. Stages in concept formation IV. A temporal analysis of effects of an extra intention to verbalize. *Scandinavian Journal of Psychology*, 1965, *6*, 75-79. (b)

Rosenbaum, M.E. Effect of direct and vicarious verbalization on retention. *Child Development*, 1962, *33*, 103-111.

Roth, B. The effect of overt verbalization on problem solving (Doctoral dissertation, New York University, 1965). *Dissertation Abstracts International*, 1966, *27*, 957-B. (University Microfilms No. 65-9321)

Routh, D.A. "Trace strength", modality and the serial position curve in immediate memory. *Psychonomic Science*, 1970, *18*, 355-357.

Ruger, H. A. The psychology of efficiency. *Archives of Psychology*, 1910, 15.

Rumelhart, D.E., & Norman, D.A. The active structural network. In D.A. Norman, D.E. Rumelhart & LNR Research Group (Eds.), *Explorations in cognition*. San Francisco, CA: W.H. Freeman, 1975.

Rundus, D. Analysis of rehearsal processes in free recall. *Journal of Experimental Psychology*, 1971, *89*, 63-77.

Rundus, D., & Atkinson, R.C. Rehearsal processes in free recall: A procedure for direct observation. *Journal of Verbal Learning and Verbal Behavior*, 1970, *9*, 99-105.

Russel, W. A., & Storms, L. H. Implicit verbal chaining in paired associate learning. *Journal of Experimental Psychology*, 1955, *49*, 287-293.

Russo, J.E., Johnson, E.J., & Stephens, D. *A comparison among protocol methods.* Manuscript in preparation.

Russo, J.E., & Rosen, L.D. An eye fixation analysis of multialternative choice. *Memory and Cognition*, 1975, *3*, 267-276.

Ryan, T.A. *Intentional behavior: An approach to human motivation.* New York: Ronald Press, 1970.

Sallows, G. O., Dawes, R. H., & Lichtenstein E. Subjective value of the reinforcer (RSv) and performance: Crux of the S-R versus cognitive mediation controversy. *Journal of Experimental Psychology*, 1971, *89*, 274-281.

Saltz, E. *The cognitive bases of human learning.* Homewood, IL: Dorsey Press, 1971.

Sargent, S. S. Thinking processes at various levels of difficulty. *Archives of Psychology*, 1940, 249.

Schank, R.C., & Abelson, R.P. *Scripts, plans, goals and understanding.* Hillsdale, NJ: Lawrence Erlbaum Associates, 1977.

Schaub, G.R., & Lindley, R.H. Effects of subject-generated recoding cues on short-term memory. *Journal of Experimental Psychology*, 1964, *68*, 171-175.

Scheerer, M., & Huling, M.D. Cognitive embeddedness in problem solving: A theoretical and experimental analysis. In B. Kaplan & S. Wapner (Eds.),

Perspectives in psychological theory. New York: International University Press, 1960, 256-302.

Schneider, W., & Shiffrin, R. M. Controlled and automatic human information processing: I. Detection, search and attention. *Psychological Review,* 1977, *84,* 1-66.

Schneider-Duker. M., & Schneider, J.F. Untersuchungen zum Beautwortungsprocess bei psychodiagnostischen Fragebogen. *Zeitschrift fur experimentelle und angewandte Psychologie,* 1977, *24,* 282-302.

Schuck, J.R. Factors affecting reports of fragmenting visual images. *Perception and Psychophysics,* 1973, *13,* 382-390.

Schuck, J.R., & Leahy, W.R. A comparison of verbal and non-verbal reports of fragmenting visual images. *Perception and Psychophysics,* 1966, *1,* 191-192.

Schuman, H. The random probe: A technique for evaluating the validity of closed questions. *American Sociological Review,* 1966, *21,* 218-222.

Schuman, H., & Johnson, M.P. Attitudes and behavior. In A. Inkles (Ed.), *Annual Review of Sociology,* 1976, *2,* 161-207.

Schuman, H., & Presser, S. *Questions and answers in attitude surveys: Experiments on question form, wording and context.* New York: Academic Press, 1981.

Schwartz, S. H. Trial-by-trial analysis of processes in simple and disjunctive concept-attainment tasks. *Journal of Experimental Psychology,* 1966, *72,* 456-465.

Scott, T.C. The retention and recognition of patterns in maze learning. *Journal of Experimental Psychology,* 1930, *13,* 164-207.

Scott, W.A. Attitude measurement. In G. Lindzey & E. Aronson (Eds.), *The handbook of social psychology (Vol. 2).* Reading, MA: Addison-Wesley, 1968, 204-273.

Segal, S.J. The Perky effect: Changes in reality judgement with changing methods of inquiry. *Psychonomic Science,* 1968, *12,* 393-394.

Segal, S.J. Processing of the stimulus in imagery and perception. In S.J. Segal (Ed.), *Imagery: Current cognitive approaches.* New York: Academic Press, 1971.

Seidenberg, M.S., & Pettito, L.A. Signing behavior in apes: A critical review. *Cognition,* 1979, *7,* 177-215.

Selz, O. *Ueber die Gesetze des geordneten Denkverlaufs.* Stuttgart: Spemann, 1913.

Shiffrin, R. M., & Schneider, W. Controlled and automatic human information processing: II. Perceptual learning, automatic attending and a general theory. *Psychological Review,* 1977, *84,* 127-189.

Shipstone, E.I. Some variables affecting pattern conception. *Psychological Monographs,* 1960, *74*(17. Whole No. 504).

Silveira, J. M. Incubation: The effects of interruption timing and length on problem solution and quality of problem processing (Doctoral dissertation, University of Oregon, 1971). *Dissertation Abstracts International,* 1972, *32,* 5500B. (University Microfilms No. 72-9560)

Simon, D.P., & Simon, H.A. Individual differences in solving physics problems.

In R.S. Siegler (Ed.), *Children's thinking: What develops?* Hillsdale, NJ: Lawrence Erlbaum Associates, 1978.

Simon, H.A. Scientific discovery and the psychology of problem solving. In R.G. Colodny (Ed.), *Mind and cosmos: Essays in contemporary science and philosophy.* Pittsburgh, PA: University of Pittsburgh Press, 1966.

Simon, H.A. How big is a chunk? *Science,* 1974, *183,* 482-488.

Simon, H.A. The functional equivalence of problem solving skills. *Cognitive Psychology,* 1975, *7,* 268-288.

Simon, H.A. The information-storage system called "human memory". In M.R. Rosenzweig & E.L. Bennett (Eds.), *Neural mechanisms of learning and memory.* Cambridge, MA: MIT Press, 1976.

Simon, H. A. *Models of discovery.* Boston, MA: D. Reidel Publishing, 1977.

Simon, H. A. *Models of thought.* New Haven, CT: Yale University Press, 1979.

Simon, H.A., & Barenfeld, M. Information-processing analysis of perceptual processes in problem solving. *Psychological Review,* 1969, *76,* 473-483.

Simon, H.A., & Feigenbaum, E.A. An information-processing theory of some effects of similarity, familiarization, and meaningfulness in verbal learning. *Journal of Verbal Learning and Verbal Behavior,* 1964, *3,* 385-396.

Simon, H.A., & Hayes, J.R. The understanding process: Problem isomorphs. *Cognitive Psychology,* 1976, *8,* 165-190.

Simon, H.A., Langley, P.W., & Bradshaw, G.L. Scientific discovery as problem solving. *Synthese,* 1981, *47,* 1-27.

Singer, J. L. *The inner world of daydreaming.* New York: Harper & Row, 1975.

Slak, S. Information, similarity and vocalization in free learning of numbers. *Psychonomic Science,* 1969, *14,* 283.

Smead, R.J., Wilcox, J.B., & Wilkes, R.E. How valid are product descriptions and protocols in choice experiments? *Journal of Consumer Research,* 1981, *8,* 37-42.

Smedslund, J. Mental processes involved in rapid logical reasoning. *Scandinavian Journal of Psychology,* 1968, *9,* 187-205.

Smedslund, J. Psychological diagnostics. *Psychological Bulletin,* 1969, *71,* 237-248.

Smirnov, A.A. *Problems of the psychology of memory.* New York: Plenum Press, 1973.

Smith, C.O. *The structure of intellect processes analyses system. A technique for the investigation and quantification of problem solving processes.* Unpublished doctoral dissertation, University of Houston, 1971.

Smith, E. R. & Miller, F. S. Limits on perception of cognitive processes: A reply to Nisbett and Wilson. *Psychological Review,* 1978, *85,* 355-362.

Smith, R.D., & Greenlaw, P.S. Simulation of a psychological decision process in personnel selection. *Management Science,* 1967, *18,* 409-419.

Smith, S.M., Brown, H.O., Toman, J.E.P., & Goodman, L.S. The lack of cerebral effects of D-Tubocurarine. *Anesthesiology,* 1947, *8,* 1-14.

Smoke, K. L. An objective study of concept formation. *Psychological Monographs*, 1932, *42*(4, Whole No. 191).

Snee, T.J., & Lush, D.E. Interaction of the narrative and interrogatory methods of obtaining testimony. *Journal of Psychology*, 1941, *11*, 229-236.

Snyder, C.R., & Larson, G.R. A further look at student acceptance of general personality interpretations. *Journal of Consulting and Clinical Psychology*, 1972, *38*, 384-388.

Snygg, D. The relative difficulty of mechanically equivalent tasks: I. Human learning. *Journal of Genetic Psychology*, 1935, *47*, 299-336.

Sokolov, A.N. *Inner speech and thought*. New York: Plenum Press, 1972.

Soliday, S.M., & Allen, J.A. *Hazard perception in automobile drivers: Age differences*. Report from Highway Safety Research Center, University of North Carolina, 1972.

Sowder, L. The influence of verbalization of discovered numerical- or sorting-task generalizations on short-term retention in connection with the Hendrix hypothesis. *Journal for Research in Mathematics Education*, 1974, *5*, 167-176.

Sperling, G. The information available in brief visual presentations. *Psychological Monographs*, 1960, *74* (Whole No. 498).

Sperling, G. Successive approximation to a model for short term memory. *Acta Psychologica*, 1967, *27*, 285-292.

Spielberger, C. D. The role of awareness in verbal conditioning. In C. W. Eriksen (Ed.), *Behavior and awareness*. Durham: Duke University Press, 1962.

Sternberg, R. J. Intelligence, information processing and analogical reasoning: The componential analysis of human abilities. Hillsdale, NJ: Lawrence Erlbaum Associates, 1977.

Svenson, O. *A note on think aloud protocols obtained during the choice of a home* (Report No. 421). Stockholm: Psychology Lab, University of Stockholm, 1974.

Svenson, O. Analysis of time required by children for simple additions. *Acta Psychologica*, 1975, *39*, 289-302.

Swaney, J.H., Janik, C.J., Bond, S.J., & Hayes, J.R. *Editing for comprehension: Improving the process through reading protocols*. Unpublished paper, Department of Psychology, Carnegie-Mellon University, 1981.

Taylor, I. Content and structure in sentence production. *Journal of Verbal Learning and Verbal Behavior*, 1969, *8*, 170-175.

Taylor, S.E., & Fiske, S.T. Salience, attention, and attribution. In L. Berkowitz (Ed.), *Advances in experimental social psychology*. New York: Academic Press, 1978.

Tell, P.M. Influence of vocalization on short-term memory. *Journal of Verbal Learning and Verbal Behavior*, 1971, *10*, 149-156.

Terrace, H.S., Petitto, L.A., Sanders, D.J., & Beaver, T.G. On the grammatical capacities of apes. In K. Nelson (Ed.), *Children's language, Vol. 2*. New York: Gardner Press, 1978.

Thomas, J.C. An analysis of behavior in the Hobbits-Orcs problem. *Cognitive Psychology*, 1974, *6*, 257-269.

Thorndike, E.L. *The fundamentals of learning.* New York: Teachers College, Columbia University, 1932.

Thorndike, E.L. A theory of the action of the after-effects of a connection upon it. *Psychological Review*, 1933, *40*, 434-439.

Thorndike, E.L., & Rock, R.T. Learning without awareness of what is being learned or intent to learn it. *Journal of Experimental Psychology*, 1934, *17*, 1-19.

Thorson, A. The relation of tongue movements to internal speech. *Journal of Experimental Psychology*, 1925, *8*, 1-32.

Titchener, E.B. *A text-book of psychology. Vol. 1.* New York: Macmillan, 1909.

Titchener, E.B. Description vs. statement of meaning. *American Journal of Psychology*, 1912, *23*, 165-182. (a)

Titchener, E. B. Prolegomena to a study of introspection. *American Journal of Psychology*, 1912, *23*, 427-448. (b)

Titchener, E.B. The schema of introspection. *American Journal of Psychology*, 1912, *23*, 485-508. (c)

Titchner, E. B. The method of examination. *American Journal of Psychology*, 1913, *24*, 429-440.

Tulving, E., & Thompson, D.M. Encoding specificity and retrieval processing in episodic memory. *Psychological Review*, 1973, *80*, 352-373.

Turner, M.B. *Philosophy and the science of behavior.* New York: Appleton-Century-Crofts, 1965.

Tversky, A. Intransitivity of preferences. *Psychological Review*, 1969, *76*, 31-48.

Tversky, A., & Kahneman, D. Availability: A heuristic for judging frequency and probability. *Cognitive Psychology*, 1973, *5*, 207-232.

Ulrich, R.E., Stachnik, T.J., & Stainton, N.R. Students acceptance of generalized personality interpretations. *Psychological Reports*, 1963, *13*, 831-834.

Underwood, B.J., & Schultz, R.W. *Meaningfulness and verbal learning.* Philadelphia, PA: Lippincott, 1960.

Uznadze, D.M. *The psychology of set.* New York: Consultants Bureau, Plenum, 1966.

van Dijk, T.A., & Kintsch, W. *Strategies of discourse comprehension.* New York: Academic Press, 1983.

Verplanck, W. S. Unaware of where's awareness: Some verbal operants—notates, monents and notants. In C. W. Eriksen (Ed.), *Behavior and awareness—A symposium of research and interpretation.* Durham: Duke University Press, 1962.

Waern, Y. *Thinking aloud during reading: A descriptive model and its application* (Report No. 546). Stockholm: Department of Psychology, University of Stockholm, 1979.

Wagner, D.A., & Scurrah, M.J. Some characteristics of human problem-solving in chess. *Cognitive Psychology*, 1971, *2*, 454-478.

Walk, R. D. Effects of discrimination reversal on human discrimination learning. *Journal of Experimental Psychology*, 1952, *44*, 410-419.

Walker, W.H. *Retrieval of knowledge from memory: A generalization of the Raaijmakers-Shiffrin retrieval model.* Unpublished doctoral dissertation, University of Colorado at Boulder, 1982.

Warden, C. J. The relative economy of various modes of attack in the mastery of a stylus maze. *Journal of Experimental Psychology*, 1924, *7*, 243-275.

Warren, R.M. Perceptual restoration of missing speech sounds. *Science*, 1970, *167*, 392-393.

Warren, R.M., & Warren, R.P. Auditory illusions and confusions. *Scientific American*, 1970, *223*, 30-36.

Wason, P.C., & Evans, J. St. B.T. Dual processes in reasoning? *Cognition*, 1975, *3*, 141-154.

Wason, P.C., & Johnson-Laird, P.N. A conflict between selecting and evaluating information in an inferential task. *British Journal of Psychology*, 1970, *61*, 509-515.

Waterman, D.A., & Newell, A. Protocol analysis as a task for artificial intelligence. *Artificial Intelligence*, 1971, *2*, 285-318.

Waterman, D.A., & Newell, A. *Preliminary results with a system for automatic protocol analysis* (C.I.P. Working Paper No. 211). Pittsburgh, PA: Carnegie-Mellon University, 1972.

Waterman, D.A., & Newell, A. PAS-II: An interactive task-free version of an automatic protocol analysis system. In *Proceedings of the Third IJCAI*. Menlo Park, CA: Stanford Research Institute, 1973, 431-445.

Watson, J. B. Psychology as the behaviorist views it. *Psychological Review*, 1913, *20*, 158-177.

Watson, J. B. Is thinking merely the action of language mechanisms? *British Journal of Psychology*, 1920, *11*, 87-104.

Watson, J. B. The place of kinesthetic, visceral and laryngeal organization in thinking. *Psychological Review*, 1924, *31*, 339-347. (a)

Watson, J. B. *Psychology: From the standpoint of a behaviorist* (2nd ed.). Philadelphia, PA: Lippincott, 1924. (b)

Watson, J.B. *Behaviorism.* New York: W.W. Norton, 1925.

Watson, J. B. *Behaviorism.* Chicago, IL: University of Chicago Press, 1930.

Waugh, N., & Norman, D.A. Primary memory. *Psychological Review*, 1965, *72*, 89-104.

Wearing, A. J. On the Adams-Bray retrieval model. *Journal of Experimental Psychology*, 1971, *89*, 96-101.

Webb, N.L. An exploration of mathematical problem-solving processes (Doctoral dissertation, Stanford University, 1975). *Dissertation Abstracts International*, 1975, *36*, 2689A. (University Microfilms No. 75-25625)

Weber, R.J., & Bach, M. Visual and speech imagery. *British Journal of Psychology*, 1969, *60*, 199-202.

Weber, R.J., & Blagowsky, J. Metered memory search with implicit and explicit scanning. *Journal of Experimental Psychology*, 1970, *80*, 343-348.

Weir, M.W., & Helgoe, R.S. Vocalization during discrimination: Effects of a mixture of two types of verbalization patterns. *Journal of Verbal Learning and Verbal Behavior*, 1968, *7*, 842-844.

Weisberg, R., & Suls, J.M. An information-processing model of Duncker's candle problem. *Cognitive Psychology*, 1973, *4*, 255-276.

Weitz, B., & Wright, P. Retrospective self-insight on factors considered in product evaluation. *Journal of Consumer Research*, 1979, *6*(3), 280-294.

Wellman, H.M. Tip of the tongue and feeling of knowing experiences: A developmental study of memory monitoring. *Child Development*, 1977, *48*, 13-21.

Werner, H., & Kaplan, B. *Symbol formation*. New York: Wiley, 1963.

Wertheimer, M. *Productive thinking*. New York: Harper & Row, 1945.

White, P. Limitations on verbal reports of internal events: A reputation of Nisbett and Wilson and of Bem. *Psychological Review*, 1980, *87*, 105-112.

Whitten, W.B., & Leonard, J.M. Directed search through autobiographical memory. *Memory and Cognition*, 1981, *9*, 566-579.

Wicker, A.W. Attitudes vs. actions: The relationship of verbal and overt behavioral responses to attitude objects. *Journal of Social Issues*, 1969, *25*, 41-78.

Wilder, L. Spoken rehearsal and verbal discrimination learning. *Speech Monographs*, 1971, *38*, 113-120.

Wilder, L., & Harvey, D. J. Overt and covert verbalization in problem solving. *Speech Monographs*, 1971, *38*, 171-176.

Williams, B. W. Verbal operant conditioning without subjects awareness of reinforcement conditions. *Canadian Journal of Psychology*, 1977, *31*, 90-101.

Williams, D.M., & Santos-Williams, S. Method for exploring retrieval processes using verbal protocols. In R.S. Nickerson (Ed.), *Attention and performance, Vol. 8*. Hillsdale, NJ: Lawrence Erlbaum Associates, 1980.

Williams, M.D., & Hollan, J.D. The process of retrieval from very long-term memory. *Cognitive Science*, 1981, *5*(2), 87-119.

Wilson, A. The verbal report of the concept in concept-learning research. (Doctoral dissertation, University of Victoria, 1973). *Dissertation Abstracts International*, 1974, *35*, 1097-B. (University Microfilms No. 1-5405)

Wilson, A. The inference of covert hypotheses by verbal reports in concept-learning research. *Quarterly Journal of Experimental Psychology*, 1975, *27*, 313-322.

Wilson, A., & Spellacy, F. Cognitive process in auditory concept acquisition. *Psychonomic Science*, 1972, *28*, 383-345.

Winikoff, A. *Eye movements as an aid to protocol analysis of problem solving behavior*. Unpublished doctoral dissertation, Carnegie-Mellon University, 1967.

Wood, D.J., & Shotter, J.D. A preliminary study of distinctive features in problem solving. *Quarterly Journal of Experimental Psychology*, 1973, *25*, 504-510.

Wood, D. J., Shotter, J. D., & Godden, D. An investigation of the relationships between problem solving strategies, representation and memory. *Quarterly Journal of Experimental Psychology*, 1974, *26*, 252-257.

Woodworth, R.S. A revision of imageless thought. *Psychological Review*, 1915, *22*, 1-29.

Woodworth, R.S. *Experimental psychology.* New York: Holt, Rinehart & Winston, 1938.

Woodworth, R.S., & Schlossberg, H. *Experimental psychology.* New York: Holt, Rinehart & Winston, 1961.

Wortman, P.M. Representation and strategy in diagnostic problem solving. *Human Factors*, 1966, *8*, 48-53.

Wright, P. Message-evoked thoughts: Persuasion research using thought verbalizations. *Journal of Consumer Research*, 1980, *7*(2), 151-175.

Wright, P., & Kriewall, M.A. State-of-mind effects on the accuracy with which utility functions predict marketplace choice. *Journal of Marketing Research*, 1980, *17*, 277-293.

Wright, P., & Rip, P. Retrospective reports on consumer decision processes. In J. Olson (Ed.), *Advances in Consumer Research (Vol. 7)*. Urbana, IL: Association for Consumer Research, 1980.

Wunderlich, D., & Reinelt, R. Telling the way. In R.J. Jarvella & W. Klein (Eds.), *Speech, place, and action: Studies of language in context*. Chichester: Wiley, 1981.

Yarmey, A.D. I recognize your face but I can't remember your name: Further evidence on the tip-of-tongue phenomenon. *Memory and Cognition*, 1973, *1*, 287-290.

Yule, G. Udny. A mathematical theory of evolution. Based on the conclusions of Dr. J.C. Willis, F.R.S. *Philosophical Transactions. B. 213*, 1924, 21-83.

Zipf, G.K. *Human behavior and the principle of least effort.* Reading, MA: Addison Wesley, 1949.

AUTHOR INDEX

SUBJECT INDEX

A-reaction, 52, 57
Access to relevant knowledge, 145-48
Accessibility to thoughts, 28
Accessing long-term memory, 13, 119. *See also* Long-term memory
Action part of production, 333
Activation, spreading, 11, 13
Adaptation-level theory, 159
Addition task, task analysis, 349-52
Aggregation by episodes, processes, and solution steps, 272-73
Algebra word problems, 176-77, 298-99
Ambiguity in encoding, 198
Anagram problem solving, 106, 155-56, 173-74, 177-79, 218, 226-27, 357-59
Analytical thinking, effect of verbalization on, 98
Anaphoric reference, 265-66. *See also* Context
Articulation in mental work, 76-77; units, 225
Articulatory structure of TA verbalizations, 227-28
Assessment, of awareness, 140-43; effectiveness of, 42-43; indirect, 42-43; of general processes, 204-15; of postulated internal states, 40-41; procedures for, 41-42; processes evoked by, 43-44; of recognition processes, 126; verbal reports in, 40-48
Associations in LTM, 13, 38, 115. *See also* Long-term memory
Assumptions, in encoding, 4-6, 179, 267-68; of model of verbalization, 221-25; of protocol analysis, 263-64
Attention, 31-32, 116, 172, 233, 243; and fixation, 116-17; control of, 14-15; focus of, 26-27; limits of, 55, 115. *See also* Heeding
Attention-control processes, verbalization of, 130

Attitudes and opinions, 38-39
Attributes, use of in naming, 230-31
Aufgabe, 56, 119, 127
Automatic encoding, 270-71, 276, 309
Automatic protocol analysis, 300-305, 355
Automation, and practice, 128-29; of cognitive processes, 14-15, 90-91, 243, 355; of responses, 126-29; of skills, 245
Average behavior, 46. *See also* Individual differences
Awareness, and automation, 126-27; of process, 34, 118-19, 143-45

B-reaction, 52, 57
Backward recall, 193-94
Basic assumptions, 4-6, 9, 179, 221-25
Bayes' Theorem, 281-84, 287
Because construction, 234-38
Behaviorism, 57-59, 137; and thinking aloud, 110-11
Bias, arising from inferences, 291; in encoding, 290-91
Biofeedback, 33

C-reaction, 52-53, 57
Causes of behavior, reports of. *See also* Goals; Reasons, reports of
Central processor (CP), 14, 16, 63
Change problems, 325
Change representation, 326-27
Chess playing, protocols of, 262
Chunking, 185-86, 189, 192-93
Clinical judgment tasks, effects of verbalization on, 100-101
Coding, of activities, 206; application of, 207-14; consistency of, 368-71; fineness of, 300; high-level, 184, 204-15; implications of Bayes' Theorem for, 282-84; interactive, 6; objectivity of, 170
Coding alternatives, a priori, 6
Coding categories, 5, 199-200, 293-94;